Arnulfo L. Oliveira Memorial Library

Cajun Breakdown

AMERICAN MUSICSPHERES

Series Editor
Mark Slobin

Fiddler on the Move:
Exploring the Klezmer World
Mark Slobin

The Lord's Song in a Strange Land:
Music and Identity in Contemporary Jewish Worship
Jeffrey A. Summit

Lydia Mendoza's Life in Music
Yolanda Broyles-González

Four Parts, No Waiting:
A Social History of American Barbershop Harmony
Gage Averill

Louisiana Hayride:
Radio Roots Music Along the Red River
Tracey E. W. Laird

Balkan Fascination:
Creating an Alternative Music Culture in America
Mirjana Lausevic

Polkabilly:
How the Goose Island Ramblers Redefined American Folk Music
James P. Leary

Cajun Breakdown
The Emergence of an American-Made Music
Ryan André Brasseaux

CAJUN BREAKDOWN

The Emergence of an American-Made Music

Ryan André Brasseaux

OXFORD
UNIVERSITY PRESS

2009

OXFORD
UNIVERSITY PRESS

Oxford University Press, Inc., publishes works that further
Oxford University's objective of excellence
in research, scholarship, and education.

Oxford   New York
Auckland   Cape Town   Dar es Salaam   Hong Kong   Karachi
Kuala Lumpur   Madrid   Melbourne   Mexico City   Nairobi
New Delhi   Shanghai   Taipei   Toronto

With offices in
Argentina   Austria   Brazil   Chile   Czech Republic   France   Greece
Guatemala   Hungary   Italy   Japan   Poland   Portugal   Singapore
South Korea   Switzerland   Thailand   Turkey   Ukraine   Vietnam

Published by Oxford University Press, Inc.
198 Madison Avenue, New York, New York 10016

www.oup.com

Oxford is a registered trademark of Oxford University Press.

Library of Congress Cataloging-in-Publication Data
Brasseaux, Ryan A.
Cajun breakdown : the emergence of an American-made music / Ryan André Brasseaux.
    p. cm. (American musicspheres)
Includes bibliographical references and index.
ISBN 978-0-19-534306-9   1. Cajun music—History and criticism.   2. Popular
music—Social aspects—United States.   3. Cajuns—History.   I. Title.
ML3560.C25B73   2009
781.62'410763—dc22   2008039178

9 8 7 6 5 4 3 2 1

Printed in the United States of America
on acid-free paper

To Jessika Ducharme Brasseaux and to our two children,
Anne Elise and Joseph Emile Brasseaux—
tenth-generation Cajuns.
Toujours dans mon coeur.

America is woven of many strands; I would recognize them and let it so remain. Our fate is to become one, and yet many . . .

—Ralph Ellison, *The Invisible Man*

We didn't have a radio or record player when I was growing up so jukeboxes were really important to me. I could hear Cajun things by Harry Choates, country singers like Ernest Tubb, and big band stuff by Glenn Miller. And I learned to play it all. I still love to play "Stardust." You know, there were no labels on the jukebox—it wasn't country or jazz or Cajun—it was just music.

—Doug Kershaw, *Fiddler Magazine*

Preface

Adaptation is a hallmark of the Cajun survival strategy. From the time the first Acadian refugees—the Cajuns' ancestral stock—set foot in the Louisiana Territory, the group began to improvise in accordance with the challenges of a new terrain and new reality. Louisiana's Acadian communities diversified as individuals adapted their lives and expressive culture through sustained interaction with neighboring groups. Musicians freely experimented with arrangements, translations, lyrical embellishments, phrasing, and syncopation with traditional materials and song styles derived from those external sources that filtered into the Bayou Country. In short, if it sounded good, Cajuns made it their own. This openness to outside stimuli thus broadened the possibility of musical expression within the community.

Some terms appearing throughout the text need clarification. The term "Cajun" is an English corruption of the French 'cadien, a contraction of Acadien (Acadian in English). The roots of the Cajun community extend to 1604, when a group of French settlers established Acadia, the first colony in New France presently centered in Nova Scotia. Over time, the European transplants developed a distinctly North American identity and mentality, in part through extensive intermarriage with local Mikmaq Indians during the first few decades of colonization.[1] Great Britain gained control of the settlement after a series of political and military disputes between the French and the British extending from the early seventeenth to the early eighteenth century. In 1755, British military forces deported approximately 6,000 of the region's estimated 15,000 Acadians during several waves of an ethnic cleansing exercise commonly known as the *Grand Dérangement* (Great Upheaval).

After a period of wandering and migration, some exiles found a new home and new cultural landscape along south Louisiana's intricate labyrinth of waterways and vast, open prairies. Between 1764 and 1900, Acadian culture evolved through interpersonal interaction, cross-cultural borrowing, transculturation, and intermarriage with other local ethnic groups. Between 1803 and 1877, this cultural fusion transformed the ethnic composition of Louisiana's Acadian community so markedly as to change the group's identification. The internal transformation from "Acadian" to "Cajun" demarcates the exiles' departure from predispersal Acadian culture, a metamorphosis that differentiated south Louisiana Acadians from exiles who sought refuge in other parts of the world.

Recorded Cajun music reflects and partly constitutes the historical influences that stimulated this behavioral change as well as the complexity of the Bayou State's cultural landscape. Folklorist Barry Ancelet describes the genre's cultural DNA through a genealogical reference that also asserts the process of transculturation at the heart of Cajun musical expression: "a blend of German, Spanish, Scottish, Irish, Anglo-American, Afro-Caribbean, and American Indian influences with a base of Western French and French Acadian folk traditions."[2] "Cajun," then, is a synthetic New World product—an amalgamation of the cultural influences that converged to varying degrees in south Louisiana.

Dewey Segura's rendition of the "New Iberia Polka," recorded in New Orleans on December 16, 1928, is perhaps the best-documented example of the interactive cross-cultural exchanges driving Cajun music's evolution. Segura was of Spanish ancestry, played the German diatonic button accordion with a distinctive syncopated style influenced by African and Afro-Caribbean musical traditions, sang in Cajun French (a North American French patois, based on seventeenth-century European grammatical structures and vocabulary), and recorded a polka, a decidedly Old World song style, for a major American record label. The Segura family immigrated to south Louisiana during the eighteenth century from Malaga, Spain, but by the twentieth century, the family participated as full members of Cajun society.

Assimilated members of other ethnic groups infused new ideas, customs, and surnames as they freely intermarried with people of Acadian ancestry. By the early twentieth century, south Louisianians considered such names as Abshire, Ancelet, Clark, Courvelle, Greely, McGee, Miller, Romero, Schenyder, Veroni, and Walker as legitimately Cajun as such authentically Acadian surnames as Babineaux, Duhon, and Thibodeaux. Working-class Cajun women who married "outsiders" ensured that their children embraced the community's values and the French language—until the emergence of mandatory education regulations in the early twentieth century. These cultural dynamics continued to evolve at an exponential rate with the introduction of mass media and a nationwide communication infrastructure.

Between 1764 and 1950, Cajun music varied significantly in terms of instrumentation, language, vocal delivery, repertory, and stylistic mode, ultimately resulting in a remarkably diverse tradition that grew increasingly complex over time. By the early twentieth century, a musician's repertoire could easily range from a cappella ballads to French interpretations of Tin Pan Alley compositions, from accordion-based dance tunes to Cajun swing, hillbilly, and blues numbers. Because the genre thrived on oral transference among family members, neighbors, acquaintances, and professional colleagues and the constant influence of mass culture, Cajun music is identified throughout *Cajun Breakdown* as a vernacular expression. Working-class musicians by and large were not "formally" trained musicians who paid for lessons from instructors or professors. Hence, many previous studies have labeled Cajun music as a "folk" expression. Yet, because of the cultural baggage attached to traditional conceptualizations of vernacular music within folklore studies, I have opted not to deploy the loaded academic term "folk," unless I am explicitly referring to traditional folk models.

The genre's commercialization and commodification and the broad spectrum of Cajun musical expression make its connection to "folk" ideology tenuous at best. Cajuns who entered the recording studio had to negotiate on a variety of cultural fronts, including song titles. I have used the original song appellations as printed on record labels to project more accurately the historical context in which Francophone musicians and Anglophone record producers negotiated French titles. Those tunes offered by local musicians, however, could range from European-derived melodic structures and French lyrics to English-language interpretations of contemporary popular music. Because the breath of the repertoire played by south Louisianians is so diverse, Cajun music is defined in this study more by ethos and social context than by a delimited set of stylistic features. Cajun musical ethos is characterized by the group's ability to interpret and selectively adapt specific cultural information—a French North American survival scheme rooted in pragmatism and openness to change. The disposition, character, and fundamental values of Cajun music are grounded in improvisation, an adaptive cultural mechanism at the very heart of the Acadian experience. In predispersal *Acadie*, the ethnic group negotiated its way through constant governmental shifts between France and Great Britain, the natural hurdles posed by the unruly maritime topography, and the ethnic cleansing operation of 1755. Like displaced African slaves who encountered a world in Louisiana completely removed from the one they left behind, Acadian refugees traversed a new cultural landscape when they arrived in Bayou Country—adapting musical ideas and stylistic traits into their repertoire. This experiment led to the development of a new regional musical form as the Acadians became acquainted with south Louisiana's cultural fabric.

Cajun musical ethos also refers to the emotional qualities of compositions born of grinding poverty and an agrarian, working-class lifestyle. Rural musicians experienced first-hand the incapacitating heat and grueling toil necessary to sustain a successful south Louisiana farm. They suffered like other Southern farmers under the weight of crop liens, the sharecropping system, and falling cotton prices during the first half of the twentieth century. Meanwhile, the transition between premechanized farming and the birth of Louisiana's industrial economy introduced new stresses and complications to the Cajun experience. These contextual scenarios are the root of the Cajun sound as working-class Cajun recordings artists cultivated a vernacular language that gave voice to these conditions.

Cajun Country, the Bayou Country, and Acadiana are used synonymously to refer to the 22-parish region that has traditionally served as the Cajun homeland in south Louisiana. The geographically diverse territory—which stretches as far east as Lafourche, St. Charles, and St. John the Baptist parishes, as far north as Avoyelles Parish, and as far west as Calcasieu and Cameron parishes—features coastal and brackish marsh along the southern coastal plains, open prairies to the west, and a complex web of bayous, streams, rivers, the expansive Atchafalaya river basin, and the Mississippi River to the east. Commercial centers such as Lafayette, Opelousas, New Iberia, Abbeville, Crowley, and Lake Charles emerged within the bounds of this territory and played important roles in the evolution of Cajun music. Despite conventional attitudes, New Orleans, which exerted a considerable cultural influence on Cajun music, is not part of Cajun Country. Rather, New Orleans has long been a Creole city.

Many New Orleanians considered their city the cultural heart of Louisiana. The city's white population in general, and upper-crust socialites in particular, maintained a condescending attitude toward provincial customs. These attitudes stymied relations between rural Cajuns and their urban white Creole counterparts. Meanwhile, steamboat commerce, and later the railroad, brought New Orleans culture and music west. That is, in part, how Cajuns stayed in tune. The city was also the state's largest commercial hub, a place where country folks could sell their wares and crops and acutely experience the pressures of marginalization and denigration. The city's character began to shift during the first half of the twentieth century when working-class Southerners left their farms in unprecedented numbers because of crop liens, poor yields, mechanization, and weak agricultural markets. These workers found employment in factories, warehouses, and new wartime industries in New Orleans. By the late 1930s and 1940s, rural transplants frequently patronized honky-tonk clubs all along Magazine Street, where the familiar strains of agrarian music thrived. This was the world where a young Cajun accordionist named Iry LeJeune would leave his mark—the interactive milieu where the urban and agrarian fused. Throughout this text, the local moniker Crescent City is used synonymously with the Creole municipality that left such an indelible mark on Cajun music.[3]

The term "Creole" is derived from the Latin *creare*, meaning "to create." During Louisiana's colonial period, "creole" translated as created or "born in the New World." The term applied to whites of European descent (*créole blanc*) and slaves born in Louisiana (*nègre créole*), and after the Civil War former free people of color adopted the moniker Creole of Color to distinguish themselves from those bondsmen freed by the 13th Amendment. I use the term "Afro-Creole" here as an umbrella term for Francophone Catholics of African decent, which includes both *nègres créoles* and members of the Creole of Color population. Afro-Creole juxtaposes the ethnic label African American, which in this study refers to Anglophone Protestants of African ancestry.[4]

I use "mainstream" American music, somewhat reluctantly, as a synonym for broadly disseminated commercially driven mass culture that gained wide acceptance in American popular culture. Of course, the "mainstream" shifted as fluidly as popular attitudes and popular culture, from styles including minstrelsy, ragtime, jazz, and Tin Pan Alley to country-and-western and rock 'n' roll. I use this terminology as a vehicle to discuss the sorts of mass culture available to, and consumed by, Cajun audiences throughout the Americanization process.

"Americanization" occurs frequently throughout the text. While the term carries significant historical and cultural baggage, it is necessary to make the distinction between Americanization and the Americanization *process* regarding its application here. The former refers to the concerted efforts of an American nationalist movement during the first quarter of the twentieth century to assimilate the unprecedented number of immigrants in the United States. Rooted in notions of white Anglo-Protestant exceptionalism, Americanization for middle- and upper-class English-speaking whites translated as the forced enculturation of "inferior" cultural communities into the mores and values of nondenominational Protestantism, republicanism, and the English language. Progressive-minded activists such as Jane Addams and Frances Kellor diligently set out to initiate immigrants into an idealized vision of American culture and society. Striking parallels exist between the working-class Cajun encounter with Louisiana's social reformers and the experience of other minority and ethnic groups during the Progressive Era. Those parallels emerged from a common progressive agenda that sought to undermine "foreign" linguistic traditions, worldviews, and folkways in the name of the proverbial American "melting pot." For instance, prohibition advocates in the Bayou Country tried their best to pass legislation to dry up some of the wettest, and often most densely populated, Cajun districts in south Louisiana. Likewise, civic-minded educators stringently enforced Louisiana's 1916 Compulsory Education Act, under which Cajun students forcibly learned English at public schools.[5]

Although the Americanization movement promised to ensure some sense of cultural homogeneity and national unity in the United States, individuals from different cultural, linguistic, and socioeconomic backgrounds interpreted and rearticulated "American culture" in accordance with their own agendas and worldviews. In essence, the Americanization *process* transpired unevenly within ethnic communities. And yet, discernable adaptations generated by sustained exposure to new technologies, industrialization, Progressive Era education, and mass culture profoundly changed the Cajun community. Group cohesiveness and an elastic ethnic identity, as historian Lizabeth Cohen has observed among other ethnics, guarded against complete cultural reorientation. By selectively interpreting and adapting cultural traits from the mainstream, Cajuns could reconcile both their French Catholic ethnicity and their place in the American national project. Moreover, the Americanization process afforded Cajuns more independence and a broader vocabulary to express themselves and their culture.

To be sure, even disenfranchised ethnics were not completely helpless at the mercy of those controlling the distribution of resources. Rather, individual agency distinguished the Americanization process from "Americanization." Ethnics quickly learned to appropriate American culture and make it their own as a means of subverting Americanization's oppressive policies and practices. Harlem's evolution is perhaps the best illustration of a diverse urban ethnic population remaking America in their own image. Some of the same principles of appropriation and adaptation hold true among rural Cajuns who selectively, and unevenly, engaged neighboring groups and various forms of mass media. Far from becoming a homogeneous whole, the intricate and complex cultural transactions that reshaped the Acadian, and later Cajun, community and the whole of America over time developed in such nuanced ways that a superficial summary here would be insufficient. Instead, I systematically discuss these themes and issues over the course of these essays that have, for the past five years, completely engrossed my imagination.

Acknowledgments

I am indebted to a long list of individuals who contributed to my understanding of Cajun music and the cultural currents affecting those traditions. This book would never have materialized without the encouragement and support of Judy McCulloh, who approached me after my first presentation at Nashville's International Country Music Conference in 2003 and planted the seed for this book in my mind. Her contagious enthusiasm spurred my writing. My father, mentor, colleague, and friend Carl Brasseaux, Director of the Center for Louisiana Studies at the University of Louisiana at Lafayette, opened his enormous personal primary source database to me, from which I was able to locate sources and materials for this book. He generously gave of his time reading dozens of drafts and offering suggestions. Likewise, my frequent collaborator Kevin Fontenot of Tulane University opened to me the exciting world of country music scholarship, a rich field of study that not only openly acknowledges Cajun music as a subcategory, but also provided a contextual framework from which to construct an argument about the currents acting on the genre. I extend many thanks to Kevin for freely sharing his resources and expansive knowledge of America's vernacular musical traditions and for profoundly shaping my thinking regarding Cajun musical traditions. Thanks to Kevin also for suggesting the title for this volume, *Cajun Breakdown*, and for generously allowing me to muse publicly about his "Honky Tonk Corridor" idea. My dear and longtime friend Erik Charpentier gave constant encouragement, numerous readings, and insight about the Cajun-American experience. His view of south Louisiana's connection to larger cultural phenomena helped provide clarity to some of the arguments featured here. I also tip my hat to James Akenson, cofounder of the International Country Music Conference. His amazing capacity to bestow compassion, unwavering intellectual support, and constant encouragement has provided the model of professionalism and friendship that I strive to emulate.

A number of Yale University's history and American studies faculty immeasurably enriched the text that follows. Thanks to insightful commentary offered by Michael Denning, John Szwed, Alicia Schmit Camacho, and Stephen Pitti, this project is immeasurably better. I am especially grateful to those graduate students who took time away from their hectic schedules and immense reading loads to offer advice, critiques, and friendship: Katherine Mooney, who dissected my arguments using her deep understanding of the American South and country-and-western music and her line-editing skills; Joseph Fronczak, whose enthusiasm and encyclopedic understanding of U.S. historiography inspired me to think more broadly and whose sharp critiques challenged me on many points; and Sara Hudson, whose loyal friendship and warm company brought a little bit of the South into my New England digs. She made me feel at home as I revised.

Archivists and librarians have enriched this project, perhaps more than they realize. I extend my thanks to Ann Mire at the Acadia Parish Library, whose enthusiasm and expertise with the Freeland Archives opened the rich cultural treasures of Crowley, Louisiana, before my eyes. Patti Threatt at McNeese State University's Frazar Memorial Library Archives and Special Collections responded with incredible expediency and professionalism to each of my queries. Steve Weiss at the University of North Carolina at Chapel Hill's Southern Folklife Collection and George Miles at Yale University's Beinecke Library helped me chase down images to illustrate this project. Sandra Himel, founder and curator of the Cajun and Creole Music Collection—one of the most extensive collections of commercial Cajun and Creole recordings at any public institution—housed in the University of Louisiana at Lafayette's Edith Garland Dupré Library, gave me full access to her resources and time, for which I am most grateful.

The Oxford University Press editorial staff and American Musicspheres series editor, Mark Slobin, were wonderfully efficient, professional, and courteous. I extend my appreciation to Professor Slobin, Suzanne Ryan, Katharine Boone, Lora Dunn, and Norman Hirschy, who generously offered their firm support for this project throughout the submission and editing processes.

I also take this opportunity to acknowledge my intellectual lineage. As an undergraduate at the University of Louisiana at Lafayette, I had the great good fortune of solidifying my comprehension of Cajun music under the tutelage of Barry Jean Ancelet, to whom I extend my gratitude. I also express my heartfelt thanks to Louisiana State University professors Carolyn Ware, Helen Regis, Heather McKillop, Jill Brody, and especially Jay Edwards for their guidance and input during my tenure as a graduate student in the university's anthropology department. They allowed me to draft what became chapters in *Cajun Breakdown* as I composed my master's thesis. My musical indoctrination, however, would not be complete without the generosity and friendship of the traditional Cajun band Les Frères Michot, who took me under their wing and molded me into a Cajun musician while demonstrating the nuances of historic Cajun music every Monday night as we performed at Prejean's Restaurant in

Lafayette, Louisiana, from 2000 to 2004. My association with the Michot family band blossomed into a lasting friendship and professional collaboration with guitarist/accordionist André and fiddler Louis Michot of the Grammy-nominated Cajun band Lost Bayou Ramblers. Their insights into early commercial Cajun music and Cajun swing have been invaluable to this project. I also thank the staff at the University of Louisiana at Lafayette's National Public Radio affiliate, KRVS 88.7 FM, which granted me the opportunity to explore on air some of the ideas put forth in these pages during my weekly radio broadcast, the *Cajun and Creole Hour*, between 2000 and 2004.

I extend many thanks to the countless other individuals who have contributed to this project—either knowingly or unknowingly—including Luderin Darbone, Hadley Castille, the Lost Bayou Ramblers, Nick Spitzer, Tracey E. W. Laird, John Mack Faragher, Jay Gitlin, Glenda Gilmore, Matthew Frey Jacobson, Michael Veal, Robin Morris, Monica Martinez, Simeon Mann, Quan Tran, Deborah Wolfe, Karylin Crockett, Ana Minian, the Southern Group and Westerners at Yale, Andrew Horowitz, Victorine Shepard, Thelma and Woody Daigle, Ray Brassieur, Norris and Evon Melancon, Ray Abshire, Ben Sandmel, Ron Brown, Ron Yule, Johnnie Allan, the Center for Louisiana Studies at the University of Louisiana at Lafayette, Archives of Cajun and Creole Folklore at the University of Louisiana at Lafayette, Library of Congress, Redell Miller, Mitch and Bob Reed, John Joyce, Aimée Brasseaux, David Brasseaux, and Christi Brasseaux.

My deepest heartfelt thanks go out to my family. My mother Glenda Melancon Brasseaux, who tolerated innumerable "business" discussions between my father and me at family functions, taught me to love Cajun music. I cherish my childhood days when I danced on her feet in the kitchen listening to French music on the transistor radio. And finally, to my strongest support, my loving companion, confidant, and best friend Jessika Ducharme Brasseaux and our two children Anne Elise and Joseph Emile, who made this book worth writing. Jessika, Ani, and Joe make me laugh from the bottom of my belly. They give me wings to explore the heights of my dreams and aspirations, and pull me back down to earth if I float too far away. They challenge me, nourish me, and make me proud to be a part of their lives.

Contents

Introduction: Framing Cajun Music   3

1. Social Music   27

2. Early Commercial Era   49

3. A Heterogeneous Tradition   73

4. Becoming the Folk   91

5. Cajun Swing Era   113

6. The Modern Cajun Sound   131

7. Cajun National Anthem   157

8. A New Mental World   179

Epilogue: Escaping Isolation   209

Appendix   219

Notes   229

Bibliography   287

Index   309

Cajun Breakdown

Introduction: Framing Cajun Music

Cajun music is woven of many strands. Like Ralph Ellison's America, this synthetic musical idiom is the product of worlds in collision. Cajuns filtered the cultural and musical systems—overlaid for centuries in Louisiana—into an intricately nuanced and wholly creolized expression that eludes stringent categorization. In the words of Cajun fiddler Doug Kershaw, it was just music: the melodic voice of a dynamic, heterogeneous, and largely invisible ethnic group. The narrative that follows spotlights the development of Cajun music, the musicians who created the art through time, and the sociocultural contexts shaping musical expression in Cajun Country to draw the genre out of the shadows of mainstream media.

I began this project as an attempt to reconnect with the soundtrack of my youth. My mind's ear can still hear the thin, processed sound of Cajun music broadcast by a local French-language AM radio station in my maternal grandfather's Chevrolet pickup truck as we traversed the gravel byways surrounding his home in rural Acadia Parish. He annotated the broadcast with tales of dancing to Lawrence Walker, Harry Choates, and Iry LeJeune, yarns that both captured my imagination as a youth and sustained my interest throughout this project. Like my grandfather, I came of age sweating and dancing all night to the latest Cajun music in poorly ventilated in south Louisiana dance halls. Indeed, my fascination with Cajun music stems directly from a personal crusade to better understand the world from whence I came.

This book is in many ways a corrective. It stands in stark contrast to previous studies of folk music in general and Cajun music in particular. My goal with this study is to expand the horizons of vernacular musical scholarship and American cultural history by presenting working-class Cajun music through a close reading of the social contexts and cultural processes driving changes in the tradition. I acknowledge the broadest scope of musical expression to emerge within the community and the mutual dialogue maintained between the ethnic group and their Anglo-American counterparts. *Cajun Breakdown* explores the heterogeneity defining Cajun society and culture. Widespread interaction among disparate groups, and the liberal consumption of cultural information disseminated from outside of the community shaped the group's perceptions and behaviors over time, and, indeed, the very contours of south Louisiana's cultural landscape. The evidence presented here suggests that Cajuns were not wholly isolated and disconnected from regional and national trends, as some scholars have argued. Rather, Cajuns were in tune with the latest developments in American popular culture, from the nineteenth-century civic brass band movement to Cajun interpretations of jazz and Broadway numbers. Many individuals, especially musicians, maintained a keen awareness of the latest mainstream trends and selectively recontextualized those cultural traits and musical styles that satisfied their fancy, values, and local aesthetics. Cajuns balanced traditional meanings and cultural production while engaging the Americanization process that transpired unevenly, even on the most basic levels, across the community at large.

America always spoke through Cajun music. In addition to local traditions, musicians were openly conversant in mainstream compositions, styles, and genres that suited their artistic sensibilities and audiences' demands. Fiddlers, singers, accordionists, and their musical colleagues encountered, selectively absorbed, and adapted American mass culture as long as it could function within expressive settings entirely of their own making. Indeed, the Bayou Country represented what anthropologist William Roseberry considers a matrix of "intersecting histories characterized by differentiation, heterogeneous cultural relations and values, and relations of power that encompass contradictions and tensions."[1] This interpretive process did not erase the ethnic community's lines of demarcation. Rather, sustained interaction compelled the group to constantly reconfigure its cultural boundaries under the weight of interethnic tension. Cajuns negotiated how and why to confront the mainstream, while being discerning about which resources to engage—a relationship characterized by "transculturation": a phenomenon, as Mary Louise Pratt suggests, that transpires when "subordinated or marginal groups select and invent from materials transmitted to them by a dominant or metropolitan culture."[2] This interactive middle ground between Cajuns and American popular culture facilitated exchange while highlighting the asymmetrical relationship between working-class Cajuns and Anglo-Americans.

A Synthetic Music

Cajun Breakdown investigates the cross-cultural discourses that gave birth to, and encouraged the evolution of, Cajun music through 1950. This vernacular Gulf Coast expression germinated across generations through interaction and adaptation. Cajun musicians drew inspiration from, and built upon, musical principles derived from their European and Canadian lineages, while readily adapting and translating a varied complex of American influences into a Franco-Southern idiom that accommodated the ethnic group's concerns, worldview, and cultural orientation. Francophone singers reframed traditional British and Anglo-American tunes such as "Billy Boy," "My Good Ole Man," and "The Butcher Boy" into French expressions that translated, respectively, as "Billy Garçon," "Mon bon vieux mari," and "Je m'ai mis aller voire une jolie brune."[3] With the rise of mass media during the course of the twentieth century, Cajuns reinterpreted and rearranged popular songs disseminated via record and radio by the likes of hillbilly crooner Jimmie Rodgers, Western swing bandleader Bob Wills, and seminal New Orleans jazzmen. Musicians performed this heterogeneous repertoire in an assortment of musical contexts that coexisted simultaneously: house dances, fairs, weddings, funerals, barns, wagon yards, taverns, dance halls, recording studios, and festivals.[4] The resulting musical amalgam often blended individualism and collectivism, propriety and carnality, vernacular and commercial idioms—a set of paradoxical combinations that reflected the complexity of the Cajun reality as the community navigated and engaged the American contexts in which they lived.

Cajuns confronted America on many fronts. Contrary to popular depictions, they were not an isolated curiosity scraping out a meager existence in a Gulf Coast backwater, but rather full participants in American culture. Individuals engaged on their own terms the varied indigenous and imported strains of cultural information circulating in south Louisiana. By the twentieth century, Cajun musicians—especially recording artists and professional entertainers—served as local culture brokers. By perching on the cultural margins of their communities, their livelihood necessitated fluency in contemporary musical trends to accommodate audience demands. Their work began in the evening, after the labor in the fields was through, on a bandstand that distinguished entertainers from the mass of dancers who patronized local dance halls. Beyond the honky-tonk, artists indulged their interest in regional and national popular music by attending performances, buying records, and listening to radio broadcasts produced hundreds of miles away from Louisiana. This collective experience united diverse individuals through the common language of music. Musicians established a social infrastructure, forming cohorts, networking, and collaborating to land higher paying jobs. They toured local dance hall circuits, and later honky-tonks and bars in east Texas after the region's petroleum boom in 1901.

As the agrarian American South mechanized and industrialization proliferated, thousands of Cajuns left their depreciating farms to work on railroads and derricks and in refineries and shipyards.[5] Here, in this new milieu, they encountered a world of differences as well as sociocultural parallels. Interchange transpired most uninhibitedly where compatibility felt familiar. During the first half of the twentieth century, well-established traditions such as Cajun dance music migrated beyond the confines of Acadiana as musicians sought work in dance halls, recording studios, and radio stations, locales that encouraged musical discourse. Over time, dance halls gave way to ballrooms, locally owned and operated independent labels such as Gold Star, Opera, and Fais Do Do emerged to meet the demands for locally produced records, and small-market radio stations such as Shreveport's KWKH became media giants syndicating such programming as *The Louisiana Hayride* to a national audience. These arenas opened the conduits of cultural communication and encouraged intercourse between well-established regional traditions such as Cajun music, Western swing, hillbilly, and blues. Dance hall circuits, record contracts, and radio programming formed foundation of the increasingly dense communication networks within the region—labeled in this book as the Honky-Tonk Corridor—that seared Cajun music into the national imagination.

The most famous song in Cajun history, "Jole Blon," catapulted to the top of the national Billboard charts and influenced generations of American musicians. The song's ascendance from an obscure French-language B-side to a novelty song embraced by Roy Acuff, Waylon Jennings, and Bruce Springsteen only came to pass when these transregional media outlets interfaced immediately after World War II. The narrative that unfolds in the pages that follow catalogues the many cultural exchanges that collectively fostered a distinctive American-made expression: Cajun music.

Cultural exchange does not mean without hostility, reservations, or misgivings. To the contrary, Cajuns navigated a complicated bilingual world that too often subjugated and denigrated the community. Cajuns were one of America's poor, uneducated, agrarian underclasses. Catholicism, their "foreign" tongue, and French customs, compounded by the many individuals who worked only to satisfy their *besoin*, or immediate needs, rather accumulating material wealth, confounded and disgusted their more affluent neighbors.[6] When Acadian refugees first settled in Louisiana, they confronted the region's Francophone elite—*les Créoles blanc*. Some immigrants embarked on an upwardly mobile trajectory toward accommodation and assimilation; the rest felt the brunt of Creole prejudice.[7] Following the Civil War, northern Anglo-Protestants who relocated to the South, either as carpetbaggers or visitors passing through, reminded those Cajuns they encountered for decades of their social, political, and economic position as a vanquished population.[8] Even Anglo-Protestant southerners in their vicinity, namely, east Texas, who also left the cotton belt for the oil patch, directed some of the most acerbic venom toward their Francophone rivals. And yet, in the face of vilification, Cajuns continued to engage, interpret, and adapt Anglophone cultural information without compromising their cultural integrity or ethnic identity.

Blue-collar Cajuns danced to the tempo of American life alongside impoverished Southerners and so-called white ethnic immigrant groups who experienced similar forms of subjugation. Suspended somewhere between blackness and whiteness, both the Anglophone and Francophone elite measured their subjugated neighbors against a white ideal exemplified by economic and political power in addition to physical characteristics.[9]

When eighteenth-century French expatriate Michel-Guillaume Jean de Crèvecoeur famously mused in 1782, "What then is the American, this new man?," the answer was resoundingly clear.[10] The new "American" was a white masculine American, to be sure, whose Protestant adherence further reinforced the notion of exceptionalism and divine purpose. Acadians and other white ethnic immigrant groups—racialized as Celts, Slavs, Nordics, Iberics, Hebrews, and Latins—threatened to destabilize Anglo-Saxonism's dominance in the United States by radically altering the nation's demographics.[11] Foreigners in America's "New Jerusalem" vexed the country's Anglo-Protestant establishment. Nativism rang from all corners of the Northeast. Even such celebrated American intellectuals as Benjamin Franklin proclaimed, "Why should Pennsylvania, founded by the English, become a Colony of Aliens, who will shortly be so numerous as to Germanize us instead of our Anglifying them, and will never adopt our language or customs any more than they can acquire our complexion?"[12] The sheer volume of immigration rose from mere thousands per year in the 1820s to hundreds of thousands in the 1840s. By 1920, America's white foreign-born immigrant population numbered more than 13.5 million, making progressive-minded Americans ever more reactionary.[13]

Progressive Louisianians sought to whiten both Cajuns and recent immigrants by "teaching the arts and habits of civilization," which translated as forced enculturation into the mores and values of nondenominational Protestantism, republicanism, and the English language.[14] To be sure, schools emphasized Progressive middle-class American values, not indigenous wisdom. After the 1916 Louisiana Compulsory Education Act, the state's "off white" children suffered the same fate as Native Americans, Mexican Americans, and other prepubescent ethnics throughout the United States who, by law, were obligated to attend English-only schools where cultural annihilation was standard policy. Blue-collar Cajuns selectively internalized some tenants of Americanization policy—including the English language, patriotism, and elements of republicanism (particularly libertarianism)— but refashioned and recalculated them according to their own cultural codes. The group actualized a synergy that allowed them to be at once recognizably American and distinctively Cajun, a sociocultural phenomenon that ultimately impeded assimilation. Indeed, American mass media certainly continued to note the difference.

Anglo-Americans constantly reminded Cajuns, particularly rural working-class denizens, that they represented the "Other" in English-only classrooms, in east Texas oil fields, and later, in movie theaters. Feature and documentary films produced in accordance with the popular American perception of the group and released between the late 1920s and the 1950s suggest that Cajuns had not succumbed to assimilation. Filmmakers ascribed ethnic stereotypes in their depictions of the group by romanticizing and highlighting "exotic" traits of Cajuns and their picturesque homeland. Directors Raoul Walsh's 1919 and Edwin Carewe's 1929 adaptation of Longfellow's epic poem *Evangeline*, pioneer documentary filmmaker Robert Flaherty's 1948 film *Louisiana Story*, and the feature film *Thunder*

Bay (1953) starring Jimmy Stewart all stereotypically portrayed Cajuns as markedly different from their Anglo counterparts, indicating that America unquestionably viewed the ethic group as the Other. The trend continued well into the late twentieth century. Adam Sandler's picture *Water Boy* racialized the ethic group by mismatching cultural symbols, exaggerating local accents, and feigning ignorance in an effort to give the comedy a "Louisiana feel."[15] In addition, the dramatic growth of Louisiana's cultural tourism industry before Hurricane Katrina, based largely on promoting the uniqueness of Cajun culture under the slogan "Come as You Are, Leave Different," also points to the distinctive character of the region's cultural landscape and musical traditions.[16]

The people and cultural processes that nurtured Cajun music's development are best understood through a nexus of relations. Musicians crafted their art via exchange and cultural transaction while performing for dancers or simply among themselves through private discourse. Local entertainers forged interactive networks linking individuals, rural neighborhoods, and the broader community at large well before they first stepped into the recording studio or stood in front of a live broadcasting microphone in a radio station. These relationships took form as early as 1764, the year the first Acadian refugees set foot on Louisiana soil.

Life before the Record

The precommercial era (1764–1927)—which I further subdivide into phase I (1764–1830), phase II (1830–1880), phase III (1880–1927)—represents Cajun music's formative and yet least understood period.[17] The historical contours and cultural processes driving change before the emergence of commercial Cajun recordings are fundamental to understanding the sequential development of the genre during the twentieth century, which serves as the primary focus of this study.

Empire sewed the seeds of Cajun music. New France clashed with New England and wrestled with New Spain in the geopolitical contests for territorial control in North America. Positioned at the crossroads of empire, Acadia and, later, Louisiana buffered the French interest on the continent.[18] The Louisiana territory became a vibrant contact zone variously blessed and cursed with porous borders through which American Indians, Africans slaves, European administrators, soldiers and sailors, merchants, smugglers, refugees, and pioneers circulated and cohabitated. Amid this global contest, musical traditions from three continents—Europe, Africa, and North America—collided in the Bayou Country. Those musical customs, which amalgamated in varying degrees within the confines of those ethnically diverse communities dotting the Gulf Coast landscape, ultimately stimulated the genesis of an indigenous form of musical expression unique to Louisiana.

Traditional Acadian music formed the rudiment of Cajun music's precommercial era. The genre's gestational stage—phase I—began when the first boatload of Acadian exiles reached the shores of Louisiana in 1764. Presumably, the refugees who established the initial Acadian settlements in the territory relied on a cappella compositions for their musical entertainment before cross-cultural exchange animated Cajun music's embryonic development. The pedigree of French ballads collected by folklorists during the twentieth century suggests that predispersal *Acadie* boasted a large repertoire of Old World compositions.[19] Yet, this argument by analogy presumes, through lyrical analysis, that Cajun musical traditions traced their roots to those European locales that boasted similar compositions in their oral repertory. The only substantiated documentation regarding Acadian music in the first years of resettlement in Louisiana, however, alludes to the popularity of the fiddle and clarinet among the immigrants. Aside from these obscure references, there is virtually no documentation of postdispersal Acadian musical traditions or repertory in Louisiana before the nineteenth century.

If data regarding the symbiotic relationship between musical development and sociocultural change during the nineteenth and twentieth centuries is any indication, the formative components of Cajun music presumably began to synthesize between 1764 and 1830 as newly arrived Acadian refuges interacted with peoples maintaining European, African, and North American cultural ties. Some upwardly mobile Acadians began to engage the region's plantation economy and acquire slaves, thereby stimulating fragmentation and diversification within the community. Historian Carl Brasseaux maintains that the Bayou Country became a "highly stratified multicultural society in which culture and language provided the basis for social distinctions. Indeed, throughout the nineteenth century, class lines and cultural boundaries coincided in rural south Louisiana."[20] As part of the nouveau bourgeoisie, genteel Acadian planters espoused formal musical training, in part, to associate with Louisiana's white Creoles and French upper classes. Their high cultural musical tastes differed significantly from rural aesthetics maintained by the region's underclasses, which are the primary focus of this book.

The music of the Cajun working classes, who originally settled Louisiana as *petits habitants* (yeoman farmers), maintained a separate and distinctive dance culture at *bals de maison*, or neighborhood house dances, from their more affluent counterparts. The first descriptions of the social setting in which working-class Cajun amusements transpired stem from phase I of the precommercial era. In 1803, French immigrant and travel writer C. C. Robin witnessed the festivities at a house dance along the Bayou Lafourche. His fascination with local customs generated a lively description of the intricate social interaction among friends, family, and dancers.[21] Customs such as dancing and musical performance would evolve slowly after Robin's visit until the onset of the Civil War, when frequent violent encounters dramatically altered the dynamics of local entertainment in rural districts.

The Americanization of south Louisiana began in earnest in 1803, following the Louisiana Purchase, when the region's Francophone population became subject to American law. In 1946, geographers Walter Kollomorgen and Robert Harrison concluded that "since 1803 [the Cajuns'] destiny has been fully identified with the destiny of our nation albeit the still common usage of the French language. They are therefore American in every sense of the word."[22] Their assertion acknowledges that Cajuns became part of a larger equation governed by American politics, economics, and law, despite the ethnic group's linguistic and cultural distinctiveness.

Louisiana's cultural landscape began to shift dramatically following the Louisiana Purchase. In 1803, the Bayou Country boasted seven times more Francophones than Anglophones in the region's free population. At the time of Louisiana's admission to the Union in 1812, an influx of Anglo-Americans moved into the territory and considerably altered that ratio, as French speakers outnumbered English speakers by only three to one. This Anglo-American invasion thus accelerated the complex cultural exchanges that transpired over the course of the nineteenth century.[23]

Americans began to exert a significant cultural influence on south Louisiana during the second phase of the precommercial era between 1830 and 1880. Life in antebellum Louisiana, the ravages of the Civil War, the virtual collapse of the American South's economy, the rise of sharecropping, and the increased interaction between the ethnic group and their black neighbors outlined the shifting cultural and social climate of the period. The combination of these forces forever altered the course of the group's sociocultural and musical landscapes. During phase II, the intrinsic nature of the Acadian community shifted in dramatic fashion that led to the emergence of splinter group that assumed the appellation "Cajun."

A number of travel reports from the mid- to late nineteenth century offer a snapshot of the musical contexts flourishing in south Louisiana. *Bals de maison* continued with great frequency, and fiddle music prospered. Phase II also witnessed the introduction of two cultural institutions that profoundly affected the sounds and social contexts associated with Cajun music. Dance halls—which eventually supplanted house dances during the twentieth century—first emerged sometime around the Civil War and expanded the space allotted for dancing and courtship. In step with the widespread violence introduced by war, *bals de maison* and dance halls became dangerous scenes of bloodshed and mayhem. The widespread dissemination of the diatonic accordion also transpired in the years following the Civil War.

Cajun music's character assumed a new attitude and feel between 1830 and 1880 as Cajuns had increased contact with their black neighbors. Historian Carl Brasseaux notes that cross-cultural interaction was common before emancipation, and that Francophone yeomen disrupted the divisions of power dividing white planters and black slaves:

American sugar planters generally viewed the Acadian small farmers and the far less numerous *petits habitants* (subsistence farmers possessing no slaves) as nuisances who "demoralized" their slaves. Not only did the small farmers' comfortable existence persuade blacks "that it was not necessary for men to work so hard as they themselves were obliged to," but the Acadians frequently hired slaves to do odd jobs, paying them with "luxuries" their masters did not wish them to have.[24]

Over time, communication between Acadians and Afro-Creoles and African Americans extended to musical interaction, particularly after the Civil War, when poor whites worked alongside their black neighbors as sharecroppers. Syncopation, call-and-response, rhythmic patterns, emotive vocals expressed with full-body release, and even repertoire became essential components of the Cajun dance music.[25]

In the wake of the Civil War, grinding poverty became a widespread reality for many Louisianians. The South's sharecropping system redistributed the ethnic components of Louisiana's population and ultimately changed the demographic complexity of the Acadian community. Tenant farmers and sharecroppers moved frequently to find work or to improve their lot with landowners who offered more congenial business arrangements. Working-class Acadian culture felt the brunt of this economic crunch as evidenced by behavioral shifts. For the first time since their arrival in Louisiana, Acadians began to practice general exogamy and absorbed portions of the region's poor white population, including Anglos, Germans, Creoles, Italians, and French. Acadian society consequently evolved from a fairly homogeneous population into a heterogeneous group that diversified within the Bayou Country's socioeconomic classification system under a common Louisiana French lingua franca.[26] As the group's social and cultural dynamics evolved, so did the group's moniker in accordance with their evolving character.

During the late 1860s and 1870s, Anglophone writers began to label this cultural and linguistic assemblage with a phonetic appellation 'cadien, derived from the French Acadien or Acadian. English corruptions appeared in print as "cagian," "cajen," and in 1879, "Cajun."[27] The term Cajun was pregnant with meaning. As early as the 1840s, Anglo attitudes toward the Acadian population disintegrated from contempt to disgust, a disposition that coincided with the nationalistic pressures leading up to the Civil War and with increasing American xenophobia following the large influx of Irish and German immigrants and competitive socioeconomic struggles between these factions. Not only did Cajun refer to the evolving ethnic group, but the term carried a negative stigma that endured until the 1960s. It translated as backward, ignorant, French-speaking peasants whose laziness and refusal to assimilate were contradictory to mainstream Anglo-Protestant mores. In response, Cajuns retorted with the slur Américains, meaning swindler, meddlesome, and haughty. Like other poor whites in the rural South and Appalachia who endured the term "hillbilly," Cajun music came under the influence of American popular culture despite overt tensions between these conflicting Franco-Catholic and Anglo-Protestant worldviews. Contrary to popular belief, Louisiana's ever-changing Acadian population was no more isolated than any other rural Southern group during the nineteenth century.[28]

Phase III of the precommercial era spanned the years between 1880 and 1927, during which new technologies such as the railroad and steamboat propulsion further connected the ethnic group to American cultural trends, and outside cultural forces altered Cajun music's dynamics.[29] By the twentieth century, the emergence of a national communications network, the development of Louisiana's petroleum industry, the state's improved road system, and the increasing availability of mass media technology profoundly shaped the discourse between Cajun and American cultures. The widespread popularity of American popular entertainment, namely, minstrelsy and musical/theatrical performances, penetrated the Bayou Country through the same channels connecting communities throughout the American South.

Popular entertainment infiltrated Cajun Country during the nineteenth and early twentieth centuries, first by rail and waterways, and later via automobile, tents, town civic centers, opera houses, and theaters. Traveling entertainers, minstrels, vaudevillians, circus performers, and the like toured throughout the South, including the Bayou Country, spreading American popular culture and music en route. Itinerant minstrel troupes were among the first such performers to arrive following the establishment of the railroad system in southwest Louisiana in the 1870s.

Anglo-Americans disseminated to Cajun audiences a particular brand of white humor, a familiar acting style, and a specific, albeit diverse, repertoire behind their burnt corked masks. One of the earliest references to black-faced performers in Acadiana dates to April 28, 1860, when a West Baton Rouge newspaper advertised the arrival of the "Banjo Minstrels."[30] By the turn of the twentieth century, troupes with names like Richard & Pringle's Famous Georgia Minstrels, Lew Tigner's Minstrels, Mahara Colored Minstrels, and Faust's Minstrels filled the playbills and provided regular entertainment at local opera houses and theaters.[31] These black-faced musicians and actors exposed south Louisianians to the same songs and stereotypes that forever changed popular culture in the United States (figure I.1).

Traveling entertainers encouraged, even facilitated, this cultural transaction by inviting local talent to share the stage. On January 27, 1877, the Morgan City *Attakapas Register* advertised a show featuring the Welch Minstrels and "three young men of this place, whose musical abilities and faculty for creating mirth are well known to our citizens."[32] Within a 20-year period, homegrown minstrel troupes had taken center stage. In 1896, the Lafayette Minstrels and orchestra entertained their fellow townsfolk at Falk's Opera House. In nearby Opelousas, residents presented the Dixie Blackbird Minstrels in the elementary school gymnasium, a troupe with local actors featuring Cajun surnames such as Comeaux, Hebert, Fontenot, Barilleaux, Guilbeau, and Castille who worked under the direction of Atlanta native Maibelle Cooks.[33]

South Louisianians loved minstrel shows and liberally patronized revues. In 1934, Thibodaux's *Lafourche Comet* newspaper hailed a local production

Figure I.1. Locally produced minstrel shows became an annual affair at the Arcade Theatre in Lake Charles, Louisiana. Courtesy of Archives and Special Collections, Frazar Memorial Library, McNeese State University.

sponsored by the city's Catholic Daughters civic organization as nothing short of a triumph. The *Comet* applauded the professionalism of the performances, which included song recitation, tap dancing, and harmonica music. The reviewer was especially taken with the costuming. "Mr. Phil. J. Naquin, as the make-up artist," the newspaper extolled, "could not have gotten the girls' faces blacker or shinier, if he had taken them to the Kongo Free State of Africa and transformed them into African negroes."[34] These Cajun interpretations of the Anglo-American and African-American minstrelsy traditions illustrate one of the Americanizing cultural undercurrents that shaped artistic expression in the Bayou Country. Minstrelsy proved such an influential factor within south Louisiana that locals organized school plays and little theater performances well into the first half of the twentieth century. As late as the 1960s, Judice Elementary School sporadically sponsored local minstrel productions featuring Cajun recording artists to raise funds for their facility.[35] Meanwhile, as field recordings collected in the late 1960s illustrate, working-class Cajun musicians absorbed portions of the common American minstrelsy repertoire and performed tunes at performances and at home for amusement.[36] Soon after the first black-faced performers captivated local audiences on land, showboats conveniently delivered outside entertainment to communities living along the region's rivers and bayous.

"Steamboats on the river a coming or a going/Splashing the night away/ Hear those banjos ringing, the people are singing/They dance til the break of day" go the lyrics to the jazz standard "When It's Sleepy Time Down South," a song that serves as a sort of lyrical snapshot of the tremendous impact that steamboats and, more important, showboats had along the American South's waterways. Dramatic entertainment, singing, and instrumental arrangements exposed curious individuals living along water routes to new compositions and the latest trends in entertainment. Traditional trade routes such as the Mississippi River and bayous Lafourche and Têche became information highways trafficking mercantile and cultural wares from northern ports to southern landings.

Showboats radiated music. Every aspect of the floating cabaret centered on a melody, from the floorshows to the boat's main marketing scheme. Piercing steam-driven strains of minstrel, ragtime, and Broadway tunes, such as "Oh Dem Golden Slippers," "Turkey in the Straw," "Dixie," "I'm a Yankee Doodle Dandy," "Goodbye, My Lover, Goodbye," "The Blue Alsatian Mountains," and "Out of the Wilderness" whistled from the boat's calliope and bellowed across the water far inland, announcing the arrival of show.[37] From the instant the lilting strains of the calliope reached Cajun ears, the thought of the forthcoming entertainment stirred the Bayou Country's landing communities into a commotion. Cajuns may not have had the chance to enjoy this popular form of entertainment without the technological advances in propulsion that allowed showboats to creep through the murky silt-laden waters of Cajun Country.

Beginning in the early 1830s, flatboats modified into small theater settings traveled south from northern ports along the Mississippi and Ohio valleys during the spring in high-water season, stopping to perform at metropolitan ports before terminating the voyage in New Orleans. Early showboats relied on river currents for propulsion, leaving captains with little choice but to sell their vessels for scrap lumber in the Crescent City, before retreating upstream to their northern headquarters to repeat the circuit the following year. By the late nineteenth century, showboats had become tremendous and ornate theaters towed or tugged by smaller transport vessels, offering captains the necessary mobility to explore unexploited markets along smaller tributaries. Governing locomotion granted showboats the freedom to ply bayou waters in search of new audiences.[38]

In 1882, Captain Augustus Byron French towed his showboat the Sensation to the Pittsburgh area just long enough to hire a team of actors, rehearse his new acts, and restock his boat. The Sensation traveled down the Ohio and Mississippi rivers entertaining locals until Captain French reached Cajun Country. The showboat discovered a lucrative market along the densely Cajun-populated Bayou Lafourche, where an anxious audience with cash in hand from sugarcane and cotton harvests eagerly paid for their chance to catch a glimpse of the entertainment featured on the boat. Though the slow-moving bayou could be treacherous for steamboats, the captain "had discovered the finest showboat territory in the whole country."[39]

Four years later, French returned to the Lafourche region and then headed north along the Bayou Têche.[40] Every night, the showboat's auditorium filled to capacity with curious Cajuns interested in an amusing evening, much to the chagrin of the actors and musicians on board. Historian Philip Graham explains:

> Performers on the stage began complaining that excessive talking in the audience was interfering with their acts. Spectators persisted in grouping themselves in excited little knots instead of remaining seated in the new opera chairs. Captain French employed special ushers to secure quiet and order. Then it was discovered that each of the

noisy little groups had its interpreter, who was translating the words spoken in English on the stage into the *cajun* of his fellows. . . . They were watching the action on the stage and getting the words through their more gifted brother.[41]

Captain French promptly edited subsequent performances by replacing spoken word with musical interludes and exaggerated action to bridge the language barrier between Bayou Country's Francophone audiences and the Anglophone actors.

During the first three decades of the twentieth century, Cajuns flocked to vaudeville performances and circuses, where, like most forms of contemporary public entertainment, music was an integral part of the show. Imaginations ran wild as such exotic animals as zebras and elephants paraded down town streets and trapeze artists hurled their bodies in death defying leaps through the thick Louisiana air. On November 16, 1901, the Campbell Brothers Great Consolidated Shows presented their circus in Lafayette. In addition to an "open den of ferocious lions," the performance included two brass bands performing an assortment of popular tunes and the "Finest Steam Calliope in America."[42] Adept local musicians absorbed popular melodies from these outside sources and learned to translate them onto the available instrumentation, shaping the sounds of Cajun music.

Evolution of Instrumentation

The introduction of new instruments within local arrangements also signaled shifts in musical direction and the extent to which Cajuns interacted with extraneous influences. Although the calliope did not become a standard feature in Cajun music, the precommercial era witnessed significant changes in instrumentation over time. The earliest material evidence regarding Acadian musical culture dates to a secession record filed in 1782. The document acknowledges that at least one Acadian refugee owned a fiddle and clarinet.[43] A second reference to an Acadian multi-instrumentalist who played the fiddle and clarinet appears three years later in a letter written by Attakapas District commandant Alexandre DeClouet to Louisiana's Spanish Governor Estevan Miró. On October 8, 1785, DeClouet explained in his correspondence that he was attempting to locate a renowned Acadian musician named Prejean, who lived somewhere in Baton Rouge. Prejean's remarkable skill with both the fiddle and the clarinet captivated the imagination of the region's top administrators.[44] For approximately 75 years after DeClouet's correspondence, descriptions of music in the Bayou Country slip into obscurity before reappearing during the mid-nineteenth century, when travel writers began to document their experiences there.

The fiddle remained at the heart of Cajun music, while the sound of the clarinet slipped underground and faded from the vernacular musical landscape.[45] The violin had indeed emerged as the dominate instrument in the region when late-nineteenth-century travel writers visited south Louisiana. In 1859, French writer Alexander Barde journeyed to Bayou Country to document vigilante activity in the Attakapas district. Barde punctuates his narrative about paramilitary violence with frequent descriptions of the instrumentation available in the region before the Civil War. He contends that musicians played a variety of string instruments, including fiddles, mandolins, banjos, and guitars.[46] The dominance of the violin is apparent in the number of active fiddlers in towns and rural neighborhoods. A writer for *Frank Leslie's Popular Monthly* encountered a prairie settlement of approximately 150 Cajun families in 1881, which boasted "no less than sixty fiddlers."[47] Less than 10 years later, Louisiana folklorist Alcée Fortier noted the dominance of the instrument in St. Mary Parish: "Every Saturday evening there was a ball in the prairie. The ballroom was a large hall . . . crowded with persons dancing to the music of three fiddles."[48] Fiddle music and neighborhood balls continued well into the first half of the twentieth century in such communities as the Grande Pointe settlement on east bank of the Bayou Têche. Cultural geographer Lauren Post counted more than 60 fiddlers in the rural community during the Great Depression.[49] Dancers amused themselves to the melody of violins at house dances, early dance halls, and significant public events. Vermillion Parish native Alice Reaux Blanchet, born 1867, recalled in an interview with Cajun musicologist Catherine Blanchet that the band that performed at her wedding dance consisted of fiddles and a cornet.[50] The fiddle remained the instrument of choice in some Cajun communities in the southwestern half of the state until the 1920s, when the accordion became the dominant melodic voice of Cajun music (figure I.2).[51]

Rhythmic accompaniment from other stringed and percussive voices may have accompanied fiddle music as early as the nineteenth century. The guitar has been in the Bayou Country since at least 1819. Travel writer James Leander Cathcart encountered in the Opelousas district a Francophone musician who "played the guitar, and sung several airs very well."[52] Local advertisements further indicate the guitar's distribution in mid-nineteenth-century Louisiana. On January 26, 1856, Washington, Louisiana, shopkeeper A. Millspaugh advertised in *The Opelousas Courier* that her Ladies and Children's Shoe Store also carried strings and sheet music for guitar. Millspaugh's ad suggests that formally trained and musically literate guitarists lived and played in Cajun Country; however, the role of the guitar as a rhythmic accompaniment for fiddles and other vernacular instruments used in nineteenth-century Cajun music remains unclear.[53] In 1901, local merchants marketed the guitar alongside fiddles and accordions, implying a possible shift in arranging styles.[54] Cleoma Breaux's rhythm guitar work on the first commercial Cajun recording in 1928, however, provides the first authenticated and audible account of the instrument's position within local arrangements.[55]

The role of percussive instrumentation—such as the triangle, which flourished in early-twentieth-century Cajun music—is rarely discussed in the documentary record, and then only in passing. What little information is

Figure I.2. When the 1927 Mississippi River flood displaced thousands of Cajuns, Red Cross tent cities housing disparate refugees became breeding grounds for musical interaction. Courtesy of the Center for Louisiana Studies, University of Louisiana at Lafayette.

available regarding these percussive implements suggests that triangles diffused across racial and ethnic boundaries from the Afro-Creole or African-American traditions into Cajun arrangements by virtue of cross-cultural borrowing. According to music historian Dena Epstein, the triangle was a regular component of African-American string bands (fiddle, banjo, triangle) throughout the South before the Civil War.[56] The first accounts of the instrument in Louisiana appear in two fictional works by local color writers dating from the late 1880s. Author George Washington Cable described the triangle as part of a slave orchestra—consisting of a four-string banjo, an extensive percussion section featuring drums, a jew's harp, a converted animal jawbone used like a washboard in modern zydeco bands, and triangle—that performed in New Orleans' famed Place Congo.[57] Black percussionists in Cajun Country also seemingly employed the triangle at local dances during the late nineteenth century. St. Martinville native Sidonie de la Houssaye created the first fictional account to place the instrument within a Cajun setting in her novella *Pouponne et Balthazar*:

All around the dance hall they had improvised benches by putting planks on tree trunks carried in for the [wedding dance]. The orchestra was composed, first of all, of the settlement's [Cajun] violin player, the handsome Etienne Aucoin, who on this memorable day had taken on as helpers three of Monsieur Bossier's Negroes, who were considered first-class musicians. They were all standing up, each on a different barrel, and the orchestra leader, Etienne, the violin player, all the while waving his bow, was beating time with his foot and head at the same time. One of the Negroes also played the violin: as for the two others, one was holding a triangle which he was hitting with an iron rod, while the other was shaking a fistful of bones and making the most grotesque contortions.[58]

Both de la Houssaye and Cable drew inspiration for their fiction from the cultural contours of their immediate environment and clearly place the triangle in the hands of Afro-Creoles, who gave rhythmic accompaniment to a stringed melodic voice. The support instrument may have indeed diffused from the Afro-Creole community into the Cajun musical tradition, because interracial band combos like the one described by de la Houssaye were not uncommon during the late nineteenth and early twentieth centuries. References to the triangle do not appear again until a handful of commercial recordings surfaced in 1928, when Cajuns used the rhythmic instrument as an accompaniment for the accordion.[59]

The diatonic button accordion revolutionized Cajun music, following its introduction to south Louisiana during the mid-nineteenth century. The volume, the diatonic chord structures, and tonal limitations dramatically altered the sound and the perception of ensemble arrangements in south Louisiana. Musicians quickly learned to adapt the instrument to local aesthetics, and fused European song styles such as polkas and mazurkas with the choppiness and syncopation heard among Afro-Creole accordionists.

Travel writers penned one of the earliest descriptions of an accordion performance in south Louisiana, a yarn that suggests the instrument's cross-cultural legacy in the Bayou Country. While traversing South Bay at the mouth of the Mississippi River one night in 1871, Ralph Keeler and A. R. Waud encountered barking dogs and a gray-haired German lighthouse keeper—standing armed with a gun—on a rotting wharf near his one-room shack. The lighthouse keeper, a disabled Civil War veteran, shouted into the moonlight to locate the source of his dogs' agitated barking. "He was frank enough to say," the travelers wrote, "that [if] he had received no answer to his summons he was going to fire at us." The party nimbly defused the situation and retired upon invitation into the German's solitary digs. "In reply to our question as to how he passed the time alone, he said he had music for company, and pointed to an accordion which from its unwieldy size and mysterious age, was a very megatherium of musical instruments." With his spirits elevated thanks to cheap claret wine,

he began to line out the famous old German hymn, *Nun danket alle Gott*, accompanying himself on the instrument when he sang [figure I.3]. By the time he had reached the second stanza he was so carried away with his own music that he forgot to give out the lines in advance. . . . It was surely an impressive thing in that swampy wilderness to come upon the words and air which have been heroic ever since the night when they were both food and sleep to the Great Frederick's army.[60]

Figure I.3. Lithograph artist A. R. Waud sketched one of the earliest depictions of the accordion in Louisiana in June 1871—a German lighthouse keeper at the mouth of the Mississippi River. Reproduction courtesy of the Beinecke Rare Book and Manuscript Library, Yale University.

Imported accordions would have followed Louisiana's normal trade routes beginning at the lighthouse and pilot town at the mouth of the Mississippi River, and then upstream to the port in New Orleans. The German lighthouse keeper, then, literally and figuratively represents south Louisiana's cultural gatekeeper marking the entrance to commercial and cultural exchange.

The diatonic cries of the button accordion were not completely foreign to Cajun musicians. By the Civil War, the harmonica became an important part of the Southern musical landscape and eventually swept through south Louisiana as a popular form of personal entertainment. Like other poor white Southerners, many of south Louisiana's vernacular musicians were accomplished harmonica players. The mouth organ was conveniently small, inexpensive, widely available at general merchandise stores, and, more important, diatonic. Singers could easily alternate between vocal deliveries and several bars of self-accompaniment. Mechanically, harmonicas and accordions were engineered by the same free-reed technology. Reeds arranged in diatonic chords vibrate, producing musical strains when affected by an ample amount of air pressure. Rather than blowing to produce the effect, accordions utilized a bellow-button system that exposed specific reeds to air pressure, thus determining the pitch and tone produced. Several accordionists from Cajun music's first generation of recording artists, including Amédé Breaux and Dewey Segura, cited their parents' harmonica playing as an early influence.[61] Vestiges of this harmonic tradition could be heard as late as the 1960s on field recordings of Isom Fontenot collected by folklorist Ralph Rinzler. During the first two decades of the twentieth century, the squeezebox helped phase out harmonica playing in both popular arranging styles and commercial recordings.[62]

According to cultural geographer Malcolm Comeaux, Afro-Creoles and African Americans "had access to accordions, and probably played a major role in acceptance of accordions in south Louisiana."[63] Afro-Creoles may have adapted the accordion to local musical tradition before their white counterparts. The first images of the instrument in Louisiana depict the accordion in the hands of black musicians (figure I.4).[64] In addition, a large number of references to musicians of color playing the squeezebox further illustrate the popularity of the accordion among the Bayou State's black population.

African Americans adapted the accordion to local musical traditions throughout the South, from West Virginia and Virginia, to Mississippi and Louisiana.[65] In the Bayou Country, the squeezebox flourished in New Orleans during the late nineteenth century before the emergence of hot jazz, and, by the turn of the twentieth century, in black English-speaking Protestant communities as far north as Louisiana's Bible Belt

IN THE STORE.

Figure I.4. Evidence suggests that accordionists of color, such as the individual in this illustration, constituted the first musicians to introduce the squeezebox into south Louisiana's musical traditions. Courtesy of the Center for Louisiana Studies, University of Louisiana at Lafayette.

along the Texas–Arkansas border.[66] Huddie "Leadbelly" Ledbetter learned to play button accordion as a child north of Shreveport in Mooringsport, Louisiana, where he played popular and folk tunes at country dances and spirituals at Baptist church services.[67] In 1972, West Virginian and African-American musician Clarence Tross remembered at 92 years of age that "it was mostly the colored man playing the accordion. . . . Fiddle, banjo, accordion all used to play together for dances."[68] Tross's statement about instrumentation in the Upper South parallels the reminiscences of Afro-Creole Eraste Carriere (b. 1901), who told French music writer and musician Gérard Dole that *only* blacks played accordion in Cajun Country during his father's lifetime.[69]

On Saturday nights at the turn of the twentieth century, Opelousas' Afro-Creole community flocked to dance halls and nightclubs to dance, drink, or find companionship in one of the city's bordellos. At the town's most notorious African-American prostitution racket, Emile Elias's famed Hoochy Koochy Dance Hall, "women danced to the ever enticing melodies of a 'go-to-and-come-from' as the accordeon [*sic*] is often called these days."[70] The widespread popularity of the instrument among Louisiana's black communities, and the choppy syncopated technique heard on the first commercial Cajun recordings, suggests that the Africanized Creole accordion style diffused along with the instrument into the Cajun repertoire. Comeaux emphasizes that whites living on southwest Louisiana's prairies "developed a style of playing that was not smooth and easy, as was done in Europe, but rather they began playing with fast choppy rhythms in a syncopated style that had many fast runs. It evolved into a style not found elsewhere in the world, and based on the style, probably first developed by black Creoles and then taught to Cajuns."[71]

While Cajuns may have learned their technique from Afro-Creoles, local musicians obtained their accordions either through local merchants or via mail order. In the mid-nineteenth century, New Orleans shopkeepers advertised their selection of musical equipment. During the 1860s, retailer Stevens and Seymour imported a variety of musical instruments from France and Germany, including a large assortment of violins and accordions at a range of prices, "Low price, medium, and fine," at their retail outlet opposite the City Hotel on Common Street, New Orleans.[72] Cajuns with money and access to the city could have purchased melodeons from Stevens and Seymour. Others may have indulged their fancy with the help of illustrated newspapers and mail order catalogues that offered a selection of musical instruments, including guitars, harmonicas, violins, and button accordions. *Frank Leslie's Illustrated Newspaper* advertised the instrument as early as 1886, followed by Sears and Roebuck's broad inventory of makes, styles, and manufacturers. Working-class Cajuns, many of whom were illiterate during the late nineteenth century, probably did not order many squeezeboxes by mail, "and certainly not before they had acquired some prior knowledge of accordions and how to play them."[73] Rather, working-class musicians probably purchased their first accordions from local retailers.

Although local German Jewish merchants at F. M. Levy's general store in Rayne, Louisiana, posted general advertisements for musical instruments as early as 1886, Mason McBride's shop in Opelousas became one of the earliest retailers to advertise his imported accordion stock.[74] In February 1901, the *Opelousas Clarion* declared,

> Mason McBride has just received a full line of musical instruments—guitars, violins, harps, accordeons [*sic*], etc.,—and the artistic display in his show window reminds one of a miniature Grunewald [music store in New Orleans]. His prices are reasonable, and he invites those musically inclined to call and see his line.[75]

The growing popularity and widespread dissemination of accordions among the general populace seemingly coincides with the turn of the twentieth century advertisements that specifically tried to attract accordion customers. Malcolm Comeaux believes that German-Jewish merchants like the Levys and the Kahns played an important role in the importation of the diatonic accordion. He explains in his landmark essay "Introduction and Use of Accordions in Cajun Music":

> There were Jewish merchants with stores in all Cajun towns, and probably the best example was the Mervine Kahn store in Rayne, established in 1884 only four years after the railroad arrived. Many Cajuns bought their accordions from Mervine Kahn prior to World War II. . . . These merchants, with close connections to Eastern firms, and possibly directly with German manufacturing companies, began importing accordions to their rural, unsophisticated, French-speaking customers.[76]

Railroads increased the range of communication and commerce in Cajun Country, triggering in the process a substantial cultural metamorphosis that included the diffusion of the accordion. According to Comeaux and music writer Ann Savoy, however, accordions imported before the 1920s were tuned to the keys of A and F, well beyond a fiddle's natural tuning range, making the squeeze box a suitable solo instrument for formal and casual amusements.[77] And indeed, one of the earliest accounts of an accordion performance in south Louisiana describes a single musician. On December 20, 1900, the doors of the Grand Coteau hall opened for a grand fair sponsored by the town's genteel Cajun faction. "At 7:30 the doors were opened," the *Opelousas Clarion* reported, "and the gay notes of 'Bol's Accordeon [*sic*] floated through the well decorated hall."[78] Some accordion performances may have included rhythmic accompaniment from the metered cadence of a triangle or spoons.[79]

By the 1920s and 1930s, importers distributed German-manufactured "Monarch," and later "Sterling" and "Eagle" brand accordions aptly labeled *les 'tit noirs* (literally "the little blacks") by the Cajun community in reference to the instrument's size and color. Comeaux maintains that no accordions were imported during World War II, and few were imported for many years after the war because German factories were devastated, and some accordion factories were located in the Russian sphere of influence. Since no new accordions could be purchased for a considerable time, local Cajuns began repairing and refurbished old accordions, and soon began making accordions.[80]

As the accordion led, the rhythm section followed.

The Jazz Age left its mark on Cajun music by radically altering the Cajun rhythm section. Local jazz drummers became the first to introduce the trap drum kit—snare, bass, and cymbal—into a subgenre of Cajun music categorized as Cajun swing. Upright bass and Dixieland-styled tenor banjo also followed suit in the formation of Cajun swing orchestras, which drew inspiration from both Texas Western swing and New Orleans jazz. These rhythm instruments substantially enriched the sonic backdrop over which fiddlers elaborated and improvised on Cajun, pop, Western swing, blues, and jazz melodies. The Cajun swing era also ushered in the use of steel guitars. Used in the Hawaiian lap steel style, local guitarists fashioned their approach after those American artists who pioneered the instrument's use in country-and-western. Drums, bass, electric guitars, and amplification subsequently became standard components in the Cajun musical equation, modernizing the sounds of Cajun music during the Great Depression.

Cajun Breakdown

The evolution Cajun music's instrumentation represents but a single dimension within the larger matrix of cultural negotiation that defines the genre's transformation through time. Those sociocultural and economic stimuli fostering change are analyzed throughout the remaining essays comprising *Cajun Breakdown*. The first chapter of this volume, titled "Social Music," analyzes the contexts that informed Cajun musical traditions. Cajun music is, first and foremost, social music. It offered the ethnic group an outlet for entertainment and courtship, while reinforcing the communal ties that gave form to the community. The social and cultural contexts in which this vernacular expression thrived—intimate home performances, weddings and funerals, public house dances, and dance halls—are all examined in chapter 1.

Chapter 2, "Early Commercial Era," outlines the birth of commercial Cajun music between 1928 and 1934. This chapter considers commercial Cajun music as a natural extension of the ethnic, race, and hillbilly markets. It examines the evolution and impact of recorded sound technology in Cajun Country and the repercussions of the first record, "Lafayette," on the Cajun community. I use the prolific careers of Joe Falcon, Cleoma Breaux Falcon, and Leo Soileau as representative examples of the accordion sides that dominated the early commercial period.

Chapters 3 and 4 portray Cajun society as a heterogeneous, socially and economically stratified bilingual community, thriving within a diverse cultural and musical milieu. Chapter 3, "A Heterogeneous Tradition," is a treatise on the protean nature of recorded Cajun music between 1928 and 1934. I use instrumentation, song style, and biographical sketches of select recording artists to demonstrate the breadth of musical expression within the commercial repertoire. Chapter 4, "Becoming the Folk," on the other hand, complements chapter 3 by offering a glimpse of the regional repertoire not represented by commercial recordings issued before 1935. This chapter demonstrates the profound effect of Americanization and the English language on musical trends and the diversity of the Depression-era Cajun repertoire by examining the field recordings and publications of folklorists interested in vernacular music before World War II. These phenomena are then framed by the different definitions of "folk" imposed on the group by folklorists, song hunters, and academics in search of authentic American culture.

Chapter 5, "Cajun Swing Era," chronicles the emergence and evolution of Cajun swing, from its earliest incarnations—small string band combos and proto-swing ensembles—to the polished orchestral sound of Cajun-inflected Western swing during World War II. Cajun Country was as a cultural crossroads, the fertile territory where the musical legacies of Texas and New Orleans overlapped most directly. Those external cultural and musical forces acting on Cajun culture from 1935 to 1946, such as the Gulf Coast's booming petroleum industry, the impact of radio, and jazz, are points of departure to discuss the musical diversity represented by bands active during the Cajun swing era. The contributions of groundbreaking musicians who transformed and modernized the genre, such as fiddler Leo Soileau and percussionist Tony Gonzales (arguably the first drummer to record country music), are used to support my claim that the Cajun swing era was the most innovative period in Cajun music.

The discussion of Cajun swing continues in chapter 6, "The Modern Cajun Sound." The careers of such prolific artists as the Hackberry Ramblers and Leo Soileau, and lesser-known groups such as the Alley Boys of Abbeville demonstrate Cajun music's adaptation to an increasingly industrialized south Louisiana economy during the first half of the twentieth century. This chapter traces the relationship between socioeconomic and musical shifts in Cajun music. It focuses on those upwardly mobile musicians, with working-class roots, who ushered in Cajun swing.

The final two chapters outline the wonderfully rich and diverse musical terrain that capitalized on the increasingly dense mass media networks stretching from western Louisiana to east Texas. For the first time in Cajun musical history, neighboring mass culture infrastructures intertwined in such a way as to slingshot locally produced music to a receptive national audience. "Jole Blon," the most famous Cajun song to emerge from the Honky-Tonk Corridor, is the focus of chapter 7, "Cajun National Anthem."[81] Cajun swing fiddler Harry Choates popularized the French waltz in 1946, when the tune transcended local and regional boundaries and changed the course of American music. This chapter traces the evolution of the composition, considers the song's meaning within both Cajun and Anglo-American contexts, and demonstrates why it is the most influential song in the Cajun repertoire. This chapter sheds some light on the nation's view of Cajuns, ethnic women, and sexuality in the years following World War II.

This volume concludes with a detailed examination of the psychological effects of the sustained engagement with the mass communication networks crisscrossing Cajun Country during the late 1940s and early 1950s, in chapter 8, "A New Mental World." Mass communication, as contemporary observers Hadley Catlin and George Allport assert, created an auditory world that that compelled listeners to create this "new mental world" through which they imagined their connection to the American mainstream.[82] Radio and records, the rise of Cajun honky-tonk and independent record labels, and the more famous musicians to capitalize on the region's mass media outlets illustrate the dynamics of the shifting post–World War II Cajun worldview. This final chapter argues that through sustained engagement with the technologies of mass communication and the group's appropriation of the iconographic symbols of popular culture, Cajuns began to imagine themselves as part of the American mainstream.

This book seeks to elevate Cajun music's position from an American musical footnote to its rightful place as a distinctive American-made music, a profoundly vibrant genre created by a passionate people with a complex history. All of the chapters in *Cajun Breakdown* are built on the foundation laid by Irène Whitfield Holmes, Harry Oster, John Broven, Malcolm Comeaux, Barry Ancelet, Ann Allen Savoy, and other researchers and writers who established a Cajun music literature.[83] I offer extensive citations as a resource for future study, while the interpretation included in this volume aims to supplant the popular conception that Cajuns were an isolated, homogeneous ethnic group living in Francophone world beyond the intrusive tentacles of American popular culture. Rather, this study takes the view that Cajuns were proactive participants who shaped their own culture by engaging, and ultimately appropriating, the mass cultural information disseminated within the United States. These individual decisions affected their everyday lives and, in effect, the direction of their culture.

This book focuses specifically on the sociocultural forces acting on south Louisiana's vernacular musical traditions and those musicians who played roles as regional culture brokers. Music makers were highly mobile compared to other members of the community and displayed a general tendency toward eclecticism, borrowing freely from local traditions and American pop culture. Musicians often found themselves positioned at interstices of several cultural currents, both indigenous and extraneous. Their symbiotic relationship with the cosmopolitan demands of diverse audiences across Cajun Country and east Texas, to some extent, dictated the ebb and flow of shifts in style and repertoire. Hence, public musical performances became the arena where the Cajun community symbolically negotiated continuity and change.

1

Social Music

he cultural friction underlying the struggle of the French and British
empires for North American hegemony during the Seven Years War
had grave repercussions for the thousands of Acadian deportees caught
in the crossfire. Scholars estimate that between one-half and two-thirds
of the deported Acadian population perished as a result of deplorable
conditions aboard transport vessels and in the dreadful physical envi-
ronments the deportees encountered in France, England, the American
colonies, and the Caribbean.[1] Between 1755 and 1763, both the French
and the English openly regarded Acadians as prisoners of war—but the
British refused the exiles in their care the rights and privileges generally
accorded such military detainees, who had a right to expect food, clothing, and shelter under prevailing international law. Instead, exposure,
malnutrition, and death defined the grim reality facing these outcasts.

The Acadians enjoyed some independence following the Treaty of Paris
of 1763, which granted the exiles an 18-month grace period to resettle.
The French government seized the opportunity afforded by the momentary lapse in British control of the Acadian population to coax—through
promises of a better life—hundreds of deportees to settle in the French An-
tilles. Between 1763 and 1764, more than 2,000 weary Acadians arrived in
Saint-Domingue (present-day Haiti), Martinique, Guadeloupe, and Saint
Lucia, where they became the unsuspecting victims of a devious colonial
experiment. After several hundred exiles debarked at Saint-Domingue,
French colonial officials herded the Acadian immigrants to Môle Saint-
Nicolas, approximately 100 miles northwest of Port-au-Prince. In an effort to diminish the labor costs associated with African slaves, the French
colonial government coerced the expendable lot into service as laborers to
carve a naval base from jungles along the island's northern coast. Most of
Môle Saint-Nicolas's Acadian population endured inhospitable work conditions, and the transplanted Canadians succumbed to malaria, malnutrition, exposure, and eventually starvation, when local officials embezzled

27

the funds allocated for provisions to feed their effectively enslaved work force. The nightmare at Môle Saint-Nicolas concluded another dark chapter in the Acadian ethnic cleansing operation.[2]

But one life-affirming moment briefly illuminated the ethnic group's uncanny ability to make the best of a bad situation before the dismal conditions at Môle Saint-Nicolas ultimately decimated their community. After facing adversity for nine years, surviving on substandard rations, without proper shelter or clothing, the first exiles to arrive in the Caribbean colony in the spring of 1764 persuaded the local French officials to grant them a two-day repose. The Acadians used the time to organize a wedding Mass for 23 couples and a lavish nuptial feast. "It took place on Monday before Ash Wednesday," before Lenten restrictions prohibited dancing and indulgence, witnessed the naval scribe Saltoris, who lived among the laborers.[3]

Approximately 400 men, women, and children broke bread under a makeshift arbor, savoring a banquet prepared from a young calf, twelve pigs, three barrels of flour, and two and a half barrels of wine. The group completed this celebration of life with one of the most vital and exuberant components of Acadian social life—dancing. As Saltoris observed, "They danced, the old and the young alike, all dancing to a fast step."[4] The merriment continued into the night and again the next day. In the wake of disaster, dancing emphasized, even nourished, the cohesive ties that held Acadian society together.

The jovial atmosphere on Saint-Domingue in the spring of 1764 offers a rare window of insight into the meaning of music and dance among Acadian refugees at the same historical moment that the first exiles landed in Louisiana. Dancing breathed new life into established relationships and gave birth to new unions. It offered temporary balm to an ethnic group reeling from the throes of despair. Tuberculosis, typhoid, small pox, exposure, and malnutrition ravaged the human cargo below the deck of British transports. Anguished cries haunted the darkened, overcrowded hulls as mothers sobbed holding their lifeless infants. The elderly and frail were the next to expire, before the healthy fell ill. By the time British vessels dropped anchor and unloaded their captives, every passenger was afflicted either by disease or by heartbreak. It would take two generations before the Acadian population worldwide would match predispersal population figures. Hence dance, as the Môle Saint-Nicolas episode demonstrates, served a fundamental social and emotional role among the Acadians, even in the midst of diaspora.[5]

Dancing was a tangible manifestation of the cultural and social dialogue existing for centuries between Acadian musicians and the larger community. Dance carried deep meaning for Acadians as a means of psychologically escaping the toil of peasant life, a way to reinforce relationships within the group, and an acceptable social convention through which courtship occurred. It was indeed an essential component of social discourse for those Acadian exiles who found refuge in Louisiana, and their Cajun progeny, as dance's profound significance transferred across time and generations.[6]

Figure 1.1. Dancing created a socially sanctioned space for courtship, familial allegiances, and neighborhood bonding. Photograph by Russell Lee, October 1938. Courtesy of Farm Security Administration, Library of Congress.

In step, the spaces in which dancing transpired also evolved organically. Cajun music's natural contexts—at home, parties, weddings and funerals, house dances, and later dance halls—bound the group and kept taut the community's social fabric (figure 1.1). Dance culture thrived on interaction. This social music and its contexts had the power to stimulate edifying exchanges such as courtship and communal celebration, and the capacity to incite grinding friction when placed against competing cultural agendas structured by unequal power dynamics.

The Cajun worldview differed markedly from that of their Anglo-Protestant neighbors. Patterned behavior, particularly those associated with land tenure and social networking, illustrate how subtly different notions of commercial activity created divergent cultural conceptions of what constitutes social space. Anglo-Americans settled on rectangular plots, fenced in their cattle, and established commercial networks among yeoman based on unequal access to water sources, firewood, and other necessities. As literary historian Edward Watts demonstrates, "Anglos viewed commercial activity *as* a way of life."[7] Franco-Catholic *habitants*, on the other hand, traditionally defined their farmsteads based on the arpent system—thin ribbons of land stretching from waterways to woodlands—as branded cattle roamed freely in open fields. "French and American approaches to the land reveal a marked contrast in values," Watts continues, "the French viewed the land as a way of supporting a way of life—neighborly, egalitarian, and village-based. The Anglos viewed it as a means to wealth—individualistic, acquisitive, and farm-as-property-based."[8] Louisiana Francophones used their property and commercial endeavors as a means of supporting a social life that centered on dance and music.

When Anglo and Cajun worlds collided and interfaced in the Bayou Country, complicated exchanges and seemingly contradictory cultural syntheses ensued, particularly when the threat of Civil War reached Louisiana. Slaveless and conscripted Cajun soldiers often disserted en masse, eschewing a war in which they had little stake—that is, until fighting broke out in their front yards. Confederate and Union forces raided local farms, demolished homes, and killed farmers. Bloody clashes continued through Reconstruction. With life in disarray, and violent disruptions ever-present on the surface of social exchange, Southern honor culture structured the ways in which Cajuns handled internal disputes.[9]

Between the 1860s and 1950, working-class Cajuns threatened to dismantle the very institution that nurtured and refreshed the lifeblood of the ethnic group. Violence at Cajun dances increased exponentially when the Civil War and its immediate aftermath forced the entanglement of heterogeneous sociocultural values in the Bayou Country. The war hardened Cajuns to brutality and vehemence, which translated at house dances and dance halls into gun and knife play. To be sure, Cajun behavior shifted in step with the evolving contexts affecting Cajun life, a phenomenon that was particularly visible during the 1860s. The socioeconomic decay infecting the American South eroded the ethnic group's standard of living, while straining community networks and personal relationships. Working-class denizens took out the frustrations of their physical and economic circumstances on each other through the prescribed codes of Southern honor culture.

The tension between socially reinforcing and antisocial behavior that defined dance culture and the social dynamics that molded Cajun musical traditions through 1950 collectively constitute the primary focus of this chapter. Social context is a crucial factor in the Cajun musical equation that ultimately shapes and defines this brand of ethnic cultural expression. Indeed, its importance transcends that of a delimited set of stylistic features. Throughout its evolution, Cajun music shifted, transformed, and grew in direct relation to environmental fluctuations. Cajun musical expression is considered here, in relation to the varied social dynamics acting on the genre, through an analytical lens categorizing musical expression into one of three distinct, but complementary roles within its host community: home music, sung a cappella for pleasure in a domestic setting for friends, family, or personal enjoyment; ritualistic ballad recitations at significant events straddling secular and religious social spheres; and dance music performed at *bals de maison* (house dances) and later dance halls—a distinctive style that would be exploited commercially in the early twentieth century. The contexts surrounding this vernacular American music satisfied the group's basic needs for self-expression, social interaction, courtship, and entertainment.

A Cappella Traditions and Home Music

A cappella singing was presumably one of the first forms of musical expression used by the Bayou Country's first destitute Acadian refugees.[10] Ballads, laments, drinking songs, *chansons rondes*, *reels à bouche*, *complaintes*, and *cantiques* formed the foundation of what musicologists have defined as "home music," compositions "sung unaccompanied for pleasure, while working or visiting friends and relatives."[11] Unlike the metered approach that characterizes much of south Louisiana's dance repertoire, home music allowed singers to explore the poetry of text-rich compositions by improvising phrasing and rhythmic structures. Unrestrained by instrumental accompaniment, vocalists enjoyed the freedom to abbreviate or extend their performances, sometimes changing mode and meter mid-song.

Home music represented a complementary repertoire to the dance compositions that thrived at *bals de maison*. Ballads, laments, and *complaintes* synthesized oral history and amusement into a single performance, which subsequently crossed generational lines through both deliberate instruction and by means of repetitive exposure to these compositions. These songs reinforced family and cultural ties, bonds that were particularly strong among the women who dominated domestic life and helped maintain home music in rural districts.[12]

Patriarchal, rural, working-class Cajun society dissuaded women from creating music in the male-dominated dance arena. Indeed, such an infraction constituted a serious violation of the strict gendered mores regulating interaction—regulations that were maintained and enforced by women who chaperoned their marriageable daughters at public events. As in other parts of the American South, the community regarded female participation in male spaces, particularly where men had been drinking, as a breach of propriety.[13] While not exclusively a feminine tradition, home music performed at intimate family gatherings, Christmas and New Years parties, communal butcheries, funerals, and wedding parties signified the only respectable musical outlet for working-class Acadian women. Within these contexts, men generally congregated and socialized in one space and women in another.[14]

When performed at important social events carrying both secular and religious significance—such as weddings, funerals, Mardi Gras, and Lenten celebrations—unaccompanied singing assumed ritual form. For example, at Cajun weddings, singers ritualistically serenaded the married couple with a *complainte* lamenting the bride's loss of innocence: "Adieu, fleur de jeunesse! / Il faut enfin t'abandonner / La noble qualité de fille / Me faut aujourd'hui la quitter" (Farewell, flower of youth / At last I must leave you / The noble calling of maidenhood / Today I must quit it).[15] Some expressions were less poetic and more melodramatic: "Tite fille, tu quittes ton papa et ta maman pour aller dans la misère / Bye-bye tite fille" (Little girl, you are leaving your father and mother to begin a life of misery / Bye-bye little girl).[16] These spontaneous and heart-wrenching performances punctuated the wedding festivities and articulated the sorrow of some parents at the disintegration of their tightly knit family. But more important, they underlined the ramifications of the *rite de passage*—that the bride would indeed leave the comforts of youth in her parents' household for a new life of adult responsibilities. Wedding *complaintes* generally ended with a flood of tears streaming down the bride's cheeks, which then stirred an emotional response from the rest of the party. In some instances, the bride performed at her own wedding in a self-conscious verbalization of her forthcoming marital responsibilities. Functional ballads also took the form of *cantiques*, or specialized religious ballads that straddled secular and religious life and accompanied Cajun funerals.

During the course of the Cajun music's evolution, frequent cultural intersections linked Cajun Country to the musical traditions of the American South. Instrumentation, repertory, song, and dance styles were manifestations of a shared agrarian lifestyle inferring cross-cultural pollination transcending the Franco-Anglo linguistic, cultural, and religious divides. The relative lack of religious themes and motifs within the Cajun repertoire, however, represents a pronounced difference between Catholic south Louisianians and their Protestant neighbors. In contrast to the rich gospel music tradition that percolated throughout the South during the nineteenth century, some working-class Cajuns assumed an anticlerical disposition that hindered the development of a religious musical repertoire.[17]

Marginalization factors prominently into the relative lack of Cajun gospel music. Catholic clergymen had remarkably little influence on the Acadian immigrants and their descendants during the late eighteenth and the nineteenth centuries.[18] The church had neither the resources to accommodate nor the full support of the burgeoning Cajun community to affect the Bayou Country's vernacular musical traditions. In 1834, there were only 24 Catholic priests and 26 churches in all of Louisiana, leaving the church little opportunity for proselytizing outside of urban districts.[19] By the early twentieth century, the Catholic Church aggressively attempted to establish a significant presence within the Cajun population. The Church did gain ground and made devout Christians out of many Cajuns. Working-class locals, however, did not compromise their social and cultural needs. They found common ground between the secular and sacred by synthesizing religious symbolism, rhetoric, and ritual with communal institutions such as Mardi Gras and *danse rondes*, which existed beyond the pulpit and pew. These Cajuns did not take issue with religion and spirituality per se, but with those authoritarian clergymen who pontifically admonished working-class behaviors. For instance, the Church's efforts met resistance when zealous priests alienated their flocks by sometimes forcefully imposing pious restrictions on secular activities, particularly dancing.

Distinctive parallels between Acadian settlements in early-twentieth-century Maritime Canada and Cajun enclaves in south Louisiana illustrate the Catholic church's increasingly strident stand against public dances. Cultural geographer Malcolm Comeaux maintains that in *Acadie* "the 'civilizing' effect of the clergy was felt, and changes occurred in [Acadian] culture. Foreign priests, usually from France or Belgium (or sometimes Quebec), played a major role in lives of these Catholics, and dancing was frowned upon," with the exception of rare instances when clergy allowed and encouraged communal solidarity by means of dancing.[20] A similar situation arose in the Bayou Country. In early-twentieth-century Louisiana, a priest along the Mississippi River in St. John the Baptist Parish refused absolution to Cajun Catholics who danced. The parishioners ferried across the river and confessed in the neighboring parish to a more liberal priest.[21] The lingering antagonism between the Catholic clergymen and their working-class congregations accounted for the small corpus of religious material in Cajun music and the seemingly contradictory overlap between anticlericalism and the selective maintenance of religious custom. The ethnic group reconciled these complications by selectively embracing religious conventions such as *cantiques* that could serve the community's spiritual and social needs in lieu of the clergy.

The *cantiques* are one of the few examples of religious compositions maintained within Bayou Country's vernacular musical landscape. The *cantique* is a European-based musical genre that set to music scripture passages describing Jesus Christ and the Catholic litany of saints.[22] *Cantiques* played a complementary role to secular home music performed for amusement in domestic contexts. Working-class Cajuns generally performed these a cappella hymns at funerals and during Christian holidays, contexts that called for a spiritual or religious effect, thereby obviating the need for priests (and the possibility of condescension) at such intimate social gatherings.[23]

Documentation of the musical form's role before the twentieth century is scant. During the late 1870s, R. L. Daniel observed a Cajun wake and described what appears to be a *cantique* recitation: "The singing of indescribably mournful hymns is kept up during the night by some of the numerous watchers."[24] At the turn of the twentieth century, the so-called anonymous Breaux manuscript acknowledged that both young and old maintained the custom of "singing hymns in the house of the deceased."[25] Although these hymns are often overlooked by scholars, who prefer to focus on the large body of secular work documented on commercial recordings, musicologists Elizabeth Brandon and Harry Oster collected a small body of *cantiques* from both the Cajun and Afro-Creole communities during the 1950s.[26] The hymns featured in these field recordings blended secular French folklore and religious imagery and musical stylings derived from Catholic French musical traditions and African-American Protestant spirituals.[27] *Cantiques* assumed ceremonial form during funerals and religious holidays and paralleled a separate repertoire reserved for other secular celebrations with religious implications.

Immediately before the Lenten season, a cappella singing again assumed ritualistic form in Cajun communities during the rather hedonistic Mardi Gras celebration—a custom loosely associated with the Christian liturgical calendar designed to exaggerate, and thereby reinforce, communal ties through song, dance, ritualized inebriation, and comic revelry.[28] Mardi Gras took root in Louisiana at the dawn of the territory's colonial history. Two days before Lent in 1699, Pierre Le Moyne, Sieur d'Iberville's exploratory French naval expedition disembarked at the mouth of the Mississippi River and made camp at a location the commandant christened "Pointe du Mardi Gras" (Mardi Gras Point). The role of the custom in the New World following Iberville's initial visit is difficult to ascertain. There is virtually no documentation in Louisiana's colonial literature concerning the provenance of Mardi Gras songs among Cajuns. Ethnographic research conducted in Acadia Parish during the late twentieth century offers the only evidence of these compositions' historical reach in Bayou Country. Anthropologist Rocky Sexton and musicologist Harry Oster maintain that "oral history indicates that Mardi Gras and Mardi Gras songs were a long-standing tradition by the mid-19th century."[29] Sexton and Oster collected two accounts linking this musical tradition to the Civil War era, including a chronicle of Cajun and Creole renegade marauders locally known as Jayhawkers singing the Mardi Gras song on raids when approaching the homes of their victims. By the end of the nineteenth century, Louisiana boasted at least two distinct variants of Mardi Gras, an urban celebration featuring parades and floats carrying New Orleans' Creole and Anglo elite, and a rural festival—the *courir de Mardi Gras*[30]—supported by working-class Cajun communities on the southwest Louisiana prairies. The rural variant differed significantly from its urban counterpart in both form and function. As in Irish mumming traditions, small bands of masked revelers drank and sang their way across the countryside within their respective rural neighborhoods on a begging quest, asking for provisions for a communal gumbo held at the end of the ritual.[31] Mardi Gras celebrants worked for their supper by entertaining their hosts with song and dance.

Two Mardi Gras song types, both derived from French and French Canadian antecedents, flourished in rural communities in southwest Louisiana—one lyrically outlining the begging quest (sometimes accompanied by instrumental music), and the other a kind of a cappella drinking song describing a dwindling bottle of alcohol. The begging rendition shared themes and lyrical structures with European and French Canadian Chandeleur and Mardi Gras songs and thrived in the northern parishes of Acadiana, home to large numbers of non-Acadian Francophones. According to Oster, the gapped and modal structure of this vernacular composition represents the arrangement's ancient European provenance and its lyrical similarities to nineteenth-century Guignolée songs.[32] On the other hand, the drinking song thrived in parishes boasting high Acadian concentrations.[33]

Both compositions served similar purposes. Revelers, depending on their affiliation with a particular enclave, sang one of the Mardi Gras song variants as a means of simultaneously entertaining and communicating with host families along the revelers' predetermined route. The recitation of these songs served as a ritualized and theatrical statement of purpose that explained both the nature of the group and the reason for their visit. For instance, celebrants chanting the begging version sang "Les Mardi Gras se rassemblent une fois par an / Pour demander la charité / Ça va aller en porte en porte / Tout à l'entour du moyeu" (The Mardi Gras riders come together once a year / To ask for charity / They travel door-to-door all / Around the community).[34] A more whimsical explanation was offered in an Acadia Parish interpretation of the drinking song during the early part of the twentieth century. In several lines that mirror portions of *Guignolée* songs from the upper Mississippi Valley and Quebec, Mardi Gras riders requested "Bonjour le maître and la maîtresse / Et tout le monde du logis / Nous vous demandons seulement la fille aînée / Nous lui ferons faire bonne chère / Et nous lui ferons chauffer les pieds" (Greetings to the master and mistress / And everyone in the household / We have come to ask only for your eldest daughter / We will make her be a good girl / And we are going to warm her feet as we dance with her).[35] Both songs assert the objective of the *courir de Mardi Gras*: to solidify the social networks that sustained the rural community during the planting season, harvest, and times of famine or disaster. Costumed jesters playfully invaded personal space to force interaction, such as dancing with the eldest daughter of a household.

Like the nature of the celebration itself, Mardi Gras songs in Louisiana followed an evolutionary path parallel to that of their European antecedents. These songs evolved over time as Cajun revelers transmitted these compositions orally across generational lines, at times under the influence of particular captains—the official leaders of these marauding bands—who influenced the vocal deliverance or lyrical components of the performance. The insertion of a lyric concerning the communal gumbo, the quintessential Cajun dish, in Louisiana's variation of the begging arrangement indicates that locals adapted to suit their New World realities. Other local adaptations included a Cajun *bal de Mardi Gras* (Mardi Gras dance), where gumbo was served to the revelers and those community members who contributed ingredients until the stroke of midnight, thus marking the beginning of Lent.

While some pious Cajuns adhered to their interpretation of the rigorous penance prescribed by the Catholic Church during the Lenten season, most of the community had to be reminded. According to Church doctrine, south Louisiana Catholics should cease all secular frivolities and profane amusements such as drinking alcohol and public balls for 40 days. In 1879, the Abbeville *Meridional* obliged the Church by emphasizing the religious convention in print: "Balls will be a discount now that the Lenten season has set in. Our fair dancers may turn their attentions to nobler things than the waltz and Jenny Lind polka."[36] By the early twentieth century, local newspapers published annually the diocese's restrictions encouraging local Catholics "to abstain from intoxicating beverages, public amusements, the theater, moving picture shows and dances."[37] Under the Church's growing influence during the twentieth century, the Cajun community interpreted these Lenten restrictions as specifically referring to instrumental music performed at *bals de maison* and dance halls. During the nineteenth century, Cajuns regarded dancing to music provided solely by the human voice an acceptable form of entertainment within the bounds of Lenten restrictions.

Locals maintained Lent-specific dances and a cappella songs outside the instrumental dance music repertoire performed at *bals de maison*. After Sunday church services, folks gathered at Lenten play parties called *soirées de Carême* and danced in circular formations to renditions of *les chansons rondes* without instrumental accompaniment. Like a square dance caller, a lead singer commanded the audience with lighthearted compositions such as "Le Joli Rosier," "Les Oeufs," and "Papillon" while the circle of dancers sang along and acted out specialized movements that coincided with particular verses of specific songs. Folklorists Marie del Norte Thériot and Catherine Blanchet offer a detailed scenario outlining the contexts that defined this particular brand of social dance music in their monograph *Les Danse Rondes*:

> There people of all ages would dance until midnight. The group would keep changing constantly throughout the day, no one person remaining for the whole time except the host. His duty was to furnish the guests with coffee, or, if the crowd grew too large, with cool well-water; with the empty front rooms of this home, moving furniture to attic or barn; with a front yard, if the weather permitted dancing on the grass; and with some simple method of illumination after sun-down. Often a ring of as many as a hundred dancers would circle around a huge oak in the moonlight, or by the light of lanterns and lamps with reflectors, attached to tree or house corners. If the group divided into more than one circle, it usually formed three rings of dancers. It seems that anyone able to walk took part in the "danse rondes" from the very young to the very old; but it was chiefly the pleasure of those of marrying age, for these "rondes" are actually courting dances.[38]

The Cajun community abandoned *danse rondes* by the Great Depression.

Danse rondes, like Mardi Gras, represented the functional overlap between religious observance, albeit a selective one, and the need for social interaction. Other vernacular musical customs reserved exclusively for the Lenten season and performed outside of church operated in the same fashion. According to the anonymous Breaux manuscript, before the Civil War Cajun men and children living along the Bayou Lafourche sang a religious *complainte* while promenading door to door on Good Friday evening. The French composition recounted "La passion du doux Jésus" (The passion of sweet Jesus) and the biblical accounts leading up to his crucifixion. During the occasion, which paralleled the pre-Lenten Mardi Gras procession in form and function, host families set aside eggs, butter, and other foodstuffs to distribute among the carolers.[39] Like *cantiques*, Cajuns folded "La passion du doux Jésus" into their repertoire precisely because it could be deployed to bolster the cultural mechanisms driving social cohesion. Whether religious and secular in theme, Cajuns employed music in a functional manner. Context, then, determined social music's meaning.

From *Bals de maison* to Dance Halls

Cajuns created clearly defined and structured social spaces at weekend house parties called *bals de maison*. These soirees served as the group's primary source of entertainment and generally featured live music, couple dancing, and refreshments including coffee, gumbo, and alcohol. The phenomenon was so widespread by the end of the nineteenth century that S. S. Prentiss commented in his memoirs that Cajuns "have balls almost every day."[40] Though exaggerated, Prentiss' remark alluded to the frequency of the *bals de maison* during both the hot and cold seasons, and the party's significance as a social vehicle for renewing and reinvigorating communal ties.[41]

News of a *bal de maison* spread quickly throughout the community by word of mouth, and in the Lafourche region with the help of a courier. During the 1820s, a representative of the host family traveled along the banks of the Bayou Lafourche and fired a gun in front of each residence to attract attention before announcing in a loud voice "bal ce soir chez. . . . " (ball tonight at the home of . . .).[42] Young envoys also advertised an upcoming dance by riding a pony throughout the settlement waving a red or white flag while passing each neighbor's dwelling. Upon his return, the messenger tied the flag above the gate to his house as a final identification of the party site. Every Saturday night, the community came together dressed in their best hand-sewn attire.[43]

Whole families attended dances. Young and old alike shared the ballroom as dancing helped forge romantic relationships and reaffirmed established familial alliances. During the sweltering summer months, *bals* sometimes took place on porches or in the front yard. Otherwise, these social events occurred within the confines of modest farm houses. Host families pushed aside their sparse furnishings before lining the walls with benches for capacity seating. Mothers with young children placed their infants and toddlers in a back room designated as *le parc aux petits* (literally children's park), where babies slept while their parents socialized (figure 1.2). Before electricity, candles in pendent tin candlesticks, or situated in empty bottles on special occasions, cast their ambient glow onto the dancers while chaperones carefully scrutinized the advances of young suitors trying to court their unwed daughters.[44] Small acoustic combos consisting of no more than three or four musicians generally sat at the

Figure 1.2. Working-class Cajun women created domestic space within the confines of Louisiana dance halls, including *parc aux petits*, or sleeping quarters for children. Photograph by Russell Lee, October 1938. Courtesy of Farm Security Administration, Library of Congress.

far corner of the dance floor, scratching out tunes over the assembly's stomping, laughter, and conversation. Fiddlers, and later accordionists, sometimes charged a marginal fee for their services. *Bals de maison* represented the Cajun manifestation of the dance culture pervading the American Southwest, where string bands generally consisting of fiddle and guitar entertained ranchers and farmers at house and barn dances.[45]

Between 1764 and 1950, the Cajun dance repertoire evolved in accordance with both local tradition and those popular external cultural forces acting on music culture in Louisiana. Dance styles fell into one of two general categories—European and American varieties—which spoke directly to the Cajun community's Old World past reframed within a North American context. The polkas, mazurkas, quadrilles, *contradanses*, *lanciers*, two-steps, jigs, waltzes, and *valses à deux temps* (waltzes in two times) that entertained the Cajun community signified the ethnic group's European cultural pedigree. A sort of dignified square dance with complicated choreography accompanied the courtly *contradance* and *lancier* song styles. These complementary dances consisted of upward of five different dance steps corresponding to particular musical movements.[46] *Valses à deux temps* also featured involved choreography. Cajun fiddler Dennis McGee, who performed for hundreds of dances during the early twentieth century, recalled: "They danced in couples for a while, then they would move away from one another and turn in one direction, then in the other direction. . . . That is why it is called the waltz in two times, because they turned in alternating directions."[47]

Uniquely American dances also thrived in some Cajun halls. During the "Jim Crow" dance, "They would jump from one side to the other," McGee explained about the minstrel-tinged hop. "The men and the women would jump together, like a toad! Yes, it was a strange dance but it was pretty for those who knew how to dance it."[48] Under the influence of the Jazz Age, Cajuns swirled around club floors while following the steps to national dance crazes like the Charleston and Big Apple. The jitterbug had become a widespread phenomenon in the Bayou Country immediately before World War II and signified the impression of African-American culture on the region's white population. In 1939, local organizers at Crowley's National Rice Festival, the state's largest harvest festival, held one of the region's first public jitterbug dance contests—"Nat'l Rice Festival Negro Jitterbug Contest"—amid programming that also featured a Cajun band contest.[49] The following year, the dance style had clearly diffused across racial lines, as the festival sponsored a jitterbug contest for Crowley's white citizens.[50]

Men and women danced exclusively together, with the exception of Mardi Gras, when social taboos regarding men dancing together were relaxed. McGee witnessed a type of solo performance that fell outside the parameters of couple dancing—a dance contest that the participants called the "dance of the four corners of the handkerchief":

> This dance was for the best dancer that walked. You see each man would dance each turn so that they could choose the best, of them

all. The best would then be the King of the dancers. Each one would spread a handkerchief on the floor, a white handkerchief about 24 inches square, on which he danced. The man would start dancing in one corner of the, handkerchief [the one nearest] and then progress to a leap into the opposite corner. He continued to dance this way until the judge allowed him to stop. Then they would decide upon who had made up the most artistic and beautiful steps.[51]

The broad range of dance styles executed in south Louisiana spoke to the region's inclusive aesthetic.

Travel writers provide the earliest documentation of community dances in Louisiana. These observers were so fascinated by Cajun music's social contexts that their texts universally described the settings they encountered, never the music they heard. In 1803, the year of the Louisiana Purchase, French immigrant C. C. Robin attended a Cajun dance and described in his memoirs,

> they love to dance most of all; more than any other people in the colony . . . everyone dances, even *Grandmère* and *Grandpère* no matter what the difficulties they must bear. There may be only a couple of fiddles to play for the crowd, there may be only four candles for light, placed on wooden arms attached to the wall; nothing but long wooden benches to sit on, and only exceptionally a few bottles of *Tafia* diluted with water for refreshment.[52]

The festivities concluded with gumbo before the guests made their way home singing and laughing.

South Carolina native W. W. Pugh was nine years old in 1820, when he first visited south Louisiana's Bayou Lafourche region. Cajun Country's natural and cultural landscapes imprinted in Pugh's childhood memories images of the simple, weather-beaten farmhouses where house dances occurred.[53] He returned to a radically different Bayou Lafourche in 1835, transformed by the "many Americans" who settled along the waterway. While newly arrived Anglo-American migrants transformed the countryside by displacing some small Cajun homesteads and cotton farms with sprawling sugar plantations, the social contexts associated with music continued to flourish at weekly dances held in Cajun homes. Pugh attended a *bal de maison* during this second excursion to Bayou Country and published a detailed account of his experience:

> The balls were well conducted, and the contrast in manner and deference towards the fair sex was marked when compared with a similar assemblage among Americans of the same class. All kinds of vehicles used on the farm were pressed into service to accommodate the people who attended these parties. There were no aristocrats of either sex, whose superior toilets could create envy or bad feelings. All attended with a view to enjoying themselves and carried out their

intentions with a will. The waltz and old-fashioned contre dance, with which all were familiar from childhood, was the fashion of the country, and they desired nothing better. Shoes were not in such general demand as a part of the every day toilet as at present, and many of the belles of those days, in the words of the old song, came to the house in which the party was given "with shoes and stockings in their hands, and feet upon the ground," which they did not fail to put on before their entrance into the ball room. . . . The dancing master was an unknown and unnecessary institution among these people, for they danced from the cradle to the grave, and danced gracefully [at] that.[54]

Like other eyewitnesses who observed and wrote about the behaviors associated with house dances, the social attitudes and cultural contexts that defined interaction at these events impressed Pugh more than the music and musicians. His fascination was well founded. Beneath the jovial façade of these seemingly simple parties, the organizational structure of local dances mirrored and partially constituted in ritualistic form important aspects social life within the community.

Etiquette at house dances was but one component of a larger cultural convention that dictated interaction in Cajun society. At work and play, two distinct but complementary gendered social spheres shaped the ethnic group's interaction. Like in other parts of the rural South, women controlled a domestic space in and around the home, while male responsibilities centered on labor beyond the home and hearth.[55] Cajuns transposed these behaviors at balls. Men and women sat apart at dances. Many of the older men in attendance played cards in an adjoining room or loitered outside the home drinking alcohol, smoking, gossiping, conducting community business, and organizing the coming week's house party. Inside the house, women visited amongst themselves between dances. More important, mothers chaperoned their unwed daughters and enforced stringent conventions regarding public displays of sexuality. Dancing then constituted the only form of sustained interaction between the sexes at *bals de maison*. When travel writer R. L. Daniels visited Cajun Country during the 1880s, he observed, "Even then the girls must be sedate, speak only when spoken to, and keep their eyes modestly lowered. I once heard an Acadian woman remark, 'It ess permeet of *les Americaine* to look at de mans in de face, *mais nos demoiselles!*' finishing off with a significant shrug of her shoulders" (figure 1.3).[56]

Until the post-World War II era, rural working-class Cajuns restricted wooing and courtship to public balls or prearranged appointments, where chaperones were always present. At least one household representative escorted the family's unmarried girls to dances to maintain the family honor. Indeed, for a woman to be alone for a few moments with a member of the opposite sex other than male relatives was a gross breach of the community's proprieties.[57] R. L. Daniels keenly observed the demanding process through which young lovers became married couples:

Figure 1.3. Gendered divisions of labor mirrored the structured social space inside of dance halls—unmarried women separated from unmarried men. Photograph by Russell Lee, October 1938. Courtesy of Farm Security Administration, Library of Congress.

Flirting being impracticable, it is always understood that the wooer means marriage. . . . The ball-room is generally the place; when the pleasurable excitement of the waltz has reached its climax, while her slender waist is encircled by his arm, and her head almost leans upon his shoulder, then comes the opportunity. If the coy maid favors his suit, he instantly seeks the approval of her parents. With that, one might think the affair settled. But no; he must obtain the permission of the numerous relatives of the bride-elect, even to the cousins, who may be of no special importance. Dressed in his nattiest suit, he proudly prances around on the grand tour, and formally asks the consent of each in turn. Advances from the dubious position of suitor to that of *fiancé*, he and his betrothed are still under a strict surveillance that is anything but agreeable; so he naturally hastens the wedding-day that is to convert the tantalized lover into the proud and happy husband.[58]

Each ball was an opportunity for matchmaking. At the turn of the twentieth century, some Cajuns hosted dances to mark a daughter's fifteenth birthday, or to celebrate her name-day, at which time suitors worked to forge alliances with potential brides and their families.[59] The cycle continued when children emerged from the *parc aux petits* and came of age on the ballroom dance floor. Indeed, stringent courtship restrictions continued well into the first half of the twentieth century. "We danced holding close," fiddler Dennis McGee recalled of his courting days,

> but we had to have a handkerchief tied around our hand. You had to have a handkerchief tied around your hand because the girls used to wear corsets and out of respect for them the man wrapped a handkerchief around his hand so she would know no man had felt her corset bones through her dress.[60]

Codes of courtship were not folly, but a serious protocol that frequently impeded personal freedom and desire. It pervaded dance culture and inspired the lyrical themes cried from the bandstand. The genre and its milieu were so inextricably intertwined that composers frequently embedded lessons from their romantic encounters into their arrangements and the emotional intensity of their performances. A case of art imitating life, themes of heartbreak and loss of love so prevalent in the twentieth century Cajun dance repertoire are directly linked to the fragile nature of romantic relationships before World War II. Cajun mores dictated that courtship be confined exclusively to marriage, not casual sexual relationships. Thus, love only blossomed when a female accepted a suitor's advances. Without reciprocation, a young man's affection was destined to die on the vine. If parents decided that a suitor was not right for their daughter, the courtship process terminated immediately—without hope of ever resuming, no matter how strong the emotional bond between the would-be lovers.

Musicologist Irène Whitfield recounted a tale of love gone astray between a musician and an elusive woman during the early twentieth century. Accordionist Léonce Trahan composed a melancholy lament about longing and despair titled "Bye-Bye Fédora" when his only love, Fédora Uzée, married another. Trahan first performed the arrangement at her *bal de noce* (wedding dance) and sang,

> Fédora, it pains us to see you leave so far away.
> The good times are over, for the rest of your life.
> Don't cry, Fédora; don't cry, Fédora.
> You are leaving us forever,
> but all we ask is that you never forget us.[61]

While the accordionist's composition parallels other wedding *complaintes*, the lyrical content delivered a particularly personal message to the bride, who lowered her head after hearing the song to conceal her tears for a love that could never have been. Trahan translated musically the heartache generated by the social codes that circumscribed his life.

Before the social and economic turmoil spawned by the Civil War, Cajun *bals de maison* were, by all accounts, peaceful affairs that effectively celebrated the intercommunity networks sustaining rural neighborhoods. Hosts ensured everyone in attendance felt welcome and supervised the participants' strict adherence to prevailing social conventions. "Nothing boisterous was ever known," commented travel writer W. H. Sparks on the civility that defined Cajun behavior at house dances before the war, "no disputing or angry wrangling, for there was no cause given."[62] Sparks's depiction of community balls lends credence to George Washington Cable's Gilded Age assertion that "only since the war" did violence escalate along with the use of deadly weapons.[63] Most Cajun men armed themselves with daggers and revolvers in case of trouble during the post-Civil War era.[64]

The culture of violence that became so commonplace at local dances stemmed directly from the Cajun community's intimate connection to forces affecting America's socioeconomic climate. A common language, culture, and ethnic identity structured Cajun society at large. Yet, an essential component of that ethnic identity was firmly rooted in a sense of place and an abiding allegiance to one's rural neighborhood, where economic subsistence lived and died by reciprocity. Neighbors supported each other through hard times; they worked together and played together. When a member of the community was too ill or frail to bring in a crop, neighborhoods organized *ramasseries*, or communal harvesting ventures, to ensure the family's survival. Social responsibility, then, became an affair of honor and could literally mean life or death.[65]

When total war ravaged the foundational tenants of Cajun society and commerce during the mid-nineteenth century, communities turned to their social networks for support. The Civil War and its aftermath beset the South's economy, peeled away civility, and contributed to a general breakdown of law and order. With nothing else to lose, the socioeconomic collapse plaguing the Cajun community magnified the importance of self-dignity and honor. To be sure, honor became a significant component of social intercourse, particularly among the most impoverished Cajuns, who ironically and increasingly engaged the lesson they learned during the war—spilling blood. Violence often ensued when someone in a rural neighborhood failed to receive an invitation to a house dance, signifying a breech in the reciprocal social contract and a slight to one's honor. In other instances, bullies openly insulted a fellow Cajun's self-dignity to measure their bravado and self-worth. By the 1860s, *bals de maison* had indeed become microcosms of the evolving and increasingly violent cultural climate in the South.[66]

One of the earliest accounts of house party violence dates from January 30, 1869, only four years after the conclusion of the Civil War. At a Saturday night soiree in Lafourche Parish, a personal dispute between T. Vicknair and two brothers, Paulin and Joseph Benoit, turned deadly. Vicknair allegedly defended himself against the Benoits' advances with a knife, leaving Paulin dead and Joseph severely wounded. In accordance with the community's code of honor, Vicknair gave himself up to the authorities in Thibodaux the next morning.[67]

A similar incident transpired on the night of July 23, 1870, in the Assumption Parish hamlet of Bruslée St. Martin. During the course of a dance, Charles Landry insulted a young lady in attendance, a daughter of Euzelieu Theriot, during a dispute over a quadrille. The young lady turned to her brother Camille Theriot, who promptly confronted Landry to defend his sister's honor. The parties dropped the matter until the next morning, when Charles and his brother Catoir Landry walked approximately one mile to Euzelieu Theriot's home between 7 and 8 A.M., "to settle the difficulty of the night previous." Catoir vociferously insulted the family from the road in front of the house. Euzelieu emerged and met the antagonist, who then drew a pistol and aimed it at the old man's head. The elder Theriot grabbed the muzzle with his hand and sufficiently lowered the firearm in time to narrowly escape the discharged bullet that passed between his legs. Euzelieu's son Nichols Theriot positioned himself between the two combatants and begged the assailant not to shoot his father. Catoir promptly fired and fatally wounded Nichols before fleeing the scene, screaming, "I've killed a bull." Landry surrendered to the authorities, claiming self-defense.[68] Even with the rising number of violent incidents, many Cajuns invoked the code of honor that encouraged perpetrators and murderers to surrender themselves to local authorities.

The number of conflicts and deaths at dances increased dramatically during the twentieth century, prompting reporters at the *New Iberia Enterprise* to address the pervasive regional social malaise. In July 1924, the newspaper noted that "disturbances occur at almost every ball" in some neighborhoods.[69] Cajun Country newspaper articles from the early twentieth century are filled with accounts of mayhem and bloodshed at *bals de maison*. Newspapers frequently punctuated these tragic scenarios with such headlines as "Youth Is Stabbed At Country Dance,"[70] "After-Dance Fight Leads To Arrests,"[71] "Killed At Sunday Ball,"[72] and "Youth Shoots Down Three Brothers At Country Ball In Evangeline On Easter."[73] Some violent outbursts stemmed from defending a woman's honor or from long-standing family feuds and outstanding vendettas. Others resulted from courtship conflicts, public drunkenness, or simply brash displays of machismo following the phrase, "I am the best man on the grounds."[74] Men sometimes fought outside out of respect for the homeowner and ball hosts. Otherwise, patrons ran for cover as angry and inebriated combatants sprayed bullets around the dance floor during heated clashes.[75] In some instances, such as the battle between Jack Fontenot and John Legier in April of 1910, several complicated motivations erupted into violence. Fontenot and Legier, who shared a long-standing disdain of each other, crossed paths at a ball in Church Point, began to quarrel, and then moved outside and began fighting. The Jennings *Daily Times-Record* reported, "Fontenot drew his knife during the fight and commencing stabbing Legier about the head and face inflicting nearly a dozen ugly wounds."[76] Legier responded with his pistol and fired three shots, one of which killed Fontenot instantly. The scars that disfigured the victor's face served as a constant reminder of the increasingly treacherous circumstances associated with music and dance culture in south Louisiana. Cajuns took their lives into their own hands every time they attended a local dance.

The relationship between social context and Cajun music comes into clearer focus with the Dixie Ramblers' Depression-era composition "The

Death of Oswald." Modeled after hillbilly murder ballads, accordionist Lester Lalonde's composition recounted the events surrounding the homicide of a Breaux Bridge man. As Lalonde's song became increasingly popular, word reached the accused murders upon their release from prison. Fiddler and Rambler front man Hector Duhon explained to folklorist Nicholas Spitzer, "They had got out of the pen and they came to the dance one night and told us, 'Don't play that number if you want to stay here tonight!'"[77] The same violent reality that inspired the composer to pen "The Death of Oswald" promptly extinguished the song's career on the south Louisiana dance hall circuit.

Cajun dance halls complicated the violent contexts that shaped house dances and perpetuated, even increased, the fighting and homicide rate during the twentieth century. *Bals de maison* were generally confined to one rural neighborhood. Audiences who flocked to dance halls, however, crossed territorial lines to attend dances in these large wooden honkytonks. These new milieus placed violence on a hair-trigger. Suddenly, dozens of young men from competing communities clashed while vying for the same girls at this neutral site. Others found sport in dethroning bullies or boxing champions, while still others sometimes used knives or pistols to even the playing field against their tormentors. Casual infractions, such as accidentally stepping on another man's foot or bumping into another couple while dancing, frequently sparked fights. The bloody repercussions of these altercations often extended well beyond the Saturday night dance. For instance, a free-for-all erupted at a Mamou dance hall on December 6, 1923, that led to the arrest of four young Cajun men. The gruesome aftermath also involved a series of fatalities resulting from the murder of a teenage bystander. A stray bullet from the gunfight instantly killed Willie Guillory's fifteen-year-old son, sending the distraught father into a severe bout of depression. Months later, Guillory wandered the streets of Mamou and randomly opened fire. The next morning, law enforcement agents found the grieving father at his home, where they shot and killed him after an extended gun battle. This tragic scenario illustrates the unfortunate domino effect that could transfer violence from the Cajun dance hall into the middle of neighborhood life.[78]

Dance halls first appeared in the region's cultural landscape in the nineteenth century. Self-styled vigilante apologist Alexandre Barde maintains that Cajuns congregated at dance halls on Saturday evenings as early as 1859.[79] In the late 1880s, Charles Dudley visited local club owner Simonette LeBlanc's bayou-side ballroom, "which had benches along the wall, and at one end a high dais for the fiddlers, and a little counter where the gombo [sic] filé (the common refreshment) is served."[80] Lithographs from illustrated magazines adorned the walls of the wooden structure and gave something of a contemporary and distinctly American character to the Cajun social space. LeBlanc's early dance hall assumed the structure and form of the traditional *bals de maison*, only on a grand scale, and foreshadowed the widespread commercialization that so dramatically shaped the community's primary form of entertainment following the genre's debut on record.

Food and alcohol consumption, music and dancing, courtship, and gambling translated easily into the dance hall setting. Men consumed intoxicants outside of the building and played cards in a designated room adjacent to the dance floor. Locals maintained the *parc aux petits*—at least through the 1930s—and mothers continued to scrutinize carefully the interaction between suitors and their unwed daughters.[81] Violence continued to pervade dance culture in halls, despite the presence of local constables, who frequented larger establishments to maintain order.[82] In contrast to house dances, however, dance halls were commercial enterprises that represented the Americanization of vernacular social space in the Bayou Country. Club owners charged admission, paid performers, and sold refreshments, thereby imposing capitalistic ideals onto a formerly reciprocal form of traditional culture. These businesses supplanted the individual's responsibility for hosting such events, standardized dance schedules, and centralizing the community's dancing locale. Halls also altered the dynamics of community interaction and musical performance by increasing the parameters that once defined the boundaries of enclaves and small rural neighborhoods.

By the twentieth century, dozens of families from rival districts descended on halls, rather than the three or four clans from within an insular rural neighborhood that might have constituted attendance at a *bal de maison*.[83] Large dance halls could accommodate as many as 200–300 dancers, thereby prompting Cajuns to establish new social conventions to maintain the group's stringent courtship standards. For instance, when unmarried teenage boys were not dancing, they stood in a partitioned space designated as *la cage aux chiens* (dog cage) or "bullpen"—a controlled staging area where chaperones corralled, and thus controlled, interaction between the sexes (figure 1.4).[84] Musical performance evolved in step with its milieu. The sheer number of patrons in attendance forced musicians to strain their vocal deliveries and musical performances in an attempt to pierce the background noise generated by large crowds. Barry Jean Ancelet maintains that these conditions affected the stylings of such musicians as fiddler Dennis McGee, who developed an unusual playing technique that increased the bow's pressure on his fiddle strings, thereby amplifying the volume of his instrument.

Legislation stunted the development of dance halls in some communities and thereby temporarily extended the dominance of *bals de maison*.[85] In November 1912, the St. Martinville *Weekly Messenger* reported that Acadia Parish entrepreneurs who charged admission and sold refreshments while giving public balls were compelled to pay a parish licensing fee of $250 beginning on January 1, 1913.[86] The exorbitant tariff impeded the establishment of dance halls, particularly in working-class neighborhoods where house dances flourished, and retarded the evolution of the phenomenon. Dance halls eventually supplanted *bals de maison* following the

Figure 1.4. This *cage aux chiens* at the Leleux dance hall near Crowley corralled young unmarried men to preserve sexual mores and propriety. Photograph by Russell Lee, October 1938. Courtesy of the Center for Louisiana Studies, University of Louisiana at Lafayette.

repeal of prohibition, when beer joints and honky-tonks that attracted patrons with live music mushroomed throughout the South (figure 1.5).[87]

Cajun music bobbed like a cork against the ebb-and-flow of social activity in south Louisiana. It accompanied life's most profound moments and fell silent during the community's darkest hour. R. L. Daniels acknowledged this dichotomy in his memoirs published in the late 1870s: "No feasting and dancing no wedding," the travel writer wrote, acknowledging music's central and essential role during the key high points in Cajun life. Families in mourning, on the other hand, forfeited all amusements, and "[dance] music, either vocal or instrumental, [was] considered sacrilegious."[88]

Working-class Cajuns made music on their own terms, according to their own sociocultural codes. That does not mean, however, in isolation. Instead, Cajun dance culture developed through sustained interaction with members of their community and through cultural clashes with external influences. Constructive and destructive social forces mutually structured the space in which working-class Cajuns cultivated communal relationships, the same space where Cajuns eradicated their enemies and antagonists through clouds of gun smoke. These tensions complicated the cultural contexts surrounding musical expression, whether they were sober a cappella recitations or boisterous dance tunes.

Figure 1.5. Cajuns in a Raceland, Louisiana, bar keeping in step with the latest dance crazes, such as the "Big Apple." Courtesy of the Center for Louisiana Studies, University of Louisiana at Lafayette.

Unaccompanied French ballad traditions in Cajun Country satisfied an individual's need for expression and entertainment and, at times, served the community at large through ritualistic presentations at weddings, funerals, and religious holidays. By the end of the twentieth century, shifts in social norms, expectations, and the intrusion of mass media, which rendered a cappella ballad traditions obsolete, erased from public memory such song styles as *cantiques* and *complaintes*. In contrast, dance music translated across generational lines with relative ease precisely because it facilitated courtship rituals. Dance stood at the nexus of inter- and intra-community solidarity, which infuriated recalcitrant factions to the point of violence. Not all sectors of Louisiana society shared in the working-class enthusiasm for *bals de maison* or rustic dance halls where congregations of impoverished and ignorant farmers engaged in, according to middle-class perspectives, debauchery and hedonism. During the 1920s, the expression *fais do do* (literally "go to sleep")—referencing the *parc aux petits*—came into common use among champions of heritage tourism, who hoped to dignify what they viewed as a provincial custom. Working-class Cajuns who attended dances in local dance halls continued to refer to the social event as *les bals*, not by the now popular moniker *fais do-do*.[89]

Contextualization is the key to understanding Cajun music. Audiences and musicians collectively created meaning around this form of cultural production. Meaning, however, did not remain static, tangled in a web of significance spun by the Cajun community. Rather, Cajuns continually wove new meaning around their social music as new influences, economic circumstances, and technologies transformed what constituted being French in North American. Cajun music is an unfinished tapestry of signification constantly under construction, an art form created on a loom driven by interaction, socioeconomic leverage, migration, and the larger historical processes affecting the whole of America.

2

Early Commercial Era

During the late 1920s, native New Orleanian George Burrow enjoyed privilege and power as a police juror in Rayne, Louisiana. Occasionally dabbling in record sales, the politician witnessed the growing demand for American popular releases and imagined Cajun music's commercial potential. In 1928, he decided to sponsor a musical trio—vocalist Leon Meche, accordionist Joe Falcon, and guitarist Cleoma Breaux—and contacted representatives from the New York–based Columbia Record Company. Burrow negotiated a recording session and agreed to purchase 250 records in hopes of capitalizing on the musicians' popularity at house dances and dance halls.

On April 27, 1928, Burrow, Meche, Falcon, and Breaux embarked on the daylong journey from Acadia Parish to Columbia's satellite recording facility in New Orleans. Upon arrival, an apprehensive group of record executives took one look at the unsophisticated rural musicians and immediately rescinded their offer. "They used to record with big orchestras," remembered Falcon. "They looked at us and said, 'That's not enough music to make a record.' And it was all them stiff collars with coats on in there . . . with their high falutin'."[1] Burrow interjected emphatically, underscoring his knowledge of Louisiana's musical landscape, "We've got to run it through because that man there . . . is popular in Rayne; the people are crazy about his music and they want his records."[2] The local investor quickly increased his order by writing a check for 500 records.

The production team agreed to issue one record, if a test recording proved acceptable. Meche buttoned his coat and tried to compose himself as he approached the microphone. With a pallid expression, he turned to Falcon and nervously declared, "You better sing it yourself, I might make a mistake," forcing the accordionist to assume the singing responsibilities.[3] Left alone in the studio, Falcon and Breaux performed as Columbia engineers cut a master wax disk of "Lafayette (Allon a Luafette)" to evaluate the duo's fidelity. Falcon remembered, "I opened that accordion, and that

Figure 2.1. Cajun music's first stars, Cleoma Breaux and Joseph Falcon, cultivated an expressly modern American stage persona. Courtesy of Johnnie Allan.

thing was sounding like it wanted to take the roof off!"[4] The duet's accordion and guitar saturated the full expanse of the New Orleans hotel suite serving as Columbia's recording studio. The executives gathered to hear the master and listen critically to the performance, exclaiming, "Lord, but boy, that's more music out of two instruments than I ain't ever heard in my life."[5] Satisfied with the quality of the group's sound, Columbia recorded permanent versions of the domestic popular release "Lafayette (Allon a Luafette)"/"The Waltz That Carried Me to My Grave" (figure 2.1). Allowing for the volume of Falcon's accordion, engineers distanced the microphone from the performers, producing in the process a swollen sound rich with ambient echo. Falcon's warm vocal quivered under the strain of nerves and exertion, thus endowing the first Cajun record with a sense of urgency. And it was compelling. Falcon and Breaux's debut session ignited a recording revolution in south Louisiana and marks Cajun music's entrance in America's musical marketplace.

Cajun music's transformation from a vernacular idiom to a marketable musical expression transpired through the genre's emergence in three distinct forms of media—concert performances, 78 rpm records, and later radio. As folk music historian Norm Cohen observes, "Men with talent for making music found outlets for it even before the advent of the phonograph as a new medium for dissemination of their skills. These artists had made names for themselves performing at neighborhood parties, dances."[6] Proficient Cajun musicians quickly cultivated reputations before the release of "Lafayette," first at local neighborhood dances, and then on a larger regional dance hall circuit. A network of musicians, including Joe Falcon, Cleoma Breaux, Leo Soileau, Dennis McGee, Amédé Ardoin, and Angelas LeJeune worked together upward of five nights a week, performing as far away as central Texas.[7] Recording raised performers' profiles on the dance circuit while subsidizing their incomes.

Recording contracts generally stipulated that Cajuns did not receive royalties for their performances, but rather earned a flat fee—between $25 and $50—per record. Considering a musician would earn on average four to five dollars per dance, everyone reaped the benefits of this mutually beneficial relationship. Record companies profited by skirting around royalty negotiations with Cajuns, who gladly accepted and often made more money at a single session than a month's wages working as a day laborer. Likewise, investors had no trouble pushing the records to their clientele, who were anxious to hear the latest local releases.

With the aid of local sponsors and investors like George Burrow, who negotiated and arranged recording deals, the first Cajun recording artists carved a niche for their art by reacting to, and consciously participating in, the latest trends in America's recording industry. The 1920s witnessed the rapid development of specialized markets capitalizing on ethnic and Southern vernacular music, including a Cajun market after 1928, which placed the earliest Cajun recordings squarely within the boundaries of the nation's commercial musical infrastructure.[8] None of the commercial releases published between 1928 and 1934 were recorded in Cajun Country.[9] Instead, local musicians traveled to regional recording centers, both in the South—Atlanta, Memphis, New Orleans, and San Antonio—and as far away as Chicago and New York. Recording companies leased entire floors in opulent hotels to house their bulky sound equipment and transformed suites into makeshift studios. Musicians gathered around a single microphone and performed in concert as a diamond or sapphire stylus engraved their recital into thick wax master disks used to mass produce 78 rpm issues.

Cajun music's early commercial era issues represented the involved engagement between vernacular tradition and mass culture.[10] Studios forced Cajun musicians to recontextualize their performances in a space where demanding engineers, intimidating microphones, and rigid time constraints replaced dancing farmers, kerosene lamps, and expansive arrangements. Some musicians had difficulty creating their art in austere hotel rooms hundreds of miles from Cajun music's natural social contexts. In this alien environment, record men trying to control the pace and tempo of the session challenged the authority of bandleaders who were used to managing their own repertoire and performances. In response, recording companies sometimes provided alcohol to ease the uncomfortable process that transformed vernacular expression into a commercial idiom.

Records commodified local custom through the artifacts of mass culture. Shellac disks gave permanent material form to ephemeral performance traditions. By fixing sound information, records helped standardize lyrics and song arrangements in Cajun music while popularizing compositions on an unprecedented scale. More profound, these issues forever altered the local perception of the genre. The mere material existence of familiar black disks imprinted with local French names gave Cajun records intrinsic value and validation: that local cultural expression, so often denigrated and marginalized, was important enough to be mass produced in the same manner as the music of the heroes of American popular music. Physical uniformity was key. Cajun records looked the same as hillbilly and race record issues and reproduced performances with the same fidelity. Cajun music had indeed risen to the occasion as a recognizably mainstream form of American mass culture.

The rise of mass consumerism in the United States magnified the significance of 78 rpm Cajun records on sale at south Louisiana furniture stores, pharmacies, and specialty music shops. Standardization, brand-name products, and widespread distribution stimulated a movement across the country driven by Americans who increasingly viewed themselves as consumers. By the end of the 1920s, "Americans, regardless of how much money they had to spend," explains historian Lizabeth Cohen, "recognized the growing dominance of mass consumption in the nation's purchasing."[11] Cajun consumers, like their counterparts across America, faced a paradoxical conundrum—a growing reliance on mass-produced goods despite scarce economic resources in the first years of the Great Depression. Impulsive purchases such as records and radios continued throughout the early commercial era despite hard times. Local consumption of Cajun records, though, all flowed from one source: the Falcon–Breaux debut. "Lafayette" was the Cajun tributary into the mainstream where the local became a bone fide extension of the commercial American music project.

Cajun music's commercialization began in earnest during the nineteenth century, when musicians began to perform in exchange for money at house dances and dance halls. Recorded Cajun music expanded commercialization in the working-class community by emphasizing mass consumption. In the pages that follow, the Cajun community's relationship to recording technology, the evolving nature of America's recording industry, and Cajun music's relationship to the recording industry's niche markets illustrate the cultural intersections between the Bayou Country and America writ large. The pioneering recording careers of Joe Falcon, Cleoma Breaux Falcon, and Leo Soileau are also offered as further examples of the recording industry's impact on local traditions and perceptions of Cajun music.

Phonographs and Niche Markets

The commercial recordings pressed between 1928 and 1934 illustrate that Cajun music existed as a diverse and constantly evolving art form incorporating musical ingredients from local and national sources. "Lafayette" opened doors for important figures in the genre's history, including Leo Soileau, the Breaux family band, and Dennis McGee, by proving the viability of a Cajun niche market. By the early commercial period, Anglo-American music further established its presence in south Louisiana following the emergence of the gramophone and, later, radio broadcasts. To be sure, by the time Joe Falcon and Cleoma Breaux made their first recordings, Cajuns were already well versed in America's mainstream music.[12]

As early as 1878, only one year after Thomas Edison invented the phonograph, local newspapers helped raise popular awareness regarding the scientific marvel. The Opelousas *Courier* published a short editorial sketch announcing the public exhibition of the gramophone, "an instrument which reproduces the voice, accent and words and records the same with the fidelity of perfection itself."[13] By the early twentieth century, furniture and jewelry storeowners provided their customers in Cajun country with the latest technological advances in recorded music, including Columbia's indestructible cylinder records. The Opelousas jeweler R. Mornhiveg and Sons also offered a "splendid repertoire" of wax cylinders at their store on Main Street, in addition to a variety of music machines ranging in price from $17.50 to $100.00. Though the poorest rural Cajun families did not have enough disposable income to acquire a cylinder player, Mornhiveg and Sons enticed potential customers and curious onlookers on the 28th of each month by demonstrating free of charge the entire catalogue of Columbia Records' latest releases. The store liberally disseminated popular American compositions, a self-serving act of generosity that offered even the most impoverished musicians an opportunity to build an extensive and varied repertoire. Such public commercial musical presentations plugged Cajun directly into contemporary popular musical trends (figure 2.2).[14]

By 1912, some Cajuns proved so familiar with phonograph equipment that they made innovations to the machine's design. In Jeanerette, Louisiana, a small agrarian settlement along the western banks of Bayou Têche, inventor Emile C. Geneaux earned critical acclaim for his "improved sounding box," designed to enhance graphophone resonance. He marketed his idea to manufacturers and music stores in New Orleans, where he received several promising offers.[15] Geneaux's invention was indicative of both the Cajun community's intimacy with sound technology and the widespread availability of mass media in the region.

Figure 2.2. Local retailers like Lake Charles's J. S. Smith Music Store (established 1898) disseminated American popular music through sheet music and phonographs, while selling violins and other assorted instruments. Courtesy of Archives and Special Collections, Frazar Memorial Library, McNeese State University.

Curio storekeepers lured music lovers to storerooms from Bayou La-fourche to Abbeville with a broad range of wares. They advertised regularly in local newspapers emphasizing the accessibility of consumerism. During World War I, Lafayette businessman T. M. Biossat struck a nationalistic chord when he offered his customers Victrolas and Edison Phonographs "to fit every pocket book." He hoped that the joyful sounds of patriotic melodies would "bring a smile, or make it possible to write 'cheerier' letters to the front."[16] Other advertisements boasted the breadth of their inventory. "Everything pertaining to the artistic and musical side of life will be found at the store located at 204 St. Phililp [sic] street," announced A. E. Malhiot's 1919 advertisement in Thibodaux, Louisiana's *Lafourche Comet*.[17] In addition to sheet music and player piano rolls, Malhiot's store carried both Columbia Grafonolas and Victrolas, and a choice selection of recordings by nationally renowned orchestras and soloists. Farther west, along the southern fringe of Cajun Country's prairie region, Bourque's Furniture Company of Abbeville carried a complete line of Edison Phonographs and records. The store attracted potential Edison customers with a free trial period to entertain their families and friends for a few days in their homes with no obligation to buy.[18] Before the release of local music, affluent Cajuns who did purchase record players listened to a variety of musical styles from classical compositions to popular American dance music from Tin Pan Alley at parties, social engagements, or alone for personal amusement.[19] Record companies understood that popular releases catered to a particular demographic—well-to-do Americans—which prompted these businesses to expand their strategy to include the nation's neglected ethnic market.

During the first three decades of the twentieth century, the recording industry diversified by exploiting new markets beyond the realm of popular issues representing the classical and American music hall canons. In an effort to increase phonograph sales, the industry's primary profit winner, record producers carved out a series of niche markets that specifically catered to groups on the periphery of mainstream America. The shift began by targeting the large concentrations of immigrant and minority groups living in America's northern commercial centers, and then moved to the South's untapped musical wellspring. Industry executives reasoned that foreign-language ethnic groups, African Americans, and rural white Southerners would purchase phonographs if they could listen to familiar sounds from their respective musical heritages.[20]

Between 1900 and 1920, independent startup labels effectively saturated the mainstream market with popular releases, thereby forcing recording giants like Victor and Columbia and smaller but well-financed labels like Okeh, Vocalion, Brunswick, and Gennett to exploit the lucrative minority and ethnic fields among immigrant populations, causing the number of foreign-language releases to increase.[21] In 1921, Okeh representative Ralph Peer helped to expand the commercialization of urban ethnic music by creating a "race record" market with popular releases by Harlem blues singer Mamie Smith. Race records filled a commercial void, an economic innovation that developed in New York City as a means of promoting African-American artists to an African-American consumer base.[22] In 1922, old-time Texas fiddlers Eck Robertson and Henry Gilliland, dressed respectively in cowboy garb and Confederate uniform, traveled to Manhattan on a whim in hopes of convincing Victor Records to give them a recording contract. Victor helped launch the commercialization of hillbilly music in the same urban realm that sustained the foreign record and race markets by recording their interpretations of "Turkey in the Straw" and "Arkansas Traveler," expanding the commercial possibilities for rural white musicians.[23] Record companies had successfully mined the resources available in Harlem and in urban immigrant neighborhoods, but the Robertson and Gilliland release revealed that an untapped market with an abundance of untold cultural riches existed in the rural sharecropper shanties, cotton fields, mountain villages, and cattle ranches of the American South. Music executives subsequently established regional recording facilities in Memphis, San Antonio, New Orleans, and other cities to expand their catalogues.[24]

Field man Ralph Peer, who led the charge out of the Big Apple, arranged the most significant sessions during the early exploratory period that launched the widespread commercialization of hillbilly music. On June 14, 1923, acting on a recommendation from Atlanta record dealer Polk Brockman, Peer reluctantly recorded Georgia fiddler John Carson at the first commercial hillbilly field session outside New York. In 1927, the producer forever expanded the commercial horizons for white Southern musicians by organizing the famous Bristol, Tennessee, sessions that jumpstarted the recording careers of the Carter family and Jimmie Rodgers.[25]

Hillbilly and race records became a viable component of the recording industry, thereby embedding Southern music into the fabric of America's popular musical discourse.[26] In 1926, minority groups and rural white Southerners bought talking machines to play their favorite records along with the rest of the nation, catapulting phonograph profits to near the $70 million mark. One million record players were sold in 1927 alone.[27] Joe Falcon and Cleoma Breaux's 1928 debut came on the heels of the hillbilly boom and stimulated a new niche market that embodied aspects of the latest fads in the nation's commercial musical landscape. Cajuns were white ethnics, many of whom lived an agrarian lifestyle and cultivated a distinctive form of French music that was infused with aspects of the African-American and hillbilly traditions. Consequently, record labels promoted the earliest Cajun records using the same marketing schemes that successfully sold the work of foreign-language and African-American artists, by specifically targeting marginalized ethnic groups on the periphery of mainstream American culture.[28]

Many of the recordings issued during Cajun music's early commercial era came to fruition under the guidance of Bayou Country's phonograph and record retailers, who knew intimately both the musical tastes of their customers and the skills of the region's popular musicians. Recognizing the potential returns that local recordings could generate, retailers often arranged recording sessions for, and invested in, the first commercial Cajun artists. In turn, record companies agreed to record almost anyone the phonograph retailer suggested.[29] Between 1928 and 1934, eight record labels—Columbia, Victor, Brunswick, Vocalion, Paramount, Bluebird, Decca, and Okeh—produced 280 Cajun recordings documenting popular musical trends and instrumentation prevalent in southwest Louisiana during the first years of the Great Depression.[30] The assorted material featured on 78 rpm disks ranged from accordion-based arrangements and harmonica performances to twin fiddle and solo guitar selections. Small accordion-driven dance bands represent an overwhelming 62 percent (174 recordings) of the instrumental arrangements during the early commercial era. Cajun musicians recorded a diverse array of arranging styles such as blues-laden one-steps, two-steps, waltzes, and French interpretations of Anglo-American compositions, along with now obsolete polka and mazurka arrangements in groups no larger than trios, reflecting the local convention employed at house dances.

Brilliant musicians and bizarre south Louisiana characters relished adventures on the open road in pursuit of making their own records. Lesser-known Cajun artists such as accordionists Bixy Guidry, Joe Credeur, Adam Trahan, and Oscar Doucet produced only a handful of records, retreating back into their hometowns where they performed for pleasure and neighborhood dances. On the other hand, prolific recording artists such as the notoriously rowdy Breaux Family Band, which developed a reputation for disrupting their own dances by brawling among themselves during drunken rampages, recorded some of the most sublime examples of acoustic accordion music during the early commercial period.[31]

Cajun commercial artists remained in lock-step with national recording trends (figure 2.3). The birth of commercial Cajun music began modestly in 1928, as record companies pressed only 27 sides ranging from accordion-based tunes to obscure French interpretations of Anglo-American string band arrangements. With the record industry in top form in 1929, record companies increased the production of commercial Cajun music by recording 176 sides. That same year, Vocalion and Columbia launched the sounds of rural Afro-Creole music in the commercial documentary record. On October 2, 1929, Douglas Bellard and Kirby Riley became the first rural Afro-Creoles from southwest Louisiana to record. Vocalion released four Bellard–Riley sides, including the classic *la la* lament "La Valse de la Prison" and "Les Flammes d'Enfer," which by the late twentieth century was a standard in the Cajun repertoire.[32] Amédé Ardoin followed his cohort's lead approximately two months later when he entered the Columbia studios to record with Cajun fiddler Dennis McGee. These Afro-Creole recording artists' extensive use of blue notes, highly syncopated melodic phrasing, crying vocal, and repertoire diversified the Cajun portfolio by generating a sort of race record subgenre under the auspices of the commercial Cajun umbrella. Production peaked in the autumn of 1929, after which the number of

Figure 2.3. Dressed in contemporary garb, accordionist Anatole Credeur and his dapper band recorded four sides for the Brunswick label in Dallas, Texas, on November 1, 1929. Ron Yule Collection, courtesy of the Wilson Granger Family.

Cajun issues tapered off in the wake of the famous stock market crash that sent the nation reeling into the Great Depression.

During the first years of the Depression, the recording industry became progressively more centralized, a reaction to economic stresses that would fully crystallize by the onset of the World War II. "Initially national record companies sold folk music back to the folk communities in the Twenties and Thirties because it would sell," argues folklorist and Louisiana music expert Nicholas Spitzer. "In seeking broader markets the companies often altered and eventually ignored the folk traditions to serve their commercial interests."[33] Several strains of American music, including accordion-based Cajun music, eventually evaporated from the documentary record as the economic crisis virtually collapsed niche markets, including the race record business.[34] In 1932, explain commercial music historians Rick Kennedy and Randy McNutt, "the record industry sold only six million records, one-sixth the volume sold in 1927."[35] Consequently, in an attempt to economize, companies became extraordinarily selective about promoting only the best-selling Cajun artists.

Local musicians recorded only 32 sides in 1930 before economic pressures brought production of commercial Cajun music to a screeching halt. In line with the sharply curtailed production of hillbilly and race records in the early 1930s, Cajun music began a three-year recording hiatus following Afro-Creole Amédé Ardoin and Cajun fiddler Dennis McGee's interracial recording session on November 20, 1930. Ardoin and McGee also helped to break the dry spell on August 8, 1934, in San Antonio, Texas, by waxing several sides for the Bluebird label, thereby resurrecting the accordion-based sounds that dominated Cajun music in the years before the interruption. Only the most popular Cajun recording artists—Joe Falcon and Cleoma Breaux Falcon and the Breaux Brothers—and influential Afro-Creole Ardoin returned to the studio between October and December 1934 to record material for the newly established discounted 35-cent record lines issued by the Bluebird, Vocalion, and Decca labels. During the last year of Cajun music's early commercial era, these labels collectively released 46 Cajun sides, before shifting their attention to the sounds of Cajun Swing that had been incubating in south Louisiana during the recording hiatus.

Situating the First Cajun Recordings

The first documented attempts to capitalize on Cajun music were made by Crescent City socialites doubling as part-time musicians. By the mid-1920s, an operatically trained physician from St. Louis, Missouri, Dr. James F. Roach, had built a regional reputation as an accomplished amateur musician during his frequent radio appearances in his adopted home, New Orleans. In January 1925, Dr. Roach, accompanied by his wife, pianist Agnes Farrell Roach, recorded what the trade magazine *Talking Machine World* referred to as the first "Cajan" recording—"Gué Gué Solingaie" (Song of the Crocodile)—at the Hart Piano House for the General Phonograph Company's Okeh record label. Agnes Roach's solo performance of Claude Debussy's high-culture composition "Reflets Dans L'Eau" (Reflections in the Water) served as the recording's flip side. On July 15, 1925, *Talking Machine World* proclaimed that the record's success would encourage future exploration of Acadian French music in south Louisiana.[36]

"Gué Gué Solingaie" was actually a vernacular Afro-Creole song prevalent in the Crescent City area. Music writer Mina Monroe recalled hearing the song as a child from the domestics who worked on her family's plantation home in St. Charles Parish. She explained in her 1921 publication *Bayou Ballads* that the song "is almost an incantation, in which the ending phrase of each couplet, 'li connain parlé,' etc., is whispered in hushed tones. In a sort of weird lullaby the little ones are urged to 'balié chimin-là,' literally to 'sweep the path clear,' the path being the tiny mind preparing for dreams."[37]

Anthropomorphic animals display the same mysterious and enchanting qualities found in Afro-Creole fairy tales, as the tortoise speaks and the *cocodril* (alligator) lures children to the edge of the swamp. Servants sang the Creole French tune to emphasize that children under their watch should not stray beyond their caregiver's protection.[38] Despite the article's enthusiastic review of the release, Roach's English rendition (which perfectly followed Monroe's English-language lyric translation line for line) intersected with Cajun musical culture only as far as the print of *Talking*

Machine World's expose. The unidentified author seemingly issued the niche marketing ploy on behalf of the General Phonograph Corporation, aimed at exploiting the exoticism attached to a little-known vernacular American music. To be sure, the release's B-side paid respects to Debussy's impressionism, while the minimalist arrangement of "Gué Gué Solingaie" fuses the American vernacular and classical tradition in the way Roach's more famous contemporaries—such as Charles Ives and George Gershwin—flirted with folk expression in their immediate environs. The Roaches' release was an experiment that failed to generate interest in the Cajun community, and apparently much interest beyond the confines of his immediate social circle. Though the initial niche market may not have developed, it foreshadowed developments that would forever alter the course of vernacular Cajun music.

Cultures clashed when Joe Falcon, Cleoma Breaux, and Leon Meche repulsed Columbia's engineers in their makeshift New Orleans studio in April 1928. The reluctant New Yorkers impelled George Burrow to haggle for the ensemble's opportunity to record.[39] The surprisingly successful venture, unlike the Roach recording, ignited a viable Cajun music niche market aimed at working-class Francophones in Louisiana. Falcon and Breaux's recording proved that Cajun music could be profitable, thereby encouraging other south Louisiana musicians and major record companies to produce an assortment of regional 78 rpm releases. "Lafayette's" cultural ramifications reverberated for years in south Louisiana, by substantiating the move toward standardized song lyrics while according Cajun recording artists unprecedented regional fame.[40]

Music had long been an outlet for individual expression in a culture that, until the twentieth century, was largely illiterate. Cajun songwriters composed tunes and lyrics articulating the passions, tribulations, and elations of a people and transferred those songs orally across generational lines. As musicians learned songs by oral transmission, they often adapted lyrics to suit their own reality or replaced forgotten words within song texts with their own language. Particularly adept vocalists could spontaneously generate melodies and texts at will.[41] The emergence of recorded music set Cajun compositions in a stable, concrete format.[42] The whole community listened with anticipation as vernacular Cajun music entered the commercial market.

"The first time I heard recorded music," remembered Cajun music enthusiast and cultural activist Pierre Varmon Daigle, "was when I heard Joe Falcon's record of 'Lafayette' played on a small record player. . . . Nothing since has so completely held my attention."[43] Like many Cajuns, both the music and the mechanics of the gramophone captivated Daigle's imagination. As an adolescent in rural Acadia Parish, Joe Falcon spent hours cutting and selling stove wood with his sisters at a dollar a chord to raise enough money to buy a record player. The siblings pooled their earnings and purchased a Victrola from Montgomery Ward's mail order catalogue. When the gramophone arrived with twelve complimentary disks, the whole neighborhood descended on the Falcon home in hopes of hearing the mysterious contraption. The machine perplexed Falcon and his sisters. The young consumers had only seen pictures of Victrolas in catalogues and had no idea how to operate their new acquisition. After a bit of experimentation, the Falcons cranked the handle, wound the spring mechanism, and spun their first records. Some neighbors stayed until midnight in complete awe of recorded sound. The collection of popular tunes, orchestrated arrangements, and novelty records—particularly "A Scene at a Dog Fight" by celebrated New York comedian and animal imitator Len Spenser—enthralled the guests. His fascination with recording technology came full circle for Falcon and the Cajun community following the release of his Columbia Records debut, "Lafayette."[44]

The initial impact of the release made Joe Falcon an Acadiana household name, as his celebrity quickly surpassed that of more proficient accordion players. "After he recorded," recalled Cajun fiddler Leo Soileau, "[Joe Falcon] was Jesus Christ." He continued, acknowledging Falcon's new-found fame, "You know, it's just like, well, Bing Crosby's going to be here tonight. I sure will try to go see him."[45] The Columbia release offered the denigrated ethnic group outside validation by equating vernacular Cajun music with the nation's top artists on south Louisiana's record shelves. Joe Falcon remembered that even some of the poorest Cajuns would buy as many as two records—despite the fact that they did not own a phonograph—to play at a neighbor's house.[46]

Joe Falcon and Cleoma Breaux's celebrity reached social heights previously unknown in the largely egalitarian working-class Cajun community. By late 1928, the two lived together. Crowds of dance hall owners and fans frequently gathered on their front lawn to book dances. Because of the overwhelming public demand for concerts and public appearances, the musicians were able to escape the rigors of manual farm labor to pursue a professional musical career. "I had to!," exclaimed Joe Falcon to folklorist Ralph Rinzler in 1965. "Playing every night, coming back at two, three, four o'clock in the morning." Not only did late-night performances physically drain the musicians, but the money they collected at dances was too good to justify continuing their agrarian lifestyle. The Falcons' popularity extended as far as east Texas, where the duo performed regularly at nightclubs between Beaumont and Port Arthur. In south Louisiana, Joe Falcon made appearances at local accordion contests, in which area musicians eagerly sought to compete against the new star.[47] Recording opened a new world of possibilities to the celebrity couple. Contracts with Columbia, Bluebird, and Decca served as passports to travel across ethnic boundaries beyond the confines of south Louisiana.

The second Cajun recording session took place when Columbia invited Falcon and Breaux to record again in New York City on August 27, 1928. The couple traveled to the record company's headquarters and recorded six tunes, including a French interpretation of the English ballad "My Good Ol' Man." The female protagonist in the tune laments the excesses of her notorious husband, who has earned the title "le meillieur buveur du pays" (the region's best drinker), an image that underscored Joe Falcon's affinity for alcohol.[48] The playful call-and-response structuring "La Vieux Soullard Et Sa Femme" (The Old Drunkard and His Wife) animates the tension between domesticity and the male-dominated world of bars and honky-tonks where the couple made their living. Simulating a drunken stupor, Falcon's gasping accordion stumbles through the looping riff-based melody, while exasperating his instrument's base chords with his left hand between phrases. When Breaux enters with the crisp treble of her commanding vocal—representing the voice of domestic reason—she interrupts her partner's rambling accordion. Meanwhile, Falcon, in the role of the drunkard, spurts deadpan French ripostes to perforate the melodic flow of his partner's call-and-response vocals.

Musicologist Harry Oster cited Americanization as the centripetal force that generated "hybrid folksongs" like "La Vieux Soullard et Sa Femme," "which combine lyrics in Cajun French with elements from one or more outside sources (southern mountain folksongs, commercial popular music of the country-and-western type, and Negro folk music of the blues variety)."[49] The Falcons interpreted the Anglo composition through a Cajun lens and rearranged the tune to conform to the Cajun aesthetic. What is more, the ditty took on new meaning when performed in the Cajun context. Conservative Anglo Southerners could have viewed the song's bawdy theme and off-color humor as departing from prevailing standards of social order. However, in Cajun Country, drinking songs spoke to the ethnic group's relatively liberal Mediterranean mores that openly accepted alcohol consumption in certain contexts.

The couple recorded several other arrangements, including another anglicized tune titled "A Cowboy Rider," a song that spoke to south Louisiana's deeply rooted ranching traditions, and "La Marche de la Noce (Wedding March)," traditionally played at working-class Cajun wedding dances as the bride and groom present themselves for the first time to the congregation as man and wife. Breaux's singing and guitar work took center stage once again during her performance of the driving *valse à deux temps* "Marie Buller" [Marais Bouleur].[50] Her nasal vocal delivery, though at an uncomfortably low key for the singer, represented the first session to feature prominently a female Cajun vocalist.

Cleoma Breaux Falcon sang frequently around her home, at dances, and again on records when Decca Records invited her to record. The four Decca sessions she recorded between December 22, 1934, and December 15, 1937, proved to be her most artistic. Her broad musical inclinations became apparent as she sang French-language interpretations of such popular and country-western songs as "Pin Solitaire (Lonesome Pine)," "L'Amour Indifferent (Careless Love)," "Lettres D'Amour dans le Sable" (Love Letters in the Sand) and Jimmie Davis's hit "Pas la Belle de Personne Que Moi" (Nobody's Darling but Mine). She also rendered French versions of popular Harlem jazz numbers, such as Fats Waller's "Lulu's Back in Town" and "It's a Sin to Tell a Lie." Joe took a back seat while his wife sang on most of the recordings. Just as her star shone its brightest, Cleoma Breaux Falcon returned to Louisiana in 1938 following her final recording session in New York only to meet with tragedy. A moving vehicle snagged her sweater and dragged the helpless pedestrian a quarter mile, leaving her maimed body beyond medical repair. She remained in frail health until her death in 1941.[51]

Cleoma Breaux Falcon's unprecedented musical career grew out of the overlapping, often contradictory, value systems forced together under the weight of mass culture, consumerism, and the sustained interaction between a traditional Cajun world and American popular culture. Falcon made a living on the turbulent male-dominated dance hall circuit. At home, she created a domestic shelter as tranquil as the eye of a storm. And, before her untimely death, the force of her creative energy breached conventional social strictures. The guitarist broke etiquette in Cajun musical tradition by desegregating those gendered divisions structuring labor and dance culture in Cajun society. She defiantly challenged the custom relegating female musicians to the home while consciously developing an urbane feminine persona that nodded to contemporary Hollywood American starlets. Before each performance, she bathed, coiffed her hair like Clara Bow, primped in her dresses, donned pointed-toe spiked heels, and applied rouge before entering the violent dance hall milieu that sustained her career. Her genteel exterior shrouded the guitarist's tough and obstinate constitution. During one club performance, a drunken patron approached the elevated bandstand and aggressively barked obscenities at Falcon. Without hesitation, she kicked the dancer in the face mid-song, put his eye out with her spiked heel, and then continued her concert.[52] Her efforts served to revolutionize the potential options available to women, a career path that few opted to follow.[53]

While her accordion-playing partner enjoyed a prominent place in south Louisiana's male-dominated dance music scene, Cleoma Breaux Falcon carved out a feminine space in commercial Cajun music. She spent the course of her career working to rectify the traditional and progressive aspects of her life. At home, she cultivated a domestic sanctuary removed from the violent contexts she experienced at work. On the bandstand, however, she performed both music and gender. The novelty of a female musician in south Louisiana's male-dominated dance band scene enhanced the ensemble's popularity. Dancers traveled for miles to ogle and hear the petite woman's performances. Respectable women in Cajun society did not drink alcohol in public, nor did they pursue such marginally acceptable occupations as music. Falcon, on the other, assumed a sort of Cajun flapper persona, wearing stylish dresses and short hair, while frequenting the nightclubs, bars, and dance halls that embraced her music.[54]

Cleoma Breaux Falcon was a dynamic woman with frizzy black hair, piercing black eyes, and an empathetic vocal delivery as enchanting as her porcelain skin. She grew up in Crowley, Louisiana, surrounded by music. Her father, accordionist Auguste Breaux, and her musical brothers Amédé, Ophy, and Clifford were all part of the region's accordion-based musical tradition. Yet, when Auguste deserted his family, eleven-year-old Cleoma assumed the role of surrogate mother—cooking, cleaning, and watching over her indolent brothers—while their mother Mathilde Schexnayder Breaux sought domestic work around town. It was then, during her adolescence, that the budding guitarist learned the significance of domesticity. She provided structure and stability to her broken home. Meanwhile, music came to represent an escape from poverty and the pain of abandonment, and a source of family cohesion and income that the Breaux family sorely needed.[55]

Joe Falcon frequently called on the Breaux home and sat in on family jam sessions, playing the triangle. He recalled her rock-steady rhythm guitar and superior musicianship, proclaiming that she was the only guitarist with whom he had played that actually changed chords. Cleoma Breaux eventually became a member of Falcon's band and the accordionist's fiancée.[56] In 1931, Breaux and Falcon married and adopted their only daughter, Loula. The guitarist went through great pains to ensure Loula would know a kind of stable family life that the musician never had. Every morning, regardless of the hour they returned from their dance engagements, both parents greeted Loula at the breakfast table and escorted her to school. The Falcon's also invited Mathilde Breaux and Amédé's son Preston Breaux to live with them. Mathilde shared the chores and babysat while her daughter and son-in-law performed or traveled to record.[57]

Her union with Falcon was not Cleoma's first experience with love. As a young woman, Breaux married guitarist Oliver Hanks. When their marriage dissolved, she pursued a relationship with Joe, though the almost universally Catholic early-twentieth-century Cajun society condemned divorce. The guitarist was a liberal-minded woman who at times challenged the traditional contexts dictating courtship, marriage rites, and womanhood. The guitarist lived on the periphery of mainstream Cajun society, like several of her fellow Cajun musicians who became professional entertainers following their commercial debuts.[58]

During the early twentieth century, few Southern women affiliated with family-oriented music enjoyed recording careers.[59] Like Mexican American guitarist Lydia Mendoza and the Carter Family women—particularly Sara—Falcon challenged the boundaries of male-dominated genres (at least in public) by taking their traditions beyond the confines of the home and into the studio. Both Mendoza and Falcon waxed their debut recordings in 1928. Mendoza recalled, "when I first got to San Antonio—in those years—there were no women who sang [publicly] or would dare to sing. There was none of that. I think I was the one who encouraged them."[60] Not all women in the South felt so eager to become professional entertainers, though. Cajun women certainly did not follow Falcon's lead. Some admired her resolve from the dance floor, while other maintained an acerbic jealousy for the attention she received on stage.[61] Thus, Falcon's professional orientation simultaneously aligned the guitarist more readily with other contemporary female recordings artists and marginalized her within Cajun society.

In contrast to the burgeoning country crooner tradition popularized by Jimmie Rodgers, Cleoma Breaux Falcon and Sara and Maybelle Carter straddled home music and commercialization while projecting an image of feminine respectability to American audiences. The Carters marketed their brand of entertainment as "morally good" and performed ballads, gospel compositions, and sentimental tunes that catered to a conservative Anglo-Protestant middle-class aesthetic that privileged sobriety and chastity. However, Cleoma's Carter Family counterpoint, Sara, divorced her husband and fellow musician A. P. Carter and remarried despite conservative Southern social mores.[62] In addition to solidifying the commercial viability of two distinctive American commercial music markets (hillbilly and Cajun), Sara Carter and Cleoma Breaux Falcon developed parallel guitar styles in their respective genres. Both provided firm rhythmic support and simple but appropriate musical accompaniment, in sharp contrast to the many Cajun guitarists who did not change chords at all while strumming. Perhaps most important, both guitarists displayed a solid sense of rhythm, an essential quality in the dance band music she helped popularize. The musical and cultural intersection linking these influential women comes into clearer focus in Falcon's Cajun interpretation of the Carter Family arrangement "Bonnie Blue Eyes," marketed to local audiences in 1937. The recording signifies Cleoma Breaux Falcon's conscious and deliberate imitation of America's popular and seemingly wholesome family band.[63] Furthermore, both artists ended their careers during the 1940s, albeit for different reasons.[64]

The parallels between the commercialization of white Southern and Cajun music extend beyond gender comparisons. Leo Soileau's early recording career further illustrates Cajun music's ascendance as part of the nation's commercial music revolution. In the summer of 1927, the Victor Talking Machine Company decided to expand its market share in vernacular American music. Victor hired talent scout Ralph S. Peer and appropriated $60,000 to develop the company's hillbilly catalogue, in an effort to compete with rivals Okeh and Columbia. Already legendary for helping to launch the race record market in 1921 and "discovering" Fiddlin' John Carson in 1923, Peer single-handedly launched the recording career of the Carter Family and Jimmie Rodgers during the 1927 "Bristol Sessions."[65] The success of the Carters and Rodgers was due, in part, to the time and special care taken by Peer's engineers in creating a quality product during the Bristol Sessions, meticulously adjusting their state-of-the-art equipment for hours over multiple takes. In 1928, the Victor Recording Company decided to venture into the Cajun market, presumably because of the Falcons' success with Columbia. The company dipped its toe into Louisiana waters when Victor recorded Cajun fiddler Leo Soileau and accordionist Mayeuse LaFleur only three months after the release of "Lafayette."

Life as a Cajun Recording Artist

Leo Soileau began to nurture his professional musical career at the age of twelve earning upward of four to five dollars per nightly performance.[66]

Even at such an early age, show business consumed his mind. "You couldn't make me do anything else but play music," exclaimed Soileau.[67] In the 1920s, Louisiana farmers experienced an economic depression. As the price of cotton plummeted, so did the morale of many small farmers, and some financially beleaguered individuals—including Soileau—opted to find an easier way to make a living. "So that's when I started," explained Soileau to folklorist Ralph Rinzler, "[I] decided I would haul off and play some music. Really, you know? Going brass tacks. Make a living out of it."[68] Soileau organized a duet in 1920 with accordionist Mayeuse LaFleur, a childhood acquaintance. "Me and him, we was practically born, you know, on the same place, same farm," explained the fiddler.[69] The group performed an assorted repertoire that included traditional Cajun numbers and such popular hillbilly tunes as "Casey Jones" and "Roving Gamblers" at Maxine Ledoux's dance hall in Basile, Louisiana, for eight years before they became the second Cajun musical act to make commercial recordings, and the first to record Cajun fiddling.[70]

In 1928, Opelousas jeweler and part-time record retailer Frank J. Dietlein[71] sponsored a recording session for Soileau and LaFleur at the Victor Recording Company's regional field studios in Atlanta, Georgia. Dietlein approached Victor with the news of two musicians who could potentially compete with Columbia recording artist Joe Falcon. The record company dispatched a field agent to Basile, where he invited the musicians to record.[72] The duo jumped at the chance. Soileau convinced his cousin and notorious St. Landry Parish Sheriff "Cat" Doucet to escort the musicians.[73]

"I loaned [Mayeuse] one of my suits," Doucet confided to biographer Mary Alice Fontenot. "And we went first class. Stayed at one of the biggest hotels in Atlanta. I had told those people we didn't want to be put up at no joint. And we went on the train and had sleepers."[74] Recording sessions, which always required travel during the early commercial era, opened a new world to Cajun musicians. Not only were musicians obliged to venture beyond their immediate environs, but their adventures abroad centered around a Cajun dialogue with Anglo-American popular culture. LaFleur and Soileau tapped into the pulse of popular culture during their sojourn in Georgia, for Victor's recording symposium attracted regional, even national talent. The record company provided most of the traveling musicians with hotel accommodations in Atlanta, where the two Cajun musicians met the legendary hillbilly crooner Jimmie Rodgers. "We stayed at the same hotel as the great Jimmie Rogers [sic], the old 'Blue Yodeler,'" Soileau remembered fondly. "And it was really a thrill for us to meet him."[75] The Jimmie Rodgers' celebrity loomed large in Cajun Country (figure 2.4). South Louisianians related to the Blue Yodeler's honest song writing and musical perspective, which fused combinations of African-American and white Southern musical elements, a cultural amalgam that paralleled the cross-cultural pollination taking place for generations in the Bayou Country. Rodgers and the two Louisianians spent the night exchanging stories and imbibing a stash of quality moonshine that the country star secured from his Atlanta connection.[76]

Figure 2.4. Boudreaux Electric Piano Shop advertised Jimmie Rogers's latest releases alongside "French records" by Joe Falcon, Bixy Guidry, and Angelas LeJeune. Courtesy of the Center for Louisiana Studies, University of Louisiana at Lafayette.

The following morning, Soileau and LaFleur were escorted to an improvised studio that doubled as a Ku Klux Klan headquarters. A single suspended microphone dangled above the musicians as the engineers prepared to record. Surrounded by Klan paraphernalia and sound-dampening curtains, the duet anxiously began the first number with the enthusiasm and volume of a dance hall performance, overwhelming the sound engineer and his equipment. The record executives concluded that the duo needed to remedy their edginess and secured a pint of 190 proof "prescription liquor" at a nearby pharmacy. The relaxant proved effective during Soileau and LaFleur's initial offering, the "Basile Waltz," but the session took five hours as the engineers worked tediously to perfect the vocal levels.[77] LaFleur played his accordion with the syncopation of an Afro-Creole, belting out powerful raspy vocals. Soileau's lilting fiddle traced the meter and phrasing of LaFleur's accordion as Soileau mimicked the melodic progression of tunes, rather then assuming the *seconder* position (or rhythmic accompaniment) employed by accordion–fiddle ensembles during the 1920s. The four sides waxed during this historic session represented Leo Soileau and Mayeuse LaFleur's first recordings, and the first recording session by Cajun musicians other than the Falcons. The Victor sessions also preserved the songwriting abilities of Mayeuse LaFleur.[78]

Mayeuse recorded two autobiographical pieces during his session with Soileau. Seated underneath Victor's dangling microphone, LaFleur performed for the first time publicly "Mama, Where You At?," an original composition that addressed his lingering sense of abandonment wrought by his mother Zola LaFleur, who abruptly relinquished parental responsibilities when the accordionist was an infant. The accordionist's Afro-Creole–inspired vocals sliced through the melody with an emotive tension that both articulated his psychological scars and appealed to the Cajun aesthetic. On the other hand, the sentiment of loss in "Ton Pere a Mit D'Eor" (Your Father Put Me Out) spoke directly to LaFleur's marital problems.[79] Though small compensation for the painful experiences behind LaFleur's compositions, each musician received $100.00 from Victor for his services. The duo celebrated their successful venture by attending a showing of the Al Jolson picture "The Jazz Singer," further expanding the duo's cultural horizons before returning to Louisiana.[80]

On Sunday October 28, 1929, only weeks after their debut session, moonshiners violently gunned down LaFleur outside of a Basile speakeasy. Seven weeks later, as a jury sentenced the accordionist's murderer to life in prison, the Evangeline Pharmacy in Ville Platte advertised the release of a new Victor recording by Leo Soileau and Mayeuse LaFleur. Pharmacy employees placed a phonograph in the middle of the street and repeatedly played the duo's records at full volume to attract customers. The accordionist's father Henry LaFleur obtained copies of the disks and listened to them in heartbroken solitude. On the other hand, the late LaFleur's former father-in-law—the protagonist of "Ton Pere a Mit D'Eor" (Your Father Put Me Out)—broke any Mayeuse LaFleur record he encountered, regardless of who owned it.[81]

The loss of his musical partner devastated Leo Soileau. When he decided to reenter the musical world, he tried to reinvent the sound he had forged with his childhood friend by hiring seventeen-year-old accordionist and LaFleur admirer Moïse Robin. "I saw Mayeuse play a house dance for the Richard family in Pacaniere," Robin remembered. "It was Christmas day. I was five years younger than he was, and he inspired me. He had a big red accordion and he would cry on that thing."[82] Soileau and Robin produced 14 sides in 1929 at three different sessions for the Paramount, Victor, and Vocalion labels. The revamped duet became part of the tremendous surge of Cajun recordings waxed in 1929 following Cajun music's rise as a commercially viable market after the genre's lucrative first year.

In the summer of 1929, Frank Dietlein negotiated a recording deal for Leo Soileau and his new accordion player. Paramount Records agreed to accommodate the Cajun musicians at the Gennett studios in Richmond, Indiana, where trumpeter and fellow Louisianian Louis Armstrong made his first recordings with King Oliver's Creole Jazz Band only six years earlier.[83] Crowley native Roy Gonzales, who sang French interpretations of Jimmie Rodgers songs, went along for the ride with an old four-string guitar. Paramount expected all three musicians to perform, having invested

$700 to transport them on a fast mail train to Indiana. When Gonzales arrived at the studios on July 13, 1929, he had a change of heart and pleaded with the producers not to record. The record executives insisted, and the Louisianian produced six Cajun adaptations of tunes popularized by Jimmie Rodgers, including a rejected French version of "Sleep, Baby, Sleep," waxed by the Singing Brakeman during the Bristol Sessions.[84] Gonzales approached the microphone, four-stringed guitar in hand, and proceeded to strum through several familiar Rodgers-styled blues. The accomplished vocalist confidently swung his warm vibrato-laden baritone through the material, embellishing his vocal with yodeling.

Soileau and Robin recorded six sides, including a couple of original compositions. Soileau's English-language lament "Easy Rider Blues" featured the intricate interplay between the fiddle and accordion voices. Moïse kept time with his left hand on the accordion's two bass chords, while interjecting syncopated riffs between Soileau's crying fiddle runs. The fiddler's experimental composition represented the collision of conflicting instrumental styles. Their bluesy interplay sounded like a tense debate between the fiddle and Robin's aggressive accordion rebuttals. The session also produced "La Valse De La Rue Canal," an ode to Canal Street, New Orleans' major commercial and Americanized cultural thoroughfare.

Blues structures, Soileau and Robin's reference to Canal Street, and cross-country travel cut through the constrictive characterizations that scholars and music critics deploy to paint Cajuns as an isolated group. Cajun musicians engaged the wide world of American consumerism when they set foot in recording studios to create shellac disks garnering their names. Furthermore, traveling musicians pierced through Cajun Country's porous borders on the open roads leading to record label headquarters in major metropolitan districts. In Indiana, Victor paid each musician $25 per record, thereby completing the cycle of consumerism that began to define commercial Cajun music during the 1920s. Local musicians not only generated products by harnessing their talents but, at times, economized by reserving their earnings to one day own the amenities of modern America. For instance, while Gonzales and Soileau rented a sleeper car and ate well on the train ride home, Moïse Robin opted to keep his $75 to put toward a $150 Model T Ford. He refused to eat on the trip to Louisiana and slept hunched over in his seat while milling over the American dream of freedom and ownership that only an automobile could bestow.

In September 1929, Robin and Soileau left Cajun Country to record again, this time with accordionist Columbus Fruge in tow. The three musicians traveled to Victor's Memphis, Tennessee, field sessions with the promise of $50 per record. On September 18, 1929, Fruge recorded four sides, including a solo performance of the popular folksong "Saute Crapaud" (Jump Frog), during which he accompanied himself by stomping on a wooden Coca-Cola crate. The accordionist earned $100 for his services, and specifically asked for his fee to be paid in $1 bills. Upon his return, Columbus's wife, who according to Robin did not understand money, stared in awe at the wad of cash, believing the sum to be an enormous fortune.[85] His wife's reaction stemmed, in part, from the grinding poverty Cajuns—and the rural South writ large—experienced at the beginning of the twentieth century. Aside from small amounts of cash (generally in the form of coins) circulating among impoverished farmers, monetary exchanges often transpired in the form of credit.[86]

As Leo Soileau's early recording career indicates, the first commercial Cajun musicians were cultural actors who helped steer their own careers. They intentionally left behind *bals de maison* and the local dance hall scene in search of recording sessions with national companies to produce a series of releases that would increase their exposure at home and supplement their incomes through performance stipends. Those Cajuns in step with the latest trends in American music made a conscious decision to engage in a dialogue with American musical culture. Yet, Cajun music's commercialization took place despite the frank and open condescension of industry executives and recording engineers. If anything, record industry executives were reluctant to record Joe Falcon and Cleoma Breaux at the first Cajun recordings session on April 4, 1928. Like investor Polk Brockman, who persuaded Okeh executives to record Fiddlin' John Carson only after doubling the size of his record order, the first Cajun record came to pass only when George Burrow guaranteed the purchase of 500 copies of the Falcon–Breaux release. Burrow's gamble paid off handsomely. No other Cajun musicians, before or since, enjoyed such instant fame. Their success inspired other musicians to leave home in hope of imprinting their talent in wax.

Moonshiner and accordionist Dewey Segura could not wait to hear his music on a record (figure 2.5). During a whiskey run to Port Arthur, Texas, in 1928, Segura read an editorial in a local newspaper reporting that recording companies were making Cajun records in New Orleans. The accordionist contacted a distant relative who had connections with Columbia records and luckily made last-minute arrangements to record at the end of the company's scheduled session in New Orleans late that year. Following his initial Columbia session on December 16, 1928, Segura sporadically trekked to the Crescent City, at times hoboing by train, in hopes of pinpointing Columbia's return to negotiate another record deal.[87] His perseverance paid off in December 1929, when he sat down to record again. During Segura's second session, the linguistic divide partially separating Cajun and Anglo-American cultures became apparent in the studio as the label's monolingual engineers emphatically insisted that Segura not "sing anything dirty," because they could not comprehend the accordionist's lyrics. Though the obvious linguistic differences between the artists and engineers required some negotiation in the studio, Cajuns recording artists helped bridge the cultural gap with record companies through sustained interaction at multiple sessions as they consciously etched their mark in American shellac.

As a product of mass consumption, the first Cajun recordings stood somewhere between African-American race recordings, issues by foreign-language ethnic groups, and rural white Southern sides in the American

Figure 2.5. Accordionist Dewey Segura and his brother Eddie recorded both commercially and for the Lomaxes' "folk" field recordings. Courtesy of the Acadian Museum, Erath, Louisiana.

commercial music matrix of the late 1920s. Cajun recordings conspicuously embodied characteristics of all three categories. They represented a foreign-language niche market that catered to a marginalized ethnic group that engaged both an agrarian lifestyle and the burgeoning industry as it spread across the Deep South. Through negotiations commonly established by a third party (generally a local record retailer), record companies also offered Cajun musicians economic relief from the crippling effects of both the agricultural depression of 1920 and later the onset of the Great Depression. Recording artists thankfully accepted the set monetary contribution that label executives issued to sidestep royalty negotiations, considering that the one-time payoff represented more income than a sharecropper could generate in one month picking cotton.

Commercial recordings changed the way Cajuns understood their own traditions. These recordings acted as a mirror through which Cajuns could view themselves from an alternative perspective. Artists like Joe and Cleoma Breaux Falcon, the Breaux Brothers, Dennis McGee, and Leo Soileau found validation for their artistic endeavors, first in makeshift recording studios in New York, Chicago, Dallas and New Orleans, and then within their own communities, when shellac disks bearing their names became available, and sold well, to an enthusiastic record-buying Cajun audience. Curious throngs packed dance halls just to catch a glimpse of Joe and Cleoma Breaux Falcon in the wake of "Lafayette." The overflow spilled into the streets, while others scaled club walls and congregated on rooftops, in hopes of getting within earshot of the duo's unamplified performances.

Yet, fame came at a price. The Breaux Brothers' overwhelming popularity following the release of their commercial recordings stimulated troubles within the family band. Accordionist and bandleader Amédé Breaux developed an ornery disposition that frequently translated into fisticuffs with his brothers, both en route to and during dance hall performances, where alcohol fueled his fire.[88]

Amateur musicians watching starry-eyed from the sidelines longed for recognition and a recording contract. Nineteen-year-old Adam Trahan practiced his accordion assiduously after hearing "Lafayette" and eventually landed a deal with Columbia Records—$100 plus travel expenses—with the help of a local record retailer with ties to the New York–based company. In December 1928, Columbia records released two Trahan records, before the disenchanted musician slipped into obscurity, never to step foot into a studio again. Fans and club owners bombarded the musician with requests to perform for dances following Trahan's debut release, explains music writer Ron Brown. "The excessive demands upon his time conflicted with his plans to marry and get a 'responsible' job."[89] Cajun musicians either fully embraced commercialization and its fringe benefits—fame, money, and the chance to become a professional musician—or skirted the periphery like Adam Trahan, disillusioned with the lifestyle. Record-buying audiences, on the other hand, suddenly found homegrown records in the same retail stores that sold the sorts of popular music regularly consumed by the community at large. In essence, Cajuns solidified a new commercial consciousness about their own musical traditions, which had indeed become part of a national phenomenon.

3

A Heterogeneous Tradition

"Acadian Musicians Sing for Records," read a headline from the Lafayette *Daily Advertiser* on March 23, 1929. The newspaper also printed a related photograph featuring six local musicians just returned from performing "French Acadian songs for Okeh records, at Atlanta, Ga."[1] This eclectic group, which included accordionist Oscar "Slim" Doucet, guitarist Chester Hawkins, pianist Jeanne LeBlanc, vocalist Christine Mufzar, and banjoist Patrick Pellerin, waxed eight contrasting sides from opposite ends of the Cajun music spectrum at the same Okeh session—from common accordion dance arrangements to French interpretations of popular American compositions rendered on banjo and piano.[2] Doucet and Hawkins paired up on two sides—"Waxia Special" and "Chere Yeux Noirs" (Dear Dark Eyes)—that typified the rural working-class dance band sound prevalent in Acadiana during the early commercial era. Doucet's accordion playing stood in sharp contrast, however, to the sounds of Acadiana's middle-class performed by Pellerin, Mufzar, and LeBlanc. The selections offered by these recordings artists, particularly Pellerin, Mufzar, and LeBlanc's unusual arrangements, signified the breadth of diversity at the Okeh session and, indeed, the scope of Cajun musical expression between 1928 and 1934 during the early commercial era.

Patrick "Dak" Pellerin's banjo was the Cajun embodiment of America's waning minstrelsy traditions and the escalating jazz fervor sweeping the nation during the roaring twenties. Consequently, Pellerin's musical performance was absolutely cutting edge. Accompanied by pianist Mina Stubbs, the banjo player performed a French interpretation of Fats Waller and Andy Razaf's showstopper "Ain't Misbehavin,'" made famous by Broadway's all-African-American musical revue "Hot Chocolates," starring Louis Armstrong in June 1929. The duet recorded "Ain't Misbehavin'" on December 15, 1929, just as the song became a national phenomenon.[3] Indeed, Pellerin and Stubb's release was contemporary and extremely up-to-date even in a national context. This modern Cajun

ACADIAN MUSICIANS SING FOR RECORDS

Figure 3.1. "Acadian Musicians Sing for Records," announced a local newspaper after Dr. A. J. Boudreaux, Oscar Doucet, Christine Mufzar, Jeanne LeBlanc, S. Hawkins, and Patrick Pellerin traveled to Atlanta to record for Okeh records in 1929. Courtesy of the Center for Louisiana Studies, University of Louisiana at Lafayette.

interpretation of the African-American composition should come as no surprise, considering that the duet recorded for the New York–based label that launched the race record market in the United States and that Cajun musicians were acutely aware of innovations in American popular culture (figure 3.1).

Mufzar and LeBlanc's collaboration titled "Chanson d'Evangeline" (Song of Evangeline)—celebrating Henry Wadsworth Longfellow's fictional Acadian heroine—engaged local and national stereotypes of Louisiana's Acadian/Cajun population. This forgotten manifestation of America's renewed interest in Longfellow's epic poem *Evangeline* (1847) during the first half of the twentieth century represented the musical culmination of two competing interpretations of this American literary classic. Although Mufzar probably read Longfellow's *Evangeline* in grade school, like most American children during the early twentieth century, the vocalist hailed from St. Martinville, Louisiana, a Bayou Têche town that boasted a thriving tourism industry based on genteel Cajun Judge Felix Voorhies' *Acadian Reminiscences*, a local spinoff of Longfellow's famous poem.[4] In 1907, Voorhies recast the epic to include new Cajun protagonists, shifted the climactic conclusion from Philadelphia to St. Martinville, and marketed his fictional interpretation as the authentic tale upon which Longfellow modeled his masterwork. The American cinema also interpreted Longfellow. In 1919, Raoul Walsh released a silent version of *Evangeline* starring Miriam Cooper. Ten years later, the same year that Mufzar and LeBlanc made their way into the studio, Edwin Carewe filmed the most famous film adaptation of Longfellow's poem on location in St. Martin Parish. Mufzar could not escape the excitement in her small hometown with Hollywood on hand, especially as the local press buzzed around Carewe's leading lady, Mexican starlet Dolores del Rio.[5] "Chanson d'Evangeline" thus bridged the divide between south Louisiana's and American mass culture's interpretations of a quintessential piece of Americana in an Okeh recording studio in Atlanta.

The cultural information encoded in Mufzar's Longfellow-inspired recording, Pellerin's jazz-inflected banjo rendition of the African-American classic "Ain't Misbehaving," and the accordion dance numbers waxed by Doucet gave musical form to the kaleidoscopic complexities inherent in Cajun musical expression during the early commercial era. Cajun music's breadth, like the dynamic cultural forces shaping the Cajun reality, was remarkably heterogeneous. Diversity stemmed not from isolation but from integration. Individuals engaged outside stimuli with varying enthusiasm, adapting or dismissing diverse traits at irregular rates. However, geography and occupation diversified the Cajun community's socioeconomic complexity as much as the region's ethic tapestry and one's affinity for mass consumption. Louisiana's varied topography shaped traditional subsistence: cotton, rice, and ranching on the western Cajun prairies, fishing and trapping along the coastal marshes, and sugarcane near the southeastern bayous. Industrial sectors later diversified Acadiana's economy as locals found employment on the railroad, in the oil patch and in canneries, rice mills, cotton gins, sulfur and salt mines, and lumber camps.[6] Early commercial-era issues ranging from polkas and waltzes to ballads and the blues, featuring such titles "Valse de Vacher" (Cowboy Waltz), "Blues de Texas," and "Valse de Puit D'Huile" (Oil Well Waltz) are indeed commentaries about the circumstances that shaped Cajun life during the first years of the Great Depression.

The collective heterogeneous body of recorded Cajun music dating from 1928 to 1934 represents a microcosm of the stylistic and musical corpus falling under the heading of "Cajun music." Issues by string band combos, harmonica players, solo guitarists, accordion-based dance bands, and balladeers provide the earliest aural evidence of the Cajun repertory's range and the simultaneity of protean musical trends and traditions.[7] Although major recording corporations were rather fickle about material that strayed from lucrative accordion dance records, guitarist Alcide "Blind Uncle" Gaspard and fiddler Dennis McGee enjoyed prolific careers as either front men or accompanists.

Bayou Country's musical terrain and the cultural and historical undercurrents that expanded the genre's repertoire, stylistic range, and instrumental conventions are outlined here. Three factors encouraged heterogeneity in the Bayou Country's musical traditions: a musical network that stimulated exchange between musicians, thereby diversifying

Louisiana's soundscape; the historical idiosyncrasies and ethnic variation shaping cultural production in rural enclaves; and the tension between traditional and innovative tendencies within the genre. In what follows, I use residual colonial song structures performed by guitarist Blind Uncle Gaspard; Dennis McGee's enigmatic fiddling, which crossed stylistic and racial boundaries; the friction between conservative and progressive inclinations in regional Cajun popular culture, as performed by Leo Soileau; and Cajun readings of American popular culture as interpreted by accordionists Lawrence Walker and Nathan Abshire as points of departure in this discussion of heterogeneous musical expression on 78 rpm records.

A Musical Cohort

Working-class Cajun musicians assumed the role of culture brokers. They interpreted and disseminated cultural information to the community at large through public performances, while simultaneously sharing ideas and songs among colleagues within a complex matrix of interpersonal relationships that connected many of Cajun music's luminaries. Performers moved in and out of ensembles so frequently that this informal network facilitated considerable cross-pollination across stylistic inclination and repertoire. Musicians also encountered new cultural and musical terrain while traveling along a dance circuit that thrived in homes and dance halls as far west as east Texas. This interaction encouraged stylistic dynamism and heterogeneity within Cajun music and ultimately expanded an individual's repertoire.

Musicians, especially professional performers, worked as a closely knit occupational group at intimate house dances and boisterous dance halls for amusement and to generate income. By the early commercial era, the lucrative financial incentives associated with dance music encouraged impromptu collaborations among musicians who united through the common goal of making money. The dance hall circuit allowed musicians to perform regularly during the week, which in turn acted as a springboard into the recording studio. Working-class audiences who liberally patronized dance halls kept Acadiana's popular traveling performers in business and, more profoundly, out of the cotton fields. Ethnographers affiliated with the Works Progress Administration acknowledged that professional Cajun musicians transcended the low wages and grueling manual labor that shaped life in the region's rural working-class ghettos, observing that they "live a life comparable to that of medieval troubadours, traveling about the Cajun settlements, living on the bounty of those who enjoy their music."[8]

This musical network transcended stylistic and ethnic boundaries. During the late 1920s, Cajun fiddler Dennis McGee collaborated with Afro-Creole accordionist Amédé Ardoin at local dances and in the recording studio.[9] Joe and Cleoma Breaux Falcon became well acquainted with McGee's colleague while playing the same dance circuit and escorted the black accordionist to the Decca Studios in New York City in 1934. "I took

Amédé Ardoin myself on a bus, way down to New York," Joe Falcon told Lauren Post, "me and my wife, and he recorded by himself."[10] McGee's brother-in-law and fiddling companion Sady Courville also performed across stylistic and racial lines with the region's top artists. Courville remembered, "I played with Dennis, with Angelas LeJeune, Amédée Ardoin, Leo Soileau . . . a lot of music with Leo Soileau."[11] Many up-and-coming musicians developed their skills within a familial setting before cultivating their talents beyond kinship boundaries through contact with established musicians.

Like many of his contemporaries, fiddler Leo Soileau fostered his talent in two complementary milieus—at home, and then later on the dance hall circuit. In the first two decades of the twentieth century, Leo's father Thaddeus Soileau farmed cotton, sweet potatoes, and corn and supplemented his income performing for rural neighborhood dances for 75 cents per gig in rural Evangeline Parish.[12] He also amused his 10 children at home with his musical ability, often playing late into the evening after the day's labor. "We'd have a little piece of wood in the fireplace and I'd sit right by him," the fiddler recalled, "sometimes with my head against him. And, boy, he'd play that fiddle until twelve o'clock."[13] Young Leo studied his father's technique intently and secretly retrieved his father's fiddle from under his bed to practice while Thaddeus worked outside.

In 1916, Thaddeus Soileau hired iterant day laborer and fiddle master Dennis McGee to work on the family farm. McGee also found time to give music lessons to Thaddeus's adolescent son, who, under McGee's tutelage, quickly developed a penchant for lead fiddle and a love for melody.[14] By 15 years of age, Leo Soileau had become an active participant in the Cajun musical network and performed regularly at large dance halls with the most popular musicians of the day. One evening, he scheduled a performance at a hall in Chatagnier, a rural hamlet 10 miles northeast of Eunice, Louisiana. Approximately 300 dancers filed into the hall as the teenage fiddler took center stage with Amédé Ardoin. Until that night, Soileau had never met the petit black man, whose brisk, syncopated accordion playing and powerful vocals penetrated the noise of shuffling feet and ambient conversation. The two performers commanded the dance floor, churning out music from Ardoin's extensive repertoire to incite the dancers into a swirling mass.[15]

By World War I, teenage accordionist Angelas LeJeune had become part of the region's musical network, collaborating and interacting with both Ardoin and McGee. LeJeune developed into a visible figure on southwest Louisiana's dance circuit, sometimes performing five nights a week at house dances in and around the rural Pointe Noire community. Demand for French music also called the accordionist away to play lucrative gigs as far away as Texas. After playing a dance in Lake Charles, Louisiana, McGee, LeJeune, and fiddler Ernest Fruge continued west to perform in Shiner, Texas. "And over there, they tapped their feet," recalled McGee, "they jumped up, they cried out . . . they danced, danced, sweated, sweated."[16] The receptive Texas audience paid the three musicians $80 for their appearance. The group's extraordinary musicianship also commanded the attention of the Brunswick label's recording scouts back home in Bayou Country.[17]

In September 1929, St. Landry Parish Sheriff Charles Thibodeaux and pharmacist Abe Boudreaux encouraged further interaction within the network by concentrating local talent at an accordion contest in Opelousas. With the Brunswick scouts on hand and the promise of a record contract at stake, LeJeune and fiddlers McGee and Fruge outplayed 33 contestants. The next morning, Boudreaux chauffeured the contest champions and Sady Courville to the label's regional recording facility in New Orleans, marking the beginning of LeJeune's recording career and McGee's second session as a studio musician.[18]

McGee's diverse repertoire represented a musical style somewhat removed from the popular accordion-based compositions that dominated the early commercial period. His early commercial recordings reflected his varied influences and differ markedly from mainstream arrangements in instrumentation, textual content, and stylistic technique. In addition to ornamental fills, mazurka arrangements, and melodies he learned from his Irish relatives, McGee apprenticed under Gustave Ardoin, a fiddler versed in nineteenth-century dance music. Ardoin was almost 100 years old when McGee became his student, a detail that delighted late twentieth-century folklorists and musicologists interested in the ancestral roots of Cajun music.[19] Scholars, musicians, documentarians, and cultural activists exalted McGee as the "Dean of Cajun fiddlers" during the 1970s and 1980s, in part because they viewed the fiddler as a way to touch the past. Musicologists relied heavily on McGee as an informant and eventually canonized the fiddler as a Cajun musical icon through publications, documentary films, public appearances, reissues, and updated interpretations of his compositions.[20]

Yet McGee hardly represented the model Cajun musician. On the contrary, as William Spires illustrates, the fiddler's highly specialized style was unique to Cajun music in almost every way. The musician employed more than seven different tunings and a variety of remarkable fingering patterns when playing lead fiddle. His unusual hand positioning and bowing technique—McGee placed both his thumb and little finger between the bow and hair—allowed the fiddler to increase the bow's tension on the strings, while maintaining enough control for both clear articulation and his trademark glissando. McGee's unique style is fingerprinted on 53 sides waxed for the Brunswick, Bluebird, Columbia, and Vocalion labels.[21] The fiddler's most profound and enduring influence on Cajun music, however, came after his debut at the *Hommage de la Musique Acadienne* in 1974, an event organized by the same individuals who deified the fiddler.[22]

McGee's musical legacy is one of the dominant threads binding the fabric of twentieth-century Cajun music. His musical prowess granted the fiddler the flexibility of playing with a broad range of musicians in string band settings and in small accordion combos. His contemporary Blind Uncle Gaspard also maneuvered between ensembles within an Avoyelles Parish network, performing and recording in a string band led by fiddler

Delma Lachney. While both musicians left a deep impression on Cajun music during the later half of the twentieth century, Gaspard's and Mc-Gee's respective French and Irish ancestries informed their contributions to the region's musical landscape. Their cultural baggage lends insight into the role of non-Acadian ethnic groups, particularly in such ethnically diverse parishes as Avoyelles and Evangeline, in the formation of the regional musical form known as Cajun music.

On the Margins of Commercial Cajun Music

Historical provenance and ethnic diversity molded Cajun music as much as the contours of American popular culture at the dawn of the early commercial era. The idiosyncratic historical experiences and demographic profiles of specific enclaves and parishes contributed to radically different patterns of interaction, cultural sharing, and thus the range of Cajun musical expression in south Louisiana. Avoyelles and Evangeline parishes form part of the permeable cultural border on the northern outer rim of Cajun country, where cultural exchange took place between French south Louisiana and the state's northern Anglo Bible Belt. As in most south Louisiana communities, African Americans, Afro-Creoles, American Indians, Acadians, French, and Anglo-Americans had coexisted and intermarried for centuries in these ethnically diverse regions. However, unlike the southern portions of Cajun Country, a large non-Acadian Francophone faction shaped the parishes' French constituency and musical repertoire.[23]

Much of Avoyelle Parish's musical legacy is rooted in colonial French North America. The establishment of the French presence in the region began during the 1760s, as a series of European diplomatic maneuvers dramatically transformed Francophone demographics in the Louisiana territory.[24] France, through the 1763 Treaty of Paris, ceded the French-owned Louisiana territory east of the Mississippi River to the British. The provincial government encouraged colonial refugees and their Indian allies fleeing British rule to settle in present-day Avoyelles, Evangeline, Rapides, St. Landry, and St. Martin parishes. In the 1770s, the population shifted again as the overflow of French settlers from Pointe Coupee trickled into the territory originally occupied by the Avoyelles Indians. Enlisted men, retired soldiers, expatriates, and French sympathizers who participated in the exodus to *les Avoyelles* transplanted into the region a rich musical repertoire that expressed the Franco-European experience in the New World. These French songs, which were distinctive from the Acadian tradition, flourished in French colonial settlements. By the time of the first commercial Cajun recordings, musicians from those northern fringe parishes continued to sing and eventually record compositions rooted in French colonial North America. Mass media, including commercial releases and phonographs, then disseminated the vernacular material to other parts of Cajun Country, where communities with higher concentrations of Acadian descendents filtered the songs into their musical inventories.[25]

Guitarist Blind Uncle Gaspard and fiddler Delma Lachney are two relatively unknown Cajun musicians affiliated with the Avoyelles Parish tradition whose short recording careers offer a glimpse into the extremities of the Cajun repertoire. These musicians, Gaspard in particular, represent another side of Cajun music based in older European styles that differ melodically from other recordings between 1928 and 1934.[26]

The son of a Civil War veteran, Alcide "Blind Uncle" Gaspard was born into a musical family in 1880 in Dupont, Avoyelles Parish, where he learned to play a variety of instruments, including accordion, upright bass, fiddle, and guitar. In 1887, a degenerative nerve disease left Gaspard almost completely blind. Like other visually impaired musicians of the period, music became his main source of income. He traveled around Avoyelles Parish playing house dances and occasionally at a dance hall in his hometown.

A sort of Cajun troubadour, Blind Uncle Gaspard often walked alone along parish roads with his Montgomery Ward guitar, delighting neighbors with his skills as a raconteur. Music writer Ron Brown maintains that the musician had extraordinary olfactory and auditory senses that facilitated his mobility. "He invariably knew whose house he was walking past even when several miles from his own home," Brown explains, "and could also identify the type and location of various objects ahead of him on the road such as parked automobiles."[27] Years later, following a bout of blood poisoning, doctors amputated a portion of Gaspard's right index finger. The guitarist nevertheless learned to compensate for his missing appendage and played flawlessly on the recordings he made with fiddler Delma Lachney.

Born in 1896 in Egg Bend near Marksville, Lachney became an accomplished instrumentalist, perfecting a left-handed fiddling style. The fiddler learned to play from his father, Lorena, whose repertoire of quadrilles and old dance tunes spoke to the family's French Canadian heritage.[28] While coming of age, Delma performed with his brother Philogene, who often provided accompaniment with spoons or fiddlesticks. By the mid-1920s, Delma had organized a small twin-fiddle string combo featuring fiddler Clifton Mayeux and guitarist Philmore Lachney. The group performed at *bals de maison* and dance halls around Marksville, when Delma was not farming or selling freshly butchered meat from his barnyard.[29]

Gaspard and Lachney crossed paths in early January 1929, when Marksville furniture storeowner and phonograph retailer Guy Goudeau sponsored a recording session for the musicians. Goudeau agreed to pay Jules Moreau, the proud owner of a new Pontiac, $100 plus expenses to drive the musicians to the Brunswick-Collender Company's Chicago headquarters. With Goudeau's son Larry and friend Charles Bordelon in tow, Blind Uncle Gaspard entertained his fellow journeymen by strumming his guitar and singing during the long trek.[30]

Up north, the barometer dropped and the icy weather grew more severe as five men reached the Windy City, where, to earn extra money, Gaspard and Lachney decided to perform on the streets despite the freezing weather. Not only did Gaspard drop his guitar—which somehow survived undamaged as it hit the frozen pavement—but Lachney came down with a cold and punctuated the recording session with several sneezing bouts. On January 26, 1929, the musicians laid down nine tracks together for the Vocalion label, including the hillbilly influenced "Riviere Rouge" (Red River) and a few original compositions such as "Baoille."[31] A duo of solo performances by Gaspard rounded out the session.[32]

Alone with his guitar and ethereal voice, Gaspard recorded the most remarkable material during the Chicago session, including a pair of French ballads with guitar accompaniment: "Mercredi Soir Passé" (Last Wednesday Night) and "Assi dans la Fenetre da Ma Chambre."[33] The instrumentation, European-based melodies, and unusually vocal delivery of his recordings contrast starkly with the syncopated, punchy dance numbers recorded by accordion-based ensembles such as the Breaux Brothers and Joe Falcon. Gaspard's melancholy tenor flowed warmly in a gentle vibrato through the opening phrases of "Assi dans la Fenetre da Ma Chambre," as he strummed his guitar through the minor chord progression of the waltz. Unlike other songs from the period, his vocals are used as a continuous melodic expression throughout the song as the ballad describes a dejected man peering through the window of his room, watching his lover leave forever. Gaspard's solo performances are linked by a common historical thread to vernacular material collected in Evangeline Parish during the 1950s and 1960s, respectively, by folklorist-musicologists Harry Oster and Ralph Rinzler.[34] The repertoire shared by these neighboring parishes is most evident in three songs—"Aux Natchitoches" (In Natchitoches), "Mercredi Soir Passé" (Last Wednesday Night), and "Assi dans la Fenetre de Ma Chamber" (Sitting in the Window of My Room)—introduced into the commercial Cajun repertoire by Gaspard.

The guitarist's rendition of "Aux Natchitoches" referred to Natchitoches, Louisiana, the oldest permanent French settlement west of the Mississippi River and a product of the same colonial society that shaped the music in Avoyelles and Evangeline parishes. Founded in 1714, the town began its existence as an important trading post along the same Red River that Gaspard and Lachney celebrated in song. Gaspard's ballad recitation in 1929 was presumably a colonial-era composition handed down for generations in families of French extraction on the northern fringes of Cajun Country. In his characteristic eerie intonation, the guitarist bewailed: "Aux Natchitoches il y a une brune/et je la vois pas autant que je veux/Par un beau dimanche, mais j'ai mis aller la voir/je l'ai trouvé au lit malade" (In Natchitoches there is a brunette/I don't see her as much as I would want/One beautiful Sunday I went to see her/I found her confined to her sick bed).[35] While most Cajun composers wrote about their immediate environs, "Aux Natchitoches" is a conscious reference to historic Louisiana settlement. Between 1956 and 1957, ethnographer Harry Oster recorded an almost identical adaptation of this early commercial recording. In search of non-commercial folkloric material in Evangeline Parish between the farming towns of Eunice and Mamou, Oster discovered vocalist and guitarist Bee Deshotels, who sang the ballad a cappella. According to Oster, the thematic integrity of the composition places the songs squarely in the French ballad tradition. And, by virtue of his 1929 recordings, Gaspard's sides also fit squarely into the American context through their association with Cajun music's early commercial era. The guitarist also recorded such ballads as "Mercredi Soir Passé," whose melody also appears in Evangeline Parish.[36]

Between 1964 and 1967, Smithsonian Institute Fellow Ralph Rinzler made three fieldtrips to Louisiana in search of the state's underground music. Like Oster, the folklorist encountered on one of his expeditions fragments of the same colonial repertoire shared by Deshotels and Gaspard. With his tape recorder in tow, Rinzler visited septuagenarian Edius Naquin, a Cajun fiddler and balladeer, at his home in rural Evangeline Parish. The aging school bus driver entertained the folklorist's requests for old-time material by unveiling his interpretations of "Mercredi Soir Passé" and the melody to "Assi dans la Fenetre de Ma Chamber," reframed as a waltz titled "Ma Mule Dessus Mes Quatres Roues." While Naquin could very well have adapted Gaspard's arrangements, striking similarities in the ethnic composition of both Avoyelles and Evangeline parishes suggest that these melodies were fixtures in specific locations within the musical landscape, where persons of French, white Creole, and French-Canadian extraction freely interacted with one another.[37]

Other non-Acadian groups, Anglos in particular, also dramatically shaped the sounds of Cajun music. In the early part of the twentieth century, Irish cultural traits permeated Evangeline Parish. Dancers faced off, nose to nose, and step-danced to reels and jigs. Irish musical traits diffused across ethnic boundaries when Cajuns intermarried with peoples of Gaelic descent. For instance, the Courville family boasted two of the most famous fiddlers in the region, Eraste and his brother Arville, who also played hornpipes and tin whistle before Dennis McGee married into the family, further reinforcing Irish musical traits in the Cajun repertoire.[38]

Diversity in the Studio

Dennis McGee was born into a musical family on January 26, 1893, in Bayou Marron, Louisiana. Although his grandfather John McGee immigrated to the United States from Donegal County, Ireland, a district famous for mazurkas and its unique style of fiddling, Dennis's first language was French. In addition, he participated as a member of Cajun society and fully identified himself as Cajun. As a young man, the fiddler was one of the few working-class Cajuns to successfully make the transition from laborer to full-time musician. McGee performed regularly on weekends at rural house dances to earn money. During the week, he found employment in towns in Evangeline and St. Landry parishes—by day, McGee provided music for the silent film theaters in Mamou and Eunice; by night, he supplied the musical entertainment at local whorehouses.[39]

McGee was an enigmatic fiddler and one of the most prolific and influential recording artists during the early commercial era, performing as accompanist or front man with fiddlers Sady Courville and Ernest Fruge, and accordionists Angelas LeJeune and Amédé Ardoin. Compared with such contemporary fiddlers as Ophy Breaux, James Fawvor, and Lawrence Walker, McGee's unique technique dispels any notion that an archetypal Cajun fiddle style existed between 1928 and 1934. Likewise, his recording career was the embodiment of heterogeneous Cajun musical expression during the Great Depression. McGee and his brother-in-law, fiddler Sady Courville, launched the twin fiddle sound in the commercial documentary record at his first session on March 5, 1929, at the Roosevelt Hotel in New Orleans. The duo recorded eight sides for the Vocalion label, featuring McGee playing the melody as lead fiddle, with Courville accompanying in the *seconder* position.[40] McGee made his way into the studio again later that year, playing across ensembles, musical styles, and racial boundaries for steady work.

McGee freely crossed the racial divide working with Afro-Creole prodigy Amédé Ardoin as the musicians famously appeared at both white and black dances throughout Jim Crow Louisiana. McGee's musical flexibility allowed him to alternate between the Ardoin's punchy syncopation and Angelas LeJeune's languid style. "I played with Amédé and Angelas, one every other week, at Luma Artin's club" before the interracial duo recorded their influential sides for Columbia, the fiddler recalled.[41] Ardoin astonished audiences with his accordion playing and vibrant voice, as McGee nimbly followed along performing the melody in unison with Ardoin's accordion and vocals.

Although the lore enveloping Ardoin's life and career is as grandiose as legends cloaking the escapades of such seminal American musical figures as Buddy Bolden and Robert Johnson, Ardoin's influence on Cajun music cannot be overstated. His blues-driven compositions and pulsing syncopation left an incalculable impact on the sounds and form of Cajun music. In the wake of his commercial recordings, music writer Ann Savoy maintains that Ardoin formulated the equation for all of the accordion-based Cajun arrangements that would follow.[42] His virtuosity and regional popularity allowed the petit Creole accordionist to become one of the first professional musicians to perform regularly in Cajun country. He traveled frequently with his accordion in a burlap flour sack entertaining white audiences, who had the financial resources to sustain his musical career. He was in demand and commanded top dollar for his services. When working-class locals caught word that he was performing, they traveled for miles in horse and buggy to hear Ardoin play. "He was well aware of his talents," observes music writer Michael Tisserand. "He carried a lemon in his pocket for his voice, and greased his throat with a mixture of oil and honey."[43]

Ardoin and McGee brought their act to New Orleans to record for Columbia on December 9, 1929.[44] For the first time in commercial Cajun and Afro-Creole music, themes focusing on heartbreak, loss of love, place, and family met the aggressive and exaggerated syncopation that distinguished Ardoin's accordion style. The duet reunited in the studio almost a year later on November 19–20, 1930, to wax 10 sides for the Brunswick label.[45] The new sound forged by the interracial duo would live on generations later in the wake of World War II through the Cajun accordion styles of such Ardoin admirers as Iry LeJeune and Marc Savoy.

Interracial collaborations were not unusual in French Louisiana, or in other Southern musical contexts. In defiance of segregation laws during the first half of the twentieth century, Southern musicians collaborated to produce a series of cross-pollinated recordings that mixed and matched white and black personnel and such diverse styles as jazz and hillbilly. The resulting amalgam produced some of America's greatest recordings: Jimmie Rodgers with Louis and Lili Armstrong, the New Orleans Rhythm Kings and Afro-Creole pianist Jelly Roll Morton, and guitar duets by Eddie Lang and New Orleans blues artist Lonny Johnson. Likewise, Achille Baquet recorded with Jimmy Durantes' ensemble, Al Dexter performed with a black band, and even Louisiana's segregationist governor Jimmie Davis recorded with black musicians as early as the 1920s. Likewise, Cajun and Afro-Creole cultures intersected in complicated ways through a meaningful and complex interracial dialogue framed by Southern notions of white supremacy. Even at the height of Jim Crow, Ardoin openly performed with a white accompanist for both white and black audiences. McGee and his Creole friend shared music, money, and corn liquor together, a relationship that conformed to the unwritten regulations and codes of conduct in early twentieth-century Cajun society.[46] On the other hand, musicians throughout south Louisiana, who sometimes skirted the periphery of social norms, openly recognized musical interaction—whether at dances or recording sessions—as an acceptable form of discourse across the racial divide.[47]

Like many Cajun musicians, McGee freely interpreted and adapted Afro-Creole compositions from south Louisiana's musical inventory. The fiddler and his partner Sady Courville adapted the melody to the Afro-Creole arrangement "Colinda," a song and dance associated with slave culture in New Orleans' Place Congo, for their composition "Madame Young."[48] Not only did McGee embrace the Afro-Creole melody, but subsequent Cajun adaptations of the tune helped to transplant the song into the rich context of south Louisiana's musical landscape.[49] McGee continued to communicate musically cultural information about the influences and institutions that defined Cajun life before the Great Depression. The fiddlers also recorded a tune titled "Mon Chère Bébé Créole" (My Creole Sweet Mama), again reflecting the interracial dialogue between Cajuns and their Afro-Creole counterparts.

Recurring motifs in McGee's musical corpus also outline the south Louisiana's evolving social and cultural landscape, including the clash between traditional occupations and the industrialization that defined the early-twentieth-century Cajun experience. Three of his commercial sides spoke directly to Texas's role in the Americanization of Cajun culture. Cajuns interacted with residents of the Lone Star State since the colonial period, igniting a cultural and musical dialogue that grew and intensified at such a furious pace following the birth of large-scale oil production in 1901 at Spindletop, Texas, that the Louisiana–Texas border became purely symbolic. Between 1901 and 1940, south Louisianians left the Bayou State in droves to find work in east Texas oil fields, refineries, and shipyards, thereby effectively extending Cajun Country as far west as Houston. McGee's compositions "Blues de Texas" and "Valse de Puit D'Huile" (Oil Well Waltz) stem directly from the cross-cultural interaction that took place across ethnic and geographic boundaries between Cajuns and Anglo-Texans. After the Spindletop oil boom, the Lone Star State represented a land of opportunities for many Cajuns. Popular musicians such as McGee often traveled considerable distances between 1928 and 1934, performing at house dances and dance halls in both states. In "Blues de Texas," the protagonist describes himself as an orphan who wanders to greener pastures in Texas, pointedly drawing a parallel to the plight of many Cajun struggling economically during the Great Depression. Ernest Fruge provided a second fiddle accompaniment, as McGee sang the tune as a talking blues, a prevalent song style throughout the African-American South.[50] Many Cajuns found those greener pastures through opportunities provided by the petroleum industry both across the Sabine and in their own backyards as fields cropped up throughout Acadiana, inspiring "Valse de Puit D'Huile" (Oil Field Waltz) and later Amédé Ardoin's 1934 Decca recording "Valse des Chantiers Pétro-lipères" (Waltz of the Oil Field).

The petroleum industry, improved mobility provided by the automobile and new state roads, and mass media were some of the stimuli that stirred the Cajun imagination and inspired songs. These same cultural phenomena radically transformed the dynamics of south Louisiana's agrarian, working-class population by promptly introducing an industrialized perspective that diffused unevenly into the Cajun community's worldview, thereby generating tension between conservative and progressive factions. This stress translated into musical electricity as performers sonically interpreted the evolving cultural climate. Lawrence Walker's and Nathan Abshire's 1935 issues document the genre's shift toward the progressive sounds of Cajun swing and the tug-of-war between tradition and innovation at the end of the early commercial era.[51]

Swinging Out of the Early Commercial Era

The winds of change began to blow a little harder within the commercial Cajun infrastructure by 1934. The Breaux family, which had not recorded since their landmark session in 1929, preserved the largest sampling of their assorted repertoire in 1934. Amédé, Ophy, and Clifford recorded one mazurka and several old-time waltzes, blues numbers, and one-steps during their stint at Vocalion's regional recording facility in San Antonio, Texas.

The Breaux Brothers' "Mazurka de la Louisiane" and "Valse D'Auguste Breaux" represented nineteenth-century song styles popular in Cajun Country that endured in family repertoires through the middle of the twentieth century. Blues arrangements and one-steps, on the other hand, acted as a cultural weathervane indicating the direction of commercial Cajun music. African-American and Afro-Creole blues seeped into Cajun music's bloodstream through a musical dialogue based on intensive personal interaction that transpired despite overt racial tensions. For instance, Joe Falcon, Cleoma Falcon, and Ophy Breaux had several days to bond with Amédé Ardoin in the winter of 1934, when the Cajun trio escorted the Creole accordionist to New York City for a Decca recording session. The musicians made the journey by bus. Ardoin opted to record alone after his accompaniment, 17-year-old Afro-Creole fiddler Canray Fontenot, backed out of the engagement.[52] Three days before Christmas, Ardoin recorded his first solo performances, while the Falcons waxed a bona fide Louisiana French blues number ironically titled "Blues Nègre" (Nigger Blues).[53] Blues-influenced compositions became a standard fixture in south Louisiana's musical landscape as more Cajuns drew inspiration from popular American commercial music. Indeed, the enormous popularity of Jimmie Rodgers in Cajun Country reinforced the blues' presence in the Cajun repertoire. This musical fusion persisted as Cajuns created a variety of transitional musical hybrids and the pendulum swung from the early commercial era into the Cajun swing era.

By 1935, small acoustic accordion-based ensembles began to give way to more substantial string-based orchestras. Lawrence Walker and Nathan Abshire, a pair of experimental accordionists who would become two of the leading proponents of the post-World War II dance hall sound, recorded the clearest example of the shift to Cajun swing on the Bluebird record label. On January 18, 1935, Walker waxed a pair of bluesy English compositions, "What's the Matter Now?" and "Alberta"—his interpretation of the popular composition "Corinna"—at Bluebird's mobile recording facility in New Orleans.[54] "Corinna" was a "blues with a touch of jazz and a flavour of hillbilly" that by the 1930s was widely popular among blues and hillbilly artists, who also recorded the arrangement under the titles "Alberta" and "Roberta."[55] The tune later became a fixture in the Western swing repertoire largely through the popularity of Bob Wills and His Texas Playboys' adaptation. While the blues genre was well established in south Louisiana's musical landscape, Cajuns generally rendered their interpretations in French. Walker's explicit use of English lyrics is a linguistic manifestation of American popular culture's infusion into Cajun life. It also signaled the decided shift from customary stylistic protocol in the commercial setting, although the thematic orientation of "Alberta" could position the song squarely in the early commercial era inventory. In essence, "Alberta" can be equated with the Breaux family composition "Ma Blonde Est Parti," because both tunes describe an inconsolable man lamenting about the impenetrable boundaries that separate the protagonist from his belle—a coincidence that alludes to the Cajun musicians' fondness of American popular music. Nine months after Walker recorded his English blues sides, Bluebird documented the best example of south Louisiana's evolving musical scene, when Nathan Abshire's blues-drenched accordion stylings merged on record with the swinging intensity of the Rayne-Bo Ramblers, a pioneer Cajun swing ensemble. Record-buying audiences could indubitably hear the momentum shifting from accordion-based arrangements to the fiddle-driven string band combos that dominated the commercial landscape during the World War II era (figure 3.2).

During the mid-1930s, the Bluebird record label was in the vanguard of commercial Cajun music. In their search for contemporary crossover artists, Bluebird documented the transition between the early commercial era and the Cajun-inflected Western swing that would later dominate the commercial market. On August 10, 1935, veteran bandleader and accordionist Nathan Abshire traveled to New Orleans to record his first commercial sides with the Rayne Bo Ramblers, a string band trio featuring fiddler Norris Savoy and guitarists LeRoy "Happy Fats" LeBlanc and Simon Schexnyder. The group fused traditional and fashionable musical elements from the Cajun repertoire and American popular musical scene. The resulting musical expression embodied the collision of two competing cultural trends. Indeed, the tension between tradition and progress transferred onto the Abshire sides. The accordion assumed its traditional position at the forefront of the recordings, while the revamped Western swing-style rhythm section created space for an improvisational jazzlike interplay between the squeezebox and the guitar voices.

Abshire's experimental recordings were a sonic premonition of the emerging developments in the Cajun musical genre. At times, his accordion work and characteristic Cajun vocals struggled for the dominant position within the song with rhythm section guitarists LeBlanc and Schexnyder. The double-guitar arrangement freed one of the stringed voices from the shackles of its support instrument status, allowing the rhythm section to periodically poke its head into the limelight. LeBlanc's and Schexnyder's

Figure 3.2. After experimenting with accordionist Nathan Abshire in the Bluebird studios, LeRoy "Happy Fats" LeBlanc (right) and the Rayne-Bo Ramblers transformed their stringed trio into a polished seven-piece Cajun swing orchestra. Courtesy of the Center for Louisiana Studies, University of Louisiana at Lafayette.

blues slide guitar embellishments and swinging 2/4 backbeat put a revolutionary twist on the traditional accordion arrangement. Even Abshire's sustained vocal outbursts, commonly used for emotional emphasis in traditional accordion-based Cajun music, stood in sharp contrast to the Rayne-Bo Ramblers' abbreviated staccato interjections, such as "ah hah," "yee ha," and "yeah boy" that the band borrowed from the Western swing tradition. These experimental recordings may have been too far removed from convention for Cajun audiences, because Bluebird never attempted to match accordionists with Cajun swing groups following Abshire's debut session.

The ensemble recorded only six sides during the session.[56] Two of the selections presaged the bluesy melodies that would become Abshire's trademark during the post-World War II dance hall era. The "One-Step de Lacassine," for example, is a vibrant romp that flirts with the melody that would become "Pine Grove Blues," the accordionist's seminal postwar smash hit. The ensemble also waxed the "French Blues," another Abshire arrangement that would achieve classic status during the 1950s. Abshire and the Rayne-Bo Ramblers also drew inspiration from tunes from the early commercial repertoire. "La Valse de Riceville," a homage to Nathan Abshire's native hamlet, is a rough adaptation of the Breaux family's "Ma Blonde Est Parti." Abshire borrows several lines directly from Amédé Breaux's waltz, including "tu m'as quitté . . . pour t'en aller chez ta famille" (you left me to go to your parent's house). Like the Breaux family and Lawrence Walker, Nathan composed his blues numbers from the cross-cultural fodder that nourished Cajun music's evolutionary mechanisms. These imaginative composers followed their ears to the permeable boundaries of their own traditions where fresh ideas and sounds seethed in the Gulf Coast's cross-cultural marinade.

Nathan Abshire and the Rayne-Bo Ramblers' collaboration is the proverbial "missing link" in the documentary record that bridges the gap between the early commercial and Cajun swing eras. Their recordings were on the cutting edge of commercial Cajun music, boldly carving a new path for other musicians to follow. The blistering energy at the core of Abshire's and the Rayne-Bo Rambler's cross-pollinated sound stemmed from the friction between two contrary stylistic paradigms that espoused two contrasting musical philosophies—French, rural, and traditional, on one hand, and Anglo, urban, and contemporary, on the other. As the French blues collided with Western swing, the awkward marriage of the two regional forms generated the same electric atmosphere that surrounded rock 'n' roll.

The early commercial recordings waxed between 1928 and 1934 during Cajun music's early commercial era were part of the constant dialogue between tradition and popular culture. The cross-pollinated vibrations embedded in the grooves of Lawrence Walker's and Nathan Abshire's releases, and the shellac records themselves, represented tangible manifestations of Cajun music's Americanization. Musicians freely explored arrangements from their own traditions while absorbing and adapting musical elements from American popular culture. Singers and instrumentalists performing during the 1920s and 1930s did not have to look far. New mass media technology and traveling musicians enriched Bayou Country's already pregnant musical landscape while the region's traditional music teemed with such diversity, complexity, and constant cross-cultural interaction that the arbitrary lines separating musical styles frequently blurred into new sounds and subgenres falling under the Cajun musical umbrella.

Historians and social scientists have customarily exaggerated the degree of cultural and social isolation among the Cajuns. While relative isolation shaped and constrained the lives of some Louisianians, the heterogeneity expressed within the musical documentary record suggests that the ethnic group constantly exchanged ideas and information with their neighbors. Artists such as Nathan Abshire, Lawrence Walker, and Dennis McGee mixed and contrasted unlikely musical combinations that reflected the availability of traditional ethnic and popular sounds at their fingertips. The development of a nationwide communications network accelerated and ameliorated the Cajun-American discourse. In essence, Cajuns adapted their behaviors to accommodate the evolving contexts surrounding traditional south Louisiana culture and reconstructed musically their changing reality.

4

Becoming the Folk

In the depths of the Great Depression, song collectors John and Alan Lomax visited "the Evangeline country" for practically the whole month of June 1934 as part of a nationwide folksong survey to document America's musical legacy for the Library of Congress's Archive of American Folk Song (AAFS).[1] Like other federally funded Depression-era cultural programs, the AAFS worked to document vernacular American culture in the name of public interest to boost morale by validating and celebrating, in this case, the nation's indigenous music.[2] Equipped with a 300-pound "portable" electronic disk recorder in the trunk of their Model A Ford, the research team established their headquarters in New Iberia, Louisiana, and traveled around the surrounding countryside in search of informants.[3] A weighted needle etched the vibrations of music and spoken word into the face of aluminum disks, capturing a side of the Cajun repertoire neglected by the commercial documentary record. Alan took the recording reins and bore the brunt of the fieldwork load, recording sometimes into the early morning. Meanwhile, his father wrote his autobiography, attended showings of John Barrymore films, and visited avid ballad hunter E. A. McIlhenny, maker of the famous Tabasco Sauce.[4]

Advances in sound recording technology helped distinguished the Lomax excursion as part of a revolutionary trend in ethnographic and folklore research.[5] By the 1930s, a number of American social scientists had already experimented with recording Native American folksongs with a variety of devices and recording machines that obviated the need for tedious lyric transcriptions, a technique then popular among folklorists who captured only a one-dimensional skeleton of songs on paper.[6] This technology allowed ethnographers combing the Bayou Country to present a sonic snapshot of contemporary musical trends and the linguistic climate of both French and English among Cajuns within their natural social contexts—in homes, dance halls, local hangouts, beer joints, and anywhere else field-workers found willing participants. In the spirit of uplift, Alan

Lomax wired his recording equipment to a loud speaker powered by large alkaline batteries and played the newly minted disk for his informants. He remembered witnessing, with deep satisfaction, "the pride and pleasure of the folk community in hearing its own music played back for the first time and to realize that this artistry had been permanently preserved."[7]

During the mid-1930s, as folklorists and ethnographers made initial forays into French Louisiana, numerous academicians raised the national profile of working-class Cajuns by stamping these individuals with the label American "folk." By inference, this distinction portrayed Cajuns as an isolated and unchanging people whose ancestors laid a distinctive portion of the nation's cultural bedrock. In turn, the ethnic group became a hot topic of discussion in folklore circles when field-workers crossed each other's paths and networked.

This intellectual history of Cajun music's folk categorization surveys the field excursions and folk festival performances that gave rise to the genre's conflation with the "folk" label. Between 1934 and 1937, Cajun cultural production would take on a new layer of significance—one that came to define all things Cajun. John and Alan Lomax conducted the most famous of Louisiana's early ethnographic field expeditions in 1934 under the guidance of Acadia Parish native and folk song hunter Irène Thérèse Whitfield. The Lomaxes helped introduce the notion of Cajuns as folk to intellectual circles across the United States through their Library of Congress field recordings. If their work helped solidify the Cajuns' folk categorization, however, it also illuminates the incompatibility of the "folk" label's ideological constraints and the ethnic group's Depression-era reality.

The Cajun presence at the 1936 National Folk Festival in Dallas, Texas—where local musicians stood on a national stage as formal representatives of Louisiana folklife—amplified the Lomaxes' categorization beyond academic circles into the public sphere. Geographer Lauren C. Post escorted the largely Cajun "Louisiana delegation" to Dallas at festival founder Sarah Gertrude Knott's request. The Louisiana delegation represented one of the many cultural curiosities on display at Knott's spectacle.

Post and Knott's public collaboration help set the boundaries of Cajun folklore by overlooking musical styles and cultural traits deemed inauthentic. Unlike the Lomaxes, who documented various aspects of the community's heterogeneity, Post and Knott carefully moderated their Cajun performers so that only select characteristics made it on stage. Would-be folklorists in attendance, such as William Owens, watched with wide eyes. As a National Folk Festival stage manager, Owens facilitated Post's stage announcements and the performances by his Cajun musicians. He ultimately embraced festival's definition of cultural survival and set out to make his own field recordings in Cajun Country a year later.

Cultural mediation was part of the implementation process as ethnographers applied the "folk" label to Cajun culture. Folklorists in search of cultural data entered into a social contract with their Louisiana subjects, who, compelled by curiosity and local mores demanding hospitality, agreed to shake hands with field-workers across the theoretical boundaries distinguishing ethnographer from informant. The protocol of ethnographic fieldwork rubbed against local expectations about social intercourse and structured interaction through what historian Richard White identifies as the "mutual need or a desire for what the other possesses, and an inability by either side to commandeer enough force to compel the other to change."[8] Cultural negotiation inevitably ensued. Field-workers hoped to persuade musicians to demonstrate their art by offering money, liquor, or other consumable goods. Cajuns obliged with the added benefit of outside validation. These compromises and exchanges, however, transpired through a process of creative misunderstanding. The Lomaxes, Whitfield, Post, Knott, and Owens conceptualized the Cajun musician as the Jeffersonian yeoman and "noble savage," who, despite his or her socioeconomic shortcomings, represented the laboring backbone of America. In the process, field researchers spun a new stereotype by imposing onto Cajuns the quaint, genteel label "folk," which carried a connotation that translated as isolated, primitive, uneducated, homogeneous, and delightfully backward. The tension between perception and reality created a static Cajun caricature in the national imagination that distinctly characterized the ethnic group as the "Other."

"'Folk' and 'modern' are both mutually dependent concepts," contends historian Robin D. G. Kelley. The term "folk," connoting pre-mass-mediated cultural practices and preindustrial social organizations, and its antithesis, "modern," are both "socially constructed categories that have something to do with the reproduction of race, class, and gender hierarchies and the policing of the boundaries of modernism."[9] Before 1950, academics and public intellectuals whose very existence depended on modern scholarship coarsely outlined the distinction between less modern, and hence less "sophisticated," forms of cultural expression generally defined under the rubric folklore. These same individuals marshaled the boundaries of modernism by selectively ignoring cultural characteristics that did not fit their models.

Even when aligned with progressive and uplifting agendas, the theoretical assumptions embedded in the "folk" label assigned to Cajuns subtly maligned the group as unsophisticated and ultimately ignorant of modernity's complexity—a distinction that persists today. The Lomaxes set the precedent in 1934. The father and son fieldwork team emerged as the most influential architects of a Cajun folk stereotype that relied on ethnic, racial, linguistic, and socioeconomic distinctions. They reinforced the commercial industry's exploitation of vernacular music by rendering "folk" cultural production as a consumable commodity in exchange for academic credibility, university positions, and book contracts. Knott took their work a step further. Beginning in 1936, she capitalized on the perpetuation of those social hierarchies that contrasted working-class Cajuns against a modernist backdrop on the National Folk Festival stage. Exceptionalism and cultural purity rendered through isolation was a trope that sold well. American audiences paid good money to hear and read about undiluted folk music performed by authentic mountaineers, dandy Negroes, and isolated Cajuns. Owens' ethnographic excursions into Cajun Country in 1937 represent the perpetuation of selective ignorance—that arbitrator of boundary maintenance that defined Cajun music as folk music throughout the twentieth century. The disparity between this conflated, rose-colored rendering of the Cajun "folk" during the 1930s and cultural production in south Louisiana beyond the commercial marketplace cultivated by record labels forms the basis of "Becoming the Folk."

John and Alan Lomax's Louisiana Expedition, 1934

The recorded sound collections amassed by the Lomaxes in Louisiana are indeed impressive. Diverse performance and repertory styles not only suggest the breadth of Cajun music in 1934 but also illuminate the shortcomings and misleading implications of the "folk" label. The cultural complexity highlighted in this collection stand in direct opposition to Cajun folk categorization that the Lomaxes help establish among academicians and the nation's intelligentsia.

John and Alan Lomax equated their vision of the folk with authenticity—that is, working-class people who supposedly lived beyond the corrosive influence of American popular culture. John Lomax's brand of salvage ethnography tended to focus on male informants. Indeed, the workingman was the sole purveyor of "pure" folk culture, vestigial behaviors, and songs that eluded both assimilation and the temptations of popular culture. Untainted by education and high culture, his music represented what John Lomax biographer Nolan Porterfield dubs the "native mind of the frontiersman."[10]

During a period when academia dismissed provincial working-class peoples as inconsequential research material, John looked to the "isolated" and impoverished as the wellspring for vernacular music. His methodological innovation targeted "actual folk," the working-class architects who constructed folk tradition. Therefore, John and, by association, Alan became visible proponents of a new American ethnography.[11] A folksong's pedigree no longer represented the single criterion for authenticity, but rather a combination of song and singer that had to conform to the Lomaxes' standards. Their pioneering efforts stimulated what cultural historian Benjamin Filene dubbed a "'cult of authenticity,' a thicket of expectations and valuations that American roots musicians and their audiences have been negotiating ever since."[12] The elder Lomax's groundbreaking achievements were not without methodological inconsistencies. The erratic strategy that characterized his French Louisiana fieldwork was closely related to his membership in two distinctive American sociocultural spheres.

Although he was born in Mississippi and raised on a Texas ranch, John Lomax's lifestyle became a balancing act between his marginal inclusion in two juxtaposed and contradictory social spheres—the rural South and the Ivy League elite. As a student at Harvard University, Lomax cloaked himself with a romantic urban cowboy persona, portraying himself as "a hard-bitten ex-cowboy, now turned civilized and sophisticated, dressed up in coat and tie and gone East."[13] In the field, Lomax emphasized his rural roots to facilitate the collection process with working-class informants, who would not have identified with traditional academicians.

Taking a page from his own experience, marginality became John Lomax's prerequisite for uncovering examples of pure indigenous music in America. He looked to the periphery of mainstream trends, for instance, cowboys, who engaged in an insular, vagabond lifestyle, and African-American inmates, sheltered from jazz, radio, and the white world outside the prison walls. In his opinion, French ballads and Louisiana's anachronistic repertoire proved another fertile hunting ground where "pure" musical traditions flourished. Hence, by virtue of the ethnographer's assumption, working-class Cajuns conformed to the Lomaxian isolation model: they lived on the economic, linguistic, and cultural periphery of the American mainstream where they presumably maintained cultural homogeneity. In their 1941 publication *Our Singing Country*, only the second book-length study to include a scholarly examination of Cajun music, John and Alan Lomax solidified this stereotype by only including ballad material with Old World pedigrees—a portrayal perpetuated in academic circles well into the twentieth century. And yet, even as the father and son team constructed a Cajun folk identity based on cultural "isolation" in print, the body of unpublished field recordings produced during their Louisiana expedition revealed complicated sociocultural processes driving the evolution of the Cajun repertoire. The researchers stumbled across a diverse cross section of the local population, including "an accordion player who also sang; a blind Cajun minstrel; a Negro play party; a four-foot hunchback—'a merry old maid of 45 years'; and a rural quartet of accordion, guitar, violin, and 'iron,'" and a bilingual vocalist, who rendered "four English and three French songs of considerable interest."[14] Blatant contradictions between the Lomaxian folk model, the unpublished material that they collected, and the discrepancies in their analyses of local cultural production that actually made it to print expose the working mechanisms propelling the fabrication of folk stereotypes in the national imagination.

John and Alan Lomax relied heavily on neighborhood gatekeepers, guides who provided the shamelessly opportunistic researchers with access to the inner circles of rural Cajun society. Ideally, the musicologists hoped to find a respected member of the local community who could mediate for the researchers. When they could not locate a liaison or diplomacy failed, bribery usually followed. Alcohol often proved to be a seductive social lubricant, and, when used in moderation, proved to be a veritable "Open Sesame" into the vaults of the Cajun musical repertoire.[15] Gatekeeping and impromptu mediation could transpire on several levels simultaneously. The Lomaxes called on local Francophile and budding folk music scholar Irène Thérèse Whitfield, who was in the process of completing her master's thesis, "Louisiana French Folk Songs," at Louisiana State University (LSU). As an academic and native of Acadia Parish, Whitfield represented the upper tier of their gatekeeping network. She identified potential fieldwork sites and negotiated with local community representatives who could identify informants. On one of their expeditions, Whitfield procured the services of a handsome Creole from Crowley, a roughneck in the Bosco Oil Fields who allegedly knew all the musicians in the rural *Marais Bouleur* neighborhood.[16] With the aid of Whitfield and other native guides, the Lomaxes got the lay of the land, while taking a crash course on how to negotiate with locals, before embarking on their own adventures in the field.[17]

To the musicologists' great delight, home music was a viable part of social life in Depression-era Cajun society. In some cases, whole families sang traditional ballads, performing solo or singing together in unison. The Lomaxes recorded 78 unaccompanied ballads, laments, and drinking songs with French, French Canadian, and American texts by an assortment of singers, most of whom learned the songs orally from older family members.[18] Cajun Country seemingly teemed with singers like 42-year-old Luneda Comeaux, an Iberia Parish resident who contributed 12 ballads in her shrill falsetto.[19] Ballad singers, a favorite subject of inquiry among early-twentieth-century folklorists, also proved the most contradictory to the Lomaxian folk model.

Alan Lomax discovered his favorite performer at 611 Hopkins Street in the heart of New Iberia: a 15-year-old girl working in a fish-canning factory named Elita Hoffpauir.[20] Far from being isolated and untainted by capitalism, the young girl not only worked in an industrialized sector of Louisiana's economy, but she was a savvy consumer who knew how to negotiate the terms of her labor. "When I found her she was tired and not particularly crazy about singing for me," Lomax explained in 1938 to a New Iberia reporter, "but she did want a new party dress."[21] After bribing Elita Hoffpauir with a one-dollar store-bought outfit, she revealed her seemingly inexhaustible repertoire to the ballad chasers.[22]

Elita Hoffpauir contradicted the Lomaxian folk model in almost every way. Hoffpauir's gender complicated the researcher's overtly masculine prerogatives. Moreover, this young bilingual woman, who grew up in an urban district, more closely resembled the rank-and-file of America's proletariat in any canning factory or sweatshop floor in the industrialized Northeast. And yet, the Lomaxes equated her musical repertoire with a caricature of pastoral isolation. Four of her ballads appeared in *Our Singing Country*, though Elita contributed eight solo performances, and three a cappella trio arrangements with her sisters, Ella and Mary. Lomax also recorded Elita's father, Julien Hoffpauir, a renowned ballad singer who taught his daughters to perform with restraint and precise enunciation.[23] "I listened with astonishment," Alan Lomax later exclaimed, "as Hoffpauir and his daughters sang their ballads and lyrics of sea adventure, of courtly love and of ancient romance, realizing that here was a survival of Western European balladry in America quite as remarkable as that of the Scots-Irish ballads of Appalachia."[24] No doubt, part of Lomax's astonishment came from the mixed conceptions of folk and the Cajun reality as he established the boundary between modernity and the "survival of Western European balladry in America."

In 1934, Cajuns living in south Louisiana performed a wide variety of song styles, from European-based a cappella ballads and fiddle tunes to bluesy accordion one-steps, cowboys songs, and popular American compositions. The diversity of these musical styles reflects the both the ethnic composition of early twentieth-century south Louisiana and the accelerating momentum of the Americanization process spurred by mass media, increased mobility provided by trains and automobiles, and compulsory English-only education. Vernacular musical traditions stood at the center of the interactive processes driving Americanization. Musicians traversed familiar and foreign terrain, crossing boundaries while accumulating cultural baggage.

The texts of the French material collected by the Lomaxes, particularly two songs describing journeymen by the Sonnier brothers and Mr. Bornu, illuminate the mechanisms of cultural adaptation enriching cultural production in south Louisiana. They simultaneously dispel the notion of Cajun isolation imposed by folklorists during the early twentieth century.[25] Between June 19 and June 30, 1934, the Lomaxes recorded members of the Sonnier family in Erath. Three of the four Sonnier brothers—Fenelus, Cleveland, and Isaac—presented an eclectic mix of French laments, drinking songs, and ballads to the Lomaxes. Barry Ancelet maintains that Isaac and Cleveland were the most active musicians in the family, frequently performing with their hot-tempered first cousin, Fénélon Brasseaux.[26] Isaac and Fénélon experienced first-hand the America beyond south Louisiana when they served together in the U.S. military during World War I.[27] Their experiences abroad may have influenced, in part, the characters and the wandering theme that appear in the some of the compositions collected by the musicologists.

Themes and images in the Sonnier/Brasseaux arrangements ranged from gambling and wild women to drink and wanderlust. "Chanson des Savoy" describes a fugitive who travels to Louisiana's capital city, Baton Rouge, with brass knuckles and whiskey. The song's thematic material suggests the extent to which working-class Cajuns engaged the broader world in which they lived. Despite Baton Rouge's French name and small Acadian population, the state capital represented a bastion of American ideals, as Anglo political figures such as Huey Long dominated the state legislature. The Sonnier/Brasseaux arrangement is remarkably similar to Jesse Stafford's "Je M'endors," collected on June 9, 1934, when the Lomaxes visited Crowley. Stafford's song also describes outlaws with brass knuckles and jugs of whiskey "chercher à malfaire" (in search of trouble). Crowley, a town boasting a large Anglo-American population, replaces Baton Rouge in the latter composition.[28] Although all of the Sonnier/Brasseaux songs are sung in French, images and thematic structures in their compositions suggest cross-cultural interaction with Anglo-Americans. The indigenous Louisiana French ballad "Belle" further illuminates the Anglo-American cultural undercurrents prevalent among Francophones, and Cajun Country's intimate connection to east Texas.[29]

Here again, the conception of isolation and cultural purity contradicts the hybrid nature of Cajun culture. The Lomaxes recorded a singer near

Figure 4.1. The Lomaxes invariably hailed Cajun performers, such as Morse resident Mr. Bornu, as sterling examples of American "folk." Photograph by Alan Lomax. Courtesy of the Library of Congress.

Morse, Louisiana, whom they identified simply as Mr. Bornu—a thin man with olive skin, unruly hair, and a piercing gaze. Bornu's nasal tone weaves through the blues-inflected jazzy structures of "Belle," as he chronicles the plight of a man desperate to reach his dying lover in east Texas, where thousands of impoverished Cajuns had migrated to work in the booming oil industry. The protagonist hops a freight train only to find his sweetheart unconscious, a tragic event that forced him to pawn his horse, Henry, to save her life (figure 4.1).[30]

Mr. Bornu filtered his contemporary experience through a traditional medium. His French ballad "Belle" affords insight into the impact of increased mobility provided by automobiles and trains and the role of Texas in the Americanization process. Improved mobility presented the possibility of a long-distance relationship for the protagonist, who might not have otherwise found love across the Sabine River. Both his ability to travel and his interstate love affair emphasize the important role that cross-cultural borrowing, prompted by interpersonal interaction between Cajuns and their Texan neighbors, played within the Cajun community during the first half of the twentieth century. Economic opportunities lured thousands of Cajuns to the Lone Star State's oil fields and shipyards, a phenomenon that would later profoundly affect the structure and sound of commercial Cajun music. Although Texas is a major theme in "Belle," other factors in the song indicate that English-only education in Bayou Country was essential to the central character's relationship.

The song's heroine writes a letter to her lover describing the severity of her illness. His ability to read the message, which was almost certainly written in English, illuminates another underlying American cultural current in Cajun music. Although the song is composed and performed in French, the hero, and evidently Mr. Bornu, have a working knowledge of English. By the 1930s, English began to play a significant role in familiar, everyday routines. Rural working-class Cajuns adopted the practice of bestowing their draft animals with common English names. In accordance with popular trends in early-twentieth-century Bayou Country, Henry is the only character in "Belle" to receive specific appellation. Furthermore, it is the only word in the song pronounced in English, making the horse a clear linguistic manifestation of Anglo-American culture within the context of Francophone Louisiana.[31]

Although travel writers regularly encountered the English language among bilingual Cajuns during the nineteenth century, the widespread adoption of English as a second language proliferated through Progressive Era curricula that sanctioned corporal punishment as effective inducement.[32] Punishment for speaking French on the school grounds in southern Louisiana included beatings and forcing pupils to soil themselves when they did not ask permission to use the restroom in the foreign tongue. Beginning in 1921, Louisiana law required Cajun schoolteachers to implement English immersion in their classrooms in a compulsory effort to impose a local interpretation of appropriate American ethics onto a new generation.[33] Pupils improvised their way through the immersion process, in the same way that they improvised and transformed the employment of English to translate their formulating views, values, and beliefs. Although immersion was almost universally a tortuous experience for Cajun schoolchildren, students embraced, however forcibly, the foreign tongue. Singers used both French and English to express the Cajun experience, adapting English to articulate the immediate needs of the bilingual community. To be sure, the second language did not express the worldview of Anglo-America, but rather the perceptions of Cajuns as they confronted American policy and culture on their own terms. Like French, English quickly became a Cajun language in south Louisiana, an additional communicative medium that ameliorated and expanded the community's expressive capacity.[34] The song "Belle" represents only one example of the linguistic complexities that shaped the 1934 Cajun musical landscape. English material is sprinkled throughout the Lomax collection.

Traditional definitions of folk culture circumvented evidence of bilingualism or even the possibility that the English language served the Cajun community in fashion similar to French. Many of the arrangements recorded by the Lomaxes featured French lyrics, though a large number of the performers were bilingual, displaying a command of the English language both in their annotated dialogue between songs and during the performances themselves. Several French ballad singers, like Elita Hoffpauir, communicated quite easily with the Lomaxes in their second language. Other performers actually sang a variety of English-based songs.

For instance, the researchers collected a fragmented version of "The Old Chisholm Trail" performed by an unidentified singer with fiddle accompaniment. The blend of popular cultural influences from radio, record, and Western movies with the interaction between south Louisianians and the Texas cowboys resonated with the Cajuns, particularly ranchers. In south Louisiana communities with large Anglophone populations, English-language expression among Cajuns such as "The Old Chisholm Trail" increased through widespread circulation.[35] And yet outside perceptions of south Louisiana perpetuated the tensions between a homogeneous Cajun "folklore" and the Cajuns' heterogeneous reality.

In Crowley, Louisiana, the large population of Midwestern transplants dramatically enhanced the cultural complexity of Acadia Parish. The Lomaxes discovered musicians in the parish seat of justice who also displayed remarkable agility in both French and English. In June 1934, Samuel Stafford performed a variant of "The Girl I Left Behind" that he learned from his father.[36] In addition to this Cajun variation of a vernacular Anglo-American tune, the Stafford family also contributed French sides, such as "Je M'endors." The family's repertoire suggests that English arrangements played a complementary role to French compositions in south Louisiana, often existing side by side in an individual's repertoire.

Cultural hybridity infinitely complicated Cajun music by expanding the parameters of expression through bilingualism. It also illuminated the fault lines between the Cajun experience and the implications of their folk categorization. To be sure, not all of the English songs in the Lomax collection are simple regurgitations of conventional compositions. An unidentified female vocalist performed a disturbing English lullaby that recounted the story of a young girl seduced on her mother's bed by an "honest boy." Although her pronunciation is decidedly shaped by French inflection, her vocabulary is derived from the rural Anglo-Southern vernacular. Her voice wavers emotionally as the storyline progresses and actions intensify. In an unusual twist at the end of the tune, the "honest boy" uses the term "fuck" violently to reproach his victim for wearing her skirt above her knee, unacceptable behavior in polite company and particularly in the presence of distinguished strangers. The singer's poignant use of such strong language leads the listener to believe that the song may be autobiographical.

> Went downtown, like an honest girl does
> I went downtown, like an honest girl does
> Went down to the store, like an honest girl does
> Got me a pair of drawers, like an honest girl does
> Then I met a pretty boy, like an honest girl does
> And he come home with me, like an honest boy do
> He took me down in mother's room, like an honest boy do
> He laid me down on mother's bed, like an honest boy do
> Raise my dress over my head, like an honest boy do
> And then he done it to me, and he said, "To hell with you
>   little girl.

Listen to me little gal, don't ever give an inch above your
  knee.
They gone to fuck you, then give you a kick, little gal."[37]

This unusually graphic description of love gone astray is a contemporary composition illustrating the singer's ability to craft melodically her
emotional distress in a second language. The seemingly personal nature
of the ditty illustrates that English had invariably become a viable form of
communication within the Depression-era Cajun community, a new communicative medium that expanded infinitely the possibility of expression.
The bilingualism prevalent in Depression-era south Louisiana reflected
the reality of the Cajun community and the extent to which Cajuns engaged mass culture and Anglo American musical culture in the middle of
the Great Depression.

The range of instrumentation featured in the Lomax collection further
dispels the notion that isolation and cultural purity automatically relegated Cajuns as American folk. More profoundly, the stylistic diversity of
south Louisiana's musical landscape suggests the extent to which local
populations incorporated musical traits imported from beyond Cajun
Country. During a period when 78 rpm recordings only hinted at the diversity of the Cajun repertoire, the Lomaxes documented an unexplored
side of Cajun music.

Recordings of instrumentalists specializing in "colonial music," brass
band arrangements and hot jazz, and fiddle breakdowns exemplify a cross
section of the few dance bands that the Lomaxes did document.[38] Wayne
Perry, an accomplished fiddler from Indian Bayou, Louisiana, recorded
10 songs with the Lomaxes that demonstrated Anglo-American music's
profound influence on local tradition.[39] Perry's field recordings embody
the diversity of the Cajun repertoire in 1934, ranging from an "old-time
Creole Blues" to popular American compositions straddling Anglo tradition and commercial hillbilly recordings, such as "Sitting on Top of the
World," "Chickens Cackling," "Old Joe Clark," and "Kissing Catherine"
(figure 4.2).[40] Perry's rendering of Anglo-influenced tunes, particularly
"Old Joe Clark," features such Appalachian fiddle techniques as cross-
tuning and haunting drones. The musician's music, like his life, highlights
the many cultural currents shaping the sound of Cajun music and the
intimacy of Cajun culture's relationship with the rest of the United States.
In the end, that intimacy proved too much for Perry. After serving in the
military during World War II, Wayne Perry suffered a nervous breakdown
triggered by the trauma of combat. He became reclusive, isolating himself
from the music world and the community at large precisely because he
was so connected to the tense global exchanges that manifest as a World
War. Like so many returning GIs suffering from posttraumatic stress dis-
order, the weight of the world beyond Cajun Country crushed his sanity.
He died alone in his Indian Bayou home.[41] Perry's memory, preserved on
the face of an aluminum disk in the Library of Congress, points to Cajun
dance music's creative pulse in 1934.

Figure 4.2. Fiddler Wayne Perry performed instrumental renditions of American popular music and traditional Anglo American folksongs for the Lomaxes during their musical survey across Cajun Country. Photograph by Alan Lomax. Courtesy of the Library of Congress.

Columbia recording artist Eddie Segura, who played triangle with his brother Dewey in the late 1920s and early 1930s, and the Breaux Family band also appear on several of the Lomax field recordings. Their commercial and field recordings collectively bridge the arbitrary ideological distinctions between folk and commercial that folklorists often used to categorize Cajun musical expression. The fine, albeit imaginary, line separating professional entertainers from the "folk" persisted well into the later half of the twentieth century. For instance, the Segura brothers recorded several sides for the Lomaxes, including "T'en Aura Plus," a song later used by the recording artists the Balfa Brothers to close out their concerts on the national folk circuit. Although the distinctions between vernacular and popular, isolation and mass consumption blur in the Archive of American Folk Song's Cajun material, one thing remains perfectly clear: by 1934, the tentacles of American popular culture touched the lives of virtually all Cajuns.

Cultural hybridity was far less important to the Lomaxes' agenda than the cultural authority that came with being the first researchers to distinguish Cajun music as a folk expression. Alan Lomax openly acknowledged that whether singing in English or French, Cajuns adjust, decode, and manipulate outside musical influences to correspond with individual tastes and the aesthetics of the community at large. He told a newspaper reporter in 1938: "In their interpretations of all music they give it something of their own personality and characteristics that makes it unmistakably theirs."[42] The Cajun stamp could be heard on French and English arrangements through instrumentation, lyrics, phrasing, melodies, and annotations before and after performances. However, the precedent the Lomaxes established in 1934—Cajuns as American folk—continued to structure America's perception through the dawn of the twenty-first century. Cajun music's designation as folk music became the touchstone that all subsequent studies had to address. Indeed, the ink had not completely dried on Cajun music's authorization as "folk" music when the National Folk Festival reasserted the categorization in Dallas, Texas, two years later.

Lauren C. Post and the National Folk Festival, 1936

In 1936, the Texas Centennial Celebration partnered with Sarah Gertrude Knott's fledgling National Folk Festival. The event provided an opportunity for folklore to shine in the public eye as the Lone Star State consciously fashioned an unequivocally Western identity. Promoters worked desperately to move away the southern cultural legacy that linked them to the "backward slaveholding, agrarian South." Rather, by exploiting chorus girls in 10-gallon hats and chaps and Texas rangers with .45 caliber firearms, "the state's link to the Old South faded and the mythology of Texas as cowboy country, with productive oil fields as a bonus, began."[43] Identity construction and cultural mediation also extended to the Cajun performers at the festival. The event helped transform these working-class entertainers—and, by extension, the whole ethnic group—into the more attractive and consumable product: the American folk.

Festival founder Sarah Gertrude Knott traveled to the Bayou Country, "especially to Lafayette, New Orleans, and Baton Rouge for the purpose of finding out what the State has to contribute, and to get under way an organization for arranging and carrying out a program of the Festival."[44] By partnering with LSU, Knott also located a suitable candidate to coordinate and escort local performers to the festival grounds in Dallas. Major Frey C. Frey, founder of the university's Department of Sociology, nominated Lauren Chester Post as chairman of the Louisiana delegation.[45]

Compared with his contemporaries, cultural geographer Lauren Post offered a liberal definition of Cajun folk music, in part because he came of age in rural Acadia Parish. "He had noticed many of their ways of life," recalled his cousin and colleague Irène Thérèse Whitfield, "and even their little folk songs, the latter of which he considered catchy, cute, and different."[46] He considered accordion-based dance bands and commercial recording artists just as viable proponents of folk expression as ballads and home musicians. Between June 14 and 21, 1936, Post realized his interpretation in front of a national audience by including commercial recordings artists on stage at the third annual National Folk Festival.

Between March and May 1936, Post probed south Louisiana's memory banks while scouting for talent. With the help of a selection committee, he searched high and low "to determine to what extent the life of the different periods of the State's development has been reflected in the folk expressions, how well they have survived in the State, and where they are to be found." Post elaborated that the National Folk Festival wanted "to find the people who know the traditional material and can use it in presentation."[47] Negotiating between his own judgment and Knott's criteria, the chairman eventually selected performers based on their aptitude with vernacular material and amassed a talented group of 36 entertainers, textile workers, and interpreters for whom expenses were paid by LSU.[48] A multiparish "Acadian Band" composed of six working-class instrumentalists and vocalists from three different south Louisiana towns was the delegation's centerpiece. Accordionist Lawrence Walker, fiddlers Ardus Broussard and Sidney Broussard Sr., guitarist Sidney Broussard Jr., triangle player Norris Mire, and 12-year-old singer Evelyn Broussard dressed in an Evangeline costume all made the trip to Dallas.[49] Post's decision to include the "Acadian Band" in the Louisiana delegation marked a pregnant moment in Cajun music history. These performers signified the first members of the ethnic group to perform on a national stage and the nation's first glimpse of authentic "Cajun folk."

Musical programmers recognized two styles of performance at the National Folk Festival, both of which fell under the umbrella of "folk expression"—what organizers considered authentic traditional folk music (ballads, sea chanteys, cowboy songs, Native American compositions, spirituals, instrumental groups, etc.) and interpretations of folk material rendered by formally trained musicians. Post accounted for the festival programming's oblique juxtaposition of folk performance and modern interpretations of folk material by symbolically recreating the social structures that perpetuated Cajun marginalization. The National Folk Festival portrayed two versions of the Cajun folk that hinged on class divisions. Post scheduled the impoverished, and sometimes barefoot, working-class Acadian Band alongside the middle- and upper-class Evangeline troupe dressed in custom-made milkmaid costumes designed specifically for Dallas to evoke the romance of Longfellow. While class divisions within the Cajun community are conspicuously apparent in the festival's programming, neither Knott nor Post chose to address and reconcile these marked differences. Rather, they put all their effort into publically constructing the timeless folk trope. Hence, the fanciful spectacle proceeding across the festival stage reflected class divisions within delegation as much as the distinction between folk and modern musical expression.

Through Knott's management, the festival functioned like a factory mass-producing "the fine traditional customs associated with the founding of this nation."[50] With each scheduled performance coming down the production line, festival patrons inspected varying manifestations of the American experience billed as the living memory of the nation's cultural past. Knott's folklore thus represented the nationalistic threads from which the American imagination spun romantic notions about "our forefathers," whose ingenuity and resilience in the face of adversity pointed the way out of the Great Depression.

Yet, ethnic and immigrant groups featured at the festival complicated the master narrative of the United States about its white forefathers. Coming on the heals of the greatest wave of immigration the nation had ever seen and the Great Migration out of the American South, nativists projected their xenophobic anxieties onto working-class members of ethnic communities by associating them with poverty, crime, and/or subversive political circles such as radical labor or communism.[51] Knott had to devise a method of softening the public ethnic persona of her performers, a task that entailed shifting attention away from socioeconomic changes wrought by America's "nonwhite" populations. The "folk" label did the ideological work for her. The categorization selectively ignored cultural characteristics and implied changeless and uncorrupted primitivism, thus rendering groups such as Cajuns as quaintly benign. The 1936 National Folk Festival Souvenir Program clearly outlined these notions and Knott's motivations:

> The folk songs, music and dances used in this festival, came into being to meet a need for self-expression. They served our forefathers through pioneer days and during the nation's early struggles. They were used in the same way when the better days came. Now in this period of economic problems, when there is such a genuinely felt need for leisure-time activity, it is only natural that people should turn to the old ways of recreation with renewed devotion. Both Europe and America show an increasing disposition to recognize the contribution that folk expressions have made to the artistic and social life of the past, and to see the necessity for continuing folklore in its living forms for the present and for projecting it into the future. . . . It is one thing to celebrate the glorious achievement of the past and another to lay the foundation for future achievement and development. We hope that the National Folk Festival has done both.[52]

Working-class Cajun musical traditions fit Knott's narrow definition of authenticity beautifully.[53] She imagined the ethnic group as existing on the margins of mainstream society, which, by definition, made Cajun music an authentic "folk" product. Isolation allowed folklore to exist in timeless stasis, at least theoretically, a space where the American folk's preserved precapitalistic cultural survivals. In Knott's view, folklore was the clandestine solution for stability in a rapidly changing world. Creating a national consciousness about folk expressions underneath the facade of modernism could be the fulcrum on which the United States could lift itself out of depression.[54]

The festival stage brought Knott's vision for America to a national audience. The National Folk Festival placed ethnics into a national origin narrative alongside white Pilgrims "during the nation's early struggles." While this new interpretation of America celebrated the underclass in the tradition of the Popular Front, it was, in a sense, a patronizing gesture. On June 17 and 18, 1936, the Louisianians performed abbreviated programs each afternoon at 4:00 P.M., a pair of evening concerts at 8:15, and a thirty-minute radio broadcast on Dallas station KRLD that highlighted the Cajun performers' eccentricity. Cajuns made their way onto Knott's stage and across the radio airwaves, but in a diminished capacity as a cultural oddity.

"Louisiana on the air!" declared a radio announcer on KRLD Dallas Columbia Broadcasting Station at 3:15 in the afternoon on June 17, 1936. "Never before has it been played in any such authentic way outside of their own bayou country," the broadcaster continued, "as it will be played and sung this afternoon by a group of real Acadians under the sponsorship of Louisiana State University."[55] The chairman selected these musicians "as representative of a type of folk music which has remained practically unchanged for many years."[56] Staying true to his particular definition of folk music, Post directed the band to perform three selections previously recorded by Joe Falcon during their radio debut. The commercial pedigree of "J'ai Passé Devant ta Porte," "Hip et Tyho," and "Lafayette" did not deter the cultural geographer from inferring the folk qualities of the selections. Nor did the academician view the Acadian Band's appearance on radio as interfering with the parameters of folklore, perhaps because all of the musicians, with the exception of Lawrence Walker, had never set foot into a recording studio.[57] Despite Post's inclusive representation of Cajun music on the radio, it was the perspective articulated by KRLD's broadcaster that came to define the public perception of Cajun music during the twentieth century. Knott's festival provided a theatrical venue to act out fantasies about the nation's cultural heritage. The Lomaxes, Post, and America's leading folklorists acting as Knott's consultants furnished the script that painted Cajuns as a cultural enigma who "remained practically unchanged for many years."

Immediately following the radio spot, Post moderated an abbreviated performance on the fairgrounds highlighting the Evangeline troupe—who danced to classical compositions such as Clement's "Polka Militaire," Santaque's "Valse a Deux Temps," and Neuville's "Jilliling" and "Mazurka"—followed by the Acadian Band. Later that evening the working-class band took center stage and belted out six dance numbers: "Hip et Tyho," "J'ai Passé Devant ta Porte," "Lafayette," "Cajun Rag," "Valse a Deux Temps," and "Azema à la Megrin." Fiddler Ardus Broussard appeared wearing wooden sandals "which the audience though most excellent for keeping time. Ardus' friends, however, knew that his only motive in wearing the sandals was to soothe a howling 'puppy' blistered by the hot pavement of the Exposition grounds and a scorching Dallas sun. The sandals were very definitely serving two purposes."[58] Broussard's blistered bare feet simultaneously symbolized the measure of the performer's authenticity (read "detached from civilization") and his socioeconomic situation—both of which organizers emphasized on the festival stage.

Working-class members of the Acadian Band found themselves both validated alongside, and measured against, artists from 22 states. "Spontaneous applause broke out even before the orchestra had finished playing the music," Post remembered.[59] Bandleader and accordionist Lawrence Walker "drew most favorable comment for his work. Ardus Broussard from Rayne played the fiddle and sang and held his own with the old-time fiddlers from other states."[60] None other than Alan Lomax even commented that "Aldus was the best example of folk talent in the whole festival."[61] The legitimizing experience left a profound impression on Lake Arthur native Sidney Broussard, Jr., who wrote to Post after the trip on June 26, 1936, to express his gratitude:

And we are very glad to know you ~~are~~ was satisfied with our performances over in Dallas. We also wish to thinks [sic] you very much for the chance you give us in going to Dallas. And if anything comes up again in the line of music. We will be only to [sic] glad to be with you again. With my thinks [sic] to you and Mr. [Elemore] Sonnier and with kindest appreciation.[62]

Although barely literate, the bilingual Francophone felt compelled to express his thanks in writing.

For the spectators, the experience was equally as pleasing. Sarah Gertrude Knott delighted in the cross-cultural exchange among performers and the festival audience's warm reception to the Cajun programming. Knott's Cajun encounter also expanded her own horizons. "I think it has been worth our while to have our Festival this year in the Southwest," she wrote to Post, "because we have brought so many people to a consciousness of their folk expressions. I am sure that I have much more of a national viewpoint than I have had before, and it has been a very great thing for me to learn these things in order that I may lead out with better national vision."[63] Knott was so taken with the flavor and authenticity of the performances that she invited members of the Cajun dance band and the Evangeline troupe to the fourth annual National Folk Festival in Chicago, thereby further substantiating the folk categorization imposed on vernacular Cajun music.[64] Meanwhile, Crowley, Louisiana, established the National Rice Festival in 1937. Much of the festival, including the musical programming, reflected the modern attitudes of the large and diverse audiences in attendance. Jazz, hillbilly, and Cajun music filled Crowley's streets. Musical programming at the National Rice Festival's debut stood in stark contrast the fieldwork William Owens conducted in Cajun Country that same year. Owens, and later Louise Olivier, who introduced "folk" programming to the Crowley festival, followed Knott's model and perpetuated Cajun cultural production's folk categorization.

Professional Folkloring with William Owens, 1937

National Folk Festival stage manager William Owens wrote in his memoirs that the spontaneous sound of Cajun dance music stopped him in his tracks in 1936 on the festival grounds, where he encountered Irène Whitfield and an Acadian Band rehearsal. The Southern Methodist University graduate student sat enchanted by Whitfield's extensive knowledge about Louisiana's musical traditions and the melodic strains emanating from the ensemble she escorted. He expounded,

> I often sat with them listening to a kind of singing and playing that never got on the stage—too spontaneous, not professional enough. In them was the beat of the bayou I had heard in Port Arthur [Texas], in them meanings that came to me not through language but through the emotions of love and laughter, in them the story of a people full of the overtones that had been edited out of the canned version they presented on stage.[65]

Owens felt sorry for the folk performers at the Texas fairgrounds. Backstage organizing members of the Texas Centennial celebration, which hosted the Knott's festival, did not share the National Folk Festival's celebratory attitudes toward the folk. "It was difficult for Centennial officials at all levels not to be condescending or patronizing to the folk performers," he elaborated.[66] After witnessing the level of cultural manipulation that defined the stage persona of the Acadian Band, the inspired and ambitious Owens decided to venture east to Louisiana one year later to uncover what he considered authentic Cajun folk music, not "the canned version they presented on stage." William Owens may now be a forgotten proponent of early Cajun folk music studies, but the traditional folklore models he espoused and helped perpetuate became part of the genre's intellectual history during the twentieth century. To be sure, his methodology—carefully culling only information that adheres to his definition of folk music—represents the continuation of the selective ignorance embraced by the Lomaxes and Knott.

As a recently enrolled graduate student at the University of Iowa, Owens and his professor Edwin Ford Piper purchased a Vibromaster recording machine and 100 aluminum disks. "Professor Piper had never been in the Cajun section of Louisiana," Owens remembered, "but he had heard enough Cajun tunes to make him eager to add a group to the University of Iowa collection."[67] Between Christmas and New Years 1937, Owens and friend Calvin Baughn embarked on an ethnographic expedition that crossed much of Cajun Country's southern hemisphere, including stops in Lafayette, St. Martinville, and New Iberia. "In ten days we recorded over a hundred songs, setting up our machine in homes, potato kilns, saloons, or any other place where we could get electricity."[68]

Although new to "professional folkloring," Owens' inchoate definition of Cajun folk music synthesized the Lomax and Post ideals.[69] Dance music, selections drawn from the commercial Cajun and popular repertoires, and the vestiges of European traditional such as a cappella French ballads were all fair game and, indeed, composed the bulk of the budding folklorist's collection. He did make one demarcation perfectly clear—professional entertainers would not do. Owens uncovered Joe and Cleoma Falcon's Columbia release "Lafayette" in a dime store located in Lafayette, Louisiana. "[Joe Falcon] was a good singer and also a professional performer. I could enjoy his records but not use them."[70]

Owens filtered his folklore through the selective ignorance process that came to define Cajun music studies throughout the twentieth century. The research team's initial recordings served preconceived assumptions about the vernacular European roots of Cajun music. Owens' inductive methodology quickly backfired when he realized that his academic concerns regarding folklore were his alone. During his very first recording session, he asked a Cajun singer near Scott, Louisiana, to demonstrate her repertoire of "old songs." "I felt the excitement of discovery. My first recording would have the real bayou sound. The woman took off her apron and stood before the microphone . . . I turned the machine on and dropped my hand as a signal to for her to start. She began and with the first words I recognized 'La Marseillaise.'"[71] Old French songs were exactly what Owens found. Much to his chagrin, the ethnographer's preconceived notion of Cajun folk music accounted for neither the repertory breadth in the Bayou Country nor his Cajun informants' purview. The researcher refocused his questions, broadened his scope of inquiry, and eventually found near Duson, along the Bayou Têche, and near Bayou Blue, Louisiana, the styles and repertoire that better satisfied what Owens considered authentically Cajun. Like the Lomax collection, these recordings resulted from the negotiation between the researcher's aspirations and the performer's inclinations.

After his disappointing first field session, Owens solicited the aid of Cajun music's academic gatekeeper, Irène Whitfield, whom he had met in Dallas the previous year. Whitfield introduced him to local part-time musicians who labored as sugar cane cutters and sweet potato diggers. The young researcher seized the opportunity to transform a potato kiln into a makeshift recording studio. The Vibromaster captured performances by fiddler and one-time recording artist Tony Allemand, guitarist Eric Domingue, and accordionist and harmonica player Marcelle Comeaux. The ensemble displayed a tremendous knowledge of local and popular songs, including commercial Cajuns sides "Hip et Taiaut" and "Jolie Blonde"; Bob Wills' Western swing compositions "San Antonio Rose" and "Corinne, Corinna" rendered in English; a translated version of "Billy Boy" set to the Anglo tune "Cowboy Jack"; the vernacular French tune "Saute Crapaud"; and an original French composition about leaving Louisiana for east Texas. Owens also located and recorded New York–trained vocalist and former member of LSU's music department Elemore Sonnier, who rendered Cleoma Falcon's recordings "Mon Coeur T'appelle."[72] In Breaux Bridge, Owens and Baughn encountered Vavaseur Mouton, who offered such selections as "Madelon," a song that he learned in France during World War I, and "Calinda." Marie Mouton sang a cappella ballads such as "Le Marin Breton" and "Cinq Sous." In Houma, Owens collected a version of the traditional French ballad "Au Pont de Nante" and the *cantique* "Marie Magdelène"—which Irène Whitfield insisted Owens "must destroy at once . . . It is sacrilegious," because of the anticlerical context and secular manner in which Cajuns deployed *cantiques*.[73] As these field recordings suggest, Cajun culture's musical custodians managed the incredible range of song styles existing simultaneously in the Bayou Country. Artists were surrounded by variety, which they selectively embraced according to their personal tastes. Cultural mediation intervened when researchers like Owens uncovered songs such as "La Marseillaise" when asking his informants for old French tunes. The Cajun reality and theoretical assumptions of field-workers during the Great Depression never matched up. Echoing Alan Lomax's observation that Cajuns adapt musical elements from mass culture, William Owens observed during his field excursion that "Cajun French singers have borrowed 'Corine, Corina,' a white blues song, from the jukebox and made it their own, adding a 'gumbo beat' and a definite French accent. One of Irène Whitfield's prized Cajun songs turned out to be 'Cowboy Jack' translated and slightly changed."[74] And yet, selective ignorance ensued. In print, the parameters of the Cajun world shrank to conveniently fit into the folklore studies that made it into print.

Folklore studies have dominated the intellectual history of Cajun music. Folk music was the subject of the first book-length study of Cajun music—Irène Whitfield's *Louisiana French Folk Songs* published by Louisiana State University Press in 1939. Whitfield's intimate knowledge of south Louisiana's roadways and byways served members of America's folklore circles as field-workers combed the countryside in search of authentic music from the nation's forgotten past. A product of the times, she interacted with all of the architects of the Cajuns' folk categorization and embraced folklore ideology as evidenced in *Louisiana French Folk Songs*.[75]

Cajuns first became the "folk" during the Great Depression. Over time, a long list of folklorists perpetuated that sometimes dubious distinction: the Lomaxes, Sarah Gertrude Knott, Lauren Post, William Owens, Harry Oster, Ralph Rinzler, and Barry Jean Ancelet. The celebratory and inquisitive motivations spurring these researchers clearly helped raise the Cajun community's national profile. But scholars have not addressed the underlying presumptions and theoretical implications attached to the notion of "folk" that has so dramatically shaped the way Americans perceive and portray the Cajun community.

Assumptions and inferences embedded in the analytical lenses used by the first field-workers to survey south Louisiana's musical landscape, however benign their intent, positioned Cajuns in opposition to modernity. Folklore studies inherently cast the community as less sophisticated than the researchers there to study them. The Lomaxes helped introduce the notion that ballad singers and musicians, not just their repertoires, represented the living embodiment of an idealized and exoticized past.

These notions have a longer historical trajectory that grew from white supremacy and American popular amusements' deep-seated influence on the academy.

Subjects of social science inquiry have historically been "primitive" and "colored" populations encountered during imperial projects, the same cast of characters P. T. Barnum displayed as sideshow curiosities in his American Museum. Barnum's nineteenth-century marketing techniques also served scholarly circles. In 1906, the Bronx Zoological Park purchased Ota Benge, an aboriginal pigmy from the Belgian Congo, and placed him in a "scientific" display in a cage next to a trained and, by inference, more civilized orangutan. Cultural oddities also became a fixture in the realm of anthropology and folklore. Beginning in 1911, one year after John Lomax published his landmark *Cowboy Songs*, famed social scientist Alfred Kroeber curated the notorious Yahi Indian exhibit at the University of California's Museum of Anthropology. Part sideshow, part cultural laboratory, the living diorama featured "the last Stone Age man" from Northern California, "Ishi," who lived in the museum exhibit by day and cleaned the facility as janitor by night.[76] In certain respects, Knott's National Folk Festival belonged to the same tradition perpetuating cultural "sideshows" cloaked in the mantle of academic inquiry. Festival programmers paraded folk musicians across the stage as celebrated exemplars of a romanticized past—cultural curiosities that represented the multicultural bedrock of America. Like Ishi and Benge, the exotic "Other" represented by Native Americans, African Americans, and less-than-white working-class Southerners—denigrated in their home communities as "rednecks," "crackers," "hillbillies," and, in south Louisiana, "coonasses"—formed the festival's main attraction. Knott and her contemporaries selectively emphasized only those cultural traits and musical selections that distinguished Cajuns from the rest of "white" America. Indeed, the public representation of Cajuns as "folk" crystallized a stereotype that froze the community in time and space.

Filmmaker Robert Flaherty's final documentary drama, *Louisiana Story* (1948), is perhaps of the most salient example of folklore's influence on the popular perception of Cajuns as an isolated folk group detached from modernity. While the "documentary" emphasized this stereotype through moving pictures, the film's soundtrack incorporated folk melodies taken from the Cajun material deposited by the Lomaxes in the Archive of American Folk Song. *Louisiana Story* recounts the story of an insulated Cajun family in a bayou backwater that, through the introduction of the petroleum industry in their backyard, learn about the benefits of modernity. Flaherty hired composer Virgil Thomson to orchestrate the soundtrack. With Irène Whitfield's *Louisiana French Folk Songs* in hand, and copies of the Lomax recordings, Thomson melodically inferred the Cajun's folk label by folding in "tunes belonging to the people of the land" every time scenes focused on the film's Cajun protagonists.[77] The composer propelled his orchestrated interpretation of Cajun music to the forefront of the nation's arts scene. Reviewers raved. The *Philadelphia Enquirer* applauded that the film and its score so skillfully portrayed the essence of the Cajun community, "its customs and characters, involving its simple-minded natives, especially a superstitious and mystic-minded boy, and the invasion of the outside world in its mechanized march."[78] In 1949, Virgil Thomson's score to *Louisiana Story* received the Pulitzer Prize for Music, which thus validated the composer's investment in maintaining Cajun music's folk categorization.[79]

The stakes of perpetuating the genre's folk categorization are high. The ideological constructs embedded in the idea "folk," even when used without malice, perpetuate the marginalization of Cajuns and their music. Folk ignores the cultural complexities and nuances of the community's experience. It minimizes the contributions of innovative and progressive artists such as Cleoma Falcon and Cajun swing architects such as Leo Soileau. And, unfortunately, when Cajuns become the folk, popular caricatures of their stereotypical backwardness only grow stronger in the American imagination.

5

Cajun Swing Era

The latest Sears & Roebuck catalogue arrived as usual on the door-steps of the Hackberry Rambler Service Station, a small enterprise owned and operated by fiddler and bandleader Luderin Darbone during the mid-1930s. While perusing the catalogue for business supplies, the proprietor spotted a public address system and imagined amplifying his band's sound by means of the new technology. "I got to thinking," the entrepreneur and musician explained. "I had one of my musicians, his voice didn't carry too well. He was a good singer, but he didn't have a loud voice. So in my mind, I said, 'This would be just the thing.' Public address system—he could sing and his voice would carry. So I ordered it. I think it was priced about $50."[1] No Cajun band had ever attempted to enhance its performances with electric amplification. The stresses of the Great Depression left most working-class musicians scrounging for change at local dances just to scrape by, a reality that reduced any desire for such luxury items as a $50 public address system to a fleeting aspiration. Darbone, on the other hand, had the means to realize his vision, and this fortuitous purchase forever changed Cajun dances.

In 1934, south Louisiana dance halls typically reached capacity some-where between 200 and 300 dancers. The noise of shuffling feet and con-versation drowned out instrumentalists and singers who tried desperately to project through the raucous throng. While the high-pitched reeds of an accordion had an easier time cutting through the clamor, the ambient racket reduced acoustic string bands to a relative whisper. Musicians tried heavy thread on their fiddle bows, wrenching their voices, stomping their feet, and forceful guitar strumming to no avail. Hackberry Rambler vocal-ist Lennis Sonnier simply could not penetrate the wall of noise until the ensemble plugged in their new public address system. "The first dance we played with it was in Evangeline," the fiddler recalled. "We had a Saturday night there that we played. So we set that thing up, started playing and we find out that the music could go through it and also the singing. And boy it

Figure 5.1. The first group photo of the original Hackberry Ramblers: guitarist-vocalist Lennis Sonnier, guitarist Edwin Duhon, and fiddler-vocalist Luderin Darbone—in 1933, shortly before Duhon left the band to work in the South American oil patch. Copyright Luderin Darbone, used by permission.

made our day, I guarantee it!"[2] The novelty inspired curiosity. "The people couldn't understand how we played at one end of the room and the music came out at the other end. They'd talk about it during the week, and bigger crowds would show up each Saturday" (figure 5.1).[3]

As the Hackberry Ramblers' popularity increased, so did the geographic scope of their performances. Their amplification system worked well in urban dance halls that had access to municipal electrical systems, but unelectrified rural honky-tonks posed another problem. Darbone approached an electrician in Rayne, Louisiana, and commissioned a $20 custom-made 110-watt converter that translated direct current to alternating current. The contraption tapped into an existing generator on the bandleader's automobile and powered the band's amplification system when the Ford was idling.

Their modern equipment stood in stark contrast to the kerosene lamps illuminating the rustic dance hall where the Ramblers first employed their electronic public address system. Unfortunately, the converter attached to the idling car behind the hall generated too much power, burnt out tubes in the sound system's amplifiers, and forced the group to perform acoustically. Their technician subsequently modified his design by inserting a lightbulb beneath the car to divert any excess wattage to prevent another burnout. As long as Darbone and his ensemble kept the light illuminated, the Ramblers enjoyed the flexibility of performing both in town and in the country. "It was a big thing, I tell you. Because, then we could play any country dancehall. If they had electricity, fine. If not . . . well I'd have to run the car."[4]

According to music writer Ben Sandmel, the benefits of amplification in Cajun music were twofold. Aside from wowing audiences, amplification relieved the strain and stress experienced by musicians who sawed on their fiddles or screamed their vocals simply to be heard. Instrumentalists enjoyed the freedom to develop lighter techniques while exploring more sophisticated material. This new technology, in combination with an expanded rhythm section, inspired a new generation of stringed soloists, who could now soar above the other voices in the ensemble. Amplification also allowed nuanced vocalists such as Lennis Sonnier and Luderin Darbone to accentuate a broad spectrum of subtleties that were impossible to project before the advent of the group's public address system.[5]

Amplification is only one of the modern developments of the string band era. The Cajun swing era (1935–1947) was the most innovative commercial period in the history of Cajun music. By 1933, upwardly mobile Cajun musicians formed string bands sans accordion and began to interpret an amalgam of Cajun tunes, Western swing, New Orleans jazz, and popular American compositions. This new synthetic style—labeled here as Cajun swing—was a bilingual Depression-era musical form indigenous to southwest Louisiana and east Texas, that cultural Lapland where Cajun music flourished during the first half of the twentieth century. These fiddle-based ensembles completely overhauled their rhythm sections and instrumental approaches by incorporating for the first time in Cajun music drums, bass fiddle, lead and steel guitars, mandolins, and banjos. Multiple supporting voices granted fiddlers, guitarists, and steel guitarists the freedom to "take off" on improvisational rides, thereby increasing the dynamic interplay among musicians, instrumentation, and melody. Bands began to cater to both working-class and middle-class tastes, all the while separating themselves from the rural working-class aesthetic by wearing uniform outfits, developing band identities, and playing urbanized music. For the first time, Cajun musicians stood as they performed. And, perhaps most profound, south Louisiana's Francophone swingers significantly expanded the Cajun repertory, which by 1940 included French renditions of Broadway numbers, jazz arrangements such as "Tiger Rag," "Eh La-bas," and "High Society," such hillbilly tunes as "Red River Valley" and "Dear Old Sunny South By the Sea"—complete with yodeling à la Jimmie Rodgers—and new interpretations of traditional material.

The growing popularity and availability of mass media fueled the style by initiating change in the local musical aesthetic. Cajun swing also signified larger shifts in south Louisiana's contemporary cultural life. The petroleum industry, compulsory English-only education, the disruptive effects of the 1927 flood, new roads, automobiles, and two world wars exposed rural Cajuns to a larger reality, while plugging the ethnic group into the pulse of American popular culture at an unprecedented pace. Disposable incomes generated by opportunities in the oil patch augmented the stratification of Cajun society and facilitated the acquisition of technological amenities—particularly phonographs, records, and radios. America was open to the Cajun community for those who opted to avail themselves of the opportunities this access afforded.

Americanizing Currents, Local Adaptations

Cajun musicians became particularly attuned to urbanized musical genres—especially Western swing, jazz, and swing—with the increased availability and reach of records and radio through the late 1920s into the Great Depression. These styles, like Cajun swing, germinated when musicians synthesized aspects of rural and urban musical expression through a lens colored by industrialization and migration. Bob Wills, for instance, relocated from the farm to Fort Worth, where he cultivated the sounds of Western swing on the radio while employed at the Burrus Flour Mill. Likewise, African Americans made jazz the soundtrack of the Midwest by forming house bands on excursion river boats and in Chicago clubs, and later as professional entertainers in New York City, after leaving the American South en masse during the so-called Great Migration. Mass media broadly circulated the work of these migrants, thus increasing the reach and appeal of Western swing and jazz, a phenomenon that facilitated local interpretation and adaptation. Although these Americanizing currents adjusted the character of Cajun musical expression, they did not erase the Cajun from Cajun swing. Rather, Louisiana's Francophone population engaged mass culture in the industrializing South in ways that paralleled the working-class ethnic experience in industrial hubs like Chicago, where, as historian Lizabeth Cohen asserts, "mass culture did not so much tear ethnic youth from their roots as help them reconcile foreign pasts with contemporary American culture."[6] The reconciliation process entailed rearticulating string band traditions through a new cultural lexicon that included the language of jazz that diffused westward into Cajun Country and Texas.

Both Texas and Cajun swing instrumentation are rooted in small string band combos that performed at rural house parties and barn dances across the American South. String bands were a widespread phenomenon with roots in minstrelsy and vernacular instrumentation. Regional variations, however, generated a difference in repertoire and technique, thus allowing the spectrum of expression to vary greatly from Texas to the East Coast. Texans, such as fiddle champion Eck Robertson, utilized the full length of their bow hairs to sustain notes while phrasing. In contrast, Posey Rorer's shuffling fiddle work with Charlie Poole's North Carolina Ramblers represented Southeast fiddling, where musicians preferred melodic syncopation generated by continually pressing only a small portion of the bow in a repetitive up-and-down motion across the strings while phrasing. By the late 1920s, black and white "hot" country bands—including the Mississippi Sheiks, Gid Tanner and the Skillet Lickers, the Leake Country Revelers, the

Dallas String Band, and the East Texas Serenaders—incorporated elements of ragtime and hot jazz into their sound and thereby initiated the transformation of the traditional Southern string band toward the Western swing orchestra of the 1930s. Western swing surfaced in the Fort Worth area as Texans forged a new musical discourse based on an amalgam of mariachi, blues, New Orleans hot jazz, and hillbilly while building on the foundation established by these jazz-inflected string bands.[7] In Cajun Country, string musicians filtered this complex musical blend through a Cajun perspective by translating tunes into French, modifying melodies, riffs, and chord arrangements to suit local aesthetics, and by applying to Texas fiddle tunes the Southeastern short-bow fiddling techniques popular in Louisiana.

This interpretive and transformative process hinged on the reconciliation of Cajun music's agrarian past and the community's contemporary engagement with mass and regional cultures. Cajun string bands factored into the larger Southern string band phenomenon as they evolved from small rustic combos into slick swing orchestras. "There were many small string bands everywhere," remembered fiddler Varise Connor, who fronted such an ensemble along with his two brothers and a first cousin. "In Gueydan, there were the Clarks; in Lacassine, the DeRouens; in Elton, Leo Soileau, but it's as I say, when the accordions took over, the string bands faded out."[8] Fiddles acted as the main melodic voice before the emergence of the accordion, according Cajun musicians the flexibility to explore an extensive repertoire that included European song structures such as reels, jigs, and contredanses.[9] The string band era reinforced and reinvigorated this tradition while affording musicians the latitude to indulge in popular compositions, jazz, Western swing, or any other genre they fancied. String bands may have "faded out," relegated to the back porch, but commercial Cajun music documented signs of life even as the accordion reigned in studios and dance halls.

On December 17, 1928, in the inaugural year of the commercial Cajun market, guitarist Dudley and fiddler James Fawvor recorded two French sides that epitomize the impact of hillbilly and jazz on Cajun music, a sound absent in contemporary string combo sides by artists such as Dennis McGee and Sady Courville (figure 5.2). During the brothers' recordings of "T'es Petite et T'es Mignonne" (You're Petite and You're Sweet) and "Creole Waltz," James Fawvor plays *legato* Texas-style long bow while the two musicians sing in unison above Dudley's swinging guitar strumming. Particularly as he performed "T'es Petite et T'es Mignonne," James used the full length of his bow to sustain his melodic phrasing, thereby creating a smooth and languorous atmosphere uncharacteristic of other Cajun recordings hailing from the early commercial era. Although their French was admittedly limited, the Anglophone duo negotiated a record deal with a Columbia executive while acting as guides during a duck hunting expedition near their home in Grand Chenier, a coastal hamlet just across the Texas line in Cameron Parish. After an audition that included several compositions rendered in French—which the brothers

Figure 5.2. In 1929, Dudley and James Fawvor (back row) created a proto-swing sound in Cameron Parish by combining Texas-style long-bow fiddle techniques with swinging guitar. Ron Yule Collection.

learned to accommodate the predominately Francophone audiences in their neighborhood—the record company representative offered the duet a recording deal.[10] The pervasive Anglo-Texan musical influence extended well beyond Cameron Parish and the immediate environs along the eastern portion of the Texas–Louisiana state line. Lawrence Walker's recordings with Tony Alleman for the Bluebird label provide further evidence of Cajun musicians organizing Texas-tinged proto-Cajun swing string bands in south central Louisiana.

As a youngster, Walker's family migrated to Orange, Texas, where the budding musician absorbed the Anglo-Texan musical landscape around him before relocating to his native Louisiana. His affinity for Southern popular music, particularly the blues, hillbilly, and Anglo string band compositions, are evident in the two swinging hillbilly-inflected numbers he recorded with Tony Alleman. "La Femme Qui Jouvait les Cartes" and "Mon Dernier Bonsoir" bristle with energy from the interplay between the songs' Franco and Anglo components. Alleman's French vocals quiver with a slight vibrato, which adds an element of syncopation and tension that juxtaposes Walker's fluid Texas long-bow fiddle strokes. The arrangements are bound together by Alleman's relaxed swinging guitar. Walker's fiddle work on Alleman's sides preempted the first Cajun swing records released by string band ensembles like the Hackberry Ramblers and the Rayne-Bo Ramblers.[11] The Fawvor, Soileau, and Alleman proto-swing recordings presage Cajun dance music's widespread recalibration. These Cajun musicians' exploration of possible musical amalgams aligns with the novel work of the East Texas Serenaders, who, like the Fawvors, foreshadowed the Western swing movement in the late 1920s by fusing a jazz sensibility with string arrangements.

Jazz seemingly oozed from every crack and crevasse along south Louisiana's sidewalks, as orchestras found homes in commercial centers across southwestern Louisiana (figure 5.3). Jazz was largely an urban phenomenon in the Bayou Country. "Dance hall owners in most towns used [jazz] orchestras on Saturday nights while the country dance hall owners used the traditional Cajun band, which consisted of an accordion player, fiddle player, and a triangle player," maintained Darbone.[12] Excursion trains from the Crescent City transported, and sometimes transplanted, jazz musicians in such towns as New Iberia, Opelousas, Crowley, Lake Charles, Lafayette, and St. Martinville, all of whom boasted local ensembles and prostitution rings that helped firmly entrench the improvisational art form in the south Louisiana vocabulary.[13] Indeed, Cajuns were just as connected to the national jazz craze of the 1920s as were urbanites enjoying the music in New Orleans or New York City, albeit in more modest proportions. For instance, civic centers in Rayne, Opelousas, Eunice, and Oakdale cosponsored a "Charleston" dance contest in 1926 to accommodate local interest in the national dance craze.[14] Jazz was so widespread in Cajun Country by October 1929 that the author of a Lafayette newspaper editorial found solace in the comforting sounds of the accordion, fiddle, and guitar at the Opelousas "'Roi De Cajin' (King of the Cajuns) accordion contest, which "proved a delightful contrast to the jazz tunes of the modern day."[15]

By the early 1930s, the first Cajun swing musicians had embraced the genre's rhythmic approaches, instrumentation, improvisational energy, and core repertoire. Yet, they rearticulated these elementary components of jazz through the vocabulary Cajun swing. Hackberry Rambler Luderin Darbone

Figure 5.3. African-American and Afro-Creole jazz bands—like this one performing in Crowley—often performed for exclusively white audiences in Jim Crow Louisiana. Photograph by Russell Lee, October 1938. Courtesy of Farm Security Administration, Library of Congress.

Figure 5.4. Trumpeter Ike Jenkins, leader of the Crowley-based Jenkins Orchestra, mentored Cajun swing musician Luderin Darbone in the art of jazz. Courtesy of the Freeland Archives, Acadia Parish Library, Crowley, Louisiana.

learned about jazz's nuances through extended conversations with African-American trumpeter and arranger Ike Jenkins, who frequently called on Darbone's Hackberry Rambler Service Station in Crowley (figure 5.4). The trumpeter taught Darbone an assortment of standard New Orleans jazz compositions such as "Eh La Bas" that the fiddler eventually waxed with the Ramblers. In 1935, the group also recorded "You've Got to Hi-De-Hi," featuring scat lyrics based on Cab Calloway's famous improvisation. Some musicians frequently bridged the small divide between Cajun swing and jazz. Crowley resident Tony Gonzales, the first Cajun drummer featured on record, performed regularly with a jazz orchestra and later with Leo Soileau's Cajun swing band. Bandleaders not only tried to hire accomplished musicians, but also put their chops to the test in the recording studio, as illustrated by the various local adaptations of the New Orleans hot jazz standard "High Society."

Fiddler Hector Duhon, who began his career performing with accordionist Octa Clark during the 1920s, branched out in the mid-1930s by forming the Dixie Rambler string band.[16] On August 10, 1935, Duhon and the Ramblers gathered around a microphone in a New Orleans studio to record the first Cajun interpretation of "High Society" titled "Dixie's Hottest." The ensemble's crude performance spotlighted a fiddle transcription of Creole musician Alphonse Picou's famous clarinet solo rendered over a thunderous guitar belting out a tumultuous 4/4 hot jazz rhythm. The composition circulated around the Cajun swing camp. One year later, the Hackberry Ramblers adapted and released the song as "Vinton High Society."[17] On February 21, 1937, Oran "Doc" Guidry recorded yet another rendition of the jazz standard with his swing orchestra the Jolly Boys of Lafayette. With each subsequent recording, Cajun musicians became more adept in the vocabulary of jazz and the mechanics of swing.

Jazz became a measure of an ensemble's proficiency and fluency in the popular dance repertoire that audiences demanded during the mid-1930s. The musical style enriched rhythm section instrumentation and imparted solo "takeoffs" and the jitterbug dance style that remained popular even after Cajun swing phased out. As jazz's influence extended nationally, it underscored the regional culture linking Cajun swing and its Texas cousin, Western swing.

The Lone Star State was not immune to America's growing fascination with jazz. Urban centers such as Dallas, Houston, and San Antonio became an organic extension of south Louisiana jazz culture by virtue of the musical shockwaves emanating from the Crescent City. Between 1904 and 1914, seminal New Orleans jazzmen Jelly Roll Morton, Bunk Johnson, King Oliver, and Sidney Bechet reportedly ventured across the state line and stimulated a local interest in the genre. By the 1920s and 1930s, the legacy of such homegrown artists as Scott Joplin, Jack Teagarden, and Charlie Christian and lesser-known musicians such as Eddie Durham and Oran "Hot Lips" Page served as an accessible model for the Anglo-Texan derivative known as Western swing that filtered into neighboring Louisiana thanks to mass media and transient labor.[18]

Western swing, various strains of jazz, and traditional Cajun music served as the lifeblood of Cajun swing. During the early 1930s, Cajuns living in east Texas delighted in the innovative sounds of the Light Crust Doughboys, an exciting new radio band featuring vocalist Milton Brown and fiddler Bob Wills.[19] This pioneering Texas swing outfit—and its musical offspring, Milton Brown and the Musical Brownies and Bob Wills and His Texas Playboys—urbanized the rural sounds of white Southern music by fusing hillbilly, jazz, blues, and American popular music by way of a country arrangement. The Light Crust Doughboys signified the urbanization of rural musical traditions for working-class whites. The ensemble made hot string band music commercially viable and thereby ensured Brown's and Wills' divergent careers. Jazz crooner Milton Brown went on to found the popular Musical Brownies in Forth Worth during the early 1930s. The band's body of work established the rhythmic meter and instrumentation that became the precedent for aspirant string bands in Texas, Oklahoma and Louisiana by transforming hot jazz's 4/4 meter into a more danceable 2/4 time signature. Bandleader and fiddler Bob Wills, on the other hand, further emphasized the parallels between jazz, swing, and Texas string bands by incorporating extensive horn sections manned with trumpets, trombones, clarinets, and saxophones.[20] The Musical Brownies and the Texas Playboys attracted Cajun audiences on both sides of the Sabine River, partly because of their connection to jazz, danceable arrangements, and familiar instrumentation, and partly because both outfits harnessed the potential of mass media—particularly radio—to provide the soundtrack for industrializing sectors in Louisiana, Texas, and Oklahoma.

Industrialized spaces— mills, canning factories, and especially oil derricks and refineries—straddling the Texas–Louisiana border served as migratory conduits through which both Anglo and Franco itinerant laborers sought employment. To be sure, the communication networks established through industrialized labor had profound cultural implications. Cajuns stood at the crossroads where the rich musical traditions of Texas and the jazz of New Orleans overlapped most directly. Linked historically by geography, commerce, culture, and musical affinity, Anglophone east Texas and Francopone south Louisiana maintained a somewhat tenuous relationship. Animosity intensified with the birth of the region's petroleum industry. Initial strikes at Spindletop, Texas (near Beaumont), and then Evangeline, Louisiana (both in 1901), facilitated the movement of capital, laborers, and musical information between these boomtowns. Country music expert Bill Malone argues that petroleum transformed country music, including Western swing, by introducing the South to the modern age. "Most of the early discoveries came in rural, even remote areas of the Southwest—Texas, Louisiana, Oklahoma, Arkansas—and the bulk of the workers were country people who moved from one field to another."[21] Itinerant workers stressed and, at times, broke existing social barriers as they invaded rural neighborhoods. With demographics in flux, new barriers between Cajuns and Anglo-Texans emerged in the oil patch. Historian Shane Bernard maintains that the oil industry generated an Americanizing tidal wave that swept across south Louisiana, drowning traditional Cajun lifestyles with American values and mainstream culture, "from consumerism to country-and-western music to various strains of Protestantism."[22] The industrialized world of petroleum became an integral part of the landscape in such communities as Anse La Butte, Hell Hole Bayou, and Evangeline. Anglo-Texan oilmen poured into Cajun country following the initial discovery at the epicenter of the Gulf Coast's oil industry in Spindletop, Texas. Roughnecks, roustabouts, and drillers introduced to Cajun country new cultural perspectives, distinct musical tastes, and an intimate knowledge of oil production.[23]

By 1933, the same year a pair of Cajuns formed the influential Hackberry Ramblers, south Louisiana produced 44,528 barrels a day, approximately twice north Louisiana's total output.[24] The petroleum industry offered working-class Cajuns economic relief during the depths of the Great Depression as rural communities struggled to adapt from subsistence agriculture to an oil-based economy. Farmers could make more money in one month in the oil patch than they could with a year's harvest.[25] Oil revenues provided Cajuns with disposable income to buy records, gramophones, battery-operated radios, cash to spend at dance clubs, and money to purchase instruments.[26]

As Anglo workers poured into Bayou Country, Cajuns willingly migrated across the border to work in the Lone Star State's booming oil fields, thereby extending the physical boundaries of Cajun country westward. The resulting cross-cultural pollination in the oil patch gave birth to the Hackberry Ramblers, the quintessential oil-era Cajun string band. The group's musical blend of "Anglo-American country with Cajun French material" epitomized founder and oil patch baby Luderin Darbone's intimate connection to the industry that forever changed his homeland.[27] Darbone was born on January 14, 1913, in Evangeline, 12 years after the local discovery of oil.[28] Ben Sandmel notes, "His father moved the family frequently in search of jobs in the oil patch, and Luderin was raised in the east Texas town of Orangefield."[29] His parents migrated around Louisiana and Texas, working in various capacities within the industry's multistate infrastructure. "In 1931, the Darbones moved to Hackberry, LA," Sandmel explains "a remote oil-field town in the coastal marshes south of Lake Charles."[30] In 1933, Darbone began broadcasting from Beaumont, Texas's KFDM radio relay located in the Majestic Hotel in downtown Lake Charles, Louisiana.[31] Darbone's radio broadcasts constitute the culmination of Louisiana's long cultural liaison with the Lone Star State and the fledgling sounds of Western swing.

Cajun Country "Tunes In"

Radio was one of the great Americanizing forces in the Bayou Country and a crucial component of Cajun swing's rise the prominence. As radio became a conspicuous entertainment source across the United States, architects of the style tuned in to learn the latest popular compositions before eventually adopting radio as a regular performance venue.

A particularly intimate form of mass communication, radio encouraged Cajuns to imagine the America beyond Acadiana. Without pictures, images, or text, the ephemeral sounds wafting out of the mechanism's loudspeaker left individuals to interpret ball games, boxing matches, radio dramas, musical performances, and on-air announcers with their minds' eyes. Cajuns embraced the media because of the technology's novelty and communicative reach. The medium was based on orality, thus complementing the oral culture that traditionally structured Cajun interaction, which particularly appealed to the region's largely illiterate working classes. As elsewhere in America, whole families gathered around the battery-operated wonder in the mornings, evenings, and on weekends as a diversion from grueling workdays. Though radio slowly replaced *veillées* (extended social calls) and other traditional communal gatherings, the new technology came to rest on the same sociocultural scaffolding that once supported these now antiquated forms of leisure. Radio became hugely popular, in part, because of its capacity as a family-oriented cultural pastime that reinforced the resilient family ties that bound together Cajun society. It also satisfied the Cajun community's growing penchant for consumable forms of entertainment by funneling music and story directly into Cajun living rooms. Even monolingual Francophone farmers such as Duma Melancon listened intently to English-language news programs and Joe Lewis's boxing matches despite the inherent language barriers in American broadcasting (figure 5.5).

The number of radios in Louisiana households increased with the technology's popularity and affordability. Louisiana State University professor Edgar Schuler estimated that approximately 53.3 percent of Louisianians owned radios in 1940. And, by 1942, approximately 41 percent of rural Lafayette Parish homes boasted their own receivers.[32] Some working-class Cajuns who did not own radios and wanted to listen made

Figure 5.5. Bernard Brothers carried and advertised the latest 1937 Philco radio models at their auto supply company in New Iberia. Courtesy of the Center for Louisiana Studies, University of Louisiana at Lafayette.

a conscious effort to access the resources around them. Cajun swing fiddler Hadley Castille remembers going to a neighbor's home before his father purchased a battery-operated unit. "We didn't have a radio then," the musician lamented, "but I had heard the Grand Ole Opry through a friend. He used to let us go, let us go sit at his house and listen."[33] The technology acted as a conduit through which Bayou Country residents tapped into a veritable sea of ideas and cultural programming.

The first voices to cut through the static on Cajun-owned radios carried the cadenced accent of Anglo-America. On September 4, 1924, the Lafayette *Daily Advertiser* published a radio program guide listing the signals that made their way into Cajun Country. Station locations included Buffalo, New York; Chicago, Illinois; Detroit, Michigan; Des Moines, Iowa; Kansas City and St. Louis, Missouri; Louisville, Kentucky; Philadelphia and Pittsburgh, Pennsylvania; Newark, New Jersey; Omaha, Nebraska; and New York City and Schenectady, New York.[34] Locals also turned their radio knobs to find a mix of Spanish-language broadcasts, featuring Mexican and hillbilly music from enormously powerful clear-channel boarder stations in far-off places such as Coahuila, Mexico, across the Rio Grande from Del Rio, Texas.[35] More important, regarding the development of Cajun swing, local audiences frequently tuned in to hillbilly programming like the Grand Ole Opry on Nashville station WSM. "When we started playing," Darbone recalled nostalgically, "we played the stuff that they were playing in Nashville . . . Fort Worth, Tulsa, Oklahoma, and places like that." On clear nights during the early to mid-1930s, Cajun radios caught the signal from broadcast stations hundreds of miles away. Bands like the Hackberry Ramblers paid careful attention to emerging strains of American popular music like Western swing. "After we'd play a dance, I had a radio in my [Model A Ford]," the fiddler remember. "And we'd leave a dancehall and listen to Bob Wills play from Tulsa. And that's where we'd learn a lot of our tunes that we would play."[36]

Closer to home, Louisiana's most prominent stations—Loyola University's WWL in New Orleans and KWKH in Shreveport—played an important role in the transmission and dissemination of American popular music on the airwaves. Live country music performed by the likes of the Shelton Brothers, Jimmie Rodgers imitator Jerry Beherns, the Pickard Family, and J. E. Mauny and his Caroline Ramblers dominated WWL's airtime from the early 1930s until 1935, when the station attained network status and discontinued hillbilly programming.[37] Shreveport's famed KWKH, on the other hand, became the first publicly identified working-class music station in Louisiana on March 14, 1925. Over time, the broadcast hub eventually featured Tin Pan Alley selections rendered by Southern string bands, hillbilly compositions, and Cajun music.[38] In fact, the Shreveport station broadcast one of the earliest radio performances of vernacular Cajun dance music when fiddlers Sady Courville and Dennis McGee traveled to the KWKH studios in 1928 (figure 5.6). Courville's ambitions to broadcast could only be realized by traveling beyond the confines of Acadiana, where locally produced radio did not exist. "There were no radio stations

Figure 5.6. Local radio stations first went on air in the mid-1930s and broadcast a mix of Cajun swing, hillbilly, and American popular music. More powerful regional stations, such as Shreveport's KWKH (pictured here), sometimes broadcast such events as the National Rice Festival on location from Crowley. Courtesy of the Freeland Archive, Acadia Parish Library, Crowley, Louisiana.

in southwest Louisiana," explained Luderin Darbone about local programming in the early 1930s, "not until the Lafayette's KVOL and Lake Charles' KPLC came on air in 1935."[39] Radio waves emanating from Texas, Shreveport, and New Orleans ignored south Louisiana's cultural boundaries as they crisscrossed Cajun Country and spilled Western swing, hillbilly music, and jazz across the region.[40] Receptive musicians absorbed these influences and rendered them musically after migrating to one of southwest Louisiana's largest industrial centers, Crowley.

Cajun Music's Commercial Epicenter

Located in Acadia Parish, in the heart of Cajun Country, Crowley, Louisiana, was the geographic nucleus of the Cajun swing movement and, by 1935, the epicenter of commercial Cajun music (figure 5.7). Musicians naturally gravitated to the urban center, and for good reason. The railroad town boasted a diverse population and a cosmopolitan musical culture that included a thriving jazz scene and Cajun music's top entertainers. The city, which also acted as the regional rice belt's commercial hub, was a bastion of American culture thanks in large part to the municipality's large Midwestern population. More important, Crowley became home to two of the most influential swing orchestras in the history of Cajun music: Leo Soileau's Three Aces (later revamped as the Four Aces and the Rhythm Boys) and the Hackberry Ramblers. Soileau formed his seminal swing group in the Acadia Parish seat of justice after relocating from his native Ville Platte in the early 1930s. The musical cohort connecting the region's top performers eased the transition. "Me and Joe Falcon used to

Figure 5.7. Crowley, Louisiana, was a booming regional industrial center and, by the mid-1930s, the hub of commercial Cajun music. Courtesy of the Freeland Archives, Acadia Parish Library, Crowley, Louisiana.

join in together on the big jobs," Soileau admitted.[41] Luderin Darbone also relocated. After organizing the Hackberry Ramblers in the marshy oil field hamlet for which the band is named, the fiddler/bandleader packed up and moved the band and his service station to Crowley in 1935 to be centrally situated along the region's dance circuit. The town's central role as the urban nexus of activity for the Cajun swing movement came into clearer focus at band contests held during the town's largest cultural event—the National Rice Festival.

In 1938, the city implemented a "Fais Do-Do Orchestra Contest" at the second annual National Rice Festival (figure 5.8). The contestants consisted exclusively of the area's finest swing ensembles. Ohio native and Crowley high school music director P. G. Swartz, Vernon Anderson of Baton Rouge, and Frank Carroll of Lake Charles judged each musical organization's ability to play in three distinctive styles: Cajun, hillbilly, and popular arrangements. As the Crowley *Acadian-Signal* reported,

> First honors and the prize of $15 went to the Raynebo [*sic*] Ramblers of Rayne while second place with a $10 cash prize went to Leo Soileau and His Rhythm Boys of Crowley. Other musical organizations competing were the Four Aces, the Hackberry Ramblers, the Louisiana Hillbillies and Joe Werner and his orchestra of Rayne.[42]

The contest simultaneously reinforced the municipality's role as the epicenter of Cajun swing and clearly defined the criteria for success for Cajun bands in the years immediately before World War II. The level of an ensemble's dexterity when negotiating among traditional Cajun, hillbilly, and popular compositions—the basic ingredients of Cajun swing—determined an organization's musicality.

Between 11:30 A.M. and 1:00 P.M. on November 7, 1939, Louisiana State University general extension division public outreach coordinator Louise V. Olivier developed and moderated the "Creole Hour" (to avoid the negative connotations associated with the ethnic label "Cajun") at the third annual National Rice Festival. The Creole Hour consisted of French sing-alongs—including such compositions as "La Marseillaise" and "Frère Jacques"—dance demonstrations by a costumed folklore troupe, and a band

Figure 5.8. Upward of 10,000 spectators filled the streets of Crowley each year at the National Rice Festival (later the International Rice Festival) to hear Cajun musicians perform traditional, hillbilly, and popular compositions. Courtesy of the Freeland Archives, Acadia Parish Library, Crowley, Louisiana.

contest that highlighted the latest trends in Cajun music.[43] Cajun swing's top recording artists fleshed out the lineup: Sons of the Acadians, featuring fiddler Oran "Doc" Guidry; Happy Fats and His Rayne-Bo Ramblers;[44] Leo Soileau and His Rhythm Boys;[45] Louisiana Hillbillies, featuring Julius "Papa Cairo" Lamperez;[46] and the Merrymakers featuring J. B. Fuselier.[47] Joe Falcon and His Silver String Band were also scheduled to perform before a last-minute schedule change.[48] Although string bands dominated the Cajun musical scene in the late 1930s, Joe Falcon's exalted celebrity would have garnered special attention at the festival. His was the only band scheduled to feature an accordion-based selection, "Lafayette," during the 1939 Creole Hour. What is more, he had also agreed to play drums during their performance of "J'va Ete Vrai a Cila que J'aime," a French interpretation of the hot hillbilly number "I'm Going to Be True to the One I Love" popularized by Frank Luther.

By 1939, Joe and Cleoma Falcon had adapted to the Cajun swing era's evolutionary currents by reformatting and renaming their ensemble the Silver String Band, a moniker Joe maintained until his death in 1965. The famous bandleader catered to local audiences' growing predilection for swing by performing one accordion set, then stowing his squeezebox for an accordionless country set highlighting Falcon on drums and his all-Crowley supporting cast, sometimes featuring guitarist Hank Redlich and steel guitarist Julius "Papa Cairo" Lamperez.[49] Likewise, members of the Breaux family, who helped usher in the accordion era in the late 1920s, were life-long residents of the Crowley area. Recording artist Cleoma Breaux Falcon and her fiddling brother Clifford Breaux, a school traffic policeman at North Crowley Elementary, kept abreast of the changing music scene in their hometown and changed their repertoire accordingly with the times.

On February 21, 1937, Cleoma Falcon returned to Decca's recording studios and demonstrated her ability to swing on French interpretations of the popular compositions "Lulu's Back in Town" and "It's a Sin to Tell a Lie," recorded and popularized by stride-piano jazzman Fats Waller in the mid-1930s. Taking a more moderate tempo than Waller, the limiting structure of "Lulu's Back in Town" inhibited the full power and range of Cleoma's vocal abilities, as she casually swung through the tune backed by an unidentified fiddler. At the same session, the guitarist also waxed the traditional Anglo song "Hand Me Down My Walking Cane," rendered in English with accordion accompaniment. On December 15, 1937, her brother Clifford followed the trend by recording a raw French version of the jazz inflected "You Keep a Knockin'" in Dallas, Texas, for the Decca label.[50] These Americanized arrangements denote the degree to which Cajuns had access to, and effectively internalized, popular commercial materials circulated in the Bayou Country via radio and record.

Cajun swing marked the birth of the modern Cajun sound. Between 1935 and 1947, inventive musicians such as Leo Soileau, Luderin Darbone, LeRoy "Happy Fats" LeBlanc, Hector Duhon, and Harry Choates redefined the parameters of Cajun music by filtering into the genre jazz, Western swing, and American popular music through a common artistic lens colored by south Louisiana's evolving cultural climate. This period of intense creativity informed and energized Cajun music through end of the twentieth century. Cajun swing's momentum, innovations in instrumentation, and an expanded repertoire all transferred in time through the accordion-based Cajun honky-tonk sound that began to dominate Cajun music following World War II. Amplified arrangements powered by drums, steel guitars, bass, and electric guitars became standard, even as the accordion returned to its prominent position in the Cajun musical lexicon. According to Shane Bernard, Cajun swing also laid the foundation for the Cajun and Creole rhythm and blues/rock 'n' roll hybrid known as swamp pop. Bernard writes:

> Those who minimize Cajun and black Creole music's influence on swamp pop also ignore a more important fact, namely, that swamp pop draws not as heavily on Cajun and black Creole accordion music as on Cajun string band music. [Swamp pop musician and music writer Johnnie] Allan's biographical data reveal that the median year of birth for swamp poppers is 1939, which falls squarely in the string band era (circa 1935–1950). Most swamp pop artists were born to parents who courted during the height of the string band era, and who after marriage probably continued to appreciate, purchase, and perhaps even perform Cajun string band music, a sound future swamp pop artists naturally absorbed growing up in their parents' homes . . . In fact, a handful of future swamp pop artists performed in Cajun string bands during the late 1940s and early to mid-'50s—among them Rod Bernard, Warren Storm, and Joe Barry—and those who performed with accordion groups almost exclusively wielded instruments brought to Cajun music during the string band era.[51]

The connections between Cajun swing and swamp pop are immediately obvious in Warren Schexnider's musical genealogy. Performing under the stage name Warren Storm, the celebrated swamp pop drummer and vocalist, who did session work early in his career for the influential Louisiana blues man Slim Harpo, first learned to play drums from his father, Rayne-Bo Rambler drummer Simon Schexnider.

Even respective Cajun and Creole fiddlers Dewey Balfa and Canray Fontenot—held as sterling examples of traditional old-timey French Louisiana music by folklorists and folk festival organizers in the late twentieth century—claimed Western and Cajun swing as primary influences. "You know, I was influenced by J. B. Fusilier, Leo Soileau, Harry Choates," Balfa told Barry Ancelet during an interview in the early 1980s, "and I think Bob Wills and the Texas Playboys had a little effect on my fiddling."[52] Balfa's smooth long-bow fiddle style is an overt nod to Texas fiddling and the legacy of Cajun swing. Black Creole fiddler Canray Fontenot personally regarded his fiddling technique not as a traditional Creole expression, but an interpretation of Harry Choates' style.[53]

Cajun scholars have largely neglected the swing era and the musicians who popularized this essential period in Cajun music, dismissing the genre as simply an American musical expression devoid of any Cajun character. For instance, Barry Ancelet argues that during the 1930s, "Western Swing replaced Cajun music in the dance halls."[54] Rather, Cajun swing represents a synthesis of indigenous and external cultural information filtered through the Depression-era Cajun perspective. The genre existed as an autonomous cultural expression that borrowed freely from both external and internal stimuli, yet maintained a distinctly Cajun character—the product of the complex sociocultural and historical processes that worked in concert to shape south Louisiana's cultural landscape, not a second-hand imitation of Western swing. The style is also a manifestation of the increasingly cosmopolitan nature of Cajun society from the mid-1930s through the end of World War II. As the band contest at Crowley's 1938 National Rice Festival indicates, a group's measure of success was judged not only on criteria relating to traditional Louisiana styles, but also on how well an ensemble could interpret hillbilly and American popular compositions. These standards also validated bilingual expression, which naturally reflected the Bayou Country's linguistic reality. Bilingualism is the metonym for a culture becoming increasingly syncretic—the linguistic product of the same cultural processes that produced Cajun swing.

The contexts that informed Cajun music and American life shifted radically between the mid-1930s and the late 1940s. The sonic information disseminated by mass media and mass consumption changed the way locals perceived their world. Jazz became part of the Cajun vernacular and connected the group, at least through imagination, to the American mainstream. Meanwhile, roadways, industrialization, and two world wars brought the flow of American culture to the Bayou Country in more concrete ways. Cajuns changed when they plugged into the mainstream. During the swing era, a new generation of Cajun musicians came of age and gave voice to this new perspective, a voice that was uniquely Cajun-American.

6

The Modern Cajun Sound

Shortly after 11 P.M. on September 10, 1926, a fight broke out on the 400 block of Proctor Street in Port Arthur, Texas. Fisticuffs ensued when a Texan insulted a Louisiana expatriate by calling him by the pejorative ethnic epithet "Cajun." The *Port Arthur News* reported, "It's expensive to call an enemy a 'cajun,' but it's even more costly to hit him after he's applied that name to you," particularly when the fine for such an offence amounted to $25 plus court costs. The unsuspecting Texan assumed the immunity of white privilege when he applied the ethnic label, fully expecting impunity for his actions. "I called him a Cajun, Judge," the boy told the court, "and he hit me."[1] This scene described in the *Port Arthur News* illuminates the complex contexts surrounding the ethnic group's identity and the assertion of their ethnicity when confronted by hostile and condescending attitudes.

For Cajuns, Texas represented the western frontier, an industrialized land of economic opportunity, oil fields, and shipyards where one could escape Louisiana's severely depressed agricultural economy.[2] As south Louisianians left in droves in search of new financial opportunities in the Cajun Lapland, tensions escalated between expatriates and working-class Texans competing for the same jobs, a situation compounded by their juxtaposed Franco-Catholic and Anglo-Protestant worldviews. Animosity frequently led to violent exchanges between the rival groups, ultimately resulting in the denigration of the Cajun image across the Sabine River.

Since the term's emergence in the nineteenth century, a dark cloud loomed over "Cajun," which, over time, accumulated the same negative connotations as the Southern slur "hillbilly."[3] In 1879, travel writer R. L. Daniels observed that members of Bayou Country's Francophone gentry applied the ethnic label to denigrate humbler classes of French origin:

> Acadian—or rather its corruption "Cajun," as they pronounce it—is regarded as implying contempt. Indeed, the educated classes habitually designate those whom they regard as their social inferiors by the

objectionable epithet. With the lower orders it is bandied from one to another in the same spirit; and none are so humble as not to feel the implied insult. If the situation is favorable, a fist fight is the result, the contest being spiced with such volleys of oaths as, were they translatable, would excite the envy of the most accomplished blasphemer of a western mining town.[4]

Negative implications associated with the epithet persisted well into the twentieth century. In 1937, as Cajun swing began to dominate the commercial Cajun musical market, Louisianian Thad St. Martin noted in the *Yale Review* that "Cajun was a fighting word. [In Louisiana] an old Negro nanny did not say 'poor white trash.' She said 'Cajun'—or 'blue-bellied Cajun.'"[5] This cultural baggage weighed most heavily on members of the ethnic group who came into frequent contact with non-Cajuns who dominated the economic currents of industrialization supplanting traditional Cajun occupations in Depression-era Louisiana.

South Louisianians left their family farms to find employment as tool pushers, roustabouts, and roughnecks on the looming wooden oil derricks that dotted the region's wetlands and prairies. Others wandered into towns and cities to work for railroad and telephone companies or in canning factories that processed foodstuffs such as oysters, shrimp, blackberries, and sweet potatoes. Some Cajuns made a living working in the rice mills and cotton gins that transformed the Pelican State's raw agricultural riches into consumable products. The exploitive tentacles of neocolonial American industrialization rapidly encroached into the Bayou Country, despite the efforts of such Louisiana populists as demagogue Huey Long, who vowed to undermine conglomerates like Standard Oil Company that held the state in an economic stranglehold. Standard and other sizable corporations mined local resources and then exported their profits—and high-paying manufacturing jobs associated with creation of end products derived from raw materials—without reinvesting in the communities they exploited. The tension afforded by these conflicting conservative and progressive forces radically redefined life in Louisiana. Many Cajuns consequently found themselves in the awkward position of both confronting and adapting to Bayou Country's shifting economic, cultural, and social environment while remaining at the bottom of the region's socioeconomic ladder. Some adapted better than others. Savvy blue-collar musicians devised a strategy for upward mobility by carving a niche for themselves on the periphery of this encroaching industrial world. Cajun swing musicians realized that they could escape the menial labor positions open to Cajuns in factories and on oilrigs by becoming professional entertainers (figure 6.1).

Cajun swing embodied the Bayou Country's rural past and industrial present. The modern sounds of swing expressed the plight of musicians attempting to negotiate simultaneously urbanization and the bounds of traditional French and popular Anglo-American repertoires. The struggles of Cajun swing's exponents to overcome the emotional dimensions of stigmatization and poverty through the freedom afforded by economic

Figure 6.1. (*top*) Cajuns such as these wage laborers at the State Rice Mill in Abbeville, Louisiana became active participants in America's industrialized sectors by forming the rank-and-file on local factory shop floors. Photograph by Russell Lee, October 1938. Courtesy of Farm Security Administration, Library of Congress. (*bottom*) A forest of wooden derricks in the rural town of Evangeline signified the birth of Louisiana's petroleum-based economy. Courtesy of the Freeland Archives, Acadia Parish Library, Crowley, Louisiana.

independence are considered in this chapter. Self-employment became a paramount aspiration for rural working-class Cajuns during the Great Depression as this south Louisiana underclass sank deeper and deeper into the dark chasm that sharecropping had become.

Rejuvenating local musical expression provided a rare means of egress. The first wave of swing musicians devised behavioral strategies centered on a culture of respectability to escape the degrading and dehumanizing consequences of the crop lien system. The musical ramifications of this cultural shift are illustrated by the lives of prolific recording artists such as Leo Soileau, the Hackberry Ramblers, and the Rayne-Bo Ramblers. Lesser known ensembles such as the Dixie Ramblers, the Merrymakers, and the Alley Boys of Abbeville are also considered in a discussion of the varied positions Cajun swing occupied along south Louisiana's vernacular-popular culture continuum. Whether interpreting indigenous French accordion tunes or the latest popular releases, Cajun swingers represented one manifestation of the paradoxical fusion of dynamism and conservatism that defined the twentieth-century Cajun experience. Likewise, their recordings and live performances offered a means of encapsulating that experience in an aesthetically pleasing and socially relevant medium for their primary audience in south Louisiana and east Texas.

Swing allowed working-class laborers in Texas and Louisiana to escape the cotton fields and fashion new identities through opportunities provided by industrialization. Music provided an attractive employment option apart from manual labor for both Cajun sharecroppers and their Anglo counterparts, who helped sketch the blueprint for Cajun swing. The decision to start a new life as a musician came easily for Texas fiddler Cliff Bruner—perhaps the most influential Western swing bandleader to influence Cajun swing. Following a short sojourn in Oklahoma, the Bruner family returned to their native Texas to establish a cotton farm. Cliff Bruner left the family business to pursue an entertainment career, an occupation peripherally associated with the same developing east Texas petroleum economy that lured thousands of Cajuns to the region. The fiddler described his transformation from day laborer to bandleader to Western swing aficionado Cary Ginell:

> So we came back to Texas, moved out on the farm, and by this time, I was in junior high school and I started playing the fiddle for the little country shindigs they were having in different people's homes. They'd throw some corn meal on the floor and we'd have a dance. A friend of mine would play the guitar and I would play the fiddle, and we'd get on our horses, put the instruments in a flour sack, and we'd head for blue yonder. Sometimes we'd make three or four dollars, five maybe. That was a lot of money then. People worked for a dollar a day back then. You'd start work when the sun came up and you wouldn't stop until the sun went down. Pickin' cotton and choppin' bermuda grass. In the summertime that could get to around fourteen, fifteen hours. For one dollar. And I thought there just had to be an easier way to make a living.[6]

Pioneer Cajun swing fiddler Leo Soileau cited the same reasons for establishing an ensemble during an interview in 1965 with folklorist Ralph

Rinzler. Soileau exclaimed that life as a professional musician seemed much more appealing than picking cotton under the blazing Louisiana sun. Moreover, he regarded music as an occupation, not as a recreational endeavor. "I wouldn't go and get up out of bed to go play a party, just to hear myself play," Soileau explained. "You better believe that!"[7] Not all Cajuns shared the fiddler's perspective. Working-class Louisianians traditionally equated work with manual labor, and music with extracurricular activities associated with leisure and amusement. This attitude was pervasive among rural working-class whites in the Deep South. Indeed, Bob Wills's biographer Ruth Sheldon notes, "If you did not do good, hard, physical labor you were considered 'no account' and were relegated to the lowest standing in the community. That having a band and playing an instrument was hard work was something that no one could have understood or accepted as the truth."[8] Soileau, like other swing musicians in Louisiana and Texas, attempted to reconcile these conflicting views by striving to create a respectable image for his band and his music. Bob Wills took offense when someone labeled his music as "country" or "hillbilly." He also consciously worked to separate his public persona from the disdain rural white Southerners maintained for local professional performers. Cajun swing musicians fashioned their music, careers, and public image, in part, on the Wills model as a means of coping with the specific challenges that denigration posed in Cajun Country.

Respectability and the Color of "Off-White"

Beginning in the mid-nineteenth century, the marginalization and vilification Cajuns felt so acutely came from both sides of the racial binary pitting white against black in the United States. In 1866, one travel writer insisted that "so little are [Cajuns] thought of—that the niggers, when they want to express contempt for one of their own race, call him an Acadian nigger."[9] When taken into account with local color writer George Washington Cable's "Notes on Acadians in Louisiana," which contains the quote "one negro of another: Dat nigga deh he's a Cajun—I'm a Creole," Afro-Creoles slandered their Cajun neighbors, with whom they competed for resources at the bottom of the region's socioeconomic ladder during and after Reconstruction.[10]

Meanwhile, whites in Louisiana, already facing unprecedented demographic shifts thanks to immigration and regional migration, pushed hard to solidify the state's racial boundaries. "Louisiana Needs Whitening," explained one Louisiana newspaper at the end of the nineteenth century. There were "too many colored people," which also applied to poor and ignorant "off-whites" like Cajuns. Since Reconstruction, white businessmen feared economic deprivation, which only exacerbated racial and ethnic tensions between the haves and the mostly "colored" have-nots. The Baton Rouge *Weekly Truth* expressed these concerns most succinctly, declaring that none of America's white business leaders "would desire to settle in a State where trade is affected with a palsy and the people are poor and growing poorer."[11] Dominant groups ironically strove for "whitening" by labeling inappropriate or unsanctioned behavior, often associated with the lower classes, as not white. Hence pervasive poverty substantiated the sociocultural blackening process Cajuns encountered.

During the twentieth century, socioeconomic pressures generated by the Great Depression and the mechanization of agriculture, compounded by the deteriorating quality of life for tenant farmers and sharecroppers, made downward social mobility an exacerbating fear and a grim reality across the American South. The plummeting price of cotton, high cost of credit, and spiking land prices made traditional forms of subsistence untenable. Looking down from the middle rungs of the South's socioeconomic ladder, landlords and the affluent upper classes stigmatized struggling sharecroppers and tenant farmers "as white trash, crackers, and rednecks," calling into question their membership within the white community.[12] Antagonists in east Texas and Louisiana, on the other hand, used the customized slur "coonass" to virtually blacken working-class Cajuns. Blackening, which rendered the group as "off-white," effectively stripped Cajuns of white privilege within Louisiana's hierarchical racial categorizations that posited people of color, especially those with black skin, to the very bottom of this iniquitous caste system. The pejorative "coonass," generally applied by Anglo-Americans to Cajuns, became standard currency in east Texas oil fields, where thousands of poverty-stricken Cajuns migrated to escape sharecropping and farm labor. The epithet complicated the blackening process (embodied by the deployment of the African-American pejorative "coon") by also inferring unhygienic degradation at the point of defecation and sodomy.[13]

Working-class Cajuns reacted to slander in two distinctive ways that coincided with the skin color of those individuals with whom they interacted. When dealing with people of color, they "could, and did, define and accept their class positions by fashioning identities as 'not slaves' and as 'not Blacks'" by clinging to whiteness and evoking the rigid racial distinctions enforced by Jim Crow legislation.[14] However, the rigidity of racial ideology fluctuated irregularly. White Cajun fiddler Dennis McGee loved black accordionist Amédé Ardoin like a brother. "Amédé and I worked together. We worked for the same people. We were both sharecroppers," McGee remembered.[15] Even though the interracial pair intimately shared music, performing side by side in the evenings, the racial divide could oscillate between transparency and opaqueness. McGee continued, "Oh, I loved that little 'nèg's' [black's] music. He played and sang well."[16] Leo Soileau also emphasized the color line when referring to his early career performing with the Afro-Creole accordionist. "Well, I played with that little nigger there. . . . Yeah, Ardoin. Got started with him."[17] This strategy sought to eschew Cajuns' status as the "Other" by deploying whiteness as leverage against blackness. However, the black and white equation became evermore complex when Cajuns encountered other whites in oil fields, refineries, shipyards, and the dance halls that catered to the laborers employed by these industries. These milieus became the contested grounds where working-class Anglo-Protestants and blue-collar Cajuns wrestled between normalcy (whiteness) and otherness ("off-white"), power and subordinance.

Cajun recording artists devised an alternative solution to navigate the tense contexts surrounding these all-white contact zones. They countered denigration by performing whiteness and emphasizing their affiliation to the region's booming industrialized sectors. Like Western swingers, jazz entertainers, and Mexican-American *orquestas* (Tejano big bands), Cajun swing musicians channeled their energies and art into the construction of respectability—or behavioral standards based on an interpretation of the public facade and social hierarchies embraced by the white elite who controlled the region's monetary resources. Respectability entailed cleanliness, orderliness, style and fashion, familiarity with popular trends, and, most important, economic independence. Yet, as historian David Goodhew suggests, "respectability did not have a rigid nature: its starched exterior belied a surprisingly pliable body."[18] The culture of respectability conformed to regional social, linguistic, and cultural idiosyncrasies. Cajun swingers exaggerated their bodily comportment and fashion, abandoned their native patois for proper English grammar and diction, and discounted local wisdom and egalitarianism in favor of education and the metropolitan attitudes validating class structures based on the upper classes in their milieu. Their strategy successfully aimed at the economic benefits afforded to whites.[19]

With disposable income generated by musical performances, bands such as Soileau's Four Aces exploited the burgeoning industrial economy and consciously distanced themselves from working-class stereotypes by altering their appearance. Taking respectable dress—traditionally reserved for church and important social events—a step further, musicians kept their hair neat and kempt, wore *matching* tailored suits, expensive shoes, and later Western garb à la Gene Autry (Hollywood's white agrarian hero) to paint a respectable facade around a profession often equated with leisure, drinking, and carousing.[20] Appearance was an essential step toward rehabilitation. Both Leo Soileau's Four Aces and the Hackberry Ramblers, for instance, emphasized their whiteness by donning ivory uniforms early in their careers to separate themselves aesthetically from their working-class audiences (figure 6.2). In effect, Cajun swingers fit into the same category as country musicians who played "hot" country music and country jazz, what music historian Norman Cohen terms "hillbillies-turned-city-slickers,"[21] musicians, that is, who consciously cloaked themselves behind the veneer of whiteness and an urbane facade that masked their agrarian, working-class backgrounds.

Caught between blackness and whiteness, the working and middle classes, Cajun entertainers strategically deployed these behavior shifts as leverage against denigration. Yet, white society never fully accepted "respectable" ethnics during the Great Depression. Like Latinos in neighboring Texas, their "status as racially in-between, as partly colored, hybrid peoples" made

Figure 6.2. During the mid-1930s, the Hackberry Ramblers emphasized their whiteness by sporting all-white uniforms to distinguish themselves from their working-class audiences. Copyright Luderin Darbone, used by permission.

upwardly mobile Cajuns suspect in the eyes of those dominant white groups controlling resources in their community.[22] And, ironically, working-class Cajuns further marginalized these same betwixt individuals.[23] In the process, Cajun swing musicians ascended into an ambiguous social space that historian David Roediger dubs "inbetweenness," a social position floating between "the stark racial binaries structuring U.S. life and law in the years from 1890 to 1945."[24]

Inbetweenness became a cultural strategy to protect against prejudice in the American South. This behavioral pattern was particularly prevalent among ethnic musicians from bilingual, working-class Catholic communities in Louisiana and Texas, such as Cajun swing ensembles and Mexican-American *orquestas*. "Faced with continuing conflict with the Anglos and increasing alienation from their working-class peers," elaborates musicologist Manuel Peña, "the Mexican American [community] struggled doggedly to maintain its sense of purpose and direction. It did this by adopting the only logical alternative available to its contradiction-filled existence—a strongly bicultural identity."[25] Bilingual *orquestas* frequently privileged English in song, meanwhile consciously separating themselves from "'low-class' dancing and music of the type associated with the accordion conjuntos."[26] Cajun swingers also consciously worked to rectify the complicated, and sometimes contradictory, relationship between their Cajun and American identities.

Cajun swing musicians cultivated a class consciousness that paralleled their Tejano neighbors performing in *orquestas*. Anthropologist Alain Larouche maintains that those analogous outside forces acting on Cajun society led to a gradual redefinition of the group's cultural and ethnic identity that "aimed at promoting the Cajuns' integration into industrial society while creating a functional overlap between two cultures."[27] Architects of Cajun swing became master mediators between local and mass cultures. Progressively minded musicians viewed south Louisiana's evolving economic climate as an opportunity to reposition themselves advantageously by adapting to shifts in the region's social organization. Like members of the immigrant underclass in industrial America, "mass culture would not make them feel any less Polish, Jewish, or black or any less of a worker," as historian Lizabeth Cohen suggests.[28] Instead, Cajun swingers took control of, refashioned, and at times dominated various forms of expressive American culture to counteract their "vulnerability and dependence on mainstream society into a demand for respect."[29] Thus, Cajun swing emerged as the audible result of the socioeconomic pressures shoving tradition and agrarian life against innovation and Acadiana's new industrial reality.

The economics propelling mass culture, and encouraging mass consumption, during the Cajun swing era further shaped the ways Cajun musicians presented their art. Strict behavioral standards imposed by radio station administrators and commercial underwriters dramatically shaped the on-air character of ensembles that relied on the new media to secure steady dance hall work and expand their audience base. According to historian Pamela Grundy, hillbilly radio bands aspired to create a respectable image that conformed to genteel middle-class mores espoused by their corporate underwriters. Grundy maintains that by the 1930s radio bands were "sponsored by companies who saw the musicians as direct representatives of their products."[30] Investors demanded positive and wholesome marketing, insisting that their spokespersons distance themselves, or at least their public image, from the disreputable social behavior often associated with musicians' lifestyles. Ensembles like the Carter Family responded by sanitizing their repertoires and public performances. The Carters clearly catered to the conservative attitudes permeating commercial country music by promoting their entertainment as "morally good."

These same forces affected Cajun music's pioneering radio bands fronted by Cajuns swingers Luderin Darbone and Leo Soileau. Both fiddlers were well acquainted with influential radio bands such as Texas's Light Crust Doughboys, who began broadcasting daily from Fort Worth in 1931 to promote Burrus Flour Mill flour. Following in the Doughboys' footsteps, Cajun string bands became commercial mouthpieces for local retailers who wanted to promote merchandise in a professional and respectable manner. In 1936, Montgomery Ward hired the Hackberry Ramblers for one year to promote its line of Riverside automotive tires. The ensemble, dressed in matching uniforms, began broadcasting directly from the Montgomery Ward third floor showroom via a relay transmitter provided by Lafayette radio station KVOL (see figure 6.3). The promotional stunt brought the performers into intimate contact with their audience. In a display of unabashed commercialism, the national retailer held a contest, allowing customers to suggest a new name for the ensemble. After hundreds of submissions, the band assumed the moniker Riverside Ramblers. The band's new identity further highlighted the cultural threads linking capitalism, Anglo-American culture, and Louisiana's industrialized reality. In 1937, this English-only incarnation of the Ramblers released eight 78 rpm disks strictly featuring 16 hillbilly, popular, and original Anglophonic compositions under their new commercial brand name, the Riverside Ramblers.[31] Not all radio bands went so far as to change their names.

"I done half of my work on radio for my own publicity," remembered Soileau.[32] Like many Cajun swing and Western swing ensembles, the Four

Figure 6.3. Commerce and Cajun music merged
again in 1937 when the Riverside Ramblers (aka
the Hackberry Ramblers)—Joe Werner, Luderin
Darbone, and Lennis Sonnier—broadcast on
local radio station KVOL from the third floor
of Montgomery Wards in downtown Lafayette.
Copyright Luderin Darbone, used by permission.

Aces and Soileau's later ensemble the Rhythm Boys performed live radio
spots to promote upcoming dances and commercial products under the
auspices of a sponsor. During his long career, the fiddler broadcast over
KVOL in Lafayette, KPLC in Lake Charles, KWKH in Shreveport, and one
spot on WNOE in New Orleans while campaigning for country crooner
and Louisiana Governor Jimmie Davis. Opening every broadcast with
"Under the Double Eagle," Soileau recalled, "my band could really mix
'em up. We could play French, English, or Mexican songs. I don't remember any requests that we couldn't do." His radio appearances were "thirty
minutes, from 10:00 to 10:30 in the morning. People would be out hoeing
cotton, but you'd see them throw that hoe down and run from that field
to their little radio. I had a lot of Cajuns tell me, 'Boy, when you come on,
that's one time in the day when we rest.'"[33] The band also collaborated
with Baton Rouge–based Community Coffee, which sponsored a series of
transcription disks for airplay on KVOL and KPLC.[34]

Radio was fundamental to Cajun music's professionalization. By the
mid-1930s, some of the region's most industrious and talented musicians
escaped Acadiana's cotton fields by emerging as professional entertainers thanks to the reach of their on-air performances. Swing musicians,
who conducted much of their business over the radio, inherently understood the commercial dimensions of their trade. These ensembles began
to brand their music and public persona under a single banner—a band
name. A musical autograph like the Hackberry Ramblers or the Riverside
Ramblers signified a personalized commodity in the same way Jack Benny
or Amos 'n' Andy represented the voice of comedy. During public appearances and dances, bandleaders had to maintain their character. They kept

close tabs on their ensembles, making sure everyone dressed appropriately and curbing the time allotted for intermissions. "You had to work too hard!" Four Aces front man Leo Soileau declared.[35] Cajun swing musicians viewed their trade not as a pastime but as a profession.

The Godfather of Cajun Swing

Professionalization was the secret to fiddler and bandleader Leo Soileau's success. He surrounded himself with exceptional musicians and made sure to care for his employees. "I had my car. I'd pay my car expense," he explained. "Then I figured I'd split, you know what I mean. . . . That's the best way to keep your musicians together. I didn't go get and pay in the dark, you know what I mean—like some other guys did." Soileau kept close tabs on the men in his outfit, paid them equal shares minus expenses, booked gigs, and limited intermissions to 15 minutes. "We'd start at 9 [P.M.] till 2 [A.M.] in a night club" and take two intermissions, during which time Soileau made sure the musicians did not drink too heavily. "Too much is no good. It's just as bad to play music when you're drunk, than when you're driving an automobile on the road," he remembered. Unlike a *bal de maison*, where individual musicians determined their own saturation levels, the Cajun swinger worked to keep his reputation in tact. Respectability and the band's French repertoire raised the ensemble's marketability. "They called for that, man," Soileau acknowledged, "Yes sir. We's selling that from here to Houston." As audiences bestowed respectability, so did Soileau's band members. When he decided to retire in 1953, "Like to kill them, when I told them I was going to quit. . . . That's when I started working at the city service of Lake Charles. And I gave my band away. . . . I retired."[36]

His level of professionalism and the extent of his influence made Leo Soileau the godfather of Cajun swing. Not only did Soileau lead his band at the very first Cajun swing recording session, but his far-reaching influence touched the lives of the movement's greatest proponents, including Luderin Darbone and Harry Choates. The musician revitalized the role of fiddling in Cajun music by popularizing swing. Furthermore, he expanded the genre through his progressive vision by modifying his instrumentation and repertoire to stay in step with the latest trends in the nation's ongoing musical evolution. "An old fashioned Acadian music did not wholly satisfy him," maintains British music writer Tony Russell.[37] The artist felt the need to innovate beyond the parameters of tradition, convention, and the accordion.

Leo Soileau could never duplicate the cohesiveness that gelled naturally between the fiddler and his musical soul mate, Mayeuse Lafleur, following the accordionist's murder. To make matters worse, other accordion players cramped his need for expression. On October 2, 1929, mounting tension and frustration between the fiddler and accordionist Moïse Robin came to a head in Victor's makeshift studios in New Orleans's Roosevelt Hotel.[38] "Leo always wanted to take the lead when we played," recalled the resentful accordionist. "He kept the lead and I had to follow him. It's both-ersome to always follow a violin, you see. It's difficult. I had to play below his violin's volume. We didn't play too long together, about one year."[39] The problems the musicians encountered in the studio were symptomatic of a larger issue. Soileau's restive fiddle and Robin's subdued accordion represented the struggle between Soileau's progressive musical foresight and the accordion-based dance band convention that relegated the violin to the role of rhythm instrument. Robin expected the fiddle to accompany him, while Leo insisted on taking the lead. The fiddler attempted to record in a duet format one final time in November 1929 with Wilfred Fruge before turning his back forever on the restrictive idiom that hindered his vision and haunted the memory of his slain partner.

Between 1932 and 1934, Soileau divested himself of diatonic accordi-onists and reinvented himself musically in Crowley, Louisiana.[40] The city was the perfect living laboratory for Soileau, who reoriented his musical direction by assembling a neoteric outfit called the Three Aces. Soileau de-signed a fiddle-friendly rhythm section featuring twin guitars performed by Bill "Dewey" Landry and hillbilly aficionado Floyd Shreve. The bud-ding swing architect conceptualized his new sound based on his affinity for Milton Brown and the Musical Brownies' string arrangements. Brown employed multiple stringed voices, including twin guitar, banjo, and bass fiddle, to provide a rhythmic backdrop to the band's jazz-oriented dance music. Soileau took an additional step by engaging one of Crowley's young jazz drummers, Tony Gonzales, who dramatically altered the sounds and dynamics of Cajun string band music by providing a firm and brash dance cadence on his rudimentary drum kit to complement the fluid interplay between the ensemble's string voices. Soileau's connection to the Gonzales family extended as far back as 1929, when the bandleader traveled with Tony's brother and Cajun Jimmie Rodgers impersonator Roy Gonzales to the Paramount studios in Richmond, Indiana. The fiddler reconnected with the Gonzales family when he relocated to Crowley in the early 1930s (figure 6.4).

Drums solidified Cajun swing's 2/4 dance beat and harkened to jazz and popular American dance compositions. Soileau's implementation of mod-ern instrumentation was radical, not only in Cajun music, but revolution-ary within the American country music context. Like Western swing's first drummer, William "Smokey" Dacus, who played in Dixieland orchestras before joining Bob Wills's Texas Playboys in 1935, Tony Gonzales was at the absolute cutting edge of country music's modernization. "Smokey Dacus, the Playboys' first drummer," write historians Bill Malone and David Stricklin in *Southern Music/American Music*, "is commonly be-lieved to have been the first person to play such an instrument in coun-try music."[41] Although scholars recognize Dacus as the first drummer in country music, Tony Gonzales recorded with Soileau eight months before Dacus debuted in the Vocalion studios in Dallas, Texas, to record for the first time with Bob Wills on September 23, 1935. Indeed, Leo Soileau had already recorded with two different drummers before the celebrated

Figure 6.4. Leo Soileau's Four Aces novelty orchestra emphasized their affiliation with whiteness and respectability by dressing the part. Tony Gonzales, the first drumming to record with a Cajun band, sat behind his jazz kit for a rare group photo. Courtesy of Johnnie Allan.

Texas Playboy set foot into a recording studio. Considering that the Three Aces performed swinging string band compositions in the Wills style, albeit in French, and since academicians and the Grand Ole Opry widely acknowledge Cajun music as subcategory of country-and-western music, Tony Gonzales thus constitutes both the first Cajun drummer to record with a Cajun band, and the first drummer in country music history.[42]

On January 18, 1935, Leo Soileau and the Three Aces made Cajun music history by becoming the first ensemble to cut a Cajun-inflected Western swing recording and the first Cajun band to record with drums. This landmark New Orleans session produced eight titles on RCA's budget Bluebird label: "Si Voux Moi Voudrains Ame" (If You'd Only Love Me), "Le Gran Mamou," "Alons a Ville Platte" (Let's Go to Ville Platte), "Acout Vous Moi Lese" (When You Left Me), "Dites Moi Avant" (Tell Me Before), "Petit ou Gros" (Little or Big), "Hackberry Hop," and "La Valse de Gueydan." Before the session ended, executives shuffled the group slightly and featured lead guitarist Floyd Shreve singing two Jimmie Rodgers–influenced tunes, "Lonesome Blues" and "Darling of Yesterday." Bluebird released the issue as Floyd Shreve and the Three Aces among the label's mainstream hillbilly recordings. The Three Aces' efforts were well received in the Cajun community. Their version of the popular waltz "Jolie Blonde," released as "La Valse de Gueydan," was an instant success that prompted Bluebird to issue the record twice in their B-2000 Cajun series. Following the session, Soileau and the Three Aces resumed their place in the rotating dance hall circuit, performing steady two-week engagements at 14 different clubs in the vicinity of Crowley.

In May 1935, a revamped incarnation of the band (now called the Four Aces) brought their act to Chicago to record for budget record kingpin and Bluebird competitor Decca records.[43] The label had tapped into the Cajun market only five months earlier by recording Joe Falcon, Cleoma

Breaux Falcon, and Amédé Ardoin. In contrast, the Aces were such a departure from the sounds of the early commercial era that Soileau's experiment forced the befuddled engineer to anxiously and somewhat reluctantly devise a scheme to control the band's sound in the studio. Drums were still a novelty outside of jazz orchestras, and the Decca technician had never attempted to corral the overbearing sounds of a trap kit in a string band setting. Decca's engineer muffled the thunderous clamor of the snare and bass drum by building a wall of stacked pillows around the percussionist. The Four Aces recorded eight sides featuring Soileau on French vocal, and to satisfy the label's request for hillbilly material, Floyd Shreve offered "Acadian-flavoured renderings of 'My Brown Eyed Texas Rose', 'Little Dutch Mill', 'Birmingham Jail', 'My Wild Irish Rose' and other country and pop favorites of the day."[44] As Tony Russell observes, the English material recorded by the Four Aces at the Chicago session represented both a case of manipulation on the part of the label, which wanted several mainstream sides to issue in their 5000 hillbilly series, and Soileau's and Shreve's personal musical tastes, which extended well beyond the confines of traditional Cajun numbers. The bandleader prided himself on his diverse repertoire that catered to the ethnically diverse audience between southwest Louisiana and east Texas. "It's more music to it—to me," Soileau maintained, acknowledging the difference between country and Cajun. "You can play in different keys. That French music, it's just the one . . . just like that rock 'n' roll."[45] The commercial ramifications of these issues had a dramatic impact on the direction of the Cajun market as other swing outfits such as the Hackberry Ramblers, Alley Boys of Abbeville, Rayne-Bo Ramblers, Merrymakers, Sons of the Acadians, and Dixie Ramblers, and later Harry Choates followed suit and recorded for the Decca, Vocalion, and Bluebird labels. These national record companies capitalized on the region's evolving cultural landscape by capturing and marketing the dramatic, reverberating shifts in instrumentation, repertoire, and technique.

In the wake the Aces' initial and influential recordings, Soileau continued to revamp extensively the sounds of commercial Cajun music. "I had fiddle, piano, sometimes I had two guitars, a steel [guitar], electric mandolin, and saxophone [and] bass," Soileau recalled. "I have as much as eight piece bands."[46] In 1937, the bandleader renamed his ensemble the Rhythm Boys and performed between Lafayette, Louisiana, and Houston, Texas, playing for dancers, including oil field and shipyard laborers and mingling with the hottest names in Gulf Coast music, including Western swing prodigy Cliff Bruner, pioneer boogie pianist Moon Mullican, and country legend Jimmie Davis. The Rhythm Boys recorded two final sessions on February 20 and December 14, 1937, before retiring to a performing career in Cajun Country's honky-tonks, dance halls, and bars. Soileau's final sides shed some light on the direction of the group's musical tendencies and the song styles available to Cajun audiences in Bayou Country. Most of the songs waxed by the Rhythm Boys were French translations of hillbilly tunes, jazz, and popular arrangements such as Al Jolson's "Avalon," an apparent Cajun interpretation of the jazz standard "Liza Jane" rearranged as

"Chere Liza," and a French rendition of Jimmie Davis's "Nobody's Darlin' but Mine," released as "Personne N'Aime Pas." The final Rhythm Boys issues were part of an increasing number of Americanized Cajun releases by a variety of Cajun swing ensembles that frequently shifted instrumentation and personnel to keep in tune with the times.

Soileau constantly reinvented his sound by drawing from the resources available at his fingertips. During the 1940s, the bandleader introduced the chromatic piano accordion sound into Cajun swing as his Rhythm Boys remained in step with the latest developments in American country music. An accordion player identified simply as "Bill from the Ohio"—who was a regular performer in different incarnations of Soileau's later orchestras—infused into Cajun music the same Eastern European musical sensibilities that took root in the American Midwest and intersected with the evolving country-and-western scene in Nashville and on the West Coast. Peewee King, an accordion player from Abrams, Wisconsin, helped popularize the instrument as a leader of the Golden West Cowboys. Born Frank Kuczynski, the Polish American learned the accordion from his polka band–leading father before emerging as a front man in his own right. King's Cowboys enjoyed widespread popularity after joining WSM's Grand Ole Opry in June 1937, where he nationally disseminated the chromatic accordion sound and popularized the instrument in country-and-western music. California-based swing groups, especially Spade Cooley's ever-popular ensemble, recorded and broadcast regularly with accordionists in the wake of Western swing's western expansion. In neighboring Texas, the squeezebox thrived among Czech musicians living in rural enclaves and towns such as Shiner and Austin along the Cajun dance circuit, while conjunto musicians fused the instrument with Spanish-language arrangements in the southern half of the Lone Star State.[47] Closer to home, Jimmie Davis campaigned for governor across Louisiana between 1943 and 1944, including stops in Cajun Country, with Moon Mullican performing on piano accordion.[48] Although many Cajuns stowed their diatonic accordions during the Cajun swing era, Leo Soileau gravitated toward the marketable and easily accessible sounds of modern country during the late 1930s and 1940s in the fiddler's never-ending quest to expand his musical horizons. His excitement about contemporary music rubbed off on his colleagues within the Bayou Country's musical network.

Cajun Swing's Ambassadors

Soileau periodically visited relatives in Hackberry, Louisiana, and would call on Hackberry Rambler bandleader Luderin Darbone. "He was a good friend of mine," recalled Darbone, who savored the time the two musicians spent talking. The fiddlers shared mutual respect and influenced each other's sounds. "I had all his records," the Hackberry Rambler fiddler explained. "I'd try to learn his style," particularly on Soileau's traditional Cajun sides.[49] Darbone spent hours playing along with the recordings trying to copy Soileau's particular fiddling technique. Leo Soileau's issues ironically never broke into the general Southern and hillbilly markets like Hackberry Rambler arrangements, perhaps because of Darbone's intimate connection to Louisiana's industrialized economy.[50]

Luderin Darbone came of age in the region's oil patch. During the first three decades of the twentieth century, the uprooted Darbone family moved constantly between Louisiana and east Texas in response to the ebb and flow of the oil industry. He grew up with towering wooden derricks adorning his backyard and drillers, roustabouts, and roughnecks as surrogate family. Young Darbone also knew first hand the benefits of travel, transcending wage labor, disposable income, consumerism, and education, all of which were tied to his father's occupation, and all of which factored into Darbone's career as a bandleader. Luderin's Francophone parents realized through their affiliation with the Gulf Coast's industrialized petroleum culture that education and the English language were the keys to success in the modern world. The Darbones refused to speak French with their son, who later picked up some basic French grammar and vocabulary while enrolled in a Lake Charles business school during the Depression. As part of their son's formal education, the Darbone family bought their son a violin for his twelfth birthday and enrolled him in a correspondence course from the United States School of Music in New York City. Without an instructor to mimic, the curriculum forced the aspiring fiddler to quickly develop an ear for melody during his daily thirty-minute practices. He recalled, "I could learn a song from sheet music and play it by memory from then on. And I could also pick out songs that I heard on records or radio, or in person."[51] Darbone's classroom extended to the house dances he frequented as a youth in Orangefield, Texas. He watched and listened closely to the finest fiddlers in the east Texas oil patch, where classic hillbilly numbers such as "Ragtime Annie," "Over the Waves," and "Beaumont Rag" burned an imprint in the developing musician's mind. The fiddler's first real exposure to Cajun music came when his family relocated to Hackberry, Louisiana.

In March 1933, Darbone and Edwin Duhon, another young musician from a migrant oil field family, spent their spare time scratching out tunes in the Darbone family barn. The duet naturally fused the basic elements of Cajun swing during their impromptu afternoon jams. Duhon's repertoire was based almost exclusively in the Cajun tradition, while Darbone brought a pop sensibility and country styling to the collaboration. Guitarist Alvin Ellender soon joined the fold, and the three musicians dubbed themselves the Hackberry Ramblers. The string band played for spare change at small parties and dances while dreaming of becoming professional entertainers.

Darbone lived between two communities. He spent his weeks in Lake Charles studying at a local business college, and on the weekends, the fiddler traveled south to Hackberry and repeated the cycle again on Mondays when his father drove him back to school. Shortly after Darbone and Duhon founded the Hackberry Ramblers, the Beaumont, Texas–based radio station KFDM established a remote broadcasting station in the

Majestic Hotel in Lake Charles, about one block from Darbone's classes. He approached the station manager and explained that he had a band in Hackberry that played parties and occasional dances but were looking to expand their audience base over the radio. The station manager gave the band their first break by agreeing to give the trio a fifteen-minute radio spot on Monday mornings at 7:00 A.M. The ensemble subsequently became a popular fixture on KFDM. Darbone attributed the band's appeal to the group's diverse repertoire. "The listeners were tired of the accordion bands because most of them at that time were limited to a repertoire of Cajun waltz and breakdown tunes only," he explained.[52] The Hackberry Ramblers, on the other hand, played hillbilly numbers such as "Bonnie Blue Eyes," "Just Because," and "Corrine Corrina," as well as popular selections such as "Diana," "Tiger Rag," and "The Waltz You Saved for Me" and traditional Cajun compositions. Following a short stint in the radio band, Ellender decided to retire, and Duhon accepted an oil field job in South America, prompting the Ramblers to hire Floyd Rainwater, a gifted hillbilly singer, yodeler, and rhythm guitarist, and Cajun vocalist and guitarist Lennis Sonnier.

Radio ensured the Hackberry Ramblers' commercial viability by enhancing their public visibility and expanding their audience base. After only a few broadcasts, a dance hall owner from Basile, Louisiana, got in touch with the radio band and hired them to play his honky-tonk in April 1933. At intermission, the owner approached the bandstand and hired the group to a rotating two-week engagement, thereby bringing the ensemble's vision of becoming a professional band to fruition. Other engagements soon followed in and around Mamou, Ville Platte, Gueydan, Abbeville, and Crowley.

After the band relocated to Crowley, Louisiana, in 1935 to be centrally located among their audience base, Darbone learned that his colleague Leo Soileau had made several swing recordings for RCA/Victor's Bluebird subsidiary label. The Hackberry Rambler leader employed his education and business training to negotiate a recording contract. "So, I wrote to RCA, and I told them that I had a band and I'd like for them to audition us; and that we'd be real happy to record for them. They wrote me back and told me what date they were going to be in New Orleans. So we went up there. And they auditioned us and they recorded us right there."[53]

Luderin Darbone, guitarists Lennis Sonnier and Floyd Rainwater, and steel guitarist Lonnie Rainwater stood around a single microphone and played their first selection, the "Crowley Waltz," in the middle of a New Orleans hotel suite. In the studio, the band did not stray from the French interpretations of popular, hillbilly, and Cajun numbers that made them so popular on the radio and dance hall circuit. Their debut issues sold well enough that Bluebird continued to send correspondence every six months to notify the Ramblers of upcoming recording sessions in the Crescent City. The Hackberry Ramblers returned to the Bluebird studios six times between 1936 and 1938, with different incarnations of the string band as musicians such as Lennis Sonnier, former Three Ace guitarist and English

Figure 6.5. Guitarist Joe Werner's "Wondering" (1937) became the first Cajun recording to become part of the national repertoire when Webb Pierce reissued the song in 1951. Courtesy of the Freeland Archives, Acadia Parish Library, Crowley, Louisiana.

vocalist Floyd Shreve, and crooner Joe Werner oscillated between ensembles within the Crowley area's musical network.[54]

Joe Werner was easily the most famous Depression-era musician to perform with the Ramblers (figure 6.5). Werner charmed audiences. The talented multi-instrumentalist played guitar and harmonica and whistled with an unusual embouchure that gave the illusion that he was smiling. The performer became an important component in the success of the Hackberry Rambler side project, the Riverside Ramblers. The ensemble capitalized on Werner's ability to sing English numbers when they returned to New Orleans for their second Bluebird session on February 22, 1937. The band recorded 10 selections: six French and instrumental sides as the Hackberry Ramblers, and four English numbers, including the ensemble's biggest hit, "Wondering," as the Riverside Ramblers.

Like a significant portion of the Ramblers' repertoire, their most popular release was an aggregate of the extraneous influences permeating Acadiana's cultural borders. During the Depression, Joe Werner stumbled across a singing drifter in Rayne, Louisiana. The two musicians exchanged stories and songs, including an offering from the hobo called "Wondering." Werner memorized the lyrics and melody to the relaxed country waltz and later suggested the Ramblers record the song when he joined Darbone's ensemble. The band promptly incorporated the composition as part of their English repertoire and realized a hit when Bluebird issued the record in their hillbilly catalogue. The recording industry took note.

A Decca representative trekked to Crowley, where he found Darbone at his Hackberry Rambler Service Station. The artist and repertory man worked to convince the bandleader to leave Bluebird and sign with his firm. Darbone replied, "RCA has been real good to us. They call us every time to come to New Orleans to make records. . . . I don't feel like I should leave."[55] Joe Werner was not so loyal. A week later, Joe told Luderin he was quitting the band and moving to Decca, who swiftly copyrighted the tune in Werner's name and escorted the guitarist into their Chicago studios. Joe Werner and His Ramblers never achieved the same measure of success that he had enjoyed with the Hackberry and Riverside Ramblers, though his popular arrangement maintained wide circulation.[56]

Despite their differences with Werner, the Hackberry Ramblers enjoyed continued success in the Cajun Lapland between east Texas and western Louisiana. By the early 1940s, the ensemble's maturing orchestral sound included drums to provide a firm danceable backbeat. The Ramblers found regular work in Creole, Louisiana, until the whole band—steel guitarist Jack Theriot, rhythm guitarist Minos Broussard, and drummer Crawford Vincent—was drafted into military service, with the exception of Darbone, at the onset of World War II. Left without a band, Darbone reunited with founding Hackberry Rambler Edwin Duhon and added guitarist Eddie Shuler, bass fiddler Chink Widcamp, mandolin player Jim Gentry, and trumpeter Neal Roberts, performing three nights a week in clubs around Lake Charles, frequently catering to soldiers from the Camp Claiborne Army Base. After the war, the orchestra became the house band at the Silver Star Club between Sulphur and Lake Charles and stayed for a 10-year stint between 1946 and 1956. Although the band's size and sound fluctuated as they experimented with piano players and saxophonists to accompany Robert's trumpet, their influence resonated well beyond repertoire and instrumentation, as evidenced by groups within their cohort who adopted the Rambler moniker.

Rambling Orchestras and Spit-Shined Swing

The itinerant rambler is both a prevalent theme in country music and one of the most fashionable band names. According to country music historian Bill Malone, the term is a metaphor for the unbridled masculine preoccupation with freedom from the conventions of traditional Southern society. In a musical context, this elusive personal freedom allowed men to indulge a thirst for strong drink, life on the open road, gambling, and fast women in lieu of responsibility and respectability.[57] Southern songwriters have long toyed with the notion of the unruly rambler who risks everything to escape the stresses associated with manual labor, animal husbandry, and fatherhood. The theme first appeared in the early Cajun commercial documentary record in issues such as Dennis McGee's "Blues de Texas" (Texas Blues) and Amédé Breaux's "Les Tracas du Hobos" (The Hobo's Troubles). By the 1930s, the theme became a reality for itinerant professional entertainers, including the Hackberry Ramblers, the Rayne-Bo Ramblers, and the Dixie Ramblers, who traveled from dance hall to dance hall, recording session to recording session in such exotic, faraway places as New York City, Chicago, Memphis, and San Antonio. These groups openly acknowledged their transient lifestyle and the shared contexts that connected local musicians to current trends in country-and-western by christening themselves "ramblers," while, ironically, simultaneously marketing their entertainment and occupation as respectable.

No one in Cajun music seemed to be able to navigate the fine line separating respectability and impropriety, or rambling and community service, while anticipating shifts in Cajun music like charismatic Rayne-Bo Rambler bandleader "Happy Fats" LeBlanc. As a result, his ensemble became one of Cajun swing's most prolific and influential outfits. During the guitarist and bass player's long and winding career, Happy Fats became well versed in the vagabond lifestyle often associated with musicians as he earned his stripes as a rambling man. The consummate showman hit the campaign trail with Louisiana Governor Jimmie Davis, recorded racially charged material for Jay Miller's segregationist label "Reb Rebel," and issued promotional material for Dudley LeBlanc's infamous Hadacol snake oil. He performed on the *Louisiana Hayride, Grand Ole Opry*, and *Amos 'n' Andy* radio broadcasts, cowrote songs with Hank Williams, Sr., and Ernest Tubb, and became a television personality on a local Cajunized interpretation of "Hee Haw." All of LeBlanc's salient contributions to Cajun music history grew from the legacy of his famous prewar string band.

The evolution of the Rayne-Bo Ramblers, named for LeBlanc's native Rayne, Louisiana, paralleled Cajun swing's maturation before the group disbanded in 1941. From its first incarnation as a rudimentary trio featuring fiddler Norris Savoy and Warnest Schexyder and Happy Fats on guitar, the Cajun swing band developed into a polished six-, sometimes seven-piece orchestra that included piano, banjo, steel guitar, upright bass, and washboard. LeBlanc taught himself to play guitar with the help of hungry drifters who exchanged a chord or two for a round meal. The musician divulged to music writer John Broven in 1979, "If I'd see a hobo or something with a guitar, I'd go pick him up and bring him home, give him dinner. Maybe learn a few chords with him. Then there was a colored boy here in town that I learned a lot from, a fellow by the name of [Clarence] Locksley."[58] American popular music profoundly affected the young musician, who drew inspiration from the collective works of Jimmie Rodgers, the Light Crust Doughboys, and Bob Wills and His Texas Playboys. "I more or less copied them," he explained, "but Jimmie Rodgers was my favorite."[59] Like other Cajun swing outfits, the Rayne-Bo Rambler repertoire represented an amalgam of traditional Cajun material, blues, jazz, American popular music, and hillbilly to satisfy the ever-increasing sophistication of the dance community's tastes.

During the band's six-year life span (1935–1941), the swing orchestra waxed an impressive 63 sides (not all released) at six different Bluebird sessions, making the Rayne-Bo Ramblers one of Acadiana's most prolific recording outfits, after Leo Soileau and the Hackberry Ramblers, in either the early commercial or Cajun swing eras.[60] Their first foray into the recording studio took place on August 10, 1935. Happy Fats, Warnest Schexnyder, and Norris Savoy offered their services as a studio band for Nathan Abshire and as a featured string trio that performed both Cajun and hillbilly music.

In 1935, both the Ramblers and Cajun swing were in an embryonic commercial form that hinted at the style's fertile potential. Following in the footsteps of the Three Aces and Hackberry Ramblers, Happy Fats toyed with the notion of employing two guitars to expand the dynamics and potential of Cajun music's humble preswing rhythm section. As these early recordings illustrate, the result equated to boisterous glissando and powerful rhythmic strumming during fast numbers. The polished and re-fined orchestral sounds for which the Ramblers and Cajun swing became famous developed with the expansion of personnel and instrumentation.

"J'ai le pays dans une jogue, bouchon dans ma main" [I have the world in a jug of liquor, and the cork in my hand], began the metaphorical first verse of the Rayne-Bo Rambler recording "Les Blues de Bosco," waxed during the group's second foray into the studio on September 10, 1937. The vivid lyrics—borrowed from blues singer Bessie Smith's "Down-hearted Blues" and Jimmie Rodgers's "Anniversary Blue Yodel (Blue Yodel Number 7)"—complemented the Rodgers-styled blues arrangement.[61] The group's initial trio recordings paled in complexity and maturity compared to the arrangement. By their second recording session on September 10, 1937, LeBlanc and Norris Savoy more than doubled the size of the original Ramblers by recruiting fiddler Moïse Sonnier, steel guitarist Roy Romero, former Hackberry Rambler Joe Werner, washboard player Louis Arce-neaux, and guitarist Eric Arceneaux. The enlarged rhythm section stroked out a 12-bar blues that cradled the melodic voices of the fiddle and vocal, while Arceneaux's abrasive washboard playing provided a brilliant treble dynamic that complemented Werner's fluttering blue-note whistle. These extra voices gave a volume and substance to the string band that rounded out the sound on their commercial sides.

The Rayne-Bo Ramblers brought their refined orchestrated arrange-ments to the Bluebird studios four more times between 1938 and 1941. By the late 1930s, the band's evolving rhythm section had mastered the swinging 2/4 backbeat employed by Western swing outfits, despite the en-semble's numerous personnel changes. Three recordings from the band's final sessions stand out as representative illustrations of the polish and urbanity inherent in Cajun swing just before World War II: "Les Escrives Dan Platin" (Crawfish in the Pond), "Les Tete Fille Lafayette" (Girls from Lafayette), and "Les Veuve de la Coulee" (The Widows from the Gully).

"Les Escrives Dan Platin" and "Les Tit Filles de Lafayette" embody the synthetic nature of Cajun swing. Both songs contain a unique blend of Cajun fiddling, Western swing, jazz backbeats, solo "takeoffs," and tight Southern gospel harmonies rendered as French choruses. On April 2, 1938, Happy Fats brought six musicians to the label's makeshift shift sound room in the New Orleans St. Charles Hotel, where Oran "Doc" Guidry's smooth fiddling and Robert Thibodeaux's swinging stride piano solos carried the band through several sophisticated arrangements such as "Les Escrives Dan Platin." While instrumental "takeoffs" had become a prominent component of the swing sound, harmony vocals as heard in the Anglo South were a rare phenomenon in the Cajun repertoire. LeBlanc and the Ramblers reemployed the stylistic innovation two years later at a Bluebird session in Dallas, Texas.

On February 14, 1940, the Ramblers replaced "Doc" Guidry in the recording studio with a young talent named Harry Choates, a teenage veteran of the Gulf Coast music circuit and a former member of Leo Soileau's Aces. The youthful fiddler took the band's musical aptitude to new heights, particularly in the group's arrangements of "Les Tete Fille Lafayette" and "Les Veuve de la Coulee." In their ode to the belles of Lafayette, the Ramblers expanded on the arranging style employed during their recording "Les Escrives Dan Platin" by emphasizing vocal harmonies, dramatic pauses, and fiddle and steel guitar breaks. The rhythm section's bouncing 2/4 backbeat, Choates' cascading fiddle runs, and Ray Clark's bright steel guitar accents painted a jovial musical backdrop for the romantic lyrics to "Les Tete Fille Lafayette," which describe a bachelor's paradise at a Lafayette dance.

At the same session, the Ramblers recorded a Cajun interpretation of Bob Wills' "Faded Love" reframed as "La Veuve de la Coulee." The band increased the tempo and replaced the original Texas swing lyrics with a French tale about widows who "go to town to buy yellow cotton material to make their own bloomers."[62] Choates' fiddle stole the show. He replaced the languid long-bow sound employed by the Texas Playboys with his own agitated Cajun short-bow technique, thereby completely altering the character of the composition. Like the Hackberry Ramblers' "Wondering," "La Veuve de la Coulee" struck a chord with record buying audiences. In 1942, the record became a national "Hit of the Week." Happy Fats explained in an interview with music writer John Broven, "The 'Hit of the Week' I understand was a record that had sold 10,000 in the first week. We had no way of knowing the amount of records sold. As a matter of fact, we were doing them for cash, there were no royalty deals at all." LeBlanc continued, "In the 1942 edition of some big radio book they put out, we had an ad in there. Our picture came out along with people like the Sons of the Pioneers."[63] The Rayne-Bo Ramblers' highly polished sound and Cajunized interpretations of the popular musical landscape allowed the orchestra to cross over into the American mainstream, where Cajun swing found validation alongside some of the nation's most influential artists.

The Dixie Ramblers' career followed a parallel trajectory. The group began as an accordion-based ensemble that kept pace with the changing musical landscape, before evolving into a swing orchestra. Fiddler Hector Duhon began playing on a homemade cigar-box fiddle at the age of 10. After mastering the contraption's mechanics, he learned to play "Tu es Petite, Tu es Mignonne"—the same song popularized by Dudley and James Fawvor in 1929—and eventually organized a dance band during the early commercial era. In 1930, Duhon's ensemble regrouped when accordionist Octa Clark resigned as the band's popularity and commercial viability increased. "Since he used a [horse and] buggy," folklorist Nicholas Spitzer maintains, "Mr. Octa was less able to travel to dances when the popularity of the group called for jobs as far away as Texas."[64]

After performing at a band contest in Midland, a Vermilion Parish hamlet, a priest approached the group to perform a private dance. The clergyman had one stipulation: that the group would perform as a string band. The band obliged and never looked back. Hector Duhon played lead fiddle, Hector Stutes joined the group as second violin, and guitarists Jesse Duhon and Willie Vincent provided rhythmic support. Duhon remembered, "People convinced us we should just have fiddles and guitars." The band intimately understood that their marketability and longevity rested on the group's ability to satisfy public demand and the evolving community aesthetic.

> We played some French waltzes still, but also pop music like "High Society." We played a lot of Jimmie Rodgers' songs which Willie Vincent would sing. I would harmonize on these and sing some myself back then. You can see how we looked in our uniform picture in 1933. It was around the same time that the Hackberry Ramblers and Leo Soileau had started bands like this.[65]

Like other string bands, the Dixie Ramblers had trouble maintaining any kind of volume at crowded and noisy dances. Following in the Hackberry Ramblers' footsteps, Duhon commissioned local radio repairmen Joe Latour and the Bailey Brothers to build an amplification system that included a crystal microphone, speakers housed in custom-built wooden boxes, an amplifier, and a generator that ran off of Duhon's idling Dodge.[66]

The Ramblers' dance hall career acted as a springboard into the recording studio. They made their way to Eli Oberstien's Bluebird recording facilities in New Orleans on two separate occasions—August 10, 1935, and again on February 19, 1936. "I never forget," Duhon remembered, "we was on the bus and goin' over there and we sat in the back seat. We had been at a dance that night and it was late. We had had a few drinks so we started playing. Man, we had the whole bus full of people clapping with the music! The road was bad, mostly dirt and gravel in those days so we passed the time to New Orleans that way."[67] The string band recorded a total of 15 sides, although only 12 were released, consisting of hillbilly-inflected tunes such as "Barroom Blues," "I Got a Gal," "Put on Your Old Grey Bonnet," and "Dixie's Hottest," their best rendition of "High Society." Their intentionally anglicized recordings represented one extreme of the Cajun swing spectrum that musically and linguistically represents the Anglo-American undercurrents that shaped Depression-era Cajun music. Like many Cajuns, particularly those on an upwardly mobile socioeconomic trajectory, the Dixie Ramblers displayed a secure command of their second language.

Other groups such as the Merrymakers and the Alley Boys of Abbeville also performed Americanized Cajun swing compositions but felt more comfortable translating English songs into their native French. In the mid-1930s, fiddler Jean Batiste "J. B." Fuselier joined tenor banjoist Beethoven Miller and guitarist Preston Manuel to form Miller's Merrymakers. The swing ensemble recorded exclusively for the Bluebird label at four different sessions between 1936 and 1938 in New Orleans. When Miller left the ensemble in early 1938, the fiddler stepped forward and renamed the group J. B. Fuselier and the Merrymakers for their last two recording ventures. Fuselier's vocal stylings and fiddle technique and the trio's preference for Cajun material provided them with solid footing in indigenous Louisiana material and thus shifted their sound slightly toward the traditional folkloric terminus of the Cajun musical spectrum. To satisfy public demand, however, the Merrymakers relied on Manuel's command of English for popular material. The guitarist translated "Corinne, Corrina" and "Birmingham Jail," while Fuselier offered the regionally popular "Chère Tout-Toute" and "Ma Chère Bassette," written about J. B.'s wife Regina Fontenot.[68]

Though the band steered toward traditional Cajun musical expression, their instrumental arrangements and vocal delivery carried the synthetic mark of hillbilly and Western swing on occasion in the form of harmonizing and yodeling. Neither vocal delivery was characteristic of the singing technique employed during the early commercial era. Rather, Merrymaker recordings such as "Ma Chere Vieux Masion Dan Swet" (1938) set to the melody of "Dear Old Sunny South by the Sea" provides a succinct example of both harmony and yodeling within the Cajun idiom. The group continued to perform and record well after World War II, in contrast to their short-lived contemporaries, the Alley Boys of Abbeville.

The Alley Boys were regulars in dance halls and roadhouses in south central Louisiana, where they performed their brand of swing with twin rhythm guitars, drums, a National steel guitar played in the style of a Hawaiian lap steel, and lead fiddle. Keeping in step with current trends in Cajun music, the Abbeville outfit modernized their sound by employing a rudimentary public address system that operated off of a car battery during performances featuring French renditions of mainstream American tunes. In addition to maintaining club dates, the band found work on KVOL. The Tuff-Nutt Company sponsored the group's weekly broadcast, though the business could only provide the group with uniforms as payment. "You have no idea how bad times were in South Louisiana, around 1938–1939," explained guitarist Sidney Guidry. "Man, times were tough and although Tuff-Nut didn't pay us, we were happy to have the clothes."[69]

The ensemble recorded at only one session on June 30, 1939. Murphy Guidry, Frank Mailhes, and Sidney Guidry traveled to the label's regional recording facilities in Memphis, Tennessee, where the group waxed French interpretations of tunes such as "What's the Use" (1930), written by popular composers Charles Newman and Isham Jones of "It Had to Be You" fame, and the standards "Do You Ever Think of Me" (1920) and "Tu Peux Pas Me Faire Ca" (You Can't Put That Monkey on My Back) recorded that same year by the old-time music duet the Shelton Brothers. The Alley Boys mixed up the session with a French version of Bob Wills's "I Wonder If You Feel the Way I Do," "Tu Ma Quite Seul," apparently based on Vernon Dalhart's hillbilly recording "Prisoner's Song," and several Cajun numbers.[70] The ensemble's only recording session on June 30, 1939, rendered six cross-pollinated Vocalion releases before the Alley Boys of Abbeville slipped into obscurity.

Cajun swing broadened the possibility of musical expression in south Louisiana. The style threw the door to improvisation wide open and linked Cajun music to the Gulf Coast's developing industrial economy Musicians like Leo Soileau, who worked to transcend traditional musical idioms while embarking on a career as a professional entertainer, made conscious decisions to capitalize upon the opportunities available in the industrialized world. Indeed, Cajun swing became the springboard that led several musicians out of cotton fields. Yet, swing was also born of an industrialized world where a culture of respectability intertwined with social mobility. To achieve respectability, Cajun musicians strove for economic independence, orderliness, cleanliness, and style, and in the case of Luderin Darbone, education, as well. Never without a collared shirt and tie, Darbone was equally comfortable playing for roughnecks and roustabouts in a dance hall as he was writing letters to RCA/Victor in hopes of getting a recording contract. Though Soileau and Darbone hailed, respectively, from agrarian and industrial backgrounds, the two fiddlers shared a common vision based on a passion for modern music and a desire to achieve a certain level of respectability for their art.

Cajun swing evolved in exponential increments between 1933 and 1950, slowly "cooling off" with each evolutionary step in accordance with trends in jazz and Western swing. When the Great Depression virtually destroyed the race record market, curtailing hot jazz issues by African-American ensembles, white big bands that played what music writer H. F. Mooney called a "highly refined, quasi-'classical' jazz" moved in to fill the void and dominated American popular music by World War II.[71] Slick Western swing outfits such Spade Cooley's West Coast orchestra featured smooth arrangements that paralleled the pendulum shift in jazz. Jazz-oriented music such as big band orchestration, Texas swing, and Cajun swing all evolved in unison with the ebb and flow of American musical currents.

At the style's inception, small Cajun string trios that married, sometimes awkwardly, the hot sounds emanating from New Orleans jazz, Texas swing, Cajun fiddling techniques, and musical aesthetics during the early 1930s eventually gave way to substantial orchestras whose cool polished approach mimicked the palatable big band arrangements popularized by Benny Goodman's, Paul Whiteman's, and Glenn Miller's wartime orchestras. Leo Soileau's first few swing recording sessions in 1935 and 1936 documented a sort of cold fusion that anxiously synthesized American and Cajun musical traditions, particularly when session drummers clumsily negotiated their position within the string band arrangement. Tension between the conservative and dynamic tendencies in Cajun swing as heard in the Rayne-Bo Ramblers' first recordings featuring accordionist Nathan Abshire dissipated over time as musicians discovered how to balance these forces. By the end of the 1930s, Soileau's Aces, the Hackberry Ramblers, and the Rayne-Bo Ramblers realized the potential articulation points between seemingly dissimilar forms of American music.

The Hackberry Ramblers' issue "A Little Rendezvous in Honolulu" exemplifies the art of combining Cajun music with the latest trends in American music. In the wake of the Hawaiian craze that swept across America during the 1920s and 1930s, Bluebird's artist and repertory man Eli Oberstein asked Luderin Darbone to develop an arrangement for this novelty song for a recording session in 1936. The fiddler explained, "Eli sent me the sheet music, and we worked it up with Floyd Rainwater singing lead. I think it came out pretty good. It was different for us in several ways, because Oberstein usually wanted us to record peppy numbers."[72] The Rayne-Bo Rambler release "Les Tit Fille de Lafayette" also represents a high point during the Cajun swing era. Happy Fats LeBlanc and his string band combined French lyrics with Southern gospel harmonies and jazzy fiddle breaks (figure 6.6). The arrangement was sophisticated, urbane, and absolutely cosmopolitan, just like the musicians and culture from which the music sprang.

Cajun swing was perhaps the most dynamic musical expression in the history of Cajun music. Fiddlers, guitarists, steel guitarists, drummers, piano accordionists, and banjo and mandolin pickers all drew inspiration from the eclectic array of commercial musical styles available at local record stores, emitting from household battery-operated radios, and via the touring groups and jazz orchestras that provided entertainment at local clubs and honky-tonks. Like Western swing, the genre helped redefine the rural Southern experience, an experience based on interaction and exchange. Varied cultural currents flowed freely throughout the Bayou Country. Individuals only had to reach out to access the cultural innovations and mass culture available at their fingertips.

Figure 6.6. Cajun swing instrumentation revolutionized local music though the musical vision of individuals such as bassist "Happy Fats" LeBlanc and steel guitarist "Papa Cairo" Lamperez. Courtesy of the Center for Louisiana Studies, University of Louisiana at Lafayette.

7

Cajun National Anthem

In the winter of 1946, the Silver Slipper, a combination rural grocery store and barroom, buzzed with the sounds of local and popular music emanating from the establishment's jukebox. Located between Leonville and Arnaudville, the Silver Slipper served as a gathering place for local sharecroppers and Cajun GIs returning from World War II, who preferred drowning the horrors of the war to returning to the cotton fields.

Eleven-year-old Hadley Castille frequented the grocery with his family, particularly during the work lulls that followed the cotton harvest in the late fall and winter months. On one of his visits, the boy encountered a song that would forever change his life. The Silver Slipper's owner had stocked the bar's jukebox with a stunning new rendition of a local favorite, "Jole Blon" by Cajun fiddle sensation Harry Choates. The magical waltz engaged all of Castille's senses from the second he walked into the store. "I can't describe the feeling I got," he remembered fifty-seven years later. "I mean, it's hard to describe how it struck me."[1]

"Jole Blon" captivated not only Castille's imagination but the imagination of an entire generation. Cajuns who experienced the World War II era vividly recall the first time they heard "Jole Blon" with the same remarkable clarity as Americans who remember the precise moment they first heard about the assassination of President John F. Kennedy. "The first time I heard 'Jole Blon' from [Choates'] band was on the radio," recalled Norris Melancon, a longtime Harry Choates fan from Acadia Parish. "I'll never forget. It was on a Saturday."[2]

"If you've ever heard that song, that original 1946 recording, I guarantee you, you will never forget," explained acclaimed Louisiana author James Lee Burke, whose obsession with the plaintive tune became the inspiration for his 2002 novel, *Jolie Blon's Bounce*. "It stays with you the rest of your life. And you don't have to speak French to understand the tragic content of the words."[3] The ethereal fiddle work, the acoustics of the recording studio, and the haunting chord progression of the waltz burned

Figure 7.1. Fiddler and vocalist Harry Choates' interpretation of "Jole Blon" entrenched Cajun music into the American imagination. Courtesy of Johnnie Allan.

an indelible impression into the minds of many other south Louisianians. Castille remembers, "I mean there's spots where the D note and the piano chord comes together. It's like," he continued, "you've never heard that before! And people who were buying the record. They didn't know why. It was that sound that had never been played before." Harry Choates' "Jole Blon" quickly became a national phenomenon and represents the artistic apex of the Cajun swing era (figure 7.1).

Choates' interpretation of "Jole Blon" is arguably the single most important recording in the history of Cajun music. Unlike any other Cajun composition, "Jole Blon" evolved in different directions simultaneously on the local, regional, and national levels. Choates' recording also had an advantage over previous Cajun releases, because it emerged during a critical moment in history when tremendous social changes and technological advances converged. New recording technologies, the impact of a nationwide communications network, the unprecedented artistic freedom afforded by new independent record labels, and the tremendous cultural repercussions of World War II collectively created a catalyst for the song's commercial success. While Joe and Cleoma Falcon's debut release "Lafayette" changed the way Cajuns viewed their own music, the record's impact was largely limited to a regional audience. The Hackberry Ramblers' "Wondering," on the other hand, enjoyed a warm reception throughout the South, but the English-language tune never achieved the immortality of Choates' waltz.

Cajuns such as Choates broadened the scope of their influence by exploiting the region's new mass media outlets. Fledgling independent record labels and local radio increased the density of communication networks between Texas and Louisiana, a cultural phenomenon that dramatically expanded Cajun music's reach. "Jole Blon" spread through the channels carved by mass culture, transcended regional boundaries, and eventually changed the course of American music. Cajun music subsequently became a fixture in the American consciousness for the first time as the French tune crossed cultural, ethnic, racial, and socioeconomic boundaries. In the wake of the song's tremendous commercial success, French and English versions of waltz cropped up around the country. Commercial success equated to cultural validation for a denigrated working-class culture and potential economic opportunities on a national playing field for regional Cajun artists. In effect, Harry Choates opened the door for musicians from the Cajun Lapland, including crossover artists such as Jimmy C. Newman and Doug and Rusty Kershaw. Newman and the Kershaws might never have found fame beyond Cajun Country on Shreveport's nationally syndicated *Louisiana Hayride* radio program without the impact of "Jole Blon." Likewise, east Texas musicians, who shared in Choates' interstate legacy, followed suit and capitalized on the waltz's commercial potential. The song's influence also became a critical impetus in the evolution of independent record labels along the Gulf Coast. This phenomenon jump-started accordionist Iry LeJeune's recording career, marking the birth of Cajun honky-tonk and the return of accordion-based music in south Louisiana's commercial musical landscape. Independent record labels in Bayou Country provided Cajuns a communications outlet as major labels abandoned or ignored niche markets—Cajun music included.[4] The tune's national popularity stirred the imagination of the country's top musicians. For instance, as music writer Kevin Coffey argues, American icon Hank Williams Sr.'s Cajun-influenced hit "Jambalaya" is rooted in the fertile cross-cultural musical legacy created in the wake of the plaintive waltz. Indeed, Harry Choates and "Jole Blon" together constitute the exclamation point marking the zenith of the Cajun swing era.

In essence, "Jole Blon" represents a bizarre dance between Cajuns and American popular culture.[5] Cajun interpretations of the tune engaged the ethnic groups' attitudes and relationship with Anglo-American culture. The central character in the song's lyrics is blond, an "exotic" personage within the overwhelmingly brunette Cajun population. The female protagonist "Jole Blon" may represent the archetypal Anglo-American—a fair-skinned blond—though Choates never made reference to the character's ethnicity or cultural affiliation. In contrast, Anglo adaptations of the waltz portray the woman in a similar light, though she becomes the exotic ethnic "Other" who lives in a French world on the periphery of Anglo-America. Over time, the song developed multiple layers of significance determined by the context in which the song was placed. As "Jole Blon" twisted and turned along its evolutionary path and became part of the American musical repertoire, the tune transcended its original Cajun cultural context and evolved with each Anglo-American adaptation. Peeling back the layers of history and meaning that the song accumulated on its way toward becoming a classic in the American songbook is key to understanding the complexities of "Jole Blon"—or the "Cajun national anthem." Three analytical themes drive the arguments that follow. A contextual interpretation of the song's evolution in Cajun Country leads into the tensions between Cajuns and their Anglo-American counterparts as English-language versions began to circulate within the Cajun Lapland. Conflicting Cajun and Anglo-American mores structured the song's transformation from a regional Cajun sensation to a national phenomenon. The last component of this study considers the most negative and stereotypical aspect of non-Cajun variants of the Cajun national anthem: depictions of the tune's central character, labeled as "Jole" in Anglo interpretations of the Cajun waltz, that reveals an Anglo-Protestant view of ethnic groups associated with poverty and sexual deviance.

Unlike other crossover Cajun-Country tunes such as "Grand Texas" and "Colinda," "Jole Blon" exploded across the nation. Americans embraced the novelty of the Louisiana waltz. Cajuns, on the other hand, viewed the song's popularity as positive validation contrasting the prejudice that often underscored relationships between Francophones and Anglophones. The composition's enormous popularity along the Gulf Coast and in the United States coincided with the nation's blossoming ethnic consciousness.

Harry Choates recorded "Jole Blon" on the heels of an American musical and social revolution. Dramatic shifts in the United States' racial and ethnic distribution during first half of the twentieth century affected the dynamics of America's perception of ethnicity, as Southerners, both white and black, migrated to urban centers in the North and West. The U.S. involvement in World War II expanded the country's economic, technological, and social infrastructures.[6] After the war, the voice of ethnic and working-class America found new audiences thanks to hundreds of independent record labels opening for business across the United States. Cajuns became part of the national trend. Choates' recording of "Jole Blon" offered non-Cajun listeners an exotic slice of America that synthesized the sounds of established popular music genres like Western swing and hillbilly with the emotive intensity of French Louisiana. As many Americans consumed indigenous music issued by local labels following World War II, a new generation of musicians cultivated new audiences for their art.

Of all the Cajun songs recorded during the early commercial and Cajun swing eras, "Jole Blon" was perhaps the most improbable recording to achieve any notable measure of success. Although the Cajun community embraced the song in a variety of forms, the potential for any sort of national exposure seemed nil until Choates' rendition of the tune rode the crest of a cultural tidal wave generated by the nation's post-World War II independent record label boom and the nationalization of Southern music.[7] The "Jole Blon" sensation is indeed a case of "right place, right time." Five major catalysts collectively produced the waltz's success: (1) the initial 1929 Breaux family recording generated strong demand for the song within the Cajun community, a demand continuously reinforced by subsequent Cajun string band interpretations; (2) an obscure Houston-based independent record label provided a commercial outlet for Cajun music, particularly for Harry Choates, who had already refined his interpretation of "Jole Blon" in clubs around south Louisiana and east Texas; (3) the increased availability of radios and the greater reach of radio stations, as well as the emergence of jukeboxes along the Gulf Coast; (4) national record distribution for Choates' 1946 recording; (5) and remakes by non-Cajuns, many of whom were nationally acclaimed recording artists. The "Jole Blon" phenomenon began in Cajun Country before the song's popularity and influence diffused throughout America.

"Jole Blon" in Cajun Country

The composition's rise to commercial prominence began on April 18, 1929, in Atlanta, Georgia, where Amédé Breaux, Ophy Breaux, and Cleoma Breaux recorded "Ma Blonde Est Parti" for Columbia records. Ophy's droning fiddle and Amédé's haunting vocals captured the melancholy and vulnerability that underscored the harsh reality of working-class life in south Louisiana before the Great Depression. However, the origins of the Breaux arrangement are somewhat sketchy. According to Cajun fiddler Wade Fruge (b. 1916), the melody is much older than the initial 1929 commercial recording. Fruge explained to Ann Savoy: "We'd play 'Jolie Blonde' and all that . . . that's old. But they didn't call that 'Jolie Blonde.' They'd call it, like, the 'Courville Waltz' or the 'Savoy Waltz' or the "Fruge Two-Step.' They didn't have no names for them songs. They played them all. And my grandpa learned them from people before him. That makes them about 200 years old."[8] Amédé Breaux apparently blended the traditional melody with contemporary lyrics about infidelity and lost love composed by his sister Cleoma.[9] Dance bands, some of whom learned the song from their gramophone records, established the song's position in Cajun's core repertoire by performing "Ma Blonde Est Parti" on a regular basis. The haunting waltz's popularity extended well into the mid-1930s, prompting musicologist Irène Thérèse Whitfield to include the song in her subsequent study *Louisiana French Folk Song*.[10]

The Breaux family performed "Ma Blonde Est Parti" in traditional courtship settings—at both *bals de maison* and dance halls—where chaperones scrupulously regulated the public display of sexual behavior, a trend that lasted until the 1950s in some rural Cajun communities. Girls attended dances in groups chaperoned by attentive family members. Married women supervised their daughters both at dances and at home when a suitor called. Young men of marriageable age could visit the home of his sweetheart only during a supervised scheduled appointment, which ended promptly before sundown. Most Cajuns did not enjoy the freedom to marry at will. Courtship and ultimately marriage only came with the permission of the young woman's parents.[11] Indeed, working-class Cajun restrictions concerning sexuality were more stringent than mainstream

American mores. Cajun courtship rituals, however, evolved rapidly with the introduction of automobiles through industrialization and subsequent Americanization of the twentieth century.

In 1935, Leo Soileau transformed the eerie ballad into a string band arrangement under the title "La Valse de Gueydan" during the first Cajun swing recording session. He, too, remodeled earlier renditions—borrowing from the Breaux Family's "Ma Blond Est Parti" and John Bertrand's Paramount release "Valse de Gueydan" recorded in 1929 during the early commercial era. He created a slightly up-tempo fiddle-based waltz. Soileau's lyrical narrative maintained the same trajectory as earlier versions, as he recounted the tale of a heart-broken man forever losing his only love, who is affectionately identified as *jolie* (pretty). His shrill sustained vocal attack and sharp fiddle work provided the blueprint for Choates' version a decade later.

In 1936, the Hackberry Ramblers forever altered the song's identity by renaming the tune "Jolie Blond," a reference to the protagonist's lost love.[12] The Ramblers' swing version of the tune became a crowd favorite. During battle-of-the-bands competitions held at the Silver Star Club in Sulphur, Louisiana, the group often won contests against rival Texas-based string bands by simply striking up their French version of "Jolie Blonde." Hackberry Rambler Edwin Duhon recalls performing opposite a number of popular musicians, including Moon Mullican and T. "Texas" Tyler, "and we'd play 'Jolie Blond.' They'd count how many dancers. We'd win every time. Cliff Bruner, same way. We just beat the shit out of him."[13]

Just as the Cajun waltz's popularity escalated, automobiles ushered in a sexual revolution in Depression-era Louisiana that shifted cultural attitudes toward courtship in the Bayou State. The region's evolving moral standards are directly linked to Americanization—the process of interpreting and adapting mainstream Anglo-American culture and values. Like the mainstream popular music embraced by Cajun families, motorized vehicles altered local worldviews by connecting the Cajun community to distant locales and contemporary trends. A family's socioeconomic status and ability to purchase vehicles determined the fate of young lovers. Those who could afford automobiles enjoyed unprecedented mobility and sexual freedom, as eligible young men and women drove themselves—and often their friends—on unchaperoned dates. Couples trying to bypass traditional mores met with stern opposition. The city council in Thibodaux, for instance, passed an ordinance in 1921 to contain this "breach of decency." Audacious dancers would "retire at the time of intermission from said hall, unaccompanied by chaperons, and to parts unknown for automobile rides" to partake in sexual escapades, or so-called "petting parties."[14] Although new technologies reshaped traditional lifestyles and values, the Cajun perspective continued to view courtship through a morally conservative prism.

Fiddler Harry Choates' life and recording career stood as representative examples of the region's changing cultural climate. Choates' promiscuity and failed marriages cast a dark shadow behind his brilliant musicianship. Before his landmark recording, the fiddler mesmerized spectators with his unprecedented showmanship and technical prowess. Band mate and tenor banjo player Charley Slagle recalled a gig at the End O' Main club in Houston, Texas, where Harry stunned the spectators by launching into "Jole Blon." "The people quit dancing and came around the bandstand, watching him," Slagle explained to Choates' biographer Andrew Brown. "That's how good he was."[15]

Twenty-three-year-old Harry Choates was an established veteran of the Gulf Coast club scene in 1946, when independent record label owner and amateur producer Bill Quinn recorded Harry's rendition of "Jole Blon" on his Gold Star record label in Houston, Texas. Quinn's upstart label advertised itself to be the "King of the Hillbillies" and released a variety of musical genres, including Cajun, following Choates' initial recording session with Quinn.[16] On Sunday, March 31, 1946, the fiddler visited the studio as a sideman with the Texas-based group Jimmie Foster and the Swingsters.[17] The ensemble recorded two French sides, "La Value Zulbaugh" and "Jole Blon," a tune Choates learned as a teenager during his stint with Cajun swing innovator Leo Soileau's group.[18] *Jolie Blonde* required at least a dozen takes before Quinn was satisfied," Brown writes. The session took an entire afternoon, between Quinn's perfectionism and Choates' beer runs. The final result was an emotionally charged, up-tempo Cajun swing waltz, featuring wailing vocals and the genius of Choates' trademark fiddle work. Harry added additional tension to the arrangement by transposing the song from the key of G, a comfortable singing key within the tonal range of a C accordion, to the key of A, which allowed Choates to employ the full range of his upper vocal register.[19]

Choates was not conversant in French, though his recordings may suggest otherwise.[20] The few phases and grammatical structures he knew frequently appear in many of his compositions. The "tu m'as quitté pour t'en aller" motif—a theme describing the traumatic departure of loved ones, usually for east Texas—appears in a number of Cajun swing recordings, including the "Austin Special," "Port Arthur Blues," and Choates' 1946 rendition of "Jole Blon."[21] The fiddler sings: "Tu m'as laissé pour t'en aller, avec un autre, mais chère petite, dans pays de la Louisiane [You left me for another, dear girl, in Louisiana]," a verse that acknowledges the role of Texas in the Americanization of Cajun music. Not only is the song rearranged in a Cajun swing format, but the protagonist is apparently a Cajun living and working in the Golden Triangle, lamenting that his belle left to find love in his native Louisiana.

On July 17, 1946, Choates returned to Gold Star as the bandleader of the Melody Boys, a band composed of two ex-Swingsters—guitarists B. D. Williams and Eddie Pursley—and brothers, and string players, Abe and Joe Manuel and drummer Curzy "Pork Chop" Roy. That summer, the band recorded two sides, a reworked arrangement of "Jole Blon" and the "Basile Waltz," Joe Manuel's interpretation of Leo Soileau's accordion-based 1928 recording "Basile." Quinn released the Melody Boys' arrangement of the

"Basile Waltz" as the record's A-side. Apparently dissatisfied with the band's performance, the producer replaced the B-side with the Swingsters' version of "Jole Blon" recorded two and half months earlier. Unfamiliar with French, Quinn misspelled the phrase *jolie blonde*, forever changing the song's appellation to the English phonetic *jole blon*.[22] The producer also misspelled Harry's surname, which appears as "Shoates" on the original Gold Star release.

Houston, Texas, home of Gold Star records, became the launch pad for Choates' recording. Immediately after the first pressings of "Jole Blon," a Houston disk jockey created a buzz in east Texas by promoting the new record on air. Rather than broadcasting the A-side, the DJ flipped the disk, inadvertently launching an overnight sensation. The demand for "Jole Blon" increased dramatically, forcing an unprepared Quinn to reconsider his distribution options. The amateur producer ran Gold Star "in the manner of a glorified hobbyist rather than that of an organized and serious businessman."[23] Overwhelmed by his unforeseen success, Quinn followed the advice of Lester Bihari, a Galveston-based jukebox operator, and licensed the record to Modern Music—an independent label in Los Angeles managed by Bihari's brother. Through Modern's organized distribution and promotional efforts, "Jole Blon" became a bona fide part of the American musical landscape. Choates' fiddle work, emotive vocals, and Austin-based supporting cast propelled "Jole Blon" to number four on the national *Billboard*'s "Most Played Juke Box Folk Records" twice—on January 4, and March 8, 1947 (figure 7.2).[24] As Brown observes, national recognition came through a concerted effort by Cajuns and non-Cajuns alike. Anglo-Americans who had access to the recording on the Modern label embraced the tune and helped to push Choates' arrangement to the top of the charts. "Jole Blon" became a hit, not because Cajuns supported their local musicians, nor through the vision of Harry Choates' record

Figure 7.2. Harry Choates and his producer, Gold Star owner Bill Quinn, made history with the 1946 release "Jole Blon," perhaps the most famous song in Cajun musical history. Courtesy of the Cajun and Creole Music Collection, Edith Garland Dupré Library, University of Louisiana at Lafayette.

company, but precisely because Gold Star lost control of its product. The phenomenon continued to build momentum as the song reached new audiences when Quinn later licensed the record to the East Coast DeLuxe outfit in early 1947. Despite tremendous record sales, neither Choates nor Quinn received any royalties for their efforts because they never took the time to copyright "Jole Blon," an oversight that proved quite costly when other musicians began to record the tune.[25]

The waltz's long and winding history outlines a shared legacy between Cajuns and non-Cajuns, as "Jole Blon" transcended the Cajun experience and became part of American musical landscape. Nationally acclaimed musicians such as Grand Ole Opry star Roy Acuff assured "Jole Blon's" prominent place in late 1940s American songbook as they rushed to jump on the bandwagon by recording their own adaptations of the song. En route, the indigenous Louisiana tune transformed, morphing through a variety of arrangements, styles, genres, and lyrical themes as renowned performers such as Moon Mullican, Bob Wills, Hank Snow, and Waylon Jennings explored, adapted, and expanded the boundaries of the Cajun theme.

Cultural Exchange, Cultural Fault Lines

Since the nineteenth century, class tensions and ethnic anxieties between Cajun and their Anglo neighbors limited the group's cultural influence across community boundaries. Anglo-Americans dominating the socioeconomic hierarchy in the Cajun Lapland, relegating working-class Cajuns to a social status just above African Americans and Native Americans. Especially impoverished Cajuns who shunned white America's ethics and values in favor of their own belief systems became targets for ridicule and reprimand.[26] Historian Timothy Reilly demonstrates that some Anglo-Americans began to express their contempt for south Louisianians on a national level during the nineteenth century, when travel writers began to create a Cajun caricature for middle-class America. *Harper's Weekly* correspondent A. R. Waud, for instance, responded to south Louisiana's low literacy levels and poverty with truculent criticism in 1866 when he wrote: "Without energy, education, or ambition, they are good representatives of the white trash, behind the age in every thing. . . . To live without effort is their apparent aim in life, and they are satisfied with very little, and are, as a class, quite poor. . . . With a little mixture of fresh blood and some learning they might become much improved."[27] Vilifying stereotypes, which could include such components as inbreeding, became the penalty for those who chose nonconformity. These ideas continued to manifest through the twentieth century in two distinct ways: in a more benign fashion when outsiders characterized Cajuns as American folk, and through openly slanderous stereotypes in the vein of A. R. Waud. As Cajuns began to exert more cultural influence within the region, Anglo caricatures of the Cajun community became more apparent in mass cultural texts as the dominant group worked to manage their social anxieties. Locally accessible independent record labels and radio allowed musicians such as Harry Choates to take control of those media outlets channeling mass culture. In the process, Choates' "Jole Blon" circumvented the boundaries of mass culture policed by dominant groups within the region. Working-class Anglo musicians were suddenly forced to cope and react to this new Cajun presence.

The growing number of mass media outlets in the Cajun Lapland, such as Quinn's Gold Star records, opened a new market in which Cajun musicians could to circulate their work. Easier access to the increasingly saturated auditory world of mass communication allowed the marginal group to offset intermittently resistance from their Anglo neighbors. When cultural production met local mass media, Cajuns slowly began to reverse the direction of the Americanization process by capitalizing on the reach and sway of newly established independent record labels. Rather than consuming and reshaping outside influences, the ethnic group suddenly found itself providing the primary text for Anglo-American interpretations of "Jole Blon."

Anglo adaptations of the Cajun song, and the female character branded as "Jole Blon," took on new meaning within an English-language milieu. Country musicians altered the melody or scrapped it all together. In addition, new instrumental combinations changed the dynamics of the composition. Some versions retained a hint of the song's cultural origins through references to distinctively Cajun traditions—particularly foodways—such as rice and gravy, strong coffee, dirty rice, and filé gumbo. Behind their Anglo facades, these reworked versions of "Jole Blon" pinpoint the increasing influence Cajuns exerted in the region and, at times, the persistent tensions structuring relations across Cajun and Anglo cultural boundaries.

Novelty interpretations of "Jole Blon" may have amused the general English-speaking public, as evidenced by strong record sales, but Cajuns were not always receptive to "foreign" adaptations. Country-and-western musicians who performed regularly in the Golden Triangle and south Louisiana recorded some of the first, and most whimsical, interpretations of the so-called "Cajun national anthem." Pianist Aubrey "Moon" Mullican recorded a trilogy of commercially successful adaptations of "Jole Blon": "New Pretty Blond (New Jole Blon)" waxed in the Fall of 1946, "Jole Blon's Sister" (circa March 1947), and "Jole Blon Is Gone, Amen" (December 1947).[28] Music writer Kevin Coffey writes that "New Pretty Blond," the pianist's first interpretation, "appears almost certainly to have been the first cover version, although a straight (and fantastic) recording of the tune by the Louisiana Cajun swing bandleader Eddie Shuler on his fledgling Goldband label could not have been far behind."[29] Regardless of chronology, Mullican's adaptations of the waltz were easily more commercially successful than Shuler's attempt.

Mullican launched his solo career, however, at the expense of a large portion of his audience. Some Cajuns living in east Texas and southwest

Figure 7.3. Hillbilly versions of Choates' "Jole Blon" took on a new demeanor as such musicians as Moon Mullican adapted the lyrics, melody, and motifs within an Anglo-American context. Courtesy of the Cajun and Creole Music Collection, Edith Garland Dupré Library, University of Louisiana at Lafayette.

Louisiana recoiled at what they viewed as patronizing and inflammatory lyrics in his version of "Jole Blon." "Moon wasn't all that popular after he come out with that *Jole Blon* thing," explained fiddler Clyde Brewer, who was already a veteran on the Gulf Coast circuit by seventeen. "[Cajuns] were offended by it. It was like the Star-Spangled Banner being slandered."[30] Francophones living in east Texas, who dealt with the friction generated by tensions between Anglo-Protestant and Franco-Catholic factions on a day-to-day basis, evidently viewed Mullican's version as an affront because the tune poked fun at the traditional Cajun lifestyle and language (figure 7.3).[31] Intimately familiar with the lyrics and contexts, some locals explicitly understood that they owned the primary text. One Cajun from Allen Parish in western Louisiana explained, "It is funny because the Cajun side of my family all liked Moon's version and just thought it was funny that he couldn't speak French."[32] The transference of "Jole Blon" across the ethnic divide afforded members of the Cajun community the opportunity to assess their position vis-à-vis Anglo-America as they imagined their connection to the mainstream.

In the South, cultural borrowing took place across racial and ethnic lines despite overt prejudice. The emergence of jazz, Western swing, and rock 'n' roll tunes in the American repertoire clearly illustrates that racism does not equate to noncommunication. Indeed, despite the festering ethnic and class tensions between Cajuns and Texans, Mullican outlined the cross-cultural musical dialogue that frequently transpired between the groups in his quasi-autobiographical composition "Jole Blon Is Gone, Amen" (1947), his final adaptation of the Harry Choates hit.[33] The song apparently recounts the first time he heard Choates performing "Jole Blon." Clyde Brewer provides an atmospheric element to the recording by singing in French to imitate the performance described by Mullican, who

incorporates his garbled rendering of Cajun French through several lines
of incomprehensible gibberish:

> Many years ago, down Louisiana way,
> I stopped into a honky tonk and this is what I heard 'em
>   play.
> The melody was haunting, as I recall that day.
> When a little man got up and sang a song in his own
>   peculiar way:
> *Jolie Blonde 'gardé donc, mais quoi t'as fais.*
> *Tu m'as quitté pour t'en aller avec un autre.*
> *M'as laissé pour t'en aller avec un autre.*
> *Quel espoir et quel avenir que moi je vais voir.*
> These words they sound peculiar,
> No they didn't sound my way
> So I just sang this *Jole Blon* in the old Moon Mullican way.
> *Jole Blon skwa tah fay conchie panchie,*
> dirty rice and pickin' cotton
> *Tawn allay skwa tah roochie*
> *conchie panchie, seeco peeco. . . .*[34]

Though little more than a novelty song, Mullican's composition describes a scene that played out hundreds, perhaps thousands of times
in the Cajun Lapland along the southeast Texas border. Musicians and
audiences shared across the Franco-Anglo divide through the interaction
that took place in dance halls, oil fields, and shipyards along the Gulf
Coast despite language barriers. "Jole Blon's Gone, Amen" is a historical
snapshot of cross-cultural sharing preserved in America's musical landscape by way of Mullican's song about Harry Choates and vernacular
Cajun music. Although the lyrics sounded peculiar to the pianist's ears, he
adapted the tune in the same interpretive fashion as Cajuns who altered
country-and-western compositions—by making it his own: "So I just sang
this *Jole Blon* in the old Moon Mullican way." This time, however, Cajun
provided the musical touchstone leading to an Anglo adaptation.

Mullican's song illuminates not only the kinds of cultural transference
happening on a daily basis in the Cajun Lapland, but also the corresponding tension structuring those exchanges. The complications generated by
the asymmetrical relationship between Franco and Anglo factions in the
region become explicit as the song continues. The Cajun protagonist eventually lashes out at a group of Anglo-Americans, presumably east Texans,
by retorting, "What have you hillbillies done to my pretty little blonde, I've
looked this wide world over, but it seems to me she's gone."[35] This rare example of a Cajun protagonist getting the final word in an Anglo adaptation
of "Jole Blon"—by deploying the term hillbilly in the same pejorative manner as coonass—does, however, suggest the level of animosity between
Cajuns their Anglo neighbors. Other English-language variants tend to
maintain a condescending tone toward their Franco-Catholic characters.

In the wake of Mullican's efforts, the position of "Jole Blon" as an American classic became cemented through a series of lucrative adaptations by an impressive list of country stars. Red Foley's Decca release "New Jolie Blonde" (New Pretty Blonde), based on Mullican's first adaptation of the Cajun classic, peaked at number one on the national charts in 1947 and became the bestselling adaptation of "Jole Blon." His Grand Ole Opry cohorts followed suit. Roy Acuff and his Smokey Mountain Boys recorded a harmonica-driven "(Our Own) Jole Blon" on January 28, 1947, approximately two weeks after Folley's hit. His interpretation synthesized specific elements found in the Cajun "Jole Blon" lineage, including the diatonic sounds of Amédé Breaux's "Ma Blonde Est Partil" and Choates' fiddling and emotive Bob Wills-like hollers. Acuff's attempt attracted national attention after spending six weeks on the national Billboard charts, eventually peaking at number four. Later, in 1953, Hank Snow, a country legend from the Acadians' Nova Scotian homeland and member of the Country Music Hall of Fame, awkwardly combined iconographic ethnic imagery from both Texas and Louisiana. Snow recounted the adventures of Mexican Joe's encounter with the Cajun seductress in Texas, where the couple dines on "filé gumbo with enchiladas on the side."[36] Even the king of Western swing, Bob Wills, who influenced so many Cajun swing musicians, recorded a version of "Jole Blon" titled "Jolie Blonde Likes the Boogie." Released in 1950, Coffey argues that the Wills adaptation was less a tribute to Cajun music than a convenient arrangement that conformed to the post-WWII country boogie craze. Wills' recording came on the heels of the well-received Tiny Moore composition, "Ida Red Like the Boogie," a tune ironically inspired by Dickie Jones and the Skyliners' Cajun ditty "Jole Blon Likes the Boogie."

As the Cajun national anthem resonated around the country, the impact of "Jole Blon" also resonated closer to home.[37] Cajun musicians would not be outdone by national spin offs. After Harry Choates brought the Cajun classic to new heights, a variety of Cajun bands also rushed to record their own interpretations of the waltz. LeRoy "Happy Fats" LeBlanc proclaimed that his ensemble—Happy, Doc, and the Boys—was reclaiming the waltz in 1947 recording "New Jolie Blond": "Jole Blon you've been kicked around. You've been bounced around a lot. But now, you're being bounced around like you've never been bounced around before. This is the new 'Jole Blon,' the one that we're talking about; the one that we always known [sic]. The one with the pretty little golden curls."[38]

"New Jolie Blond" synthesized elements of country, Western swing, and Cajun musical traditions. The Happy Fats string band treatment highlighted Oran "Doc" Guidry's smooth fiddling, lap steel, and French lyrics laced with tight, country-inspired vocal harmonies. LeBlanc's recording was one of at least three Cajun swing renditions waxed in the wake of the Choates recording. Eddie Shuler and his All-Star Reveliers recorded the first post-Choates Cajun adaptation of "Jole Blon" in 1946. The following year, Luderin Darbone and the Hackberry Ramblers rerecorded the tune. In 1951, the song's winding and convoluted history came full circle when

Amédé Breaux—the accordionist from the original 1929 recording session that initiated the "Jole Blon" phenomenon—reinterpreted the tune with his group the Acadian Aces on the independent Crowley-based Feature label. The instrumentation featured in the accordion-based arrangement combined elements of the early commercial period (accordion and fiddle) and the Cajun swing era (bass fiddle and lap steel). By the end of the decade, "Jole Blon" plied unexplored waters as rock 'n' rollers incorporated the composition into the burgeoning genre.

Cajun rebuttals to Anglo interpretations did not deter some of the most remarkable adaptations of the Cajun national anthem. During the late 1950s, a new generation of Texas musicians further cemented "Jole Blon" place in American popular culture. The tune became part of the rock 'n' roll revolution when Dallas vocalist Charles Lee (actually Leath) reinvented the waltz with the help of fellow Texan Eddie Shuler and a cast of Cajun musicians. In 1956, Leath's Yellow Jackets coalesced in Shuler's Goldband headquarters in Lake Charles, Louisiana, and recorded the revamped, rock-based "Rock and Roll Jolie Blonde." The group abandoned "Jole Blon's" traditional chord progression, melody, and lyrics in favor of an amplified, rolling blues progression, rock 'n' roll backbeat, and original contemporary storyline. Two years after "Jole Blon's" first rock 'n' roll experience, the tune would reach a larger audience beyond the Gulf Coast through the efforts of another group of Texas musicians.

Cajun music achieved enough momentum by 1958 to reach an unprecedented level of influence. The genre's ascendance coincided with Lubbock native and rock 'n' roll pioneer Buddy Holly's decision to embark on a new career as an independent record producer for the Brunswick label. Holly's maiden effort centered on his bandmate and future country music legend Waylon Jennings' solo debut. Holly was convinced that Choates' waltz could cross over as a pop hit and encouraged Jennings to record "Jole Blon" in French. The two Anglophone Texans tediously listened to the Choates record again and again, meticulously transcribing the lyrics. In September 1958, Waylon and Buddy rendezvoused at Norman Petty's New Mexico Studio for the session. Holly not only produced the record, but also laid the guitar track on the rock 'n' roll–inflected interpretation of the Cajun classic. Their contemporary rendering of the waltz, highlighting King Curtis's driving saxophone, only vaguely resembled Choates recording and flopped on the independent market.[39] Although a financial disappointment, the historical significance of the personnel involved with the recording situates "Jole Blon" and Cajun music at the crossroads of American music. The potential market viability of Cajun music, Choates' recording in particular, tickled Holly's musical intuition. Holly biographer Ellis Amburn also places the pioneer rock 'n' roller "at the forefront of the late fifties 'country Cajun' trend,"[40] championed by Doug and Rusty Kershaw and Jimmy C. Newman. Newman and the Kershaws found a home on the periphery of mainstream Cajun music by fusing south Louisiana musical traditions with popular American genres such as country-and-western, rock 'n' roll, and rockabilly, a trend that mirrored the musical direction of Waylon Jennings's debut solo effort.

As a primary text, the appeal of "Jole Blon" was powerful enough to compel Jennings, who had no working knowledge of French, to remain unusually faithful to Choates' version. Jennings's version may have been unusually sensitive to the Cajun waltz, but it still illuminates the larger cultural processes at work. Anglo interpretations and adaptations of "Jole Blon" indeed mirrored the ways in which Cajuns engaged mass culture. Cultural exchange transpired in two directions simultaneously when local mass media allowed Cajuns to speak to a broader audience. Asymmetrical power dynamics and country musicians' stereotypical assumptions about the ethnic group, however, indicate the differences structuring the flow and reception of information.

Stereotypes, Sexuality, and "Jole Blon" in Anglo-America

A comparison of the competing perspectives that play out in French Louisiana and English adaptations of "Jole Blon" illuminates the cultural rift that distinguished the Cajun worldview from that of the rest of the Anglo South. The original 1929 version of "Ma Blonde Est Parti" describes the song's working-class heroine as a home wrecker who leaves the broken-hearted protagonist for another man, launching the immortal line "tu m'as quitté pour t'en aller, pour t'en aller avec un autre, oui, que moi" (you left me for someone else). Following the advice of her friends and family, the female character decides to embark on a new life much to the chagrin of her former lover, who proclaims "si t'aurais pas ecouté tout les conseils des autres, tu serais ici avec moi aujourd'hui" (if you would not listen to the advice of others, you would still be with me today). However, she presumably leaves her husband for another chance at love, not for a wild impulsive romp at the expense of the song's male protagonist. The heroine's departure is a difficult but rational decision based on much deliberation. The social context in which she lived forced "Jole Blon" to consider her actions wisely in order to negotiate the moral climate of early-twentieth-century Cajun society, which did not tolerate promiscuity. Hence, subsequent Cajun interpretations of "Ma Blonde Est Parti" preserved the song's original storyline, though the lyrics evolved with each adaptation. The theme and character development in French renditions of the song continued to engage the traditional Cajun cultural context.

When "Jole Blon" transcended its original milieu and became part of the national repertoire, the waltz's characters, theme, and melody evolved as non-Cajun musicians manipulated the tune to conform to the Anglo-American perspective. Many country musicians expressed both their fascination and repulsion with Cajun culture, particularly through their portrayal of the waltz's heroine, "Jole." Detached from the original Cajun context, the waltz's heroine became a hot-blooded, lascivious character, whose promiscuity is of legendary proportion. Several Anglo-American adaptations painted the iconographic character "Jole" as the sensual antithesis of the wholesome and innocent Evangeline, the stereotypical romantic image of the Acadian, and therefore Cajun, woman that captured the imagination of Americans during the late nineteenth and early twentieth centuries. The term *jolie* (pretty), a term of endearment often used by Cajun men when referring to their belles, became the first name of the exotic seductress in songs by a variety of artists. Within this new context, "Jole" equated with open and uninhibited sexuality.

Blues motifs and contemporary attitudes toward ethnic sexuality and the working classes informed the Anglo characterizations of the waltz's Cajun protagonist. Blues motifs concerning desire and sexuality, introduced to country-and-western musicians through the race record market, are perhaps the most obvious structural component of Anglo versions of "Jole Blon." However, when these themes crossed racial lines, white anxieties about the ethnic libido added new layers of complexity to the equation.[41]

Anglo-American adaptations of "Jole Blon" provided a medium for English-speaking musicians to represent and manage their sociocultural anxieties about ethnic sexuality. Anglo characterizations of Jole as a sexually suggestive working-class woman paralleled what cultural studies scholar Hazel Carby identifies as "fears of rampant and uncontrolled female sexuality" among African Americans during the Great Migration.[42] Migratory Cajuns competing for blue-collar jobs on the railroad and in oil fields, refineries, and shipyards in Texas incited a similar reaction. Stereotypes helped reinforce the status quo, at least rhetorically, by keeping Cajuns in their place as subordinates.[43] Anglo variants of "Jole Blon" thus represent the intersection of Anglo-American attitudes regarding ethnic groups, gender, sexuality, and the working classes.

Policing sexuality, especially among ethnic groups, has long been an American preoccupation. During the twentieth century, miscegenation laws enforced taboos against interracial (and interethnic) sex.[44] Progressive Era studies and social programs further fanned the flames. Reform-minded social workers such as Elsie Johnson McDougald insisted that "sex irregularities are not a matter of race, but of socioeconomic conditions."[45] Working-class women perpetuated sexual degeneracy and hence needed social and cultural uplift, according to Progressive advocates. These platitudes became mainstream dogma by mid-century. Between 1946 and 1958, mass-circulated magazines—including *Ladies' Home Journal*, *Woman's Home Companion*, and *Reader's Digest*—trumpeted the virtue of women who either stayed at home nurturing the hearth or achieved public success in the workplace through "hard work, especially without complaint."[46] This prescription left no room for foot-loose honky-tonk angels like the imaginary "Jole Blon." By frequenting working-class barrooms and indulging in promiscuity, this femme fatale became suspect by mainstream measures.

Cajuns' open acceptance of alcohol consumption, smoking, dancing, gambling, and Epicureanism flew in the conservative face of middle-class America that publically denounced such temporal pleasures. While most

Cajuns adamantly upheld the Catholic doctrine concerning premarital abstinence, they partook freely of other sensual outlets, a situation that indeed affected the Anglo perception of working-class Cajuns and their "erotic" customs. The ethnic group's cultural orientation frequently juxtaposed the attitudes among those non-Cajuns who came into contact with them. Middle- and upper-class intellectuals applied the folk label as a means of interpreting and policing these differences. Working-class Anglo-Protestants, on the other hand, who maintained more intimately contact with Cajuns in the region's oil patch, refineries, and honky-tonks, drew distinctions between themselves and their rivals with a deprecating vocabulary familiar among individuals designated as "crackers."[47]

In some renditions, the heroine in "Jole Blon" and, by association, the Cajun people fell victim to the same conventional stereotypes that molded American popular culture's portrayal of the rural South. Anglo-American songwriters burlesqued "Jole Blon" into a sexually deviant character rivaling the dissolute protagonists in Erskine Caldwell's Depression-era novel *Tobacco Road*. Jole engendered the same shameless perversion of Caldwell's South in country-and-western adaptations. She also displayed traits resembling the caricatures Daisy Mae Scragg (buxom beauty) and Sadie Hawkins (assertive sexuality) from Al Capp's comic strip *Li'l Abner*. In the context of Depression-era Southern stereotypes, Jole Blon became the most dangerous kind of character in the conservative post-World War II American context—an alluring, sexually active woman. Thus, *Tobacco Road*, *Li'l Abner*, and English interpretations of Jole Blon all evolved from an American perspective that equated perversion with poverty and assertive uninhibited sexuality with "crackers," people of color, and ethnic Catholics.[48]

Ironically, working-class country musicians deflected these same belittling attitudes onto Cajuns despite the cultural consistencies and musical parallels connecting these groups. Cajun became a step down from "cracker" as blue-collar artists emphasized musically the cultural fault lines distinguishing these rival factions. Stereotypes created rhetorical space between Anglos and Cajuns. Country singers felt safe to comment generically on cultural difference through the defensive buffer generated through typecasting. Some songs reprimanded Jole for her inappropriate behavior. In Jack Rivers's 1950 recording "Shame, Shame on Jolie," the male protagonist breaks off his relationship with the Cajun seductress because of her promiscuity and infidelity. "You wine-and-dine, that's quite alright," sings Rivers, "but you don't have to kiss good night. Shame, shame on Jolie."[49] Moon Mullican's "Jole Blon's Sister" also condemns feminine sensuality and warns against expressing such sentiments by letting the listener know that Jole Blon's sibling, who is just as wanton as her sister, had 10 bastard children. Mullican reiterates the American Protestant propensity toward the simultaneous repulsion and fascination with temporal pleasures by combining themes about food and sex in the tune. The south Louisiana undertones in the composition—Moon's signature French-based gibberish and the character "Jole Blon"—automatically condemn by association the Cajun lifestyle, a way of life quite familiar to Moon.

Not all of Anglo-American composers had the strength to ward off the seductive powers of food, drink, and sex. For instance, Bud Messner and His Sky Line Boys indulged their yearnings "Slippin' Around with Jole Blon." Tommy Thompson and the Boys, a group that toured around Austin, Texas, after the war, emphasized the siren's call of food and sex in their 1949 recording "Dinner with Jole Blon." The group's vocalist Hub Sutter launches into a convoluted story about a love triangle involving the song's hero, "Jole Blon," and her sister. The protagonist proclaims his love for fresh oysters, sauerkraut, beer, whiskey, and Jole Blon, who "gives him a thrill." The tune's male character also apparently had an affair with Jole's sister. "Jole Blon, where's your sister?," broods Sutter in a whiny voice, "Seems last night, that I kissed her."[50] After imagining how fine the sister would look in a bathing suit, the central character proposes to his true love, "Jole."

The most blatant example of Jole Blon's promiscuity is found in a song by a female vocalist from Roanoke, Virginia. A regular on the *Louisiana Hayride* radio program, Betty Amos turned the tables on the image of "Jole" by creating a character named "Jole John." Amos, apparently unaware that her hero's name translated as Pretty John, applied term "Jole" as a synonym for male unabashed sexuality to mirror the allure of his female counterpart Jole Blon, who is also perpetually in heat. A Cajun Dionysis, Jole John loves all things temporal from red wine to rice and beans, and, of course, sex with Jole Blon. In Amos's adaptation, the couple then "makes whoopee" on the Delta down in New Orleans. The singer also makes reference to oysters, a symbol of Louisiana cuisine and a supposed aphrodisiac, as the two Joles "go wild on the bayou."

Not all adaptations of the Cajun waltz described such uninhibited debauchery. Some Anglo-Americans grappled with the conflicts between Victorian morality and corporeal temptations in song. Frustrations born from the clash between constrictive religious and cultural law and forbidden pleasures sometimes led to bizarre sexual perversions. In the case of "Jole Blon," Sheb Wooley and His Calumet Indians, and later Cliffie Stone and his Barn Dance Band, employed ambiguous language and double entendre in their fantasies about voyeurism. In "Peeping Through the Key Hole (Watching Jole Blon)," Wooley learned to do the "hoochie coo" by surreptitiously watching "Jole Blon" through her keyhole. Stone took the tune a step further in 1948 by adding a verse about intimacy at the end of a date:

> And then I took my gal home, when the dance was through.
> She asked me if I'd kiss her, I said, "Don't mind if I do."
> And when the clench was finally over, she shook her pretty head.
> [She] said "where did you learn to kiss like that," and this is what I said:
> I've been a peepin' through the keyhole watching Jole Blon.[51]

Stone's version of the Wooley composition is a metaphor for the kind of cultural voyeurism at the heart of country music adaptations of "Jole Blon."

The composition's widespread popularity encouraged singers on both sides of the linguistic and cultural divide to acknowledge the ethnic group's growing influence in American mass culture. For Anglo musicians, "Jole Blon" provided a titillating keyhole that peered into Cajun culture. Yet, because the waltz represented a primary text linked to Cajun cultural agency, musicians such as Cliffie Stone displayed a certain amount of anxiety regarding ethnic cultural production. Tension between repulsion and attraction frames his adaptation, possibly because he recognized the pointed rural Southern stereotypes reflected in the Cajun caricatures he paints.

Other songs also described the attraction between the Anglo-American protagonist and the exotic Cajun Venus. The hero in California-based guitarist and vocalist Johnny Bond's "The Daughter of Jole Blon" found himself in love with the aging seductress's only daughter, a bewitching woman of 16 with far more to offer than her mother. In addition to a dozen boyfriends, whom she claims are her "cousins," Jole's daughter finds time to get together with her favorite beau. A talented young vixen, the 16-year-old knew "all the tricks that Jole taught her."

Bond's tune accentuates the derogatory undertones permeating the Anglo-American stereotype of poor rural Southerners by insinuating that Jole's daughter maintained several incestuous relationships:

> She's got boyfriends by the dozen,
> She tries to make me think that they're her cousins.
> Oh but, I don't care, 'cause when I'm there
> She makes her cousins take the air.[52]

By inferring incest in "The Daughter of Jole Blon," Bond simultaneously deflects national stereotypes about rural Southerners while lyrically painting the dark side of the Cajun isolation model espoused by folklorists. Whether articulated in *Tobacco Road* or inferred on a folk festival stage, isolation suggests a limited gene pool and thus physical and cultural degeneracy. Bond takes these characterizations a step further by giving his protagonist agency. Jole's daughter dismisses her other suitors as "her cousins." Because she is free to choose her lovers, some of whom happen to be blood relations, the country singer conflates Cajuns with the ultimate sexual taboo. Moreover, the number of beaus her daughter keeps, and the implication that she knows the "tricks" her mother taught her, alludes to the possibility that both Jole Blon and her daughter engaged in prostitution.

The long and winding history of "Jole Blon" changed the course of Cajun music by transforming a regional genre into an American musical style. Nationally famous recordings artists catapulted their interpretations of the Cajun experience into the American mind's eye. Each adaptation, interpretation, and performance of "Jole Blon," affixed a new layer of meaning to the song. The plaintive waltz began its meteoric flash through the American musical firmament in the Cajun repertoire. Along the way, the song accumulated an assortment of cultural implications that compounded and shifted over time depending on the song's context.

The song's legacy highlights the exchanges and fault lines framing the Cajun engagement with American popular culture during the first half of the twentieth century. Locally owned and operated mass media installations afforded Cajuns the opportunity to extend their influence across cultural and geographical boundaries. Cajun swingers effectively altered the currents of Americanization by disseminating at an unprecedented level their own primary text for Anglo American consumption. In the case of Harry Choates' recording of "Jole Blon," the fiddler transforms the plaintive Cajun waltz by employing American imagery embodied by the blonde protagonist and popular musical instrumentation via a Cajun swing arrangement. Cajun audiences adored the composition's storyline, lilting melody, and waltz time signature, in part, because traditional courtship practices inform the song's lyrical content. Underlying assumptions embedded in the song's motifs—the social contexts of dance halls and heartbreak—spoke broadly to the Cajuns both on the jukebox and on the dance floor. By demanding the song from local ensembles, audiences prompted musicians like Harry Choates to keep the song in circulation. American adaptations, on the other hand, modify the song to conform to an Anglo-Protestant perspective. In English renditions of the tune, "Jole Blon" came to represent prevailing attitudes toward female sexuality. American musicians filtered and burlesqued the Cajun heroine's character, turning her into a sometimes sexually deviant, sometimes perverse seductress, whose wanton ways rival the sexual escapades of other ethnic women who fell victim to stereotypes. "Jole Blon" acts as a barometer of the nation's view of sexual expression both in Southern white society and among ethnic groups. Cajuns and Anglo-Americans alike interpret and respond to national developments by interpreting, editing, and adapting cultural information through an individual's attitude and cultural lens.

"Jole Blon" broadly represents the post-World War II ethnic experience in America. New mass media outlets and increasingly dense communication networks diversified the U.S. soundscape. Cultural filtration allowed for the novel rearticulation of mass culture heard with ethnic ears. Folklorist William Owens observed parallels between Cajuns who "made [popular music] their own" and the cross-cultural exchanges defining life along the Texas-Mexican border. "On the Mexican border," Owens explains, "I found Mexican songs with rhythmic and vocal effects definitely borrowed from Negro Blues. In the *cantinas* there I heard 'Cielito Lindo' sung in variations ranging from the traditional waltz through the *huapango* and blues rhythm and winding up as a yodel."[53] Ethnic musicians throughout America naturally fused traditional music with elements of extraneous compositions. When these musicians made their way into locally operating independent record labels, individual artists began to introduce primary texts of their own making that in essence reversed the Americanization process and influenced Anglo-America.

Harry Choates' rendition of "Jole Blon" adhered to a successful formula for marketing ethnic music in America, a strategy repeated during the late 1950s by Mexican-American rock 'n' roller Ritchie Valens. Although Richard Steven Valenzuela was only five years old when Harry Choates' version of "Jole Blon" hit in early 1947, the Latino rocker and the Cajun swinger enjoyed extraordinary success in their short musical careers by reinventing traditional music. Both musicians revamped traditional songs from their respective cultural heritages by synthesizing vernacular melodies and themes with contemporary arrangements based on the sounds of American popular music. Valens combined aspects traditional Mexican music and rock 'n' roll in his million-seller "La Bamba," released as the B-side to "Donna" on the Los Angeles–based Del-Fi label.[54] Choates, on the other hand, incorporated Cajun and Western swing. Though neither musician could speak his ancestral tongue, Valens and Choates recorded their biggest hits on independent record labels situated in communities that boasted diverse ethnic populations. Disk jockeys also factored into the remarkable success of "La Bamba" and "Jole Blon" by giving the songs airtime, rather than letting them fade into obscurity as B-side oddities. Although both musicians died tragically as young men, their recordings live on as fixtures in the American musical landscape.

"Jole Blon's" legacy extended well into the later part of the twentieth century. Cajun musicians continued to celebrate the heavily requested waltz at dance halls and honky-tonks around south Louisiana. The song crossed racial boundaries in Bayou Country as black Creole musicians incorporated the song into the zydeco repertoire. For instance, "My Jolie Blonde," recorded as a duet by Cajun swamp pop legend Rod Bernard and the black Creole "King of Zydeco," Clifton Chenier, symbolically bridged the racial divide on the 1976 album *Boogie in Black and White*.[55] Beyond Cajun Country, nationally acclaimed musicians have perpetuated the song's place in Americana. In 1972, the Lubbock-based Flatlanders— featuring songsters Jimmie Dale Gilmore, Joe Ely, and Butch Hancock— took a page out of native son Buddy Holly's songbook, and reinforced the position of "Jole Blon" in Texas's musical traditions by waxing the tune on their debut album. During the early 1980s, both Gary U.S. Bonds and influential rock 'n' roller Bruce Springsteen experimented with Roy Acuff's adaptation of the Cajun waltz. Springsteen coproduced, coarranged, and provided the duet vocals on Bonds's version of "Jole Blon" released on EMI. Springsteen also performed the country-inflected tune regularly in concert with his E Street Band.[56]

"Jole Blon" occupies many positions as a cultural buffer between the Cajun and American experiences. It offered south Louisianians a ray of affirmation that pierced the looming cloud of negative stereotypes perpetuated through popular American literature. The song also became the soundtrack for the post–World War II generation that reinvented and, in some ways, modernized the Cajun experience through a Cajun interpretation of American culture. Harry Choates' rendition of "Jole Blon" is the most important song in the history of Cajun music because it simultaneously shaped the whole of Cajun society and American popular culture. The recording also opened the floodgates to the diverse array of Cajun musical expression by making Louisiana music a viable commodity for business-minded record producers and labels.

Gold Star owner and producer Bill Quinn recognized the grassroots demand and the financial potential for vernacular music and insisted that Harry record other Cajun tunes from the accordion's golden era of the late 1920s and early 1930s after the remarkable success of "Jole Blon." Choates subsequently recorded string band renditions of such songs as "Lafayette" and "Port Arthur Waltz," all previously issued before the infiltration of Texas Western swing in south Louisiana. The efforts of independent record labels such as Gold Star and Opera in Houston—and later Khoury, Lyric, Goldband, Fais Do Do, and Swallow in Louisiana—satisfied working-class Cajuns' appetite for vernacular music, which had again found a home in the commercial market. Though follow-up efforts by Harry Choates never replicated the success of "Jole Blon," Quinn continued to market swing interpretations of traditional music "in Louisiana and Texas, and that market was large enough to justify Quinn's continuing interest."[57] Indeed, the emergence of postwar independent record labels filled the musical void left by larger national companies by releasing recordings made by and marketed to the Cajun community.

The contribution of "Jole Blon" to American music lies in the song's role as a primary cultural text. Burgeoning regional mass media projected Choates' arrangement across cultural boundaries where the waltz demonstrated Cajun music's capacity to speak broadly to diverse audiences despite the persistent marginalization of the community. The wide popularity of "Jole Blon" along with Anglo adaptations by country music icons such as Roy Acuff and Bob Wills compelled Cajuns to imagine their connection to the American mainstream. The legacy of "Jole Blon" helped Cajuns understand that they, too, could contribute to the American songbook.

8

A New Mental World

A white-washed wooden honky-tonk, owned and operated by an ex-convict named Quincy Davis, decorated the rural Cajun prairie along Louisiana State Highway 190 near Basile after World War II. Davis's Avalon Club became one of many popular hangouts in Cajun Country, where blue-collar laborers congregated to socialize and dance to the region's most popular entertainers. Indeed, these smoke-filled dance halls had long served as cultural incubators for south Louisiana's cross-pollinated musical scene.

Naked light bulbs hanging from the ceiling cast a glow across the Avalon Club's oak dance floor, a milieu where a diverse clientele—drunks, tarts, fighters, family men, respectable ladies, white English-speaking soldiers from Fort Polk, and Coushatta Indians from nearby Elton—intermingled to the sounds of the house band led by accordionist Nathan Abshire. Davis convinced Abshire to relocate from rural Vermilion Parish to Basile with the promise of steady work. The accordionist quickly amassed a loyal audience in the wake of his 1949 hit recording, "Pine Grove Blues," and by 1950 performed at the club seven nights a week to a packed house.

One Saturday night, a group of well-dressed strangers, led by a conspicuous gentleman dressed all in white, entered the club and sat together at a table adjacent to the bandstand. The accordionist gazed curiously at the dapper, ivory-clad interloper—who ignored local custom by wearing his cowboy hat indoors—then continued the dance with his interpretation of "Grand Texas," a Western swing–tinged French composition about Cajuns living in the Lone Star State. After the tune, a member of the entourage approached the bandleader and declared, "Mr. Hank would like you to play that song again."[1] Abshire obliged, never realizing that "Mr. Hank" was, in fact, *Louisiana Hayride* personality and country music recording artist Hank Williams. Eight months later, the accordionist tuned his radio to a broadcast of Williams' Cajun anthem "Jambalaya." "Hank picked up on that rhythm, melody line," recounts the late accordionist's cousin and understudy Ray Abshire, "and made 'Jamba-laya' out of 'Grand Texas.'"[2]

Nathan Abshire's anecdote reads like a dream—a mysterious stranger dressed in a white suit lurking in the shadows underneath the brim of his cowboy hat, enchanted by the master accordionist. Origin stories pin-pointing the Cajun provenance of Hank Williams's "Jambalaya" (1952), and yarns recounting local encounters with the iconic singer, are a part of the shared lore among Cajuns who frequented dance halls like the Avalon Club after Word War II. Memories of meeting Williams and claims regarding "Jambalaya" signify emotional conduits through which Cajuns have imagined their relationship to the American mainstream.

Abshire's claim to have first heard Williams's tune during a radio broad-cast is especially significant. Records, radio, and the region's increasingly dense mass communication networks connected the Cajun Lapland to distant cities beyond the previous orbit of the ethnic group's experience. These emergent communication channels privileged aurality, which en-couraged listeners to create a sonic imaginary. As radio historian Susan Douglas asserts, "by compelling [listeners] to use their imaginations as part of the cultural work of being Americans, radio required people to engage in a cognitively active mode in the construction of mass culture's varied, multiple meanings."[3] Radio and records introduced rural and small-town Americans to a larger world, and, like Nathan Abshire, many quickly imag-ined their way into that sonic universe.

Substantial changes broadened radio's reach between its inception and World War II. Crystal receivers gave way to amplifying vacuum tubes that increased reception during the 1920s, and nationwide communication networks forged by such corporations as Radio Corporation of America (1919), its subsidiary the National Broadcasting Corporation (1926), and the Columbia Broadcasting System (1927) refined their use of amplitude modulation (AM) as they relayed information across the United States. By 1934, the newly established Federal Communications Commission (FCC) hoped to manage an industry so immense that it captivated the nation. Hadley Cantril and Gordon Allport documented in 1935 that "100,000 persons are now employed in the radio industry, that 78,000,000 of our citizens are more or less habitual listeners, that more than 20,000,000 of them often listen simultaneously to a single broadcast."[4] Cajun house-holds were among the 21,455,799 homes equipped with radios during the Great Depression. Moreover, radio had the uncanny ability to encapsulate the world's magnitude into easily consumable portions for those capable of translating sonic information into mental images.

Records and radio built an industry around imagination. Media tech-nologies created an auditory world where sound, language, and music expanded listeners' mental worlds. Foregrounding orality forced an-nouncers to sharpen their verbal agility, humorists to master linguistic slapstick, and musicians to polish their performances in hopes of creat-ing a receptive audience. Racial ventriloquists like the white stars of ra-dio's *Amos 'n' Andy* played minstrels without makeup, often fooling both white and black listeners who distinctly heard African-American voices with their minds' ears. Cajuns encountered a distinctive aural world that located its power in the individualized mental pictures radio and records could stimulate in listeners—a power that could transform individual imagination into a collective experience. Orson Wells's *War of the Worlds* broadcast, and the widespread panic that ensued along the Eastern Seaboard, demonstrated with force the social action radio could wield. Programmers and producers demanded that the full potential of aurality be used to good effect because audience denunciation was simply a dial turn away.[5]

The Cajun imaginary represents in this study the varied ways in which individuals understood their connection to a larger imagined community—America—through the soundscape generated by mass communication.[6] In Cajun Country, mass communication outlets assumed different forms. Newly established dance clubs and independent record labels took root in the Cajun Lapland. Meanwhile, radio broadcasts emanating from distant cities such as Dallas, Tulsa, and Shreveport, Louisiana, generated an aural matrix able to transport imaginative listeners to big-city baseball games, to Tulsa alongside Bob Wills, or to the bleachers in Shreveport's Municipal Auditorium as Hank Williams stirred the crowd into a frenzy. Unidirectional modes of transmission aimed at the psyche allowed receptive listeners to attach personalized meaning to songs, speeches, and other auditory information. Particularly for ethnic minorities, no matter if they lived in New York or New Iberia, imagination provided the tools for individuals to carry out the cultural work of making America in their own image.

My interests here lie in those communication networks directing the flow of cultural exchange between Cajuns and mainstream mass media between 1946 and 1955. I focus especially on Cajuns' mental engagement with those media technologies that made the world a smaller place. With personal networks already in place, radio airwaves afforded Cajuns in this era experienced a new sense of connectedness. If the sound of the music radiated from distant stations, the music's contours gained shape only in the minds of those tuned in at the other end. Radios hummed constantly in Cajun Country. The talking cabinet spoke with the disembodied voice of the American mainstream. This conspicuous piece of furniture opened a virtual portal into an imaginary realm where musicians called you "friend," the President of the United States spoke directly in your ear, and advertisers promised to change your life with their miracle products.

As this auditory sphere enveloped Cajun life, an emergent Cajun musical subgenre sprouted: Cajun honky-tonk. This stylistic development coincided with sociomusical developments in neighboring Texas. As country music historian Bill Malone notes, rural musicians introduced amplification, closed chords, and the percussive "shock rhythm" (striking all six guitar strings at once) as country music moved from house dances into "fightin' and dancin' clubs" termed honky-tonks by working-class patrons.[7] Cajuns not only listened to the drinking and cheating songs popularized by Ernest Tubb, Lefty Frizzell, and the region's other honky-tonkers but also created their own small but amplified string bands featuring an accordion front and center. The Cajun honky-tonk sound took hold in the Bayou Country and rapidly overwhelmed Cajun swing that had reigned supreme in Cajun country since the late 1930s. This transitional moment manifested through the emergence of several local independent record labels that profoundly shaped the region's musical currents and gave voice to Cajun musicians otherwise ignored by major recording labels. The rise in popularity of "Jole Blon" outlined the importance of these labels, a market that continued to expand after World War II. The Opera, O. T., Khoury, and Folk Star labels are discussed here in relation to the most famous and influential Cajun artists to emerge during the post-World War II era—fiddler Harry Choates and accordionist Iry LeJeune.

The premise of this study is derived from conclusions of the landmark treatise *The Psychology of Radio* compiled in 1935 by Hadley Cantril and Gordon Allport, of Columbia and Harvard universities, respectively. Cantril and Allport's study provides contemporary reactions to the emergent mass media's awesome ability to make the world a smaller place. "The scientists who first mastered the acoustical properties of ether did not know they were preparing a device that within one short generation would bind the earth in a universal network of sound," they expressed in awe.[8] The dissemination of information accelerated at such velocity as to create a sense of simultaneity, a sense that the world was suddenly at your fingertips. And, more profound, an individual's engagement with mass culture within this universal network of sound, Cantril and Allport suggest, could stimulate a "new mental world" for the listener.[9] The personalized stimulus of the human voice, the sense of participation through visualization, and the simultaneity of live radio encouraged listeners to dream about the sounds they heard. Cantril and Allport's field study suggests that radio's intimacy "made each listener feel welcome as a member of the circle."[10]

For marginalized and denigrated demographics, the auditory world of mass communication had democratic potential. Millions of people listened to the same emissions collectively in isolation, a scenario that could momentarily subvert class structures and racial hierarchies. African Americans could feel exhilarated listening to Joe Louis beat up his white opponent Max Schmeling, while disenfranchised Southern whites might find a brief instance of validation in populist demagoguery through the intimate directness afforded by radio oratory. Louisiana politician Huey Long, for instance, always began his radio addresses with, "Friends, this is Huey P. Long speaking . . . I want you to go to the phone and call up five of your fiends and tell them to listen in."[11] Meanwhile, beginning in 1943, on-air Cajun personalities began to broadcast in French. Radio democratized the Cajuns' native tongue, marginalized since the Progressive Era, by equating French with the celebrated voice of mainstream America. Live radio had the power to create a sense of belonging and emotional involvement as radio receivers piped stories about contemporary affairs into the nation's living rooms. Farmers heard the same static and voices as city dwellers as they consciously listened alone, together, in the creation of that amorphous imagined community—the "audience."

The Honky-Tonk Corridor

Construction of a new mental world began simply by tuning in. "A turn of the wrist immeasurably expands [the listener's] personal world," as Cantril and Allport so eloquently state.[12] Industrialization, itinerant labor, and the emergence of regional mass media outlets were the building blocks that forged the communication networks compelling Cajuns to move into the realm of the imaginary. These social and economic forces connected the Cajun Lapland to the center of the cultural convergence zone that transcended and traversed political boundaries and state lines. At once confined by geography and unbound by imagination, historian Kevin S. Fontenot dubs this interactive Cajun space as the "Honky Tonk Corridor." "The Honky Tonk Corridor straddles the Texas-Louisiana border and extends northward to Tulsa," Fontenot maintains. "The region is anchored on the southeast by Lafayette, LA, and on the southwest by Houston, TX. The region moves north through Shreveport and Dallas-Forth Worth and ultimately reaches its apex at Tulsa, Oklahoma."[13] Just beyond these geographical parameters, New Orleans exerted considerable influence on musical trends within the region. The urban center's media outlets also served the Honky-Tonk Corridor as a meeting ground where musicians interacted in regional recording studios.

Between 1900 and 1950, the rapid spread of industrialization and a shared dance culture facilitated the fruitful musical interaction that blossomed in the Honky-Tonk Corridor. In east Texas, Tejanos populated the south, while Germans, Czechs, Moravians, and Bohemians settled in the hill country that extended northward to Dallas. The Lone Star State also had a considerable and influential African-American and Anglo-Celtic population. Louisiana's landscape was just as diverse: Cajuns, Afro-Creoles, Midwesterners, Germans, and French/French Canadians to the south, and a largely Anglo-Protestant and African-American populace north of Acadiana. The Catholic faith, Latin and Franco factions, and "an extended 'frontier' period" complicated the corridor's ethnic equation.

Fontenot notes that a highly mobile work force composed largely of young men traveled in search of work in the corridor's lumber (1890s–1920s), petroleum (1900 on), and wartime industries, in addition to the agricultural economy sustaining much of the rural American South. Furthermore, the disposable income generated by this industrialized labor force intersected directly the Corridor's vibrant dance culture. "Dance halls often had ethnicities," Fontenot maintains, "and were popular with Czechs and Cajuns in particular. . . . Dance halls, at least on the inside, were safer havens than honky tonks which developed in the years following the end of Prohibition."[14] In Cajun Country, dance halls were, by and large, family-oriented spaces where parents took their marriageable sons and daughters. Honky-tonks, on the other hand, evolved from the seedy and violent "blind tiger" (speak-easy) scenes that attracted moonshiners, drunks, prostitutes, fighters, musicians, "and all the low types who followed the booms."[15] Both dance halls and honky-tonks catered to demanding audiences who insisted on danceable music, much of which also found an audience through newly established regional and local radios stations and independent record labels within the region.

By the 1940s, a distinctive music scene had developed in Orange, Texas, in the heart of the Honky-Tonk Corridor. Impoverished Cajuns left Louisiana in droves in hopes of finding a comfortable existence in the Golden Triangle region of east Texas bounded by Beaumont, Port Arthur, and Orange. According to geographer Dean Louder and historian Michael Leblanc, Cajuns flocked to the Golden Triangle in two successive waves during the twentieth century—the first movement ending in 1921, and the second beginning in the early 1940s—which generated lasting cultural and demographic repercussions in the region.[16] Port Arthur grew from "a mere 7,600 in 1910 to over 50,000 by 1930."[17] Meanwhile, the population of Orange exploded from 765 in 1900, to 46,140 in 1940 as a direct result of the Cajun influx.[18] This Cajun migration magnifies the significance of both industrialization and the corridor's pervasive petroleum culture. Louder and Leblanc write: "In 1902, following the establishment of the first Texas Oil Corporation refinery and a company town near Orange, Texas, Cajuns so completely dominated the facility's work force and housing units that the community became popularly known as Petite Abbeville."[19] The great Texas migration marked the decided cultural shift away from the Cajun community's agrarian values toward a new mental world structured by industrialization, mass consumption, and materialism. Southwest Louisiana's working class continued to migrate to Texas through the Second World War after the U.S. Navy awarded multimillion dollar contracts to local shipbuilding companies in Orange.[20]

Single male itinerant workers with disposable incomes populated the industrialized sprawl in the Golden Triangle. With cash in hand and a thirst for diversion from the long workweeks, this new proletariat supported an entertainment industry thriving off the Corridor's booming industrialized economy. Honky-tonks and dives emerged as interactive spaces that catered to oil workers and ship builders, Cajuns and Anglos. These clubs fostered local manifestations of the new mental world Cajuns cultivated. Mass media's influence shaped the sonic world of honky-tonks throughout the Corridor as string bands emulated the sounds they heard from radio broadcasts emanating from Dallas, Tulsa, New Orleans, and beyond. A kind of circular exchange framed the way that mass culture influenced performance styles, repertoire, and the ways in which Cajuns perceived their connection to mainstream culture. Musicians listened to broadcasts and records, interpreted what they heard, and then introduced their adaptation over the radio microphone and in the recording studio.

Honky-tonks relegated to a vice district on the eastern banks of the Sabine River (referred to as East Orange, Louisiana) served as the testing ground where audiences demanded an amalgam of local and mainstream music. Card games, cock fighting, slot machines, and other illicit forms of gambling accompanied the strip of seedy clubs that employed Cajun swing, Western swing, and country music ensembles.[21] A mammoth steamboat promoted as "America's Largest Floating Dance Pavilion," docked on the eastern banks of the Sabine, served as both a Cajun swing hotspot and the strip's most notorious honky-tonk. "If the music scene in east Texas and southwest Louisiana had a nerve center in the 1940s," explains music writer Andrew Brown, "it was East Orange. Cliff Bruner, Moon Mullican, Toby Kelley, Link Davis, all were stalwarts of the Strip, and Leo Soileau and the Rhythm Boys had been the house band at the Showboat since October, 1944" (figure 8.1).[22] The axis of the Cajun swing movement shifted during World War II from Crowley to the center of the corridor, indeed to the banks of the Sabine River. Soileau's Cajun swing outfit played an amalgam of Western swing, country, Cajun, and American popular tunes—ranging from "The Woodchopper's Ball" and "In the Mood" to "Jolie Blonde" and "Big Mamou"—to accommodate the shipyard and oil refinery workers who frequented the Showboat. Likewise, the fiddler hired a variety of musicians from either side of the state line. In different incarnations, the Rhythm Boys lineup included drummer Crawford Vincent, bassist George Duhon, guitarist D. W. Thibodeaux, pianist Gene Navarre, saxophonist Link Davis, steel guitarist Julius "Papa Cairo" Lamperez, guitarist Esmond "Eddie" Pursley, and a young upstart named Harry Choates whose fiddle skill was matched only by his Anglo-American counterpart Cliff Bruner.[23]

Fiddle virtuoso Cliff Bruner directly influenced Cajun swing bands in the Golden Triangle and in Louisiana. Andrew Brown equates the influence of the former Musical Brownie with the social and economic impact of the Spindletop oil boom. Brown elaborates:

Figure 8.1. By the 1940s, the range of instrumentation in Leo Soileau's Cajun swing orchestras afforded the fiddler the flexibility to perform French tunes, hillbilly, and popular compositions in ballrooms and honky-tonks. Courtesy of the Margie Breaux Collection, Center for Louisiana Studies, University of Louisiana at Lafayette.

The arrival, in early 1937, of Cliff Bruner and his Texas Wanderers in Beaumont transformed the entire region musically every bit as much as Spidletop [sic] had done so economically years before. While the records of people like Milton Brown, Bob Wills, and Bill Boyd had undoubtedly been staples on local jukeboxes well before this, none of these groups had actually made live appearances in the area.[24]

Harry Choates drew inspiration from Bruner's band, particularly the work of Bob Dunn, the Texas Wanderers' steel guitar player.[25] He also collaborated with Cajun crooner Buddy Duhon, who enjoyed a successful career as the longtime vocalist for Bruner.

Duhon's smooth, unassuming pop vocal delivery made him a favorite in the corridor. The Cajun singer was a Jimmie Rodgers devotee whose ability to fluctuate between styles and genres—such as popular compositions, blues, country, swing, and Cajun—boosted his stock as a professional musician in southeast Texas and southwest Louisiana.[26] In 1941, he joined the Texas Wanderers and eventually became Bruner's right-hand man, acting as bus driver, mechanic, cover-charge collector, and the bandleader's personal assistant. Duhon also acted as gatekeeper and facilitator for the Anglo Texan ensemble as the group toured Cajun Country, particularly when trouble arose in dance halls. Cliff Bruner remembered that his assistant's loyalty remained with those who ensure his financial security, rather than his cultural counterparts:

> One time we was playing this little town way down in deep Louisiana. And some of the girls had winked at the boys in the band, you know? And these [local] boys got mad about it. Naturally. So they decided that they was gonna whip us. They all gathered up—there was about 20 or 30, a flock of 'em. When it was all over and we were fixing to leave, Buddy looked out there and he saw two lines, one on each side of the walkway going to the bus. And it's just lined up with those Frenchmen!—ready to whip our band. There was enough of 'em that they should've been able to, but Buddy had news for them. He reached in that money box that he had and he had the biggest .44 you ever saw—that thing had bullets like a shotgun! He pulled that thing out and waved it at those guys. He said, "I'll tell you what: we're coming right down between you. I'm gonna count 1–2–3 and when I say three, if any of you are not running, you're gonna get a bullet between your eyes!" And he started counting—and, boy, they started running! So Buddy came in handy lots of times! He said, "I know who you are!"—they were all coon-asses, you know? He was something else.[27]

Buddy Duhon served as Cliff Bruner's middle man when in Cajun Country, precisely because Duhon imagined himself as linked to both the blue-collar patrons in attendance and his Anglo American employer. The warning, "I know who you are!," translated the musician's willingness to retaliate violently in accordance with the Cajun code of honor that governed fighting and "folk justice" at Bayou Country dances. While he privileged his allegiance to Bruner in this particular scenario, the Anglo fiddler kept Duhon in check by reminding him of this ethnic status. "They were all coon-asses," including Buddy Duhon, Bruner insisted. Cajuns such as Duhon and Choates led by example for the working-class people of Acadiana. By emphasizing their adaptability in both Cajun and Anglo contexts, they helped created space for Cajuns to feel like they belonged to the American project. Crossing over into the mainstream was neither easy nor always pleasant. Choates drowned his anxiety with alcohol, only to expire alone in an Austin, Texas jail cell at the age of 28. Duhon, who also lived off the Corridor's bounty, died in a swimming accident near Beaumont after recording his last two sides—"Old Cow Blues" and "Nobody Cares for Me"—with Choates.[28]

Harry Choates' musical legacy serves as an accurate barometer for the Cajun community's evolving mindset and cultural orientation within the Honky-Tonk Corridor. Choates, who became widely popular both in his native Louisiana and Texas, played frequently alongside several of the great string band icons, including Leo Soileau, before his rendition of the Cajun classic "Jole Blon" moved Choates into the national musical spotlight. In view of the instability plaguing the recording star's personal life—alcoholism, gambling, and extramarital affairs—his remarkable commercial success would seem something of a mystery. The interconnecting maze of communication channels available to Cajun musicians during the 1940s allowed Choates to overcome seemingly insurmountable odds when he launched his national hit on an unknown independent record label. "Neither Louisiana nor Texas can exclusively claim him," maintains the fiddler's biographer Andrew Brown, "as he vacillated between these two states, both physically and in musical terms, so often as to render their border irrelevant."[29] He fused the improvisational style of steel guitarist Bob Dunn and Gypsy jazzman Django Reinhart with the technique and repertoire of his mentor Leo Soileau. The fiddler's urbane pop sensibility and brilliant musicianship also allowed him to straddle Cajun and Anglo-American musical currents. He plugged directly into the networks of sound penetrating the Honky-Tonk Corridor.

Cajuns were active listeners, and indeed accomplished participants, in the communication networks sprawling across the region. Like Choates, locals could easily imagine their attachment to the mainstream because they effectively influenced the voice of local mass media after World War II. The war accelerated shifts in Cajuns' self-perception.[30] Bilingual Louisianians became significant players in the international conflict as French interpreters for the U.S. military. Their denigrated native tongue quickly accumulated new significance as a life-saving attribute that moved Cajun soldiers from the frontlines to the interrogation room. Locals entering military service and the broad reach of pro-American propaganda left their mark on both French- and English-language broadcasting in the Bayou Country.

Politician and entrepreneur Dudley J. LeBlanc harnessed the power of mass media to reach listening audiences across the southern portion of the Honky-Tonk Corridor. In 1943, Cajuns welcomed "Cousin Dud" into their living rooms for 30 minutes of local, national, and international news in English and French during his weekly broadcasts over the 16-station Louisiana Hadacol Network. LeBlanc set the precedent for French-language broadcasting and later raked in millions of dollars as he also promoted his notorious cure-all tonic Hadacol.[31] A familiar accent coming through the same loudspeakers that broadcast the sounds of mainstream America facilitated LeBlanc's efforts to create an imagined community. The Cajun orator used colloquialisms and friendly banter to simulate sociable interaction. But unlike political rallies, where Cajuns could provide immediate feedback, mass media disrupted the circular flow of social exchange that enriched Cajun culture and music. Rather, LeBlanc's monologues flowed in a single direction from the radio station to the audience. Cajuns embraced the opportunity to create community, even if their interaction was not face to face.

Locals consciously and enthusiastically responded to the rise of mass media outlets within the region. "We listen to your [radio] program every Thursday," wrote a fervent listener from Gueydan, Louisiana to the Hackberry Ramblers, "and we think you'er [sic] the best on the air."[32] Fan mail addressed to the Ramblers' weekly Thursday night radio broadcast from Lake Charles poured in during the war years. Cajuns engaged the radio as a way to expand their imagined community to distant corners of the world, where their sons and daughters in the service were physically becoming part of the broader American community. In 1944, active listeners from across the Cajun Lapland—from Port Arthur, Texas, to Jennings, Louisiana—mailed requests for patriotic songs like "Soldiers Last Letter" and "There's a Star Spangled Banner Waving Somewhere" dedicated to their loved ones serving overseas. Lonely girlfriends such as Rene Belle Dyke of Welsh, Louisiana, also requested sentimental songs penned by honky-tonk artists from the Corridor. "Dear Boys," Dyke wrote on June 26, 1944, "Will you please play [Tex Ritter's] 'Have I Stayed Away too Long' For Jesse P. Gautreaux in the U.S. Navy From his sweetheart." Emile Broussard, a concerned father in Lake Arthur, Louisiana, implored that the Ramblers play their best rendition of Ernest Tubb. "Please play this requested tune ["]I am walking the Floor over You["] for P.V.T. Lawrence Broussard whoes [sic] in the army, Station [sic] in North Carolina," the melancholy parent wrote. "We will be listening."[33] Radio's ability to shrink the world through a virtual community allowed Cajun listeners to imagine that their loved ones halfway around the world were still within arm's reach. Both World War II and an intensive engagement with mass communications stimulated a seismic shift in the mental life of the Cajun community. Men and women shipped off to war physically connected a segment of the community to the American mainstream. Theirs was the dangerous grunt work that allowed marginalized ethnics to feel, at least temporarily, fully American.[34] Cajun families were suddenly deeply invested in the national war effort.

Worried parents and girlfriends emphasized their imagined connection to GIs by requesting patriotic and sentimental songs over the radio waves.

Anxious families on the home front found solace in the emerging honky-tonk sounds popularized by artists such as Ernest Tubb and Tex Ritter. Songs like "Have I Stayed Away Too Long" and "I'm Walking the Floor Over You" clearly carried profound emotional significance for Cajuns to dedicate these compositions to their loved ones in harm's way. Honky-tonk therefore conveyed more salient meaning than just dance music. Singers like Tubb, Ritter, and Hank Williams filtered the American experience through a Southern musical vernacular that spoke with resonance to Cajun audiences. Records and radio firmly established honky-tonk's presence in the sonic world enveloping the ethnic community. By the mid-1940s, Cajun musicians began to interpret those sounds by synthesizing aspects of Cajun swing with the architecture of honky-tonk.

The functional overlap between swing and honky-tonk was more than just musical. Cajuns fashioned Cajun honky-tonk while exploiting the increasing dense matrix of mass communication channels within the Honky-Tonk Corridor that gave rise to such phenomena as "Jole Blon." "At one time we were on seven radio stations. Most of it was live," reported former Rayne-Bo Rambler bandleader Leroy "Happy Fats" LeBlanc. "Like on a Saturday we would play Opelousas, Lafayette and Abbeville, three stations. Two of them were live from the stage of theatres they had linked with the radio stations and we stayed together during the forties and early fifties."[35] After the Rayne-Bo Ramblers disbanded in 1941, LeBlanc played in various ensembles around the Corridor. He played for a two-year stint with Leo Soileau's outfit at the Silver Star Club in Lake Charles and announced for the band during their daily radio broadcasts from KPLC. The musician then returned to his native Rayne, where he found a regular dance job at the Hollywood Club before making the transition to radio. During the late 1940s and early 1950s, LeBlanc and fiddler Oran "Doc" Guidry secured sponsors and performed on radio stations around Cajun Country. Like their Hackberry Ramblers counterparts, Cajun musicians including Happy Fats and Doc Guidry became stalwarts of the ether. They filled the airwaves with local sounds and diversified the radio dial.

Mass cultural outlets became the fountainheads feeding the Cajuns' "new mental world." The distribution of mass media technology coincided with the reach of industrialization and profoundly affected the cultural climate in Texas, Louisiana, and Oklahoma. Influential and far-reaching radio stations emerged in Dallas (KRLD), Shreveport (KWKH), and Tulsa (KVOO). The physical dimensions of these locales are far less significant to this study than their place in the mind of the Cajun audiences who tuned in. Like Hollywood for many Americans, Dallas, Shreveport, and Tulsa were imaginary spaces for many Cajuns. They were radio hubs associated with the live performances and banter of the Light Crust Doughboys and the Musical Brownies (Dallas), Hank Williams and the *Louisiana Hayride* (Shreveport), and the warm, inviting voice of Bob Wills (Tulsa). Unlike records, these live radio venues stimulated what

Cantril and Allport termed "the sense of participation in actual events that is radio's chief psychological characteristic. It is not merely words and melodies that the listener craves. These he can obtain from a variety of mechanical contraptions. When he turns his dial he wants to enter the stream of life as it is actually lived."[36] Luderin Darbone and the Hackberry Ramblers did not have to drive to Tulsa to experience Bob Wills. Rather, the band learned a portion of their extensive repertoire from active listening to Wills's radio broadcasts during their return trip after they themselves had performed. Radio's immediacy provided enough visceral information for the "imaginative completion of the situation in the minds of the listeners."[37] Cain's Ballroom, where Bob Wills broadcast, might look more like Basile's Avalon Club in the mind's eye of some Cajun listeners, but that was the magic of mass communication. Cajuns remade American through mental images entirely of their own design. The power of an individual's imagination provided the building blocks of the Cajun's new mental world.

Cajun participation in World War II encouraged and even accelerated the process through which Cajuns imagined themselves as part of the mainstream. Tales of distant lands and military service only served to reinforce the emotive sense that Cajuns participated in the American national project. More significant, veterans returned from the global conflict with a sense of empowerment and became visible proponents in civic affairs. Some became local radio newscasters. Their worldly experience and intimate knowledge of local attitudes allowed these broadcasters to selectively determine which pieces of local, national, and international news might be of interest to local audiences. The result was a Cajunized form of mass media that directly channeled the outside world into a consumable Cajun commodity.

Bertrand DeBlanc returned to his native Louisiana after three years in the U.S. Army Signal Corps in the European Theater. Like many veterans, he applied his military training and exposure to the Army's global communications networks to local contexts that in the process changed the Cajun imaginary. On April 1, 1948, DeBlanc began broadcasting a daily French news program from KVOL in Lafayette. Dudley Bernard from Golden Meadow, Louisiana, served as an interpreter in North Africa, Southern France, and the Pacific. After five and a half years overseas, he formed a Cajun radio band named Southern Serenaders, an experience that then allowed him to shift from band member to French newscaster and disk jockey on KLFT in his hometown. Likewise, journalist Alden Sonnier enlisted in the Air Force in 1941 and rose through the ranks to captain before his discharge, when he became a newscaster in both French and English at Crowley's KSIG during the 1950s. These French-language broadcasters interpreted the news through the same selective process that informed Cajun music's evolution through time. Interpreting stories from news outlets such as local newspapers and the Associated Press wire services, broadcasters selectively translated the English-language copy into French live on the air.[38]

The rise of French-language talk radio was only one aspect of Cajuns assuming control of those mass communication outlets that so influenced their culture in their own image. The second substantial phase in local broadcasting came with the Cajun disk jockey. While largely a 1950s phenomenon, the rise of local DJs suggests the level of engagement Cajuns attained with the sonic world they helped create. Jerry Dugas, host of the program "Allons Danser" on Jennings' KJEF, explained that he "received so many requests demanding that the same French recordings be played time and time again that he completely discontinued the policy of playing requests on his program."[39] Dugas's frustration was hardly an isolated incident. Willie Bordelon, DJ for "The Cajun Hour" broadcast over station KAPB in Marksville, Louisiana, also fielded numerous repetitive song requests that inhibited programming variety. Dugas's and Bordelon's experiences signify the community's obsession with mass communication. Cajuns embraced locally produced records documenting and encouraging stylistic shifts from Cajun swing to Cajun honky-tonk following the war.

"The Rise of Cajun Honky-Tonk"

Kevin Fontenot maintains that Western swing and honky-tonk were two of the most distinctive forms of dance music to crystallize within the bounds of the Honky-Tonk Corridor. Both styles claimed small string band combos as antecedents. While Western swing bands evolved into full-blown orchestras that synthesized jazz, big band swing, country, mariachi, blues, and popular music, honky-tonk outfits remained small and employed amplification to increase their projection inside of halls. "Many of the most popular Cajun bands of the 1930s were essentially Western Swing or Honky Tonk aggregations," continues Fontenot, "such as the Hackberry Ramblers, the Alley Boys [of Abbeville], and the various bands led by Leo Soileau" (figure 8.2).[40] Between 1935 and World War II, Cajun swing bands frequently paralleled the sound and instrumentation (and at times repertoire) of their corridor counterparts like Bob Wills, Milton Brown, and Cliff Bruner. After the war, Western swing relocated its nexus to the West Coast. Developing honky-tonk bands quickly filled the void. Legendary country musicians such as Jimmie Davis, Floyd Tillman, and Hank Williams, all of whom created their legacies in the corridor, prompted Cajun bands to follow suit. The so-called "dance hall sound," championed by Iry LeJeune, Nathan Abshire, and Lawrence Walker in the late 1940s and early 1950s, paralleled in many ways the form and sound of country honky-tonk outfits, with several exceptions, including French vocal deliveries and the prominence of the diatonic accordion.

Cajun honky-tonkers cut records on the region's new independent labels. After World War II, the American record industry underwent radical decentralization as hundreds of emergent independent labels fragmented the American recording industry.[41] Music historians Rick Kennedy and Randy McNutt estimate that more than 1,000 independent labels emerged in the United States between 1948 and 1954.[42] Cajun honky-tonkers were among the creators of the independent label movement and influenced

Figures 8.2. Both Cajun swing (*top*) and Cajun honky-tonk (*bottom*) musicians consciously dressed in bandanas, oversized straw hats, and occasionally overalls, like members of the Grand Ole Opry, after World War II. Courtesy of the Freeland Archives, Acadia Parish Library, Crowley, Louisiana.

its development. Ambitious entrepreneurs in the Honky-Tonk Corridor—such as Bill Quinn, Bennie Hess, and James Bryant in Texas, and Jay Miller, George Khoury, and Eddie Shuler in Louisiana—opened recording studios that gave a voice to the shifting trends in regional music, styles that were often overlooked by major labels. In contrast to the sometimes monotonic sound of the major labels, independents brought together a cacophony of American musical traditions, making them ideal recording homes for Cajun honky-tonkers' musical experimentation (figure 8.3). Local independent labels provided space where Cajuns could construct primary texts that translated their new mental world in sonic form.

Electrical contractor and part-time musician Jay D. Miller excited extensive change in Cajun music by becoming a local mass communication mogul. "French records, apart from 'Jole Blon' and a couple of other Harry Choates records," he explained, "just were not available."[43] Miller imagined that he could satisfy the Cajun consumer's demand for local music by launching Cajun Country's first independent record label—Fais Do Do.[44] He produced his first session in June 1946 with former Rayne-Bo Rambler Happy Fats LeBlanc and swing fiddler Doc Guidry and their band "the Boys." Without recording equipment, Miller, the ensemble, and Charlie "Dago" Retlitch traveled to Cosmo Matassa's New Orleans studio to cut two sides. "With this recording session being what we thought to be one of the highlights of our lives we did a little celebrating, cajun style. There was plenty of food, plenty of drink, and plenty of music (which) lasted nearly all night. . . . The next day is when the records were cut."[45] Miller subsequently issued Happy Fats and Doc Guidry's string band offerings as "Setre Chandelle" and "Allons Dance Colinda" on his newly minted Fais Do Do label.

Figure 8.3. Like other independent producers in the Honky-Tonk Corridor, Eddie Shuler equipped his Folk Star, and later Goldband, studios in Lake Charles, Louisiana, with relatively inexpensive technology readily available to enthusiasts across the country. Courtesy of Southern Folklife Collection, Wilson Library, University of North Carolina at Chapel Hill.

Matassa's studio inspired Miller to create his own studio. The fledgling producer traveled to the retailer Gates Radio Supply in Houston, Texas, where he purchased the Magna Carter P-56 magnetic tape recorder that served as his Crowley studio centerpiece. By October 1946, he was open for business. Miller's father-in-law, Lee Sonnier, and his Acadian All-Stars became the first ensemble to record in the new Crowley studio and the first band to reintroduce accordion-based dance sound to the commercial marketplace after World War II.[46]

Sonnier was a product of Louisiana's industrial economy and the regional musical climate. A welder by trade, the part-time musician made a living working in defense plants. After World War II, he opened his own welding shop and performed for dances on the weekends. Sonnier took time away from his business to record eight songs during a session that proved to be Jay Miller's first experience as a producer and sound engineer. Sitting in with Sonnier's Acadian All-Stars, Cajun swinger Happy Fats yet again instigated radical shifts in Cajun music's architecture by reconciling the differences between Cajun swing and accordion-based Cajun music—a feat he could not accomplish with Nathan Abshire in 1935. Happy Fats took the lead vocals on the group's very first recording, "Dans les Grand Meche." LeBlanc's rhythm guitar danced between chord changes answers Sonnier's bubbly accordion while band members lifted their voices with "yeah ha" and other staccato exclamations. The Acadian All-Stars slipped into a hypnotic groove driven by the guitars, accordion bass chords, and other supporting voices accentuating in unison a 2/4 dance beat.

Time signature was key to the recording's fluidity. During the late 1930s, swingers significantly shifted away from hot jazz's pounding 4/4 rhythms toward the 2/4 permutations perfected by Western swingers Milton Brown and Bob Wills. This change facilitated the formation of Cajun honky-tonk. Sonnier's aggregate style created the space for revamped Cajun rhythm sections to sync like clockwork with the accordion's pulsing syncopation. That fateful day in October 1946, Happy Fats and Lee Sonnier fine-tuned the mechanics of Cajun music by aligning the gears driving swing and accordion-dance music. Jay D. Miller captured this historic development while inadvertently launching an accordion revival, not in the same fashion as heard during the early commercial era, but through the fresh sounds of Cajun honky-tonk.[47]

The initial Acadian All-Star releases signaled that Cajun music's quintessential features had changed profoundly by 1946. A decade of commercial Cajun swing releases had transformed the local aesthetic, while hard-wiring the style's exaggerated 2/4 rhythmic approach into the minds and fingers of local accordionists. This new approach to Cajun music related directly to Louisiana's new industrialized reality and the vicissitudes shaping the genre's commercial direction. Amplification exaggerated the sonic force of rumbling basses, pining steel guitars, and the swollen chords booming from hollow-body electric guitars. Following the drummer's lead, these supportive voices became Cajun music's deep-throated engine, firing their pistons with coordinated regularity through the wall of sound blaring out of loudspeakers in wooden dance halls and honky-tonks. Amplified rhythmic beds controlled the propulsion of a composition's forward momentum, thus relieving accordionists of the burden of carrying a song's full weight as they had during the early commercial era. Rather, like the fiddle during the Cajun swing era, reconstructed Cajun rhythm sections encouraged virtuosity, improvisation, and embellishment when the accordion took the steering wheel as lead instrument. Meanwhile, Cajun rhythm sections looked to the bare outfits backing honky-tonk crooners like Ernest Tubb who harnessed the raw power of amplification when wartime conscription gutted the regulars from his band. Hence, smaller bands with bigger sounds carried the accordion into Cajun music's postwar era.

Sonnier's release wielded little influence on the genre's direction following his initial releases with Jay Miller. But then, the accordionist rode the crest of a tidal wave about to make landfall. The growing number of independent record labels opening for business between the end of World War II and 1955 joined the cacophony stimulated by the density of mass communication networks in the Honky-Tonk Corridor. Cajuns could imagine themselves as part of the mainstream America because they actively constructed a local mass media infrastructure that generated a portion of this sonic world. Just as the rise of recording studios in the Cajun Lapland created the launching pad for Harry Choates' Gold Star release "Jole Blon," the proliferation of locally accessible independent labels created an audience for Cajun honky-tonk.

In 1948, Bill Quinn's former associates Bennie Hess and James Bryant left Gold Star to launch the Opera label in Houston. Like Quinn's outfit, Opera marketed its products to country music fans and Cajun audiences with the slogan "Hits of the Hillbillies." Hess performed regularly with a hillbilly outfit named the Oklahoma Tornadoes, which served as the

Figure 8.4. Iry LeJeune (center) helped popularize the new sounds of Cajun honky-tonk after WWII by synthesizing the Oklahoma Tornadoes' swing instrumentation with the diatonic accordion. Ron Yule Collection, courtesy of Ervin LeJeune.

label's house band. The Tornadoes lineup exemplified the regional cross-cultural interaction that influenced Cajun musical expression. Hess and guitarist Virgil Bozeman represented the Anglo-American component of the ensemble while a fiddler from Mermentau, Louisiana, named Floyd LeBlanc injected a Cajun sensibility into the Tornadoes' sound.[48] While LeBlanc enjoyed some success with Cajun audiences following his Opera release "Over the Waves," the fiddler's real contribution to Opera came when he introduced the label's managers to accordionist Iry LeJeune. Hess and Bryant witnessed first-hand the tremendous success of Harry Choates' "Jole Blon" and recognized LeJeune's promising talent with the accordion to tap the potentially lucrative Cajun market. LeJeune sat in the Opera studios with his accordion and recorded the Cajun honky-tonk anthem "Love Bridge Waltz" backed by the Oklahoma Tornadoes.[49] The song launched a renewed interest in accordion music in the commercial Cajun market and demonstrated the effects of commercialization on postwar Cajun music (figure 8.4).

Cultural activists, scholars, and music writers have often presented Iry LeJeune as an archetypal working-class Cajun contemptuously resisting assimilation into the American mainstream during the 1940s by performing (and thereby preserving) traditional music and eschewing Cajun swing.[50] Yet, contrary to popular belief, Iry LeJeune's musical legacy represents the new mental world Cajuns' constructed by imagining their connection to the mainstream. His fascination with commercial recordings stimulated his desire to record. It also suggests the extent of individual engagement with mass media at midcentury. Music writer Ann Savoy notes, "He spent many hours listening to his Uncle Angelas LeJeune's 78's of early accordion masters"—including the likes of Amédé Ardoin, Amédé Breaux, and Angelas LeJeune himself—as well as Cajun swing recordings by Happy Fats LeBlanc and Leo Soileau.[51] Unable to pick cotton on the family farm due to his poor vision, Iry spent considerable time developing his technique and repertoire by playing along with phonograph records. LeJeune's serrated vocal and virtuosic accordion sliced straight to the hearts of his Cajun audiences, who warmly embraced his synthesis of the early commercial and Cajun swing repertoire.

Around 1935, LeJeune enrolled at the Louisiana School for the Blind in Baton Rouge, where he received his first formal education, including Braille and violin instruction (figure 8.5). The School for the Blind not only provided LeJeune with skills the musician would later employ on the Goldband recording "Duralde Waltz" and financial support that would eventually help sustain the visually impaired musician's family, but also placed him in close proximity to New Orleans, where his blind half-brother Whitney found employment at the Lighthouse for the Blind broom factory in 1940.[52] LeJeune biographer Ron Yule maintains that "Whitney would check him out, and Iry would ride the Greyhound Bus to New Orleans to stay with Whitney for as much as two weeks at a time."[53] During his recurrent sojourns in the Crescent City, the young musician earned considerable amounts of money performing outside the numerous country music and honky-tonk clubs along Magazine Street's bustling music strip. LeJeune earned upwards of $60 a night playing on the street and, eventually, $75 as a featured performer when club owners realized his potential marketability.

In 1946, LeJeune encountered fiddler and fellow Cajun Floyd LeBlanc and the rest of the Oklahoma Tornadoes, who happened to be performing in an adjacent club on Magazine.[54] After several collaborations in New Orleans, Lejeune attended an Oklahoma Tornado performance at the Pine Grove Club in Evangeline, Louisiana, in the heart of the Honky-Tonk Corridor. The string band had plans to leave the following day to record on Tornadoes' vocalist and guitarist Bennie Hess's newly formed Opera record label in Houston, Texas. LeJeune commented, "I'd sure like to go. I've got some recordings I need to do."[55] Recording, the young accordionist understood, was the only way he could be on equal footing with mainstream commercial artists.

Figure 8.5. Iry LeJeune's fiddling skills enriched his understanding of the instrumental approaches introduced during the Cajun swing era, an inclination he developed while at the Louisiana School for the Blind, where he learned to play the violin. Ron Yule Collection, courtesy of Ervin LeJeune.

One of the clearest examples of LeJeune's connection to commercial music is interwoven in the melody of his now classic "Love Bridge Waltz," which turned south Louisiana's record business and musical landscape on its ear. On November 7, 1929, accordionist Delin Guillory and fiddler Lewis LaFleur recorded six sides, two of which—"Stop That" and "Alone at Home"—were issued and distributed more than 10 years later in 1940. Music writer and record collector Ron Brown speculates that "with the masters already in hand, it was relatively cost-efficient to release music they already had in house . . . perhaps also, with a marketing experiment in mind, to see if, after a long lull, the accordion material would take off again."[56] LeJeune was apparently quite familiar with the Guillory-LaFleur release. The melody to "Alone at Home" served as the basis for the "Love Bridge Waltz" eight years later. Bluebird's delayed issue, in conjunction with the Acadian All-Stars' postwar catalogue, sparked the accordion revival that thrived in Cajun Country following World War II. The songs that LeJeune recorded for producer Eddie Shuler's Lake Charles–based Folk Star and Goldband labels after leaving Opera further illustrated the accordionist's familiarity with recorded French Louisiana selections by Afro-Creole accordionist Amédé Ardoin, Cajun fiddler Dennis McGee, and Cajun swing releases by the Rayne Bo Ramblers and Leo Soileau's Four Aces. His success hinged on both repertoire diversity and newly established mass communication outlets within the region.

Cajun honky-tonkers built their audience through rousing performances, radio spots, and perhaps most important through independent record labels. By 1950, a cluster of locally owned independent labels developed in the south central portion of the Honky-Tonk Corridor in Lake Charles, Louisiana. Lake Charles was the first substantial urban center east of the Texas-Louisiana state line. Like Jay Miller, Turkish-American George Khoury became one of the many local engineers dedicated to building the Gulf Coast's mass communication networks. Khoury owned a record shop, serviced jukeboxes, and established the independent Khoury and Lyric labels by embracing the technological tools stirring the local imagination. In 1949, the entrepreneur became directly involved in production by financing former Oklahoma Tornado Virgil Bozeman's newly formed O. T. Records.[57] Khoury's investment yielded handsome returns following Nathan Abshire and the Pine Grove Boys' regional hit on O. T., the "Pinegrove Blues," which firmly cemented Cajun honky-tonk's place as a dominant style in Cajun Country.[58]

The Pine Grove Boys began in 1948 as a small Cajun honky-tonk band, featuring fiddler Will Kegely on fiddle, Kegely's sister Oziet on drums, and guitarist Ernest Thibodeaux, and performed regularly at Telesfar Istre's Pine Grove Club near the Evangeline Oil Field (figure 8.6). At the club owner's request for an accordionist, the Pine Grove Boys hired Nathan Abshire to keep up with the region's evolving musical landscape. The group quickly amassed a following, in part through their daily radio broadcasts on Lake Charles radio station KPLC. On May 23, 1949, Bozeman, Abshire, and the Pine Grove Boys made their way back into the radio studio,

Figure 8.6. Amplification and an expanded rhythm section allowed Cajun honky-tonkers such as accordionist Nathan Abshire to bridge the divide between Cajun swing and accordion-based arrangements. Courtesy of Johnnie Allan.

this time to record the "Pinegrove Blues" and "Kaplan Waltz" on acetate disk. The raw accordion-driven, honky-tonk–styled "Pine Grove Blues" borrowed the melody from Abshire's 1935 Bluebird recording "One Step de Lacassine." The raucous low-fidelity recording incorporated call and response, a riff-based melody, and a storyline about a man confronting his cheating wife. It sold approximately 3,200 copies. "Pine Grove Blues" was Abshire's first hit, which, in conjunction with LeJeune's "Love Bridge Waltz," ensured the marketability of accordion-based records and the Cajun honky-tonk sound in postwar south Louisiana.

As early as 1935, Cantril and Allport understood mass communication's "capacity for providing the listener an opportunity to extend his environment easily and inexpensively, and to participate with a feeling of personal involvement in the events of the outside world from which he would otherwise be excluded."[59] The technologies of mass culture unlocked an imaginary gateway into the auditory realm of the American mainstream. Honky-tonk represented the sound of cultural agency in postwar Cajun Country. These little bands with big sounds made use of technological advances that became widely available to the general public. Inexpensive and accessible technology such as amplification changed music at the grassroots level. Meanwhile, independent record labels created space for musical experimentation. Local record producers also took advantage of the increasingly normalized prices and availability of recording equipment to stock their studios. New releases on the Fais Do Do, Folk Star, Khoury, Lyric, and Goldband labels widely circulated and popularized the musical shifts that gave rise to Cajun honky-tonk.

Meanwhile, radio piped in live performances by Cajuns such as Happy Fats LeBlanc appearing on the nationally syndicated *Louisiana Hayride*, while records issued by locally owned and operated independent labels became fixtures alongside American popular music on the region's jukeboxes.

The propensity for cultural exposure and adaptation—both characteristics for the Cajun experience with mass culture—culminated in one place in Cajun Country: the jukebox. Like radio, these record machines blurred the distinctions between nationally distributed genres like country, pop, and jazz. Jukeboxes were Americanizing forces par excellence. They afforded listeners the freedom to imagine the relationship between the genres and musical styles shuffling in grocery stores. And, when records like "Jole Blon" became staples in the rotation, these contraptions placed Cajun music on par with national idioms. "We learned songs from local musicians like the [Nathan Abshire's] fiddler Will Kegley. But when we started playing the bars, we also began to learn the songs off the jukeboxes. . . . I could hear Cajun things by Harry Choates, country singers like Ernest Tubb, and big band stuff by Glenn Miller," Cajun fiddler Doug Kershaw recalled of his relationship with jukeboxes. These mass media outlets allowed Cajuns to imagine their music, and by inference their culture, as part of the American mainstream. "You know," Kershaw continues, "there were no labels on the jukebox—it wasn't country or jazz or Cajun—it was just music."[60] The more local artists rightly imagined themselves as active participants in national trends, the more their admiration grew for their new imaginary peers.

Jukeboxes offered listeners a democratic vision of the American musical landscape. Cajun records played for the same cost of a Glenn Miller or Hank Williams tune. Moreover, these potent imaginary tools acted as a virtual nexus where Cajun Country's increasingly dense communication networks intersected in one conveniently accessible place. Jukeboxes helped structure the boundaries of the postwar Cajun imaginary, including the connection Cajuns felt toward Hank Williams.

The Cajun Likeness of Hank Williams

Unlike any other artists before, Hank Williams, Sr., came to represent the Cajun involvement in the broader world beyond Cajun Country. His nasal yodel cut across the mass cultural networks structured by radio, record, and other audio technologies. Emotional sincerity and frequent tours across the Cajun Lapland made Hank Williams an icon in the new mental world that postwar Cajuns constructed. "With Cajun people, he hit," remembered Jimmy C. Newman. "He was telling it the way it was, you know, and the Cajun people love that real sincere story in a song."[61] In 1952, the same year Kitty Wells recorded the Jay Miller composition "It Wasn't God Who Made Honky Tonk Angels," Williams released the perennial Cajun favorite "Jambalaya (on the Bayou)" during his short stint at the Grand Ole Opry. When the Opry fired him, the country star celebrated his *Louisiana Hayride* "homecoming" during the fall of that year with a raucous rendition of "Jambalaya" live from Shreveport's Municipal Auditorium. Uninhibited eruptions from the audience punctuated Williams's performance. The capacity crowd boisterously demonstrated their appreciation of the song, which had recently topped the charts, and the fact that "the old lonesome Drifting Cowboy is coming home again."[62]

As *Hayride* historian Tracey Laird asserts, "Williams bridged north and south Louisiana with his Anglo pop variant of a Cajun tune in 'Jambalaya.'"[63]

When he sang it, Cajuns fell in love with the country star. "Jambayala (on the Bayou)" came to represent the genesis of the Cajun as American story: the community's rise from the status of marginal ethnics to the ways in which individuals perceived their participation in the American mainstream. In the process, Hank Williams became the chosen Anglo voice of the Cajun experience. After "Jole Blon," the country composition signified the community's admittance into the annals of American popular culture. Locals embraced him, in part, because they empathized with Williams's plight. Marginalized by the mainstream radio giant WSM, Williams returned "home again" to the only audiences that seemed to accept his working-class wisdom, blemishes and all—the imagined *Louisiana Hayride* community.

Cajuns adopted Williams as an ambassador between Cajun Country and the American mainstream, a connection reaffirmed through a tangle of "Jambalaya" origin stories. His time in Louisiana stimulated numerous Drifting Cowboy sightings. For instance, Williams was scheduled to play the McNeese Junior College Auditorium in Lake Charles on April 19, 1949. "Legend has it that after the show," Andrew Brown maintains, "Williams showed up at a club Harry [Choates] was appearing at, and the two kindred spirits played a jam session well into the night. Considering how often Williams toured south Louisiana and east Texas, it would hardly be surprising if their paths didn't cross more than once."[64] Williams left such an impression on budding Cajun guitarist and vocalist D. L. Menard that the Erath native embarked on a lucrative career as the self-proclaimed "Cajun Hank Williams." Roughly 10 years after meeting the Drifting Cowboy at the Teche Club in New Iberia, Menard borrowed the melody to his now classic composition "The Back Door" (1962) from Williams's "Honky Tonk Blues."[65] Williams the icon was a product that sold well to a community addicted to mass consumption. But where do the grains of truth about the origin of "Jambalaya" lie between personal contact, nostalgia, and the imaginary world stimulated by records and radio? Perhaps somewhere between the ether, jukebox, and Papa Cairo Lamperez's recordings of "Big Texas."

In 1948, brothers Joe and Jules Bihari—whose sibling Lester distributed jukeboxes in the southwestern portion of the Honky-Tonk Corridor—conducted an extensive Southern musical survey for their Los Angeles-based Modern record label and established a regional recording facility in New Orleans to record their newly found talent. The Bihari Brothers recorded Chuck Guillory and His Rhythm Boys, a young Cajun swing outfit featuring the archetypal Cajun steel guitarist and World War II veteran Julius "Papa Cairo" Lamperez, whose melody to "Big Texas" served as the foundation of Williams's 1952 hit "Jambalaya."

"Papa Cairo saw his first electric steel when he heard the Texas Wanderers at a dance in Mermentau," writes Arhoolie Records owner Chris Strachwitz, "and was sufficiently impressed to get one."[66] Presumably, Lamperez witnessed one of the legendary performances by the swing outfit's regular steel player, Bob Dunn, who worked for years in the Dallas-Fort Worth area with Milton Brown and the Musical Brownies before migrating to the

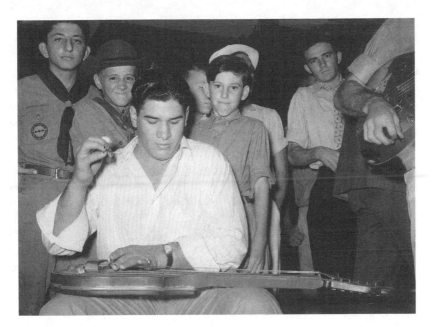

Figure 8.7. Julius "Papa Cairo" Lamperez, performing on the lap steel guitar at the Crowley Rice Festival, popularized the Cajun swing composition "Grand Texas," which subsequently served as Hank Williams's inspiration for "Jambalaya." Photograph by Russell Lee, October 1938. Courtesy of Farm Security Administration, Library of Congress.

southern portion of the Honky-Tonk Corridor as a member of Cliff Bruner's Texas Wanderers. Papa Cairo became a seasoned veteran of the region's dance circuit as a member of polished swing bands led by Harry Choates, Happy Fats LeBlanc, and Leo Soileau and was a familiar voice over Lafayette radio station KVOL (figure 8.7). In 1937, at the age of seventeen, Lamperez made his first commercial recordings for Decca Records with Joe Werner and the Louisiana Rounders, where he sang "Allons Kooche Kooche," the first incarnation of his classic "Big Texas" (also known as "Grand Texas").

The unprecedented success of Harry Choates' "Jole Blon"—released to Modern when Bill Quinn's Gold Star label could not keep up with the demand for the record—undoubtedly prompted the Bihari brothers to retest the waters in the Cajun market with Papa Cairo's "Big Texas" issues. Between 1948 and 1949, Lamperez successfully reintroduced the tune three times, each reframed under a different title—"Big Texas," "Big Texas #2," and "Kooche Kooche." He sang the most popular version, "Big Texas," as a member the Rhythm Boys backed by upstart guitarist Jimmy C. Newman, pianist Herman Durbin, fiddler Chuck Guillory, and drummer Curzy "Pork Chop" Roy.[67] Jukeboxes controlled by the Biharis broadcast Lamperez's pop-styled French vocals and familiar melody in clubs, dance halls, grocery stores, and anywhere else their strategically placed record machines were located. Radios tuned to Shreveport's *Louisiana Hayride*, on the other hand, circulated Hank Williams's honky-tonk interpretation.

Shreveport's *Louisiana Hayride* exerted tremendous influence on both Cajun and national audiences while serving as one of the most important cultural convergence zones in the Honky-Tonk Corridor. The radio emission began as a live broadcast from the north Louisiana city's Municipal Auditorium on KWKH in 1948 and developed into a nationally syndicated 50,000-watt force that nurtured so many musical careers, the program garnered the moniker "Cradle of the Stars." Hank Williams, Webb Pierce, Elvis Presley, Jimmie Davis, Kitty Wells, Johnny Cash, Jim Reeves, and Johnny Horton all made names for themselves as regulars on the radio show.[68] In addition, a host of Cajun artists shared the stage with these legendary performers. Cajun-country musician Jimmy C. Newman joined the *Hayride* in June 1954. During the mid-1950s, other Cajun performers, including Edward "Tibby Edwards" Thibodeaux (1952–1958), Allison "Al Terry" Theriot (mid-1950s), and Doug and Rusty Kershaw (1955–1956), were all featured on the program.[69] Happy Fats LeBlanc and Doc Guidry's experience on the *Hayride*, however, demonstrates the tangible connections to Hank Williams structuring the imaginary boundaries that Cajuns expressed as lore.

The evermore intricate mass media networks crisscrossing Louisiana and Texas shortened the cultural distance between Cajun and country music, especially the emerging honky-tonk style. Happy Fats LeBlanc first met Williams in 1947 during a dance hall performance in south Louisiana. In the middle of the dance, Williams approached the bandstand, introduced himself, and asked if he could sing a song. "I had never heard of this young fella and didn't know whether he could sing but after he had sung one song the audience went wild in requesting that this young man sing more," LeBlanc recalled.[70] After the engagement, LeBlanc learned that Williams was traveling and performing in the area. "I invited him to appear on my radio show to play and sing for the people of South Louisiana," the Cajun band leader continued, "[and] Hank accepted my invitation."[71]

LeBlanc and his longtime fiddling partner "Doc" Guidry maintained ties with Williams until his untimely death at the age of twenty-nine. The Cajun duo reunited with their friend in Shreveport during the late 1940s before Williams transitioned to the Grand Ole Opry.[72] LeBlanc recalled of his first appearance on the *Louisiana Hayride*:

> I had a connection with Mr. Murphy, who owns the Shreveport Syrup Company. I worked down here for him and Jay Miller had a boy by the name of Bill Hutto whom he was pushing. So Jay got him on the *Louisiana Hayride* and he got us to go back him up in a group. When we got there to put on Bill Hutto, Mr. Murphy was there and he told the station manager "I wanna hear Happy and Doc." He bought a lot of time with that station so his word was pretty strong on that station.
>
> So O.K., he fixed us up on the network program which was a half hour that went on the network but they wasn't supposed to take any repeats on it. He kinda sniggered so we played "Jole Blonde," there was a

tremendous crowd that night—Hank Williams was there playing—we got on and we played "Jole Blonde" and when we got through playing it they started clapping. Horace Logan the station manager was there so I thought he wanted us to quit. "No," he said, "play it again!" "Well, you said no repeats." We had to repeat on that network program three times!

And, after that we stayed on the whole show. We stayed on the show in place of poor Bill Hutto which I wasn't glad of 'cos he was a nice boy and everything, and Jay too. But they invited us back and we went back several times. It was good, we had some pretty lean times, which at that time gave me the feeling that Cajun music was graduating up, up to North Louisiana and all we'd play was Cajun songs.

Hank Williams had a lot of influence down here [in Cajun Country], he was on the *Louisiana Hayride*. It covered about a quarter of the nation, it was a 50,000 watt station. And Hank, you've got to give him that, he was good, he was really good. He was on like I was for Johnny Fair's Syrup, he left to go to the Grand Ole Opry. He gave me the job, the Old Syrup Sopper.[73]

Happy Fats's anecdote conflates the popularity of "Jole Blon" with his proximity to Hank Williams on the *Louisiana Hayride*. The overflow crowd, there to catch a glimpse of the Drifting Cowboy, roared until Horace Logan gave them an encore of the Cajun national anthem. It was a moment of unparalleled agency for LeBlanc and Guidry. The power of the independent Cajun text and the iconic status of the singer allowed LeBlanc to touch the mainstream. Moreover, LeBlanc's particular rhetoric about Williams set the two musicians as equals. Radio placed LeBlanc in a position to extend his influence. His claim to the Old Syrup Sopper job may have been exaggerated, or his employment short-lived, because Red Sovine assumed that mantle shortly after Williams left Shreveport. Nonetheless, LeBlanc's connection to Williams spoke to the kinds of relationships that allowed Cajuns to connect themselves, even if only in their imaginations, to the American mainstream. The Drifting Cowboy and Happy Fats LeBlanc reunited in 1952 when Williams invited the Cajun guitarist to tour around the United States. Their collaboration also resulted in a songwriting partnership culminating in "Cajinne Lulu," a ditty that recalls the imagery and ethnic flavor of "Jambalaya."[74]

Lafayette politician Dudley LeBlanc also came under the honky-tonker's charm, particularly after gauging the musician's potential as a spokesman during his Shreveport Syrup Company spots on the *Hayride*. In 1949, the politician made arrangements with Williams and advertising director Mat Hedrick of Nashville's WSM to produce a series of transcription disks to hawk LeBlanc's famous "medicinal" cure-all tonic Hadacol over the radio.[75] The transcriptions allowed Williams to craft his public image, which he aimed directly toward the imagination of his audience. The Drifting Cowboys recorded eight 15-minute programs on two consecutive Sundays in October 1949. After each song, the band clapped and cheered wildly immediately after the last chord to evoke the sound of a huge adoring audience.[76] The "Health and Happiness Shows" came on the heels of the budding country star's first major hit, "Lovesick Blues," and signified the musician's first syndicated series. Although the program did not meet LeBlanc's expectations, this initial collaboration solidified the relationship between the Williams and Louisiana's Cajun Senator, who invited his new friend to take the show on the road.

In 1950, Dudley LeBlanc organized the Hadacol Caravan, a medicine show of mammoth proportion boasting colossal talent. Nationally recognized figures such as Mickey Rooney, Bob Hope, Jimmy Dorsey, Milton Berle, George Burns, Roy Acuff, Minnie Pearl, and Hank Williams covered 3,800 miles playing one-night stands in 18 southern cities. Williams generally closed the show amid a fanfare of fireworks and antics by the cast. Like Nathan Abshire's tale of the white apparition "Mr. Hank," members of the Hadacol Caravan claimed to be the genuine architects of Cajun honky-tonk anthem "Jambalaya." Williams supposedly devised lyrics to his Cajun anthem while en route between Caravan shows in a train dining car with Dudley's son Roland, George Dupuis, and Lafayette entrepreneur George Berry. Roland provided the French lyrics and Cajun surnames as the men drank whiskey.[77] This "Jambalaya" origin narrative allowed Cajuns to touch the American mainstream through Williams by placing members of the ethnic group at the center of the hit song's creation. Tracey Laird relocates the origin of the song to yet another collaborator, pianist Moon Mullican, who toured extensively within the Honky-Tonk Corridor.[78] As for Papa Cairo, Lamperez felt jaded by the "Jambalaya" phenomenon, claiming that Williams "stole" his melody. Music writer John Broven explains, "In 1951 Cairo rerecorded 'Big Texas' in French and English for Jay Miller's Feature label, but after the 'Jambalaya' episode he turned his back on recording in disgust."[79]

If the origins of "Jambalaya" seem murky, the Cajun creation of a Hank Williams lore remains remarkably clear. Williams existed as a phantasm within the Cajun mental world. The country star's recorded legacy, the memory of his radio appearances, and the nostalgic image of the crooner rambling though the Bayou Country suggests, as *The Psychology of Radio* did during the Depression, the tenacious grip mass communication "so swiftly secured on [our] mental life" during the twentieth century.[80] Through Hank Williams the icon, Cajuns imagined themselves as part of the American mainstream.

Hadley Cantril and George Allport wrote during the early twentieth century that "there have been five major innovations of method in human communication: printing, telegraphy, the telephone, the cinema, and the radio. Each innovation has been followed by social and psychological changes of a revolutionary character."[81] Technological advances in human communication created what Cantril and Allport termed an "impression of universality." Mass communication's ability to reach so many physically separated individuals with such immediacy and simultaneity as to create a sense of unity and belonging, an impression that everyone experiences the same emotional and psychological impact when exposed to these stimuli. The impression of universality, while a potentially homogenizing notion, partially drives the power of the imagined community: the dance hall crowd, the record consumer, and the radio audience.

For Cajuns living in a world of mass communication driven by sound, the radio wielded particular power as locals imagined themselves as part of a broader America. "The daily experience of hearing the [radio] announcer say 'This program is coming to you over a coast-to-coast network,'" Cantril and Allport observed, "inevitably increases our sense of membership in the national family."[82] Mass communication grabbed Cajuns by the ears. Without pictures or moving images, records and radio compelled locals to visualize musical performances, comedy skits, politicians, international news, and sporting events through active listening. That meant not simply hearing, but applying meaning to auditory information. Connecting to this auditory world could be an act of self-perception, one that allowed individuals to participate as a member of an imagined community tuned into the same radio station.

Local meaning applied to the region's soundscape manifest as stylistic changes in Cajun music, French-language broadcasting, the rise of independent record labels, and other Cajun interpretations of mass communication. Before Jay Miller launched his Fais Do Do label in June 1946, Cajun musicians could realize their recording aspirations only by traveling across the state line to major urban centers like Houston, where a handful of upstart studios inadequately serviced the Cajun market's demand for French recordings. As evidenced by "Jole Blon" and Iry LeJeune's "Love Bridge Waltz," Louisiana's burgeoning recording industry signaled a new direction in Cajun music. Inspired by successes of Choates, LeJeune, and Miller, entrepreneurs like George Khoury and Eddie Shuler launched a number of record labels in the Bayou State to capitalize on the Cajun community's hearty appetite for local music. The experimental nature of these musical wildcatters allowed musicians inspired by traveling acts, radio broadcasts, and records the growing room to branch out. Cajun honky-tonk was one of the end results.

Instrumental conventions born during the Cajun swing era forever altered Cajun music's DNA. Leo Soileau explicitly stated that performances during the early commercial era came to a grinding halt even if only one of the two or three instrumental voices went silent. "You just can't stop. You stop," he explained, "well, everything gone stop." Cajun swing, on the other hand, layered rhythmic voices and varied soloists. Rhythm sections provided the labor propelling songs. "You got five musicians on the band stand," Soileau clarified. "Man starts singing . . . Then, we got a chorus on the guitar, a chorus with the piano. Well, I'd get off sometimes. I'd get off the bandstand and talk to a man about a job or something."[83] Under this new convention, bandleaders engaged the ensemble's autopilot while enjoying the leisure to walk off the bandstand to secure another gig, use the restroom, or order another drink. Amplification and an expanded rhythm section offered the same luxury to accordionists who fronted Cajun honky-tonk outfits. After World War II, accordions were no longer the engine driving Cajun music, but rather the chrome that made Cajun honky-tonk shine. This new approach to accordion-based material radically altered the dynamic interplay between musicians and the mechanics of performance, a custom that continues to structure Cajun music. At the dawn of the twenty-first century, traditionalist Marc Savoy closes his accordion during vocal and fiddle breaks, sometimes placing it on the floor in the middle of the performance, as the supporting cast carries the tune. The organic transference of this musical convention from swing to honky-tonk was evident by October 1946 through Lee Sonnier's pioneering collaboration with Happy Fats LeBlanc.

Accordionist Lee Sonnier and his contemporaries were attuned to, and profoundly affected by, the ever-changing musical landscape that sustained their art. They were not only products of their environment, but also cultural actors who intervened by adapting the diatonic accordion into a Cajun swing framework, a context they knew intimately well. Iry LeJeune, Nathan Abshire, and Lawrence Walker all learned to play fiddle, to find work when string bands dominated the genre, before becoming the three greatest proponents of Cajun honky-tonk after World War II.[84] Better known as an accordionist, Abshire's fiddle skills allowed him to negotiate the radical shifts in instrumentation and repertoire during the Cajun swing era. Fiddling thus allowed him to play in a succession of local swing bands before World War II.[85] Even the records that stimulated the regional demand for accordion-based music in Louisiana serve as examples of the fluid transition between Cajun swing and Cajun honky-tonk. Sonnier's collaboration with swinger Happy Fats LeBlanc set the precedent in the commercial market place two years before the regional hit "Love Bridge Waltz." Iry LeJeune further bridged the divide on his Opera label debut backed by the Oklahoma Tornadoes, a Texas-based swing outfit. He constructed an imaginary link between the direction of Cajun honky-tonk and its historical antecedents later in his career. The accordionist paid homage to his favorite Cajun swing recordings by reworking the Rayne-Bo Ramblers' classic "Les Blues de Bosco" and Leo Soileau's "Atrape Moi Je Tombe" reframed as "Donne Moi Mon Chapeau."

Iry LeJeune's ears provided much of his perception of the world. He had to rely on his hearing to compensate for his poor eyesight. Friends and relatives from his native Pointe Noire community recalled that the accordionist was an extremely imaginative youth whose exaggerated yarns amused his neighbors. The virtuosic recordings he left behind further demonstrate his cognitive prowess. He envisioned a new style of Cajun music, one that synthesized components of Cajun swing, Western swing, and the burgeoning sounds of honky-tonk. Through his foresight, he opened gates to the Cajun imaginary for audiences and other musicians to follow.

Imagination is the seed of the new mental world Cajuns cultivated. Increased exposure to various stimuli such as radio, records, and local appearances by Hank Williams animated the imaginary. An amorphous outside force did not impose these stimuli. Rather, individuals controlled the dial and applied meaning to the sonic world around them. Moreover, ambitious community members appropriated mass media in the form of local recording studios and record distribution companies, local radio stations, and Cajun DJs. The nostalgia attached to that historic moment when Cajuns felt as though they were part of the mainstream makes the point all the more salient.

D. L. Menard, the "Cajun Hank Williams," has repeatedly told the same story over the course of his career: the Drifting Cowboy spoke to Menard for five minutes in a local dance hall and offered advice about songwriting. The end result, of course, was Menard's 1962 recording "The Back Door" set to the tune of Williams's "Honky Tonk Blues." With each recitation and embellishment of how the Drifting Cowboy changed his life, Menard reactivates the mental world when Cajuns touched the mainstream. Meeting the iconic Hank Williams validated Menard as a young man. It was the moment when the budding guitarist reconciled his Cajunness with feeling American. The experience moved him so deeply that it forever structured his identity.[86]

Menard's experience speaks for many Cajuns of his generation. By the mid-twentieth century, Cajuns had finally realized their transformation as fully articulated Americans. Their increasing mastery of the English language allowed the group greater access to the mainstream. Meanwhile, the number of monolingual Francophones began to decline sharply. Cajun honky-tonk began to splinter into subgenres that included the biting accordion-driven sound of Austin Pitre, bilingual country-and-western by the likes of Jimmy C. Newman, Sun Studio–styled rockabilly by Al Ferrier, and swamp pop (Cajun rhythm and blues) by such artists as Rod Bernard. Cajun music once again diversified through sustained interaction with mass media. Contemporary American popular music sounded perfectly natural to the musicians creating local adaptations, in part, because they imagined themselves as part of the mainstream. After World War II, the sounds of Cajun music were the sounds of reconciliation, a soundtrack that articulated what it feels like to be Cajun *and* American.

Epilogue: Escaping Isolation

"We're living in God's world, and I want to thank him for willing this our way," said the Creole accordionist and St. Landry Parish native Terrance Simien during his acceptance speech from the stage of the 50th Grammy Awards ceremony. "I want to thank my wife, Cynthia Simien. She was one of the driving forces to get this category."[1] The small golden phonograph in Simien's clenched fist signified a dream come true: the first Grammy issued in "Field 14, Folk, Category 72—Best Zydeco and Cajun Music Album." That historic afternoon on February 10, 2008, the National Academy of Recording Arts and Sciences validated Louisiana music's status as a veritable American-made music.

Optimistic locals conflated cultural legitimacy, prestige, and potential financial returns in the form of record sales and concert tickets in the idea of a local Grammy category. Advocates demanded acknowledgment of Louisiana culture's place in the American mainstream. "The world is moving forward," noted one south Louisiana native after hearing about the category, "and we are moving forward with it."[2] This fresh articulation of the Cajun community's imagined connection to the mainstream suggests the perpetuation of the new mental world formulated during and after World War II. To be sure, the Grammy Association neither "discovered" nor sought engagement with Cajun music. Rather, Cynthia Simien, Terrance's wife and manager, petitioned the Academy of Recording Arts for "almost seven years to the day" before the award category became a reality.[3]

If the new Grammy category authenticates Cajun music's place in the American mainstream, it also raises questions about the genre's definition and musical boundaries. Who has the cultural authority to confer what is authentic or not? What styles and subgenres are eligible and why? Moreover, by its own volition, the Grammy category reinforces Cajun music's "folk" categorization. All of these concerns echo the major themes and issues that have followed Cajun music since its "discovery" by Columbia records in 1928. Compounded by the academic agendas of folklorists such as the John Lomax, Alan Lomax, and Sarah Gertrude Knott, the contexts surrounding the Grammy Awards' new south Louisiana category suggests that the interface between Cajuns and mainstream culture remains suspended in dynamic tension.

Escaping Isolation

Zydeco and Cajun bands received Grammy nominations in the past and actually won awards in the generic "Best Traditional Folk Album" category.[4] "For us, the nominations brought a boost," maintains fiddler Michael Doucet, whose group BeauSoleil is the only Cajun band to ever win the prestigious award, "at least an acknowledgment of our music that we were legitimate folk music."[5] The folk categorization imposed onto Cajun music infers the genre's status as a "less sophisticated" cultural commodity when compared to artists placed in, for instance, the "Rock" category. The trophy for "Field 14, Folk, Category 72" is presented during an untelevised ceremony that takes place before the star-studded marathon broadcast highlighting "mainstream" artists. The folk category's diminished importance within the broader Grammy Awards ceremony is inherently linked to the marginalization of niche markets and the perception that zydeco and Cajun music are vestigial art forms cultivated in Louisiana's isolated ethnic enclaves.

In April 2006, the St. Landry Parish cultural magazine *The Acadian* published an interview with a local Cajun music spokesperson Ann Savoy, who explained:

> when Cajun music was in its earliest days, when it was still just authentic, this was such an isolated culture. There were not a lot of outside influences. And when outside influences came in, like early country music, the Carter family and Jimmy Rodgers, the Cajun music people embraced that, translated them into French and turned them into Cajun . . . What made Cajun music Cajun? It was the certain isolation in which people had a certain lifestyle.[6]

The passage raises questions about the inherent nature of Cajun culture while illuminating the early-twentieth-century perception that has become gospel in Cajun music appreciation circles, among professional musicians, and within the general public—Cajun culture and the ethnic group's musical traditions are rendered unique and distinctive by means of isolation. "Isolation protects the essence of [Cajun] culture," maintained Louisiana's Cajun-born lieutenant governor and cultural tourism director Kathleen Babineaux Blanco in an interview with *USA Today* in 1999.[7] While the idea became an ingrained part of the popular imagination, academics also embraced this line of reasoning during the twentieth century.[8]

Contradictory threads permeate the academic literature regarding Cajun music's evolution and the alleged cultural isolation insulating the ethnic group from the "corrosive effects" associated with mainstream American culture. This isolation model ironically presupposes that the group lived in a bucolic "Longfellow-esque" backwater, blissfully ignorant of contemporary mainstream trends beyond the parameters of the community's ethnic boundary, even when analyses focus on cultural articulation points between Cajun Louisiana and American popular culture. For instance, folklorist and musicologist Harry Oster declared in 1958 that Cajuns retained a fundamentally French culture in an English-speaking nation for two centuries "because of isolation from the rest of the world,"[9] while simultaneously acknowledging the role of acculturation in the formation of "hybrid" folksongs—compositions that "combine lyrics in Cajun French with elements from one or more outside sources (southern mountain folksongs, commercial popular music of the country-and-western type, and Negro folk music of the blues variety)."[10] Folklorist and linguist Elizabeth Brandon further convoluted the historical complexities of the Cajun experience by first acknowledging Louisiana's heterogeneous population—including English, Scottish, Irish, German, Acadian, and French factions—which she claims, over time, became the foundation for the Cajun amalgam, before suggesting that isolation and insularity served as a sort of cultural preservative protecting the ethnic group from cultural erosion. In 1972, she expounded upon her interpretation through a series of contradictory arguments published as "The Socio-Cultural Traits of the French Folksong in Louisiana" in *Revue de Louisiane/Louisiana Review*:

> After the Louisiana Purchase, the non-French speaking settlers from the southern mountains and the seaboard states of English, Scottish, Irish, and German descent joined the French inhabitants.
>
> Of all these heterogeneous groups, the Acadians, colloquially called 'Cajuns', constituted the strongest unit which finished by assimilating all the rest. Because of their isolation and closely integrated family and community life, the Cajuns continued to cling to their language, their customs, and their Catholic religion. Through their marriages to Cajun girls, the young American bachelors became thoroughly assimilated. Their descendants continued the pattern of life of the bayou country without any change until the beginning of the twentieth century.[11]

Brandon explains that closely integrated families further safeguarded the group's social and cultural integrity, despite the fact that Cajun girls intermarried with "young American bachelors." This paradoxical notion persisted into the beginning of the twenty-first century through such claims as "most Cajuns remained culturally isolated from the rest of America for nearly the entire first half of the twentieth century, even as radio made its way into south Louisiana during the 1920s and 1930s."[12] This same study then includes a brief description of radio culture including a segment on the Cajun swing ensemble and radio band the Hackberry Ramblers.[13]

Academic literature and the generalized categorization of Cajun music by the Academy of Recording Arts distort the nation's view of Cajun cultural production. Francophones in Louisiana selectively adapted cultural information from a broad range of stimuli including the English language and various forms of American popular music. Individuals such as Patrick Pellerin did not stand outside of national trends, isolated and disconnected. His banjo-based recordings—especially his French rendition of Fats Waller's "Ain't Misbehavin'"—were absolutely contemporary. What is more, Happy Fats LeBlanc's and Tony Gonzales's careers, recordings by the Hackberry Ramblers and Leo Soileau, and the evolution of "Jole Blon" all suggest that new trends, new technology, and foreign concepts were readily available to Cajun Country residents who *chose to consume them.* Isolation neither made Cajun culture thrive nor accounts for the unique musical styles forged in south Louisiana. Instead, hybridity ensured cultural survival.

"Clearly, Cajuns have found a way to flourish in the modern world—but at what cost?" laments one Louisiana historian. "Many of their folk traditions have been lost, are on the verge of disappearing, or have been transformed almost beyond recognition."[14] These apprehensions echo concerns revolving around socially constructed notions of Cajun musical authenticity that are frequently folded within discussions of folk tradition.[15] Academicians and music writers alike conceive of folk expression as an anchored set of fixed core traits that are in danger of eroding "almost beyond recognition" thanks to the abrasive forces of external cultural entities, usually defined as mainstream American popular culture. However, this argument leads to the question of what exactly is traditional or authentic Cajun music? Is it a cappella home music, fiddle and clarinet duets, or commercial recordings such as "Lafayette" and "Jole Blon" (now considered part of Cajun music's "traditional" canon)? What about Cajun swing or French renditions of Jimmie Rodgers and Hank Williams songs? All of these expressions collectively form the corpus of traditional Cajun music because they carry enough meaning within the Cajun context to cross generational boundaries through successive interpretations. Such concepts as tradition and cultural purity, however, are intimately tied to theoretical models championed by twentieth-century folklorists, the same disciplinary camps responsible for skewing the nation's perception of Cajun cultural production.

Tradition is a theoretical construct that has long served as a conceptual framework for social scientists, folklorists, and historians. The paradigm evokes notions of the past as it manifests in the present—as "a set of inherited traits."[16] Scholars have generally described this "commonsense" definition as a core set of traits transmitted through time, from generation to generation. These kinds of assumptions have masked Cajun music's full breadth and complexity. Revisionists like anthropologists Richard Handler and Jocelyn Linnekin offer a more complicated way to conceive the depth of Cajun cultural production. They argue that tradition is transmitted not through a fixed corpus of unchanging traits passed through space and time but, like the Americanization process, via an ongoing interpretation of past behavior.[17] As the process unfolds, individuals reinvent customs with each new performance or reenactment of specific behaviors. In turn, when crossing generational lines, tradition changes ceaselessly in accordance with the perspective of each new protagonist. Tradition, like culture, is permeable, fluid, and constantly evolving by conforming to a society's contemporary needs, attitudes, and dispositions. These academic concerns, however, were not relevant to the pragmatic attitudes of Cajun musicians, especially professional entertainers, who catered to the whims of their audiences. Words like "tradition" and "culture" were not part of their vernacular. That kind of self-referential vocabulary only became part of Cajuns' common parlance during the latter half of the twentieth century. Rather, musicians performed music that satisfied both their personal artistic aesthetic and the demands of the musically savvy community to which they catered without concern for the imaginary boundaries of tradition. Furthermore, if antiquated styles no longer carried meaning or appeal for the general population, musicians routinely purged them from their repertoires.

Handler and Linnekin's prescription—tradition as process—helps account for the way Cajuns engaged and manipulated the memory of past cultural production within the community. When considered within the notion of Americanization as process, these complementary perspectives illuminate more completely the adaptive mechanisms of cultural filtration as ethic Americans engaged mass culture. In 1902, English journalist W. T. Stead pronounced Americanization the "Trend of the Twentieth Century," a keen observation about the growing influence of American culture—a trend that would dramatically redefine Cajun culture's boundaries.[18] Americanization, however, never quite functioned as Progressive Era activists envisioned. Cloaking ethnics with a mainstream veneer provided superficial evidence of the American melting pot. Heterogeneous cultural values, mores, and aesthetics continued to operate behind the veil. Fashion, the English language, instrumentation, and musical styles fueled the processes through which Cajuns recontextualized and rearticulated mainstream American culture "to make it function within expressive settings entirely of their own making," a process that dynamically increased societal and artistic heterogeneity.[19] The Americanization process did not erase the ethnic community's lines of demarcation, but reconfigured the group's cultural boundaries by means of sustained interaction. As new technologies became widely available— particularly mass media and transportation—communication networks became increasingly dense, facilitating interconnectivity on unprecedented levels. These transactions transpired with such velocity as to heighten the Cajuns' sense of engagement with mainstream American culture. Locals imagined a world beyond Cajun Country when tuning into mass culture. Cajuns remained as connected to the mainstream as they chose to be.[20] We should rethink the world from whence modern Cajun music emerged by escaping the trappings of cultural purity and isolation. Instead, the key to understanding Cajun music lies in the tension between the *processes* that give life to culture and tradition, and the ideological constraints imposed by those cultural authorities creating award categories and spinning grand narratives around the genre.

Questions of Cultural Authority

Voting members of the Memphis chapter of the Academy of Recording Arts, which governs the new zydeco-Cajun category, is faced with the dilemma of engaging the breadth and scope of two heterogeneous genres, whose practitioners generally characterize their music along racial lines. "It's ironic that such genres," writes zydeco and Cajun music journalist Herman Fuselier, "with related yet different styles, share the same category." The challenge also perplexes New Orleanian Reid Wick, senior membership coordinator for the Memphis chapter. "Others have wondered where swamp pop fits in, since it's the same geographic region. And divisions down black and white lines were more prevalent than I expected. There are some people who consider one to be highbrow and the other lowbrow."[21] The racial dimensions of zydeco and Cajun music, and the manifestations of Cajuns' protracted dialogue with American mainstream culture—like swamp pop and its predecessor Cajun swing—are problematic when filtered through both the isolation-exceptionalism model and award categorizations. Yet, because Grammy Awards are, by definition, valuations of the artifacts of mass consumption, south Louisiana's cultural reality will continue to grind against the limiting categorizations imposed by outside forces—including academic studies—that oversimplify these traditions.

Today, musicians and the 150 voting members of the Academy of Recording Arts representing Louisiana are coping with the repercussions of commercialization and commodification, a scenario that Cajun musicians and their audiences helped perpetuate for more than 80 years. At the heart of the issue lies the negotiation between local cultural concerns (authenticity) and those of the Academy of Recording Arts (commodity). One local journalist pinpoints some of the more pressing concerns that have emerged regarding genre boundaries: "Does the music have to be made in Louisiana to be true Cajun or zydeco? Does it even have to be made by Cajuns and Creoles? Does it have to be sung in French? Does it need certain instrumentation (notably accordions) to qualify? Or a predominance of traditional waltzes and two steps?"[22] Indeed, where are the boundaries of Cajun musical expression, and who has the authority to dictate those parameters?

In 1986, Paul Simon won a Grammy award for *Graceland*, which featured one zydeco-flavored song, "That Was Your Mother." Controversies surrounding Simon's tap dance around apartheid did not carry over into

Louisiana.[23] On the contrary, the Afro-Creole zydeco band he employed was happy with the exposure. Yet, when Hollywood-based fiddler Lisa Haley, bandleader of the Zydecats, also received a Grammy nomination in 2008 for "Best Zydeco and Cajun Album," deep emotion stirred in Cajun Country. "Many fans feared Lisa Haley, or 'that woman from California' as she was commonly called, would keep the Grammy in Los Angeles."[24]

Haley considered her inclusion from the same perspective driving the decision by the Academy of Recording Arts to create a zydeco-Cajun category. When addressing naysayers in Louisiana, she retorts that her craft represents "the very global reach of southwestern Louisiana music that was required by Grammy officials in the process of granting the category."[25] And she is absolutely correct. Turbulence, then, comes from competing Cajun and Anglo-American perspectives regarding culture and commodity.

Cajun drummer and Grammy nominee Chris Courville asserts that Cajuns "would complain if it was someone from only as far away as Shreveport," in the state's Anglo-Protestant Bible Belt.[26] Courville's statement is really about authenticity and cultural authority. During the Great Depression, folklorists and ethnographers—including the Lomaxes, Irène Whitfield, Lauren Post, and Sarah Gertrude Knott—constructed the "folk" label though which Cajuns and, later, voting members of the Academy of Recording Arts came to understand indigenous Louisiana music. America's folk represented a hardy stock from a preindustrialized world that offered a model of subsistence that did not rely on material wealth. "Traditional practices," historian Jane Becker maintains, "might be restorative, uniting body and spirit, nourishing the soul, encouraging self-reliance, and upholding the family" during the ominous economic crisis of the 1930s.[27] Amid the ethnic revival movements that emerged across the United States in the later half of the twentieth century, these same ideas resurfaced under the banner of cultural activism. Beginning in the late 1960s, Cajun Country activists associated with the so-called "French Movement" tried to bridge the gap between academics and the broader Cajun community. Activists doubling as university professors recontextualized academic parlance borrowed from folklore studies, and then introduced such terms as "culture" and "tradition" into the local vernacular to stimulate a new, introspective form of cultural conscious-ness.[28] These individuals championed the merits of preservation over change "to address shared problems, especially economic marginaliza-tion, ethnic stigma, and cultural assimilation."[29] Largely detached from their nuanced and politically charged academic definitions, "culture" and "tradition" circulate freely among Cajuns who, often unwittingly, reiterate the Lomaxian model equating authenticity with isolation.

Authenticity became of particular interest in Cajun music studies dur-ing the latter half of the twentieth century when members of southwest Louisiana's French Movement worked to define the parameters and scope of historic Cajun music. These cultural and linguistic activists sacrificed nuance to create a new, locally produced master narrative aimed at a general audience. By bucking studies produced by outside observers, this new history privileged a Cajun perspective through an act of self-assertion and cultural uplift. The ramifications of what Barry Ancelet calls "guerilla academics," however, are profound. With the gravitas of cultural authority bestowed by Ancelet's position as a university professor, guerilla academics presents historical and cultural phenomena on a bias that satisfies political agendas first and critical analysis second.[30] Historian W. Fitzhugh Brundage argues that these attempts to reeducate the local community stressed Cajun exceptionalism, a product of isolation, that effectively "placed the Acadian saga outside the flow of southern and, indeed, American history."[31] Also referred to as the "Cajun Renaissance," scholars and music writers affiliated with this faction considered French the lowest common denominator in the Cajun musical equation and, ultimately, the criterion for authenticity—an attitude that continues to shape Louisiana-based scholarship in the social sciences and folklore.[32] However, this view skews the ever-evolving Cajun experience by dismissing particular cultural traits derived (or at least perceived as being derived) from Anglo-American tradition as a clear-cut case of linear assimilation, rather than considering the interpretation of cultural information within a Cajun context as an adaptive mechanism. The combined influence of the isolation model and the search for an idealized vision of cultural authenticity was so pervasive by the early 1980s that one ethnohistorian boldly claimed that, "so far as the 'cultural stuff' of Cajun life was concerned, there were signs that the subculture was moribund if not already dead by 1955."[33] From this perspective, song lyrics rendered in English—especially performed in styles inspired by Anglo-American traditions—are considered inauthentic, and therefore not within the scope of Cajun artistic and cultural expression.[34] Ancelet described Cajun swinger Harry Choates' fiddling as a Southern-American musical expression, not a Cajun adaptation of American music. "His music no longer imitated western swing," explained Ancelet, "it *was* western swing, and good western swing at that."[35] On the contrary, the nuances of Choates' style and technique, and the social contexts in which the musician performed, suggest that the fiddler was a sublime example of Cajun swing, not its Texas cousin Western swing. Furthermore, the musician embodied all of the cross-cultural ideas permeating the Bayou Country in the years immediately before, during, and after World War II.

The French Movement presumed language and culture to be mutually exclusive (and at times seemingly one and the same), thereby oversimplifying the nuanced social, economic, racial, and linguistic complexities complicating all aspects of the region's cultural dynamic.[36] Each new foreign cultural influence introduced in the southern half of the state—including the English language—enriched the cultural landscape and provided fodder for artistic expression. Moreover, each development dramatically affected the ethnic group's view of the world and themselves. Cajuns selectively internalized extraneous traits and made them their own under the weight of denigration, a phenomenon that helped to spur the continuous evolution of the group's ethnic identity. At the end of the twentieth century, political scientist Mark Mattern observed that Cajuns straddled the varied linguistic and cultural tendencies in the region. He writes in his article "Cajun Music, Cultural Revival: Theorizing Political Action in Popular Music":

> Most Cajuns, preservationists included, live comfortably in both fran-
> cophone and Anglo worlds. More profoundly, contemporary Cajun
> identity includes a significant Anglo component, as Cajuns selectively
> adopt some of the beliefs and practices that characterize Anglo cul-
> ture and identity. It thus makes little sense to argue that Cajuns are
> opposing or resisting Anglo culture, since this would imply that they
> are at least partly at war with themselves.[37]

While Mattern refers to Cajun culture at the end of the twentieth century, the argument holds true for the first half of the century, as well. Con-structions of authenticity, then, should be called into question, as should the status of the group's isolation in relation to the notion of traditional music.[38]

Commodification amid Depression

Cajuns have long straddled the regional Franco-Anglo divide. Abundant evidence of capitalism and bilingualism during in the nineteenth century suggests that the adaptive processes driving Cajun culture's evolution were well under way by the Civil War when dance hall owners began charging admission thus opening the door for the widespread commercialization of Cajun music. Ironically, the dawn of the genre's commercialization came at an historic moment of economic deprivation. The war exhausted South ern resources, and Louisiana's limping postbellum economy virtually col-lapsed under the weight of Reconstruction. Financial security had yet to be realized in Cajun Country when Joseph Falcon and Cleoma Breaux made their recording debut in 1928, one year before the great stock mar-ket crash launched the nation into depression.

Eighty years later as the Academy of Recording Arts launched the "Best Zydeco and Cajun Album" category, local poverty and national eco-nomic instability continued to structure the cyclical patterns of Cajun music's commercialization. As Cynthia Simien lobbied, the recording industry in the United States began what *Rolling Stone* magazine calls an economic "free fall." Between 2000 and 2007, when the Academy of Recording Arts actually instituted the zydeco-Cajun category, record sales across the United States dropped by 36 percent. "After years of sinking sales," *Rolling Stone* reported, "the record business collapsed even further in 2007, with album sales down 15 percent and massive layoffs at the major labels."[39] Back in Louisiana, signs of economic dis-tress also plagued Cajun Country.

Poverty has generally been a dark reality for vernacular Cajun musicians. During the course of the twentieth century, musicians learned that life as a professional entertainer could serve as an escape hatch to financial security and respectability. Playing dances paid more than sharecropping, and recording companies offered handsome payoffs thus encouraging Cajun music's commercialization. In short, musicians came to associate their art with more than just leisure—but with economic sustenance and celebrity. In a recent interview, local accordionist Ray Landry asserted that the Grammy Awards are "one of the most important things that will happen to us—forever," at once pointing to the unprecedented degree of outside validation bestowed onto local tradition and also, unfortunately, to the persistence of pockets of deep poverty in Cajun Country.[40]

According to the 2000 U.S. census, the projected median household income in 2003 for the northernmost parishes of Cajun Country, Evangeline, St. Landry, and Avoyelles—a cultural borderland defined by the overlap between Franco-Catholics and Anglo-Protestants—collectively averaged 42.67 percent lower than the national standard.[41] Within Evangeline's Cajun community (70.2 percent of the parish demographic), less than 10 percent claimed any sort of higher education, and only 55.5 percent graduated high school. The estimated median household income peaked at $23,576 before Hurricane Katrina, compared to $43,318 in the rest of the United States.

Now, the future seems even less certain in the hurricane-ravaged state. Even more distressing, sociologists Carl Bankston III and Jacques Henry have identified a direct corollary between socioeconomic stress and language loss. They assert that Cajuns are less likely to teach French to their children in households where poverty is the norm.[42] Although activists continue to emphasize French language preservation, they do not address impoverishment's effect on language erosion in music hubs such as Evangeline and St. Landry parishes. Thus, Bankston and Henry's findings point to an unclear future for Cajun music rendered in French. Moreover, the parameters of authenticity become evermore fuzzy as Anglophone Cajun singers perform, like Lisa Haley, in a second language (French).

Thus, current debates surrounding Cajun music's commodification—and the power structures determining the parameters of Cajun music and hence who is allowed to participate—can be contentious. "The definition of just what is or what isn't eligible," maintains journalist Steve Knopper, "has caused a lot of raised eyebrows and some raised tempers."[43] As the Grammy Awards bring national attention to local artists, the balance between cultural production and commercialization remains tenuous. "Ours is a music that represents the soul of a people," elaborates Beau-Soleil bandleader Michael Doucet, "'s-o-u-l' that could turn into 's-o-l-d,'" the metamorphosis that undergirds and defines the clash of world views in south Louisiana.[44]

Appendix

Cajun Redux: A Discographic Essay of Early Cajun Music Reissues on Compact Disk

Reissues of songs first released before World War II stimulated and sustained my work through *Cajun Breakdown*. Alongside the only complete prewar Cajun discographies—woven into *Country Music Records* by Tony Russell, Bob Pinson, and Country Music Hall of Fame and Museum, and the first volume of Richard K. Spottswood's *Ethnic Music on Records*—compact disk compilations of Cajun reissues became my most significant archive. Without scores or written texts, these primary documents are the essence not only of my study but of vernacular music studies writ large. Early Cajun music's reemergence in the market place via LP compilations and later CD has not only been big business, but also a remarkably influential source of inspiration for Cajun bands during the late twentieth and early twenty-first centuries. Barry Jean Ancelet compiled the best discographic analysis of reissued material in his "Cajun Music" (*Journal of American Folklore*, 1994), written at the dawn of the compact disk age. Ancelet's sketch, however, focuses largely on 33 1/3 long-play records, which receive only a brief mention in the pages that follow. I focus instead on those Cajun materials originally issued on 78 rpm shellac disks through circa 1955, and later reissued around the world on compact disk. These CD compilations are organized according to their relationship to the major stylistic shifts presented in *Cajun Breakdown*: early commercial era (1928–1934), Cajun swing era (1935–1947), Cajun honky-tonk (1948–ca. 1955), and finally a rundown of significant field recordings available for purchase.

In 1952, Folkways Records launched the first reissues of early Cajun material as part of Harry Smith's landmark *Anthology of American Folk Music* (FA 2951). Composed of commercial songs released between 1927 and 1932, the LP anthology features selections by Joseph and Cleoma Falcon, the Breaux Brothers, Delma Lachney and Blind Uncle Gaspard, Columbus Fruge, the Hackberry Ramblers, and the remarkably unpolished French-language side "I Woke Up One Morning in May" by Didier Hebert. Smith's *Anthology of American Folk Music* stirred the American folk revival and piqued the interest of Pete Seeger, who explored Cajun music on his mid-1960s television program "Rainbow Quest." Shanachie reissued Seeger's appearance with the Mamou Cajun Band on DVD in 2005 as *Pete Seeger's Rainbow Quest—the Clancy Brothers and Tommy Makem, and Mamou Cajun Band* (Shanachie Sh-DV 609). While this early reissue compilation influenced the folk scene, the anthology did not affect Cajun music in Louisiana the way later issues by Chris Strachwitz's Arhoolie record company did.

Between 1970 and 1973, Arhoolie's Old Timey subsidiary released the first substantial wave of reissues across five LP compilations titled *Louisiana Cajun Music*, Vols. 1–5 (OT 108–111, 114). With an emphasis on selections from the early commercial and Cajun swing eras, these records helped reintroduce early compositions to traditionalists who recorded their own arrangements of songs featured on these LP compilations. Arhoolie and Old Timey's efforts to highlight the vintage sound of Depression-era ethnic music included spotlighting individual artists: Afro-Creole accordionist Amédé Ardoin circa 1981, *Amédé Ardoin, Louisiana Cajun Music*, Vol. 6, *The First Black Zydeco Recording Artist: His Original Recordings, 1928–1938* (OT 124); and a 1982 tribute to Harry Choates, *Harry Choates: The Fiddle King of Cajun Swing, Original 1946–49 Recordings* (Arhoolie 527). Leo Soileau and His Three Aces' version of "La Valse de Gueydan," the first string band version of "Jole Blon," found a new audience in the early 1980s with the release of *The Smithsonian Collection of Classic Country Music* (Smithsonian R 025, 1981). With more than 50 pages of liner notes by Bill C. Malone, the song's inclusion represented the country music scholar's interest in Cajun music and the styles inclusion as a subcategory of country music.

While Arhoolie's earliest reissues simultaneously provided fodder for contemporary musicians and shaping the scholarship on Cajun music, Swallow Records in Ville Platte, Louisiana, issued one of the most influential LP compilations, *Cajun and Creole Music: The Lomax Recordings, 1934* (Swallow 8003-2). This 1987 collection assembled by Michael Doucet and Barry Ancelet foregrounded the Lomaxes' fieldwork in Cajun Country. These aural texts created the foundation of BeauSoleil's repertoire in the 1980s and 1990s, and Ancelet's studies of Cajun music published in 1989 as *Cajun Music: Its Origins and Development* and later his music essay in the 1991 book *Cajun Country*, with Jay Dearborn Edwards, and Glen Pitre.

Early Commercial Era

The second substantial wave of reissues began in 1990 when the Country Music Foundation (CMF) in Nashville, Tennessee, and Sony Records, respectively, released a pair of Cajun music anthologies that marked the emergence of early Cajun music's appearance on compact disk. Based on a rough sense of chronology, Charlie Seaman compiled *Le Gran Mamou: A Cajun Music Anthology* (CMF 013-D, 1990) followed by *Raise Your Window: Cajun Music Anthology*, Vol. 2 (CMF 017-D, 1993), and *Cajun Music*

Anthology, Vol. 3, *The Historic Victor/Bluebird Sessions* (CMF 018-D, 1993), all of which focus on the historic Victor and Bluebird recordings from the Country Music Hall of Fame's record collection. Material on these essential collections straddles the early commercial and Cajun swing eras by including sides by Leo Soileau and Mayeuse LaFleur, rare harmonica tracks by Arteleus Mistric, Nathan Abshire's recordings with the Rayne-Bo Ramblers, the Hackberry Ramblers, and J. B. Fuselier and His Merrymakers. Likewise, Sony's first Cajun reissue collection, *Cajun*, Vol. 1, *Abbeville Breakdown 1929–1939* (Roots N' Blues, CK 46220, 1990), issued with substantive liner notes by Lawrence Cohn through the subsidiary Roots N' Blues label, compiles vintage recordings by Joe and Cleoma Falcon, the Breaux Brothers, and most of the Cajun swing sides by the Alley Boys of Abbeville. Sony followed suit in 1992 by including "La Valse des Yeux Bleus" by the Breaux Brothers and "Pourquoi " by the Alley Boys of Abbeville on the four-CD box set *Roots N' Blues: Retrospective, 1925–1950* (Columbia Legacy C4K 47911, 1992). Sony later released *Cajun Dance Party: Fais Do-Do* (Columbia Legacy CK 46784, 1994), which reintroduced some of the best sides by Joe and Cleoma Falcon, Dewey Segura, and the Breaux family band.

During the 1990s, early Cajun music became tangible once again—this time in a CD format—in the hands of those collectors who were willing to dig through CD racks in independent and specialty record stores. In effect, these releases suggested the viability of reissued Cajun material on CD. When Strachwitz partnered with documentary filmmaker Les Blank for the film and soundtrack, both titled *J'ai Été au Bal* (Brazos Films Video BF-103v, 1989; Arhoolie CD 331 and CD 332, 1993), Arhoolie seized the opportunity to issue for the first time on CD Joe Falcon and Cleoma Breaux's "Lafayette" on a two-disk set broadly defining Cajun music that coincided with the documentary's release. The composition's reemergence on CD prompted other reissues. Sony later equated "Lafayette" with American country music by including Joe Falcon and Cleoma Breaux's recording on the two-disk collection *Country: The American Tradition* (Columbia/Epic/Legacy J2K 65816, 1999). Successful marketing and appeal of Cajun reissues compelled companies like Arhoolie and Smithsonian Folkways to reformat popular LPs for the burgeoning Cajun CD market. In the mid-1990s, Strachwitz repackaged Amédé Ardoin's recordings, including his duets with Dennis McGee, as *I'm Never Comin' Back: The Roots of Zydeco* (Arhoolie 7007, 1995). And, in 1997, Harry Smith's *Anthology of American Folk Music* (SFW 40090, 1997) also made its compact disk debut. Other niche market companies like the Shanachie subsidiary Yazoo also saw Cajun reissues as a potential market. In 2006, they included the only version of Amédé Ardoin and Dennis McGee's recording "Two Step De La Prairie Soileau" available on CD as part of the two-disk compilation *The Stuff That Dreams Are Made Of: Super Rarities and Unissued Gems of the 1920s and 30s* (Yazoo 2202, 2006).

The Yazoo label also published three important CD anthologies chronicling the early commercial era work of Dennis McGee, Leo Soileau, and a single issue devoted to John Bertrand, Delma Lachney, and Blind Uncle Gaspard. The McGee reissue, *Dennis McGee: Complete Early Recordings of Dennis Mcgee with Ernest Fruge and Sady Courville, 1929–1930* (Yazoo 2012, 1994), focuses largely on his twin fiddle repertoire. Liner notes by music writers Ann Savoy and Will Spires contextualize the fiddler's collaborations with Sady Courville and Ernest Fruge, who are also featured on the compilation as McGee's accompanists. Savoy also contributed the notes for the Leo Soileau collection *Early American Cajun Music: The Early Recordings of Leo Soileau* (Yazoo 2041, 1999). While she considers Soileau an innovator regarding his Cajun swing material, the release is devoted to the musician's early commercial sides with Mayeuse LaFleur.

Record collector Ron Brown used his own archive and ethnographic work to compile the third Yazoo Cajun release, *Blind Uncle Gaspard, Delma Lachney, John Bertrand: Early American Cajun Music* (Yazoo 2042, 1999). Brown's liner notes provide the only published biographical data on these three forgotten artists. While the notes included Yazoo's packaging are solid, the sound quality leaves something to be desired. The fluctuating volume of surface noise on these recordings—particularly the Gaspard, Lachney, and Bertrand CD—often distracts from the beautifully rendered songs by these accomplished artists. Where quality falls short, T-Bone Burnett's sound track to the *Divine Secrets of the Ya Ya Sisterhood* (Sony/Columbia CK86534, 2002), which opens with a remastered version of Gaspard's "Assi Dans la Fenetre de Ma Chambre," suggests the potential of an updated edition.

Many of the other Cajun recordings presenting music from the genre's early commercial era simply saturate the market with songs and artists readily available on other compilations. For example, *Down in the Basement: Joe Bussard's Treasure Trove of Vintage 78s, 1926–1937* (Old Hat Records RCD 1004, 2003) includes only one Cajun song by Leo Soileau, "Eazy Rider Blues," which is replicated on the Yazoo Soileau anthology and the JSP box set *Cajun: Early Recordings* (JSP7726, 2004). Likewise, Rounder's *Raw Fiddle* (Rounder Select 1160, 2004) and *Squeeze Play: A World Accordion Anthology* (Rounder CD 1090, 1997), and overseas compilations *Swamp Music*, Vol. 6, *Prend Donc Courage—Early Black and White Cajun* (Trikont US-0202, 1995), *Cajun Origins* (Catfish UK, 2001), and *Cajun Hot Stuff, 1928–1940* (Acrobat 127, 2003) are rendered obsolete by previous American releases and subsequent issues by Germany's Bear Family and the British label JSP.

Although various artist compilations in the United States opened the market for Cajun recordings originally issued before World War II in North America, European record labels specializing digitally remastered anthologies of American roots and vernacular music have vastly surpassed the range and scope offered by their U.S. competitors. JSP, Proper, Krazy Kat, Ace, and Acrobat out of the United Kingdom, the Bear Family in Germany, and, to a lesser extent, Frémeaux and Associés in France are the leading charge to reissue much of the prewar Cajun discography. Thanks to less restrictive copyright laws, songs like "Blues Negre" by Cleoma Falcon became available only through the German issue *Hot Women: Women Singers from the Torrid Regions of the World* (Kein and Aber Records EFA 23284, 2003). European labels also helped broaden the scope of Cajun music's expressive capacity among aficionados. In 2003, Frémeaux et Associés issued one of the earliest European releases to examine extensively Cajun music's chronology from the early commercial era through Cajun swing on a two-disk collection titled *Cajun Louisiane, 1928–1939* (Frémeaux et Associés FA 019, 2003). Though this substantial set garnered rave reviews in France, it seemed less substantial when competitors from neighboring Great Britain upped the ante.

Without doubt, JSP's respective four-disk box sets *Cajun: Early Recordings* (JSP7726, 2004) and *Cajun Country*, Vol. 2, *More Hits from the Swamp* (JSP7749, 2005) are the most important, comprehensive, and affordable reissues of early Cajun music to date. Although there are no real substantial notes accompanying these eight disks, each song is accompanied by discographic information, including personnel, date of recording, venue, and original label information. *Cajun: Early Recordings* is organized largely by individual artists or groups, whose work is presented more or less chronologically across tracks. Joe and Cleoma Falcon's body of work from "Lafayette" through Cleoma's swing material "Lulu's Back in Town" and "It's a Sin to Tell a Lie" comprise most of disks A and B. The Breaux Family Band, Dennis McGee, and Lawrence Walker's early recordings are sprinkled throughout the collection, while Leo Soileau and the Hackberry Ramblers are the focal point of disks C and D. JSP's companion collection *Cajun Country*, Vol. 2, offers a more diverse array of performers, styles, and repertoire than its more focused predecessor. This second volume not only duplicates material featured on the early CMF issues, but also includes Dudley and James Fawvor's "T'Est Petite a Ete T'Est Meon (You Are Little and You Are Cute)," much of Amédé Ardoin and Dennis McGee's collaboration, the Didier Hebert recording "I Woke Up One Morning in May" only available heretofore on *Anthology of American Folk Music*, and obscure swing by Jolly Boys of Lafayette, Thibodeaux Boys, and Joe's Acadians. JSP has also brought to light the lost sounds of Cajun Jimmy Rodgers imitator Roy Gonzales, who traveled to Richmond, Indiana, with Leo Soileau and Moïse Robin in 1929 to record for Paramount. Disks 2 and 4 of the box set *Paramount Old Time Recordings* (JSP7774, 2006) features two rare blue yodels from Gonzales, "Choctaw Beer Blues" and "Anuiant et Bleu" (disk 2), and sides by Leo Soileau and Moïse Robin, obscure selections from John Bertrand and Milton Pitre, and Bertrand's collaboration with Roy Gonzales "Delaisser" (disk 4).

Following in JSP's footsteps, Proper's four-disk set, *Cajun Capers: Cajun Music, 1928–1954* (Proper P1462, 2005), repeats much of the material heard in the two JSP boxes, with the exception of disk 4. The last CD in this set offers an exciting array of songs and artists rarely included in Cajun reissues. Chronicling the momentum shift and functional overlap between Cajun swing and Cajun honky-tonk during the 1950s, songs and styles range from Link Davis, Eddie Shuler and his All-Star Reveliers, Vin

Bruce, Marion Marcotte and His Cajuns, Shuk Richard and the Louisiana Aces, and Jimmy C. Newman's smash hits "Cry Cry Darling" and "Diggy Liggy Lo," to Clarence "Bon Ton" Garlow's Afro-Creole romp "Bon Ton Rula" and Julius "Papa Cairo" Lamperez's "Big Texas #2." Ace Records out of London also reissued a sampling of Papa Cairo's work on the swing collection *Swingbillies: Hillbilly and Western Swing* (Ace CDCHD 893, 2004). Lamperez's original steel work and vocals are extracted from his Modern issues from the late 1940s and can now be heard in "Big Texas #2" and "Kooche Kooche [Complete Version]" and as a sideman with Chuck Guillory and His Rhythm Boys in "You Just Wait and See."

Cajun Swing

Reissues covering Cajun swing are generally more focused on one performer or ensemble than releases covering Cajun music's early commercial era. This phenomenon reflects, in part, the emergence of cohesive ensembles between 1935 and 1947 that performed under a band name, such as the "Ramblers." For instance, in 2003 Arhoolie bestowed the honor onto the Hackberry Ramblers' body of work. With insightful liner notes by Rambler drummer Ben Sandmel, *Luderin Darbone's Hackberry Ramblers, Early Recordings: 1935–1950* (Arhoolie 7050, 2003) is the most comprehensive Ramblers compilation on one CD. While some collections can be focused, there are exceptions to this pattern.

Francophone musicians in Louisiana are often lumped together, sometimes indiscriminately, with hillbilly or Western swing. Examples abound: *Black & White Hillbilly Music: Early Harmonica Recordings from the 1920s & 30s* (Trikont, 1996) which includes the only reissues of Joe Werner and the Ramblers' "Running Around" and Joe's Acadians' "Ammend la Nouville a Mamere"; *The Decca 5000 Series Classic Country Music* (British Archive of Country Music CD D 077, 2004) featuring a rare Leo Soileau and the Four Aces swing number rendered in English, "When the Moon Comes over the Mountain"; *Macy's Texas Hillbilly: The Best of Macy's Hillbilly Recordings* (Acrobat ACRCD125, 2006), includes a pair of Harry Choates songs, including the never before reissued "Korea Here We Come." A second Macy compilation on Acrobat, *Queen of Hits: The Macy's Recordings Story* (Acrobat ACRCD228, 2003), also includes some reissued gems by Choates. While these CDs focus mostly on country-and-western performers, Chris Strachwitz's overview compilation, *Cajun Breakdown: Cajun String Bands of the 1930s* (Folklyric CD 7014, 1997), is the best single disk to cover the style. *Cajun Breakdown* covers the Cajun swing stylings of Leo Soileau, J. B. Fuselier, and the only version of Clifford Breaux's "Continuez de Sonner" available on CD.

Cajun swing fiddler Harry Choates has received much attention from reissue labels. Beginning in 1993, record companies in the United States, Great Britain, Australia, and Germany issued five compilations devoted to outlining the fiddler's brief career. Reissues from the U.K.-based label

Krazy Kat (named for Cajun singer Johnnie Allan's backing group) present sonic snapshots of Harry Choates' early career. As a precursor to understanding the many sides to Choates, *Alley Cat Stomp, 1937–1941* (Krazy Kat KK CD 34, 2006) includes Choates' recording debut from October 1941—"Beer Joint Blues" and "The Big House Blues"—as a very young electric guitarist performing as a side man for Shelly Lee Alley's hot string band. Arhoolie's *Fiddle King of Cajun Swing* (CD 380, 1993) and the more inclusive Krazy Kat release *Five-Time Loser, 1940–1951* (KK CD 22, 1993) were the first Choates CD reissues on the market. *Five-Time Loser* includes Choates' early work with the Happy Fats LeBlanc and the Rayne-Bo Ramblers, such as the swinging "Tit Fille de Lafayette." In 1999, two more issues followed: the Australian release *Cajun Fiddle King* (Aim Records AIM 1205, 1999) and *Jole Blon: The Original Cajun Fiddle of Harry Choates* (Glad Records, 1999). Despite all of the attention the Cajun fiddler garnered by reissue companies, no compilation is as comprehensive as the 2002 Bear Family release *Harry Choates: Devil in the Bayou, the Gold Star Recordings* (BCD 16355, 2002). This chronological two-disk set also includes Choates' early work with the Rayne-Bo Ramblers and a 119-page biography by music writer Andrew Brown. Western swing aficionado Kevin Coffey, who also wrote the liner notes to *Five-Time Loser*, helped compile Bear Family's companion volume to their stunning Choates retrospective (Andrew Brown's *Devil in the Bayou*), which focused on the evolution of the Cajun hit song "Jole Blon"— *Jole Blon: 23 Artists One Theme* (BCD 16618, 2003).

Serious students of Cajun music will also be interested in other Bear Family box sets, including *Cliff Bruner and His Texas Wanderers* (BCD 15932 EI, 1997). This five-disk set includes brilliant Western swing by one of the most influential proponents of the genre to influence Cajun swing—Cliff Bruner. The extensive liner notes include a discussion of Cajun crooner Buddy Duhon, who sang for both Bruner and Harry Choates. In addition, the first three volumes of the colossal five-volume Bear Family CD box set series (with four compact disks per volume), *The 'D' Singles*, offer listeners a rare peak into the postwar sound of Cajun music. Work by Harry Choates, Edward "Tibby Edwards" Thibodeaux, and Rufus Thibodeaux are all featured here. Although the Choates material covers much of the same ground as the Glad Records issue *Jole Blon*, volume 1 of this set (BCD 15832 DI, 1995) reissues for the first time two rare sides by Cajun swing fiddler Rufus Thibodeaux, "Mean Autry" and "Cameron Memorial Waltz." Both Choates and Rufus Thibodeaux's D singles represent the continuation of swing even as the sounds of honky-tonk, championed by Cajuns like Tibby Edwards, came to the fore.

Cajun Honky-Tonk

Cajun honky-tonk developed between southwest Louisiana and east Texas, where Iry LeJeune made one of the first Cajun honky-tonk records, "Love

Bridge Waltz." LeJeune's monumental recordings have been the subject of two CD reissues, both of which were released in the early 1990s: *The Legendary Iry LeJune—Louisiana's Brightest Cajun Star* (Goldband, 1992) and *Iry LeJeune: The Definitive Collection* (Ace, 1994). The Goldband release, *The Legendary Iry LeJune* [*sic*], is an unusual blend of vintage recordings and Jo-El Savoy's overdubbed bass guitar that detracts from the original work. The superior Ace issue from the United Kingdom retains the original mixes from the Opera studios in Houston, Texas, and the Goldband studios in Lake Charles, Louisiana, in a remastered format. While the LeJeune recordings are a quintessential part of any Cajun record collection, its contextual companion *Cajun Honky Tonk: The Khoury Recordings—the Early 1950s* (Arhoolie 427, 1995) is essential listening and provides a broader look at the musical shift from swing to honky-tonk in Cajun Country.

The Arhoolie release, *Cajun Honky Tonk*, features poignant selections originally issued by the Khoury record label in Lake Charles, Louisiana. Musical boundaries blur in the works by Harry Choates, Floyd LeBlanc, the Musical Four Plus One, and the Texas Melody Boys featured here. The CD also includes sides by such artists as Nathan Abshire and Lawrence Walker, who grafted the accordion onto a Cajun swing rhythm section. The Khoury sound is the main attraction of another Arhoolie release, *French Blues: Nathan Abshire and His Pine Grove Boys* (Arhoolie CD 373, 1993), first released on LP in 1972. The CD highlights Abshire's raw, biting accordion and his first hit originally recorded in 1949, "The Pine Grove Blues," which solidified Cajun honky-tonk as a viable component of Louisiana's musical landscape.

Cajun honky-tonk splintered into four distinctive personalities during the early to mid-1950s: (1) the brash accordion-driven dance hall sound heard on *Opelousas Waltz* (Arhoolie CD 452, 1997) chronicling the collected works of accordionist Austin Pitre; (2) the crooning country stylings of such singers as Al Terry, *Hickory's Cajun Hillbilly* (Ace CDCHD 1159, 2007), and Jimmy C. Newman, *The Cajun Country Music of a Louisiana Man* (Edsel EDCD 572, 2001) and *Bop A Hula* (Bear Family Records BCD 15469, 1990); (3) the burgeoning rockabilly drive of *Louisiana Hayride* regular Tibby Edwards (Edward Thibodeaux), *Play It Cool Man, Play It Cool* (Bear Family Records BCD 16557, 2007), and the early works of Doug and Rusty Kershaw, *Louisiana Men: The Complete Hickory Recordings* (Ace CDCH2 992, 2004); and (4) Al Ferrier's work on *Goldband Rockabilly: Boppin' Tonight* (Ace CDCHD 442, 1994) and *Eddie's House of Hits: Story Of Goldband Records* (Ace 424, 2003). Yet, to fully comprehend honky-tonk's place in south Louisiana, there is another essential CD compilation, *I'm a Honky Tonk Daddy* (Flyright 44), available only through www.mterecords.com and the MTE Records storefront in Crowley, Louisiana. The CD features Jay D. Miller's collaborations with country music hall-of-famer Lefty Frizzell, the only recordings of Bill Hutto available on CD, and the very first recording of Miller's composition "It Wasn't God Who Made Honky Tonk," performed here by country singer Al Montgomery.

In 2000, Nashville's Music Mill Entertainment released a complementary compact disk library sampling the various aspects—country, rockabilly, gospel, and comedy—of the *Louisiana Hayride* radio program broadcast over KWKH in Shreveport. Hank Williams's triumphant return to the *Hayride* following his Grand Ole Opry dismissal is one of the highlights of disk 1 of the four-volume *Louisiana Hayride: Classic Country Radio* (MME 70015-2-MME 70018-2, 2000). In addition to a crowd-stirring rendition of "Jambalaya," the set of CDs includes vintage sounds that Cajuns tuned into over the radio loudspeaker: Ernest Tubb, Johnny Cash, Kitty Wells, Elvis Presley, and comedy skits by the likes of Minnie Pearl.

Field Recordings and Beyond

Cajun field recordings should also be a part of any serious collector's library. The essential works available on CD highlight the work of John and Alan Lomax, Harry Oster, Lauren Post, Ralph Rinzler, and Barry Jean Ancelet. Oster's Arhoolie release *Folksongs of the Louisiana Acadians*, recorded between 1956 and 1959 near Mamou and Eunice, Louisiana, first became available for commercial consumption on a two-volume LP set in 1959 (Folklyric LP A-4 and later as Arhoolie LP 5009 for Vol. 1; Vol. 2 appeared as Arhoolie LP 5015). Both volumes appeared together on a subsequent CD release in 1994 by the same title (Arhoolie CD 359).

The 1990s also witnessed the CD release of the Lomaxes' extensive body of work on Rounder Records. Two volumes of *Cajun and Creole Music: The Classic Louisiana Recordings, 1934/1937* (Rounder 11661-1843-2, 1999) and the single disk *Deep River of Song: Louisiana—Catch That Train and Testify!* (Rounder 1830, 2004) all feature so-called "folk" material from Francophone Louisiana. *Deep River of Song* contains more Afro-Creole–oriented selections that formed part of the musical world in which Cajun musicians circulated. Although beyond the temporal scope of this study, Lauren Post's field recording of one of Joe Falcon's last performances before he succumbed to cancer, *Joe Falcon: Cajun Music Pioneer* (Arhoolie CD 459, 1997), and Ralph Rinzler's two-volume *Louisiana Cajun French Music from the Southwest Prairies, 1964–1967* (Rounder Select CD 6002, 1989) are also worth a listen. Most recently, Louisiana Folk Masters—based out of the Center for Louisiana Studies at the University of Louisiana at Lafayette—has issued two anthologies of ethnographic material mostly recorded by Barry Jean Ancelet during the 1970s: *Louisiana Folk Masters—Varise Conner* (2004) and the two-disk set *Louisiana Folk Masters—Women's Home Music, 1937–1995* (2007), featuring field recordings by William Owens, Elizabeth Brandon, Harry Oster, Ralph Rinzler, Claudie Marcel-Dubois, and Barry Jean Ancelet. Although the liner notes are at times uneven (ranging from scholarly contextualization to fluffy appreciations), these reissues shed light on the contexts informing early Cajun music.

The digital age has brought the lost sounds of early Cajun music back into circulation. It accompanies listeners via radio waves, from the speakers of

CD players, and through iPod headphones. It also circulates on the Internet. David Simpson, English professor at Louisiana State University at Eunice, established the first website devoted solely to contemporary Cajun and Creole music in the summer of 1999, "Contemporary Louisiana Cajun, Creole and Zydeco Musicians" (http://www.lsue.edu/acadgate/music/musicmain. htm). The World Wide Web also provides a home for Neal Pomea's amazingly resourceful site, "Cajun Music mp3: Hadacol It Something!" (http:// npmusic.org/artists.html). Online since May 26, 2002, Pomea's website streams a number of yet-to-be-reissued songs originally issued on 78 rpm disks via mp3. His work illuminates the importance of reissued material.

Several songs by forgotten artists are made available for the first time since their original releases thanks to "Cajun Music mp3: Hadacol it Something!" including Angelas LeJeune's ignored recordings, such as "Le Petit One Step" and "La Valse de la Veuve." Moreover, Douglas Bellard and Kirby Riley, the first Afro-Creoles to record, do not have to stand in the shadow of Amédé Ardoin thanks to Pomea's efforts. His interactive site illuminates the gaping holes in the reissued Cajun discography. Vin Bruce's material from the 1950s has yet to see the light of day, with the exception of *Cajun Caper*'s last disk. The paucity of Cleoma Falcon's Decca material available on compact disk and the ignored side of Leo Soileau's English language repertoire recorded during the swing period are also conspicuous. While much of early Cajun music's legacy is alive and well and is circulated through new media, much of it is yet to be rediscovered.

Notes

Preface

1. John Mack Faragher, *A Great and Noble Scheme: The Tragic Story of the Expulsion of the French Acadians from Their American Homeland* (New York: W. W. Norton, 2005); see also W. J. Eccles, *The Canadian Frontier, 1534–1760* (Albuquerque: University of New Mexico Press, 1983).

2. Barry Jean Ancelet, *Cajun Music: Its Origins and Development* (Lafayette: Center for Louisiana Studies, University of Southwestern Louisiana, 1989), 1.

3. For a discussion of Creole attitudes toward Cajuns, see Leonard V. Huber, *Creole Collage: Reflections on the Colorful Customs of Latter-Day New Orleans Creoles* (Lafayette: Center for Louisiana Studies, University of Southwestern Louisiana, 1980); Sidonie de la Houssaye, *Pouponne and Balthazar*, trans. J. John Perret (Lafayette: Center for Louisiana Studies, University of Southwestern Louisiana, 1983); and Jacques M. Henry and Carl L. Bankston, III, *Blue Collar Bayou: Louisiana Cajuns and the New Economy of Ethnicity* (Westport, CT: Praeger, 2002). For broader discussions of cultural, social, and economic changes in the agrarian South at the turn of the twentieth century and beyond, see Lawrence Goodwyn, *The Populist Moment: A Short History of the Agrarian Revolt in America* (New York: Oxford University Press, 1978); Neil Foley, *The White Scourge: Mexicans, Blacks, and Poor Whites in Texas Cotton Culture* (Berkeley: University of California Press, 1997); and James N. Gregory, *The Southern Diaspora: How the Great Migrations of Black and White Southerners Transformed America* (Chapel Hill, NC: UNC Press, 2005), and *American Exodus: The Dust Bowl Migration and Okie Culture in California* (New York: Oxford University Press, 1989).

4. Richard A. Long, "Creole," in *Harvard Encyclopedia of American Ethnic Groups* (Cambridge, MA: Belknap Press, Harvard University Press, 1980), 247; Carl A. Brasseaux, *French, Cajun, Creole, Houma: A Primer on Francophone Louisiana* (Baton Rouge: Louisiana State University Press, 2005); Carl A. Brasseaux, Claude F. Oubre, and Keith P. Fontenot, *Creoles of Color in the Bayou Country* (Jackson: University Press of Mississippi, 1996).

229

5. Immigrant and ethnic American parallels to the Cajun experience abound in the literature of the Progressive Era. For specific references to the Cajuns in the Progressive-Era United States, see Shane K. Bernard, *The Cajuns: Americanization of a People* (Jackson: University Press of Mississippi, 2003); and Carl A. Brasseaux, "Acadian Education: From Cultural Isolation to Mainstream America," in *The Cajuns: Essays on Their History and Culture*, ed. Glenn R. Conrad (Lafayette: Center for Louisiana Studies, University of Southwestern Louisiana, 1978), 212–224. For the Americanization movement and the Progressives, see Philip Gleason, "American Identity and Americanization," in *Concepts of Ethnicity*, ed. William Peterson, Philip Gleason, and Michael Novak (Cambridge, MA: Belknap/Harvard University Press, 1982), 57–143; Michael McGerr, *A Fierce Discontent: The Rise and Fall of the Progressive Movement in America, 1870–1920* (New York: Oxford University Press, 2005); Shelton Stromquist, *Re-inventing "The People": The Progressive Movement, the Class Problem, and the Origins of Modern Liberalism* (Urbana: University of Illinois Press, 2006); K. Tsianina Lomawaima, *They Called It Prairie Light: The Story of Chilocco Indian School* (Lincoln: University of Nebraska Press, 1995); David Wallace Adams, *Education for Extinction: American Indians and the Boarding School Experience 1875–1928* (Lawrence: University of Kansas Press, 1995); Matt Garcia, *A World of Its Own: Race, Labor, and Citrus in the Making of Greater Los Angeles, 1900–1970* (Chapel Hill, NC: UNC Press, 2001).

Introduction

1. William Roseberry, *Anthropologies and Histories: Essays in Culture, History, and Political Economy* (New Brunswick, NJ: Rutgers University Press, 1989), 88.

2. Mary Louise Pratt, *Imperial Eyes: Travel Writing and Transculturation* (London: Routledge, 1992), 6; see also Ramón Saldívar, *The Borderlands of Culture: Américo Paredes and the Transnational Imaginary* (Durham, NC: Duke University Press, 2006), 190–225.

3. Harry Oster, "Acculturation in Cajun Folk Music," *McNeese Review* 10 (Winter 1958): 19–23; Elizabeth Brandon, "The Socio-Cultural Traits of the French Folksong in Louisiana," *Revue de Louisiana/Louisiana Review* 1 (1972): 23–24; Irène Thérèse Whitfield, *Louisiana French Folk Songs* (Baton Rouge: Louisiana State University Press, 1939), 42–43, 64–66 (see also the revised, 3rd edition of Whitfield's book [New York: Dover Press, 1969]).

4. Raleigh Anthony Suarez, "Rural Life in Louisiana, 1850–1860" (Ph.D. dissertation, Louisiana State University, 1954), 434–437; Grace Ulmer, "Economic and Social Development of Calcasieu Parish, Louisiana, 1840–1912," *Louisiana Historical Quarterly* 32 (July 1949): 596–599.

5. For more on the mechanization and industrialization of the Deep South, see Jack Temple Kirby, *Rural Worlds Lost: The American South, 1920–1960* (Baton Rouge: Louisiana State University Press, 1987); Neil Foley, *The White Scourge: Mexicans, Blacks, and Poor Whites in Texas Cotton Culture* (Berkeley: University of California Press, 1997); Edward L. Ayer, *The Promise of the New South: Life after Reconstruction* (New York: Oxford University Press, 2007); and C. Vann Woodward, *The Burden of Southern History* (Baton Rouge: Louisiana State University Press, 1993). For the specific reverberations in Louisiana see, William Ivy Hair, *Bourbonism*

and Agrarian Protest: Louisiana Politics, 1877–1900 (Baton Rouge: Louisiana State University Press, 1969); Carl A. Brasseaux, "Grand Texas: The Cajun Migration to Texas," in *The French in Texas*, ed. François Lagarde (Austin: University of Texas Press, 2003), 273–286; William A. Owens, *Tell Me a Story, Sing Me a Song: A Texas Chronicle* (Austin: University of Texas Press, 1983), 116–152.

6. I have borrowed Richard White's term *besoin*—which White uses to refer to a parallel historical phenomenon among the Native Americans allied with the French in New France—to convey a worldview based on reciprocity and satisfying communal need, a worldview that is distinct from the notion that wealth equated to material acquisition. Richard White, *The Middle Ground: Indians, Empires, and Republics in the Great Lakes Region, 1650–1815* (Cambridge: Cambridge University Press, 1991), 98, 129–132.

7. Vaughan B. Baker, "The Acadians in Antebellum Louisiana: A Study of Acculturation," in *The Cajuns: Essays on Their History and Culture*, ed. Glenn R. Conrad (Lafayette: Center for Louisiana Studies, University of Southwestern Louisiana, 1978), 115–128; Carl A. Brasseaux, *Acadian to Cajun: Transformation of a People, 1803–1877* (Jackson: University Press of Mississippi, 1992).

8. Woodward, *The Burden of Southern History*, 19.

9. Pablo Mitchell, *Coyote Nation: Sexuality, Race, and Conquest in Modernizing New Mexico, 1880–1920* (Chicago: University of Chicago Press, 2005), 6; George Lipsitz, *The Possessive Investment in Whiteness: How White People Profit from Identity Politics* (Philadelphia: Temple University Press, 1998); David R. Roediger, *The Wages of Whiteness: Race and the Making of the American Working Class* (London: Verso, 1991).

10. Philip Gleason, "American Identity and Americanization," in *Concepts of Ethnicity*, ed. William Peterson, Philip Gleason, and Michael Novak (Cambridge, MA: Belknap/Harvard University Press, 1982), 64.

11. Mathew Frey Jacobson, *Whiteness of a Different Color: European Immigrants and the Alchemy of Race* (Cambridge, MA: Harvard University Press, 1998).

12. Benjamin Franklin, *The Autobiography and Other Writings by Benjamin Franklin* (New York: Bantam, 1982), 226.

13. Jacobson, *Whiteness of a Different Color*, 43.

14. Gleason, "American Identity and Americanization"; Robert A. Carlson, *The Americanization Syndrome: A Quest for Conformity* (London: Croom Helm, 1987); Mel van Elteren, *Americanism and Americanization: A Critical History of Domestic and Global Influence* (Jefferson, NC: McFarland, 2006); Shane K. Bernard, *The Cajuns: Americanization of a People* (Jackson: University Press of Mississippi, 2003); Carl A. Brasseaux, "Acadian Education: From Cultural Isolation to Mainstream America," in *The Cajuns: Essays on Their History and Culture*, ed. Glenn R. Conrad (Lafayette: Center for Louisiana Studies, University of Southwestern Louisiana, 1978), 212–224; Michael McGerr, *A Fierce Discontent: The Rise and Fall of the Progressive Movement in America, 1870–1920* (New York: Oxford University Press, 2005); Shelton Stromquist, *Re-inventing "The People": The Progressive Movement, the Class Problem, and the Origins of Modern Liberalism* (Urbana: University of Illinois Press, 2006); K. Tsianina Lomawaima, *They Called It Prairie Light: The Story of Chilocco Indian School* (Lincoln: University of Nebraska Press, 1995); David Wallace Adams, *Education for Extinction: American Indians and the Boarding School Experience 1875–1928*

(Lawrence: University of Kansas Press, 1995); Matt Garcia, *A World of Its Own: Race, Labor, and Citrus in the Making of Greater Los Angeles, 1900– 1970* (Chapel Hill, NC: UNC Press, 2001). Cultural debasement, as defined by Matthew Jacobson, lies at the heart of the Americanization process. See *Barbarian Virtues: The United States Encounters Foreign Peoples at Home and Abroad, 1876–1917* (New York: Hill and Wang, 2000), 119.

15. Miriam Cooper and Bonnie Herndon, *Dark Lady of the Silents: My Life in Early Hollywood* (Indianapolis, IN: Bobbs-Merrill, 1973), 155, 156–157; "The Screen," *New York Times* (August 20, 1919); "Famous Poem Screened," *New York Times* (July 7, 1929); Crowley *Signal* (March 9, 1929; March 16, 1929; March 23, 1929); Napoleonville *Assumption Pioneer* (March 16, 1929); *Evangeline* [DVD] (Chatsworth, CA: Image Entertainment, 2001).

16. See, e.g., www.louisianatravel.com/ (accessed February 6, 2008), www.crt.state.la.us/ (accessed February 6, 2008), and ccet.louisiana.edu/ (accessed February 6, 2008).

17. The breadth of Cajun musical expression between 1764 and 1950 is conceptualized here through a periodization that categorizes the genre's evolution by pinpointing landmark developments within the tradition. The arbitrary boundaries of these conceptual frames—based on shifts in instrumentation, repertory patterns, stylistic idioms, and commercial trends—are fluid and serve only to facilitate a discussion of musical trends.

18. New France historian W. J. Eccles considers Acadia a "borderlands" in the struggle for North American hegemony. See Eccles, *The Canadian Frontier 1534–1760* (Albuquerque: University of New Mexico Press, 1983), 3. For the colonial experience in Louisiana, see Bradley G. Bond, ed., *French Colonial Louisiana and the Atlantic World* (Baton Rouge: Louisiana State University Press, 2005); Gwendolyn Midlo Hall, *Africans in Colonial Louisiana: The Development of Afro-Creole Culture in the Eighteenth Century* (Baton Rouge: Louisiana State University Press, 2005); Daniel H. Usner, Jr., *Indians, Settlers, and Slaves in a Frontier Exchange Economy: The Lower Mississippi Valley before 1783* (Chapel Hill, NC: UNC Press, 1992) and *American Indians in the Lower Mississippi Valley: Social and Economic Histories* (Lincoln: University of Nebraska Press, 2003); and Carl A. Brasseaux, *The Founding of New Acadia: The Beginnings of Acadian Life in Louisiana, 1765–1803* (Baton Rouge: Louisiana State University, 1987), and *French, Cajun, Creole, Houma: A Primer on Francophone Louisiana* (Baton Rouge: Louisiana State University, 2005).

19. Harry Oster, liner notes, *Folksongs of the Louisiana Acadians* [disk] (El Cerrito, CA: Arhoolie, 1994); Alan Lomax, liner notes, *Cajun and Creole Music: The Classic Louisiana Recordings, 1934/1937* [disk], 11661-1843-2 (Cambridge, MA: Rounder Records, 1999); Whitfield, *Louisiana French Folk Songs*; Barry Jean Ancelet, *Cajun Music: Its Origins and Development* (Lafayette: Center for Louisiana Studies, University of Southwestern Louisiana, 1989).

20. Brasseaux, *Acadian to Cajun*, 92.

21. C. C. Robin, *Voyage to Louisiana, 1803–1805*, trans. Stuart O. Landry, Jr. (New Orleans, LA: Pelican Publishing, 1966), 115.

22. Walter M. Kollomorgen and Robert W. Harrison, "French-Speaking Farmers of Southern Louisiana," *Economic Geography* 22, No. 3 (July 1946): 153.

23. Brasseaux, *Acadian to Cajun*, 92–93.

24. Ibid., 10.

25. For an example of this interracial interaction, see Shane K. Bernard and Julia Girouard, "'Colinda': Mysterious Origins of a Cajun Folksong," *Journal of Folklore Research* 29 (1992): 37–52.

26. Brasseaux, *Acadian to Cajun*, 105–109.

27. Thibodaux *Sentinel* (February 25, 1871); Jacques M. Henry and Carl L. Bankston III, *Blue Collar Bayou: Louisiana Cajuns and the New Economy of Ethnicity* (Westport, CT: Praeger, 2002), 33–43.

28. David Whisnant's study *All That Is Native and Fine: The Politics of Culture in an American Region* (Chapel Hill, NC: UNC Press, 1995) outlines the cultural politics of change in Appalachia. He, too, demonstrates that the so-called Southern isolates reside only in the American imagination.

29. See Brasseaux, *Acadian to Cajun*; Carl A. Brasseaux, personal communication with the author, 2004.

30. West Baton Rouge *Sugar Planter* (April 28, 1860).

31. Lafayette *Advertiser* (January 5, 1901; December 21, 1901); Lafayette *Daily Advertiser* (November 29, 1902; August 12, 1903); New Iberia *Enterprise* (December 17, 1904; January 24, 1906; December 2, 1910).

32. Morgan City *Attakapas Register* (January 27, 1877).

33. Lafayette *Advertiser* (August 26, 1896); Opelousas *Clarion-News* (October 13, 1932).

34. Thibodaux *Lafourche Comet* (November 1, 1934).

35. Barry Jean Ancelet and Elmore Morgan, *The Makers of Cajun Music* (Austin: University of Texas Press, 1984), 115.

36. Ann Allen Savoy, liner notes, *Edius Naquin: Ballad Master* [audio cassette] (New Orleans: New Orleans Jazz and Heritage Foundation, n.d.).

37. Philip Graham, *Showboats: The History of an American Institution* (Austin: University of Texas Press, 1951), 80–81, 141–144; Cordelle Kemper Ballard, "Steamboats on the Bayou," *Attakapas Gazette* 19 (1984): 8–10.

38. Carl A. Brasseaux and Keith P. Fontenot, *Steamboats on Louisiana's Bayous: A History and Directory* (Baton Rouge: Louisiana State University Press, 2004), 130–134.

39. Graham, *Showboats*, 63; Ballard, "Steamboats on the Bayou," 8–10.

40. Bayou Têche is one of the defining landmarks of Cajun Country. It traverses the south central portion of the state—St. Martin, Iberia, and St. Mary parishes—along some of the region's most productive sugarcane plantations.

41. Graham, *Showboats*, 63–64.

42. Lafayette *Advertiser* (November 2, 1901).

43. Ancelet, *Cajun Music*, 15.

44. Alexandre DeClouet to Estevan Miró, October 8, 1785, Archivo General de Indias, Papeles Procedentes de Cuba, legajo 198A, folio 237.

45. Ione Weiland's study of succession records in Lafayette Parish recorded between 1825 and 1835 reveals that yet another Country resident owned a clarinet, suggesting that the instrument remained in circulation—though in small number—during the first half of the nineteenth century. The clarinet resurfaces in the documentary record when musicologists John and Alan Lomax record a fiddle–clarinet ensemble in the mid-1930s. Weiland, "Typical Household: Lafayette Parish, 1825–1835," *Attakapas Gazette* 9 (March 1974): 7.

46. Alexandre Barde, *The Vigilante Committees of the Attakapas*, ed. David Edmonds and Dennis Gibson, trans. Henrietta Guilbeau Rogers (Lafayette, LA: Acadiana Press, 1981); Malcolm L. Comeaux, "Introduction

and Use of Accordions in Cajun Music," *Louisiana Folklore Miscellany* 14 (1999): 31.

47. *Frank Leslie's Popular Monthly*, 1881, 12:566

48. Alcée Fortier, *Louisiana Studies* (New Orleans: F. F. Hansell and Bros., 1894), 196.

49. Lauren C. Post, "Acadian Folkways," Louisiana State University *Alumni News* 12, No. 4 (April 1936): 9.

50. Catherine Blanchet, "Acadian Instrumental Music," *Louisiana Folklore Miscellany* 3, No. 1 (April 1970): 71.

51. Rocky L. Sexton, "Cajuns, Germans, and Les Americans: A Historical Anthropology of Cultural Demographic Transformations" (Ph.D. dissertation, University of Iowa, 1996), 157–159; Steven L. Del Sesto, "Cajun Music and Zydeco: Notes on the Music of Southern Louisiana," *Louisiana Folklore Miscellany* 4 (1976–1980): 90.

52. Walter Prichard, Fred B. Kniffen, and Clair A. Brown, eds., "Southern Louisiana and Southern Alabama in 1819: The Journal of James Leander Cathcart," *Louisiana Historical Quarterly* 28 (July 1945): 756.

53. *The Opelousas Courier* (January 26, 1856); *The Catalog of the Southwestern Louisiana Industrial Institute, Lafayette, LA., Containing List of Officers, Teachers, and Students, 1901–1902, and Announcements for the Session of 1902–1903* (New Orleans: L. Grahm Co., 1902), 26; Blanchet, "Acadian Instrumental Music," 71.

54. *Opelousas Clarion* (February 2, 1901).

55. The first Cajun record, as considered by this study, references the Columbia session that produced the sides "Lafayette" and "The Waltz That Carried Me to My Grave," recorded April 27, 1928.

56. Dena J. Polacheck Epstein, *Sinful Tunes and Spirituals: Black Folk Music to the Civil War* (Urbana: University of Illinois Press, 1977), x, 6, 144, 147, 154.

57. George Washington Cable, "Creole Slave Dances: The Dance in Place Congo," *Century Magazine* 31 (November 1885–April 1886): 519–522.

58. Sidonie de la Houssaye, *Pouponne and Balthazar*, trans. J. John Perret (Lafayette: Center for Louisiana Studies, University of Southwestern Louisiana, 1983), 75.

59. Accordionist Dewey Segura and his triangle-playing brother Edier Segura recorded four sides on December 16, 1928, for Columbia records: "A Mosquito Ate Up My Sweetheart," "New Iberia Polka" (Columbia 40507), "Bury Me in a Corner of the Yard," and "My Sweetheart Ran Away" (Columbia 40517).

60. Ralph Keeler and A. R. Waud. "On the Mississippi," *Every Saturday* 2, No. 75 (June 3, 1871): 524–525.

61. Ann Allen Savoy, *Cajun Music: A Reflection of a People*, Vol. 1 (Eunice, LA: Bluebird Press, 1984), 80; John H. Cowley, "Moonshine and Mosquitoes: The Story of Dewey Segura," in *Accordions, Fiddles, Two Step and Swing: A Cajun Music Reader*, ed. Ryan A. Brasseaux and Kevin S. Fontenot (Lafayette: Center for Louisiana Studies, University of Louisiana at Lafayette, 2006), 379–382. In 1897, the Sears and Roebuck catalogue sold a range of harmonicas beginning at five cents; the company's cheapest accordion sold for $1.85. Fred L. Israel, ed., *1897 Sears Roebuck Catalogue* (New York: Chelsea House Publishers, 1968), 526–527.

62. Robert Sacré, *Musiques cajun, créole et zydeco* (Paris: Presses Universitaires de France, 1995), 31–32.

63. Comeaux, "Introduction and Use of Accordions in Cajun Music," 31.

64. Although contested by some music scholars, the Louisiana State Museum's collection in New Orleans houses a daguerreotype of an African-American accordionist dated circa 1850, which, if the date is correct, represents the first image of an accordionist in Louisiana. Afro-Creoles and African Americans who worked as laborers on the trading steamboats that frequented Cajun Country could have potentially transplanted the instrument into the region. Ralph Keeler and Frank Waud's sketch of a German lighthouse keeper playing an accordion near the mouth of the Mississippi River, published in 1871 (see figure I.3), may prove a more definitive source. An 1877 *Frank Leslie's Illustrated Newspaper* lithograph of a black prisoner playing accordion in a prison camp along Cane River in central Louisiana and a line drawing depicting a black man dancing to the music of a black accordion player published between 1887 and 1888 in *Century Illustrated Monthly Magazine* may also shed some light on the introduction of the button accordion in Cajun Country. Keeler and Waud, "On the Mississippi," 524–526; Eugene V. Smalley, "Sugar-Making in Louisiana," *Century Illustrated Monthly Magazine* 35 (November 1887–April 1888): 109; *Frank Leslie's Illustrated Newspaper* (1877), 264; Comeaux, "Introduction and Use of Accordions in Cajun Music," 30.

65. Jared M. Snyder, "Squeezebox: The Legacy of the Afro-Mississippi Accordionists," *Black Music Research Journal* 17, No. 1 (Spring 1997): 37–58; Kip Lornell, liner notes, *Virginia Traditions: Non-Blues Secular Black Music* [disk], BRI 001 (Ferrum, VA: Blue Ridge Institute Records, 1976); Kip Lornell and J. Roderick Moore, "Clarence Tross: Hardy Country Banjoist," *Goldenseal* 2, No. 3 (1976): 7–13; Bruce Bastin, *Red River Blues: Blues Tradition in the Southeast* (Urbana: University of Illinois Press, 1986), 296.

66. See Lawrence Gushee, *Pioneers of Jazz: The Story of the Creole Band* (New York: Oxford University Press, 2005), 49, 62; Robert Tallant, *Voodoo in New Orleans* (New York: Collier Books, 1969), 87–88; Charles Raphael, interviewed by Hazel Breaux and Jacques Villeré, n.d., evidently from the Louisiana Writers' Project, 1935–1943, Federal Writers' Collection, Cammie G. Henry Research Center, Watson Memorial Library, Northwestern State University, Natchitoches, LA.

67. Charles Wolfe and Kip Lornell, *The Life and Legend of Leadbelly* (New York: HarperCollins, 1992), 16–17

68. As quoted in Lornell and Moore, "Clarence Tross," 5.

69. Gérard Dole, liner notes, *Louisiana Creole Music*, FA 2622 (Washington, DC: Folkways Records, 1978).

70. Opelousas *St. Landry Clarion* (October 18, 1913).

71. Comeaux, "Introduction and Use of Accordions in Cajun Music," 33–34.

72. New Orleans *Bee* (November 4, 1862).

73. Comeaux, "Introduction and Use of Accordions in Cajun Music," 32; Israel, *1897 Sears Roebuck Catalogue*, 5, 525–526. In 1897, Sears and Roebuck sold a range of button accordions priced between $1.85 and $11.25.

74. *Rayne Signal* (May 8, 1886; June 5, 1886; July 24, 1886).

75. *Opelousas Clarion* (February 2, 1901).

76. Comeaux, "Introduction and Use of Accordions in Cajun Music," 32.

77. Ibid., 34; Savoy, *Cajun Music*, 13. Also see Malcolm L. Comeaux, "The Cajun Accordion," *Revue de Louisiane/Louisiana Review* 7, No. 2 (Winter 1978): 117–128; Mark F. DeWitt, "In the Cajun Idiom: Mutual Influences of Dance Music Style and Diatonic Accordion Technique," *Musical Performance* 3, Parts 2–4 (2001): 185–214, and "The Diatonic Button

Accordion in Ethnic Context: Idiom and Style in Cajun Dance Music," *Popular Music and Society* 26, No. 3 (2003): 305–330.

78. *Opelousas Clarion* (December 29, 1900).

79. Early-twentieth-century accordionist Allie Young remembered, "I started playing house dances when I was about sixteen years old, just with the accordion and triangles or spoons." As quoted in Raymond François, *Yé Yaille, Chère: Traditional Cajun Dance Music* (Ville Platte, LA: Swallow Publications, 1990), 97.

80. Comeaux, "Introduction and Use of Accordions in Cajun Music," 34.

81. The term "Jole Blon" is a phonetic spelling of the French *jolie blonde* (pretty blonde). Independent record producer and Boston expatriate Bill Quinn, who recorded and published the most famous version of the tune (recorded by Harry Choates), misspelled the song's title in 1946. After the tremendous success of the record, the incorrect appellation has become part of the American lexicon. I use the term here as it appeared in the post-WWII context.

82. Hadley Cantril and Gordon Allport, *The Psychology of Radio* (New York: Harper and Brothers, 1935).

83. For a discussion of Cajun music historiography, see "Introduction," in *Accordions, Fiddles, Two Step and Swing: A Cajun Music Reader*, ed. Ryan A. Brasseaux and Kevin S. Fontenot (Lafayette: Center for Louisiana Studies, University of Louisiana at Lafayette, 2006), 9–34.

Chapter 1

1. Carl A. Brasseaux, *Scattered to the Wind: Dispersal and Wanderings of the Acadians, 1755–1809* (Lafayette: Center for Louisiana Studies, University of Southwestern Louisiana, 1991); John Mack Faragher, *A Great and Noble Scheme: The Tragic Story of the Expulsion of the French Acadians from Their American Homeland* (New York: W. W. Norton, 2005).

2. Yale historian John Mack Faragher argues that the Acadian deportation, frequently referred to as *le Grand Dérangement*, was the first episode of ethnic cleansing in North American history. Faragher, *A Great and Noble Scheme*, xiii, xix, 119, 469–481.

3. Gabrielle Debien, "The Acadians in St. Domingue," in *The Cajuns: Essay's on Their History and Culture*, ed. Glen R. Conrad (Lafayette: Center for Louisiana Studies, 1979), 45.

4. Ibid., 46.

5. Postdispersal Acadian women often gave birth to between eight and ten children over the course of their lifetimes. Carl A. Brasseaux, *The Founding of New Acadia: The Beginnings of Acadian Life in Louisiana, 1765–1803* (Baton Rouge: Louisiana State University Press, 1987), 107, 114–115.

6. See James H. Dorman, *The People Called Cajuns: An Introduction to an Ethnohistory* (Lafayette: Center for Louisiana Studies, University of Southwestern Louisiana 1983); Barry Jean Ancelet, Jay D. Edwards, and Glenn Pitre, *Cajun Country* (Jackson: University Press of Mississippi, 1991); Carl A. Brasseaux, *Acadian to Cajun: Transformation of a People, 1803–1877* (Jackson: University Press of Mississippi, 1992); Jacques M. Henry and Carl L Bankston, III, *Blue Collar Bayou: Louisiana Cajuns in the New Economy of Ethnicity* (Westport, CT: Praeger, 2002).

7. Edward Watts, *In This Remote Country: French Colonial Culture in the Anglo-American Imagination, 1780–1860* (Chapel Hill: University of North Carolina Press, 2006), 59.

8. Ibid., 57–58.

9. For the Cajun experience during the Civil War, see Carl A. Brasseaux, *Acadian to Cajun: Transformation of a People, 1803–1877* (Jackson: University Press of Mississippi, 1992); for information on Louisiana in general, see Roger Wallace Shugg, *Origins of Class Struggle in Louisiana: A Social History of White Farmers and Laborers during Slavery and After, 1840–1875* (Baton Rouge: Louisiana State University Press, 1966); for violence and Reconstruction, see Eric Foner, *Reconstruction: America's Unfinished Revolution, 1863–1877* (New York: Harper Collins, 2002); for honor culture in the American South, see Bertram Wyatt-Brown, *Southern Honor: Ethics and Behavior in the Old South* (New York: Oxford University Press, 1983); Kenneth Greenberg, *Honor and Slavery: Lies, Duels, Noses, Masks, Dressing as a Woman, Gifts, Strangers, Humanitarianism, Death, Slave Rebellions, the Proslavery Argument, Baseball, Hunting, and Gambling in the Old South* (Princeton, NJ: Princeton University Press, 1997).

10. Steven L. Del Sesto, "Cajun Music and Zydeco: Notes on the Music of Southern Louisiana," *Louisiana Folklore Miscellany* 4 (1976–1980): 89.

11. Musicologist and public folklorist Lisa E. Richardson defines both *chansons rondes* (round dance songs) and *reels à bouche* (mouth music) as forms of home music. These are regarded in this study as exceptional examples of home music, because Cajuns employed these song types during Lenten dances when the Catholic clergy frowned upon instrumental music. Richardson, "The Public and Private Domains of Cajun Women Musicians in Southwest Louisiana," in *Accordions, Fiddles, Two Step and Swing: A Cajun Music Reader*, ed. Ryan A. Brasseaux and Kevin S. Fontenot (Lafayette: Center for Louisiana Studies, University of Louisiana at Lafayette, 2006), 78. Also see Marie del Norte Thériot and Catherine Brookshire Blanchet, *Les Danse Rondes: Louisiana French Folk Dances* (Lafayette, LA: Tribune Printing Plant, 1955).

12. Richardson, "Public and Private Domains," 77–82.

13. See Ted Ownby, *Subduing Satan: Religion, Recreation, and Manhood in the Rural South, 1865–1920* (Chapel Hill, NC: UNC Press, 1990).

14. R. L. Daniels, "The Acadians of Louisiana," *Scribner's Monthly* 19 (1879–1880): 389–390; Ancelet et al , *Cajun Country*, 154; Alan A. Lomax, John A. Lomax, *Our Singing Country: A Second Volume of American Ballads and Folk Songs* (New York: Macmillan, 1941), 179; Ann Allen Savoy, *Cajun Music: Alive and Well in Louisiana* [Louisiana Folklife Festival Booklet]. (Baton Rouge: Louisiana Division of the Arts, Department of Culture, Recreation and Tourism, 1990).

15. According to the anonymous Breaux manuscript, written circa 1900,

> It was the general custom in days gone by for one of the young women-friends of the bride to come forward at dessert. When the tables were loaded with pastry, tarts and cakes, she would sing for the bride to the "romance" or "complainte" which follows, set to a melancholy tune. In it she bemoaned in the name of the bride the loss of sweet liberty beneath her father's roof and especially the forfeiting of her virginity, "la noble qualité de fille," which she had prized so much.

Jay K. Ditch, ed., and George F. Reinecke, trans., "Early Louisiana French Life and Folklore from the Anonymous Breaux Manuscript," *Louisiana Folklore Miscellany* 2, No. 3 (May 1966): 42–43. Musicologist Harry Oster documented and published a variant of the same composition in "Acculturation in Cajun Folk Music," *McNeese Review* 10 (Winter 1958): 19–23.

16. Irène Thérèse Whitfield, *Louisiana French Folk Songs* (Baton Rouge: Louisiana State University Press, 1939), 27–28.

17. For examples of anticlericalism and religiosity, see Brasseaux, *Acadian to Cajun*, 33–37; Barry Jean Ancelet, "Ote voir ta sacrée soutane: Anticlerical Humor in Louisiana French Oral Tradition," *Louisiana Folklore Miscellany* 7 (1985): 26–33; Michael P. Carroll, "Were the Acadians/Cajuns (really) devout Catholics," *Studies in Religion/Sciences Religieuse* 31 (2002): 323–337.

18. Brasseaux, *The Founding of New Acadia*, 153–166. A variety of factors working in concert probably account for the Cajun community's pervasive anticlericalism and the lack of religious material in Cajun music. The first settlers to arrive in *Acadie* in the early 1600s left France, in part, to escape the religious wars plaguing the country. Furthermore, Huguenots formed the nucleus of predispersal Acadian society, which did not facilitate a grassroots attraction to the Catholic faith. Upon arrival in Louisiana, Spanish priests alienated the Acadian population with their fanatical brand of Catholicism informed by the Inquisition movement. In addition, those few portentous immigrant clergymen who serviced the Cajun community thumbed their noses at the group's poverty and secular frontier lifestyle.

19. Roger Baudier, *The Catholic Church in Louisiana* (New Orleans: A. W. Hyatt Stationery Mfg. Co., 1939), 382.

20. Malcolm L. Comeaux, "The Cajun Dance Hall," *Material Culture* 32 (2000): 37–56. Also see Anselme Chiasson, Charlotte Cormier, Donald Deschênes, and Ronald Labelle, "Le Folklore Acadien," in *L'Acadie des Maritimes*, ed. Jean Daigle (Moncton, New Brunswick: Chaire d'études acadiennes, Université de Moncton, 1993), 701–702; and Sally Ross and J. Alphonse Deveau, *The Acadians of Nova Scotia: Past and Present* (Halifax, NS: Nimbus, 1992), 146.

21. Marcia G. Gaudet, *Tales from the Levee: The Folklore of St. John the Baptist Parish* (Lafayette: Center for Louisiana Studies, University of Southwestern Louisiana, 1984), 18.

22. By the eleventh century, *cantiques populaires* (also known as *épître farcie*) combined epistles or other biblical texts supplemented with popular vernacular interpretations of passages sung to the tune of sacred hymns. Amédée Gastoué, *Le Cantique Populaire en France* (Lyon, France: Editions Musicales Janin, 1924), 5; André Prévos, "Afro-French Spirituals about Mary Magdalene," *Louisiana Folklore Miscellany* 4 (1976–1980): 41–42. For aural examples of cantiques, see Oster Collection, OS1, Acadian and Creole Folklore and Folklife Collection, Center for Louisiana Studies, University of Louisiana at Lafayette; *Women's Home Music, Recorded 1937–1995* [disk], Louisiana Folk Masters Series LCR 2002-3 (Lafayette, LA: Louisiana Crossroads Records, 2007).

23. Marce Lacouture, personal communication [e-mail], April 20, 2004.

24. Daniels, "The Acadians of Louisiana," 389–390.

25. Ditch and Reinecke, "Early Louisiana French Life," 44.

26. André Prévos maintains that a total of 40 *cantiques* were collected by Elizabeth Brandon (8) and Harry Oster (32). The Oster collection is now housed at Laval University in Québec City, Québec, Canada. Prévos, "Afro-French Spirituals about Mary Magdalene," 43–44.

27. One *cantique* in particular demonstrates the transnational complexity of the ballad tradition in south Louisiana. The hymn combines specific biblical references (Luke 7: 36–50) and elements of an eleventh-century French legend about Mary Magdalene and her sister Martha immigrating to southern France. Prévos, "Afro-French Spirituals about Mary Magdalene," 43–44.

28. Rocky L. Sexton. "Ritualized Inebriation, Violence, and Social Control in Cajun Mardi Gras," *Anthropological Quarterly* 74, No. 1 (January 2001): 28–38.

29. Rocky Sexton and Harry Oster, "Une 'Tite Poule Grasse ou la Fille Aînée [A Little Fat Chicken or the Eldest Daughter]: A Comparative Analysis of Cajun and Creole Mardi Gras Songs," *Journal of American Folklore* 114, No. 452 (2001): 207.

30. Literally, "to run Mardi Gras."

31. For information on traditional mumming, see Henry Glassie, *All Silver and No Brass: An Irish Christmas Mumming* (Philadelphia: University of Pennsylvania Press, 1983); for more on the Cajun Mardi Gras, see Carolyn E. Ware, *Cajun Women and Mardi Gras: Reading the Rules Backwards* (Urbana: University of Illinois Press, 2006); Marcia Gaudet and James C. McDonald, eds., *Mardi Gras, Gumbo and Zydeco: Readings in Louisiana Culture* (Jackson: University Press of Mississippi, 2003).

32. Harry Oster and Revon Reed, "Cajun Mardi Gras in Louisiana," *Louisiana Folklore Miscellany* 1, No. 4 (1960): 1–17; Sexton and Oster, "Une 'Tite Poule Grasse," 219.

33. Sexton and Oster, "Une 'Tite Poule Grasse," 221–222.

34. Ibid., 214.

35. Ibid., 217.

36. Abbeville *Meridional* (March 1, 1879).

37. Thibodaux *Lafourche Comet* (March 2, 1939). Also see Crowley *Signal* (March 4, 1922; February 17, 1923); Napoleonville *Assumption Pioneer* (March 8, 1930).

38. Thériot and Blanchet, *Les Danse Rondes*, 4.

39. Irene M. Petitjean, "'Cajun' Folk Songs of Southwestern Louisiana" (Master's Thesis, Columbia University, 1930), 8–9; Ditch and Reinecke, "Early Louisiana French Life," 32–34.

40. George Lewis Prentiss, *A Memoir of S. S. Prentiss*, Vol. 1, (New York: Scribner, 1899), 95.

41. Pierre Clément de Laussat, *Memoirs of My Life to My Son During the Years 1803 and After, Which I Spent in Public Service in Louisiana as Commissioner of the French Government for the Retrocession to France of That Colony and for Its Transfer to the United States* (Baton Rouge: Louisiana State University Press, 1978), 53–54; William Darby, *A Geographical Description of Louisiana Presenting a View of the Soil, Climate, Animal, Vegetable and Mineral Productions: Illustrative of Its Natural Physiognomy, Its Geographical Configuration, and Relative Situation: With an Account of the Character and Manners of the Inhabitants: Being an Accompaniment to the Map of Louisiana* (Philadelphia: John Melish, 1816), 270; Prentiss, *A Memoir of S. S. Prentiss*, 95; Frederick Law Olmsted, *A Journey in the Seaboard Slave States in the Years 1853–1854, with Remarks on Their Economy* Vol. 2 (New York: G. P. Putnam's Sons, 1904), 305.

42. W. W. Pugh, "Bayou Lafourche from 1820 to 1825—Its Inhabitants, Customs and Pursuits," *Louisiana Planter and Sugar Manufacturer* (September 29, 1888), 143.

43. W. H. Sparks, *The Memories of Fifty Years: Containing Brief Biographical Notices of Distinguished Americans, and Anecdotes of Remarkable Men; Interspersed with Scenes and Incidents Occurring during a Long Life of Observation Chiefly Spent in the Southwest* (Philadelphia: E. Claxton and Co., 1882), 376.

44. Daniels, "The Acadians of Louisiana," 386; Marguerite Roman, "Les Acadiens au XXe Siècle," *Comptes Rendus de l'Athénée Louisianais* (March 1924): 19; Petitjean, "'Cajun' Folk Songs," 7; Louisiana Writers' Project, Lyle Saxon, Edward Dreyer, and Robert Tallant, *Gumbo Ya-Ya: A Collection of Louisiana Folk Tales* (New York: Johnson Reprint Corporation, 1969), 197; Harry Hansen, ed., *Louisiana: A Guide to the State* (New York: Hastings House, 1971), 86.

45. Bill C. Malone, *Country Music U.S.A.: A Fifty-Year History* (Austin: University of Texas Press, 1968), 172.

46. Lauren C. Post, *Cajun Sketches from the Prairies of Southwest Louisiana* (Baton Rouge: Louisiana State University Press, 1974), 115.

47. The "petit gallop" (small gallop) appears to have paralleled the alternating movement that defined the choreography in *contradanses*, *lanciers*, and *valses a deux temps*. Dennis McGee remembered, "The couples would move in one direction and then change direction [opposite direction]. They danced, four or five couples together. They called it the gallop you know 'Ti gallop, Ti gallop.'" As quoted in Brenda Daigle, "Acadian Fiddler Dennis McGee and Acadian Dances," *Attakapas Gazette* 7, No. 3 (1972): 124–143.

48. As quoted in Raymond François, *Yé Yaille, Chère: Traditional Cajun Dance Music* (Ville Platte, LA: Swallow Publications, 1990), 94.

49. Cajun music was provided on the same bill by Happy Fats and His Rayne-Bo Ramblers. National Rice Festival Program, November 7, 1939, Acadia Parish Library, Crowley Branch, Freeland Archive.

50. With its roots in the 1940s, jitterbugging continues to be the most popular dance style among younger Cajuns. National Rice Festival Program, November 7, 1940, Acadia Parish Library, Crowley Branch, Freeland Archive.

51. Daigle, "Acadian Fiddler Dennis McGee," 124–143.

52. C. C. Robin, *Voyage to Louisiana by C. C. Robin, 1803–1805*, trans. Stuart O. Landry, Jr. (New Orleans: Pelican Publishing, 1966), 115.

53. Pugh, "Bayou Lafourche from 1820 to 1825," 143.

54. Ibid.

55. Marcelle Bienvenu, Carl A. Brasseaux, and Ryan A. Brasseaux, *Stir the Pot: The History of Cajun Cuisine* (New York: Hippocrene Books, 2005), 67–69.

56. Daniels, "The Acadians of Louisiana," 387.

57. See Post, *Cajun Sketches*, 154.

58. Daniels, "The Acadians of Louisiana," 387–388.

59. Ditch and Reinecke, "Early Louisiana French Life," 38.

60. Daigle, "Acadian Fiddler Dennis McGee," 127.

61. Whitfield, *Louisiana French Folk Songs*, 74–75. English translation by author.

62. Sparks, *The Memories of Fifty Years*, 376.

63. George Washington Cable, "Notes on Acadians in Louisiana," 158, Cable Collection, Manuscripts Division, Tulane University Library, New Orleans, LA. Beginning with sporadic reports dating from the late nineteenth century through the mid-twentieth century, newspapers documented the

increasingly violent Cajun cultural landscape, particularly in such towns as Ville Platte and Mamou, which represented the northern frontier of Cajun Country. *Thibodaux Sentinel* (June 5, 1875); Lafayette *Gazette* (August 18, 1894); Crowley *Signal* (January 11, 1896); "Life Sentences for Murderers, Janesse Case," Jennings *Daily Times-Record* (January 26, 1910); *New Iberia Enterprise* (June 3, 1911); Ville Platte *Weekly Gazette* (December 9, 1922).

64. Firearms were generally concealed in buggies and carriages because of their size. Ditch and Reinecke, "Early Louisiana French Life," 7; Lee and Irene Stelly, Jody Ancelet, and Elmo and Maude Ancelet, interviewed by Barry Jean Ancelet, Lafayette, LA, April 18, 1977, accession No. A-0.143, Acadian and Creole Folklore and Folklife Collection, Center for Cultural and Eco-Tourism, University of Louisiana at Lafayette.

65. For more on communal work parties and folk justice, see Ancelet et al., *Cajun Country*, 34–65, 101–114.

66. There is an extensive literature within Southern historiography that outlines the social turmoil between 1861 and 1865 south of the Mason-Dixon Line and the incredibly violent nature of Reconstruction that ensued after the Civil War. Cajuns were connected to these cultural, economic, and social forces, particularly as Confederate forces drafted local men and war spread to Cajun Country. For a discussion of violence stimulated by war and Reconstruction in Appalachia, see Altina L. Waller, *Feud: Hatfields, McCoys, and Social Change in Appalachia, 1860–1900* (Chapel Hill, NC: UNC Press, 1988). For a discussion of violence in Cajun Country during the mid- to late nineteenth century, see Brasseaux, *Acadian to Cajun*, 26, 29, 36–37, 55 73, 76, 113–128, 130–132, 173, 175–179; Gilles Vandal, *Rethinking Southern Violence: Homicides in Post-Civil War Louisiana, 1866–1884* (Columbus: Ohio State University Press, 2000); Samuel C. Hyde, Jr., *Pistols and Politics: The Dilemma of Democracy in Louisiana's Florida Parishes* (Baton Rouge: Louisiana State University Press, 1996).

67. *Thibodaux Sentinel* (February 6, 1869).

68. *Thibodaux Sentinel* (May 29, 1875).

69. New Iberia Enterprise (July 12, 1924).

70. Ville Platte *Weekly Gazette* (June 3, 1922).

71. Crowley *Signal* (August 18, 1923).

72. *Opelousas Clarion* (June 17, 1905).

73. Opelousas *Clarion-Progress* (April 26, 1924).

74. *Opelousas Clarion* (July 21, 1900).

75. Ibid.; *Opelousas Courier* (June 17, 1905); "Fatal Shooting in St. Landry," Jennings *Daily Times Record* (January 20, 1910); "Life Sentences for Murderers, Janesse Case," Jennings *Daily Times-Record* (January 26, 1910); *New Iberia Enterprise* (June 3, 1911); Crowley *Signal* (January 13, 1923; September 29, 1923; May 9, 1925); Ville Platte *Weekly Gazette* (May 28, 1921; April 26, 1924; May 31, 1924; May 9, 1925); *Opelousas Clarion-Progress* (November 8, 1924; March 28, 1925). Also see, for fighting and folk justice, Ancelet et al., *Cajun Country*, 101–111.

76. "Jack Fontenot Killed in Bloody Duel in Acadia," Jennings *Daily Times-Record* (April 26, 1910).

77. Nicholas R. Spitzer, liner notes, *Octa Clark and Hector Duhon: The Dixie Ramblers, Ensemble Encore, the Men and Their Music* [disk], LP 6011 (Cambridge, MA: Rounder Records, 1983).

78. Ville Platte *Weekly Gazette* (December 16, 1922; April 7, 1923; May 12, 1923). A similar scenario transpired in September 1923, when Lucien

Leger murdered his cousins Cesare and Lozin Leger following a dispute at an Acadia Parish dance hall. Crowley *Signal* (September 15, 1923).

79. Alexandre Barde, *The Vigilante Committees of the Attakapas*, ed. David Edmonds and Dennis Gibson, trans. Henrietta Guilbeau Rogers (Lafayette, LA: Acadiana Press, 1981), 39, 106.

80. James H. Dormon, "A Late Nineteenth Century View of Acadiana: Charles Dudley Warner's 'The Acadian Land,'" *Attakapas Gazette* 7 (1972): 167–168.

81. Cultural geographer Lauren Post witnessed the continued use of the *parc aux petits* during his fieldwork expeditions during the 1930s. Post, *Cajun Sketches*, 156.

82. Norris Melancon, informally interviewed by Ryan A. Brasseaux, July 30, 2005; Steven LeJeune, interviewed by Barry Jean Ancelet, Pointe Noire, LA, April 7, 1979, accession No. A-0.134, Acadian and Creole Folklore and Folklife Collection, Center for Cultural and Eco-Tourism, University of Louisiana at Lafayette.

83. The repercussions of incorporating factions from rival neighborhoods in the same space were generally violent. Ancelet et al., *Cajun Country*, 101–111.

84. Ibid., 48–49; Ann Allen Savoy, *Cajun Music: A Reflection of a People*, Vol. 1 (Eunice, LA: Bluebird Press, 1984), 80, 240.

85. 1910 Census, Vermilion Parish, p. 192, and Household 243, ward 6. The 1910 census reveals only two dance halls (owned, respectively, by Simon Breaux, Jr., and Michael Nunez) operating in rural Vermilion Parish.

86. St. Martinville *Weekly Messenger* (November 30, 1912).

87. *Bals de maison* and dance halls coexisted in the first half of the twentieth century through World War II, after which house dances had virtually disappeared from the cultural landscape. Cultural geographer Malcolm Comeaux maintains that *bals de maison* had fallen out of favor by 1960. Comeaux, "The Cajun Dance Hall," 41; Bill C. Maloneand David Stricklin, *Southern Music, American Music* (Lexington: University of Kentucky Press, 2003), 86.

88. Daniels, "The Acadians of Louisiana," 388–390.

89. Sabry Guidry (b. 1894), interviewed by Barry Jean Ancelet, Abbeville, LA, May 5, 1977, A-0.144, Ancelet Collection, Archive of Cajun and Creole Folklore, University of Louisiana at Lafayette.

Chapter 2

1. Les Blank and Chris Strachwitz, *Jai Été au Bal (I Went to the Dance Last Night): The Cajun and Zydeco Music of Louisiana* [film] (Brazos Films, 1989); Mark Humphrey, liner notes, *Cajun Dance Party: Fais Do-Do* [disk], CK 46784 (New York: Roots N' Blues, 1994).

2. Chris A. Strachwitz, "Cajun Country," in *The American Folk Music Occasional*, ed. Strachwitz and Pete Welding, Vol. 1 (New York: Oak Publishers, 1970), 15.

3. Ann Allen Savoy, *Cajun Music: A Reflection of a People*, Vol. 1 (Eunice, LA: Bluebird Press, 1984), 93.

4. Columbia release 15275-D misspelled the French "Allons à Lafayette" with the phonetic "Allon a Laufette." Throughout the text, I have used the title printed on the original record label, "Lafayette," for the recording and composition commonly referred to as "Allons à Lafayette" in Louisiana. Blank and Strachwitz, *Jai Été au Bal*; Humphrey, *Cajun Dance Party*.

5. Joe Falcon interpreted the executive's disbelief by explaining the event in his own terms. Blank and Strachwitz, *Jai Été au Bal*.

6. Norm Cohen, "Early Pioneers," in *Stars of Country Music: Uncle Dave Macon to Johnny Rodriguez*, ed. Bill C. Malone and Judith McCulloh (Urbana: University of Illinois Press, 1975), 5.

7. Leo Soileau, interviewed by Ralph Rinzler, October 20, 1965, RI1.024, Ralph Rinzler Collection, Archive of Cajun and Creole Folklore, University of Louisiana at Lafayette (hereafter cited as Soileau interview); Savoy, *Cajun Music*, 54.

8. Norm Cohen and Paul F. Wells, "Recorded Ethic Music: A Guide to Resources," in *Ethnic Recordings in America: A Neglected Heritage* (Washington, DC: American Folklife Center, Library of Congress, 1982), 200.

9. Richard Keith Spottswood, *Ethnic Music on Records: A Discography of Ethnic Recordings Produced in the United States, 1893 to 1942*, 7 vols. (Urbana: University of Illinois Press, 1990); Shane K. Bernard, "J. D. Miller and Floyd Soileau: A Comparison of Two Small Town Recordmen of Acadiana," *Louisiana Folklife Journal* 15 (December 1991): 12–20; John Broven, *South to Louisiana: The Music of the Cajun Bayous* (Gretna, LA: Pelican Publishing, 1983); Andrew Brown, liner notes, *Harry Choates: Devil in the Bayou, the Gold Star Recordings* [disk], BCD 16355 (Hambergen, Germany: Bear Family Records, 2002).

10. Like recorded hillbilly and ethnic music, commercial Cajun music is a synthetic cultural product rooted in what Archie Green calls "genuine folk elements which have intruded into the mechanism of popular culture." Green, "Hillbilly Music: Source and Symbol," *Journal of American Folklore* 78, No. 309 (July–September 1965): 205; Nicholas R. Spitzer, ed., *Louisiana Folklife: A Guide to the State* (Baton Rouge: Louisiana Folklife Program, 1985), 212.

11. Lizabeth Cohen, *A Consumers' Republic: The Politics of Mass Consumption in Postwar America* (New York: Alfred A. Knopf, 2003), 22.

12. Joe Falcon, interviewed by Ralph Rinzler, October 10, 1965, RI.065, Ralph Rinzler Collection, Archive of Cajun and Creole Folklore, University of Louisiana at Lafayette (hereafter cited as Falcon interview); *Lafayette Advertiser* (January 5, 1901; December 21, 1901; January 24, 1906; December 2, 1910); *Opelousas Courier* (September 29, 1906).

13. Opelousas *Courier* (May 4, 1878).

14. Regular cylinders sold for 35 cents, whereas four-minute indestructibles sold for 50 cents, and the disks with music on both sides cost 65 cents. Opelousas *St. Landry Clarion* (March 11, 1911).

15. St. Martinville *Weekly Messenger* (April 27, 1912).

16. Lafayette *Daily Advertiser* (December 27, 1917).

17. Thibodaux *Lafourche Comet* (July 10, 1919).

18. Abbeville *Meridional* (December 16, 1922); Abbeville *Progress* (May 19, 1923).

19. Period newspapers indicate that socialites employed the phonograph for parties and other social engagements. *Crowley Signal* (August 16, 1924); Ryan A. Brasseaux, "Early Twentieth-Century Reminiscences of Eve Lavergne Castille," *Louisiana History* 66, No. 1 (Winter 2005): 65–88. In 1931, the Lafayette *Daily Advertiser* published an advertisement for Boudreaux's Electric Piano shop suggesting the range of musical styles available to Cajun consumers: "Here comes—The Peanut vender Mama Ines! Everybody's doing it! Doing what? The RUMBA, of course . . . that mean, voluptuous dance hall twister from old Havana. And everybody's buying

'em. Buying what? These brand-new RUMBA tunes, of course. Tunes that are hot from the Victor Record Press—and when we say hot, we mean HOT. Step up and get 'em, folks! They're both on hearing at this store." Lafayette *Daily Advertiser* (February 11, 1931).

20. Pekka Gronow, "Ethnic Recordings: An Introduction," in *Ethnic Recordings in America: A Neglected Heritage* (Washington, DC: American Folklife Center, Library of Congress, 1982), 1–9.

21. Ibid., 6.

22. Rick Kennedy and Randy McNutt, *Little Labels—Big Sound: Small Record Companies and the Rise of American Music* (Bloomington: Indiana University Press, 1999), xiv.

23. Kevin S. Fontenot, "Country Music's Confederate Grandfather: Henry C. Gilliland," in *Country Music Annual 2001*, ed. Charles K. Wolfe and James E. Akenson (Lexington: University Press of Kentucky, 2001), 190–206.

24. Green, "Hillbilly Music," 204–228; Bill C. Malone, *Country Music U.S.A.: A Fifty Year History* (Austin: University of Texas Press, 1968), 33–78; Norm Cohen, "Early Pioneers," 3–39; Gronow, "Ethnic Recordings," 1–9.

25. Charles Wolfe and Ted Olson, eds., *The Bristol Sessions: Writings about the Big Bang of Country Music* (Jefferson, NC: McFarland, 2005).

26. Bill C. Malone and David Stricklin, *Southern Music, American Music* (Lexington: University of Kentucky Press, 1979).

27. Gronow, "Ethnic Recordings," 1–3.

28. Though the literature is rather sparce, the best surveys relating to the commercialization of Cajun musical traditions are Broven *South to Louisiana*; and Stephen R. Tucker, "Louisiana Folk and Regional Popular Music Traditions on Records and the Radio," in *Louisiana Folklife: A Guide to the State*, ed. Nicholas R. Spitzer (Baton Rouge: Louisiana Folklife Program, 1985), 223–40.

29. Gronow, "Ethnic Recordings," 7.

30. For the complete pre–World War II Cajun discography, consult Spottswood, *Ethnic Music on Records*.

31. The Breaux ensemble consisted of accordionist Amédé, fiddler Ophy, occasionally guitarists Clifford, and Cleoma Breaux Falcon.

32. *La la* is a form of Afro-Creole dance music that mirrors the instrumentation and presentation of Cajun music. It is a possible antecedent to the modern Afro-Creole expression, zydeco. Michael Tisserand, *The Kingdom of Zydeco* (New York: Arcade, 1999), 51–65, 69–70, 75; Barry Jean Ancelet, "Zydeco/Zarico: Beans, Blues and Beyond," *Black Music Research Journal* 8 (1988): 33–49; for a discussion of juré, a contemporary form of AfroCreole music, largely performed among French-speaking black protestants in Louisiana, see Doris White, "Jouré My Lord," *Louisiana Folklore Miscellany* 4 (1976–1980): 143–145.

33. Nicholas R. Spitzer, "Documenting Tradition: Louisiana Folklife and Media," in *Louisiana Folklife: A Guide to the State*, ed. Spitzer (Baton Rouge: Louisiana Folklife Program, 1985), 212.

34. Malone, *Southern Music, American Music*, 71; Tony Russell, "Leo Soileau," *Old Time Music* 27 (1977): 6; Broven, *South to Louisiana*, 29; Kennedy and McNutt, *Little Labels—Big Sound*, 22.

35. Kennedy and McNutt, *Little Labels—Big Sound*, xv.

36. Benno Häupl of Riga, Latvia, owns one of the only surviving copies of the Roach issue. He shared the details of the Roach recording—descriptions of the aural information on the 78 rpm disk and printed label information—with Patrick J. Huber and Kevin S. Fontenot, who

kindly forwarded the correspondence to the author. Kevin S. Fontenot to Ryan André Brasseaux, personal communication [e-mail], December 29, 2007; Patrick J. Huber and Kevin S. Fontenot, "A 'Cajan' Music Mystery: Dr. James F. Roach and the Commercial Recording of 'Gué Gué Solingaie,'" unpublished paper, in author's possession, n.d.; Mark Zwonitzer and Charles Hirshberg, *Will You Miss Me When I'm Gone?: The Carter Family and Their Legacy in American Music* (New York: Simon and Schuster, 2002), 87; Gronow, "Ethnic Recordings," 9; Lawrence Cohn, liner notes, *Cajun*, Vol. 1, *Abbeville Breakdown 1929–1939* [disk], CK 46220 (New York: Roots N' Blues, 1990), 6–7.

37. Mina Monroe and Kurt Schindler, *Bayou Ballads: Twelve Folk-Songs from Louisiana* (New York: G. Schirmer, 1921), vi.

38. In Louisiana French, "cocodril" is the term for alligator. Monroe, *Bayou Ballads*, vi, 22–25; Barry Jean Ancelet, *Cajun and Creole Folktales: The French Oral Tradition of South Louisiana* (Jackson: University Press of Mississippi, 1994); Louisiana Writers' Project, Lyle Saxon, Edward Dreyer, and Robert Tallant, *Gumbo Ya-Ya: A Collection of Louisiana Folk Tales* (New York: Johnson Reprint Corporation, 1969).

39. Cohn, *Cajun Vol. 1*, 7; Gronow, "Ethnic Recordings," 8; Barry Jean Ancelet, *Cajun Music: Its Origins and Development* (Lafayette: Center for Louisiana Studies, University of Southwestern Louisiana, 1989), 19–20; Barry Jean Ancelet, Jay D. Edwards, and Glen Pitre, *Cajun Country* (Jackson: University Press of Mississippi, 1991), 150; Savoy, *Cajun Music*, 91; Charlie Seemann, liner notes, *Le Gran Mamou: A Cajun Music Anthology, the Historic Victor/Bluebird Sessions 1928–1941* [disk] (Nashville, TN: Country Music Foundation, 1990).

40. Gronow ("Ethnic Recordings," 8) maintains that the success of Falcon's recording supports the hypothesis that record companies did not have to sell thousands of recordings to realize a satisfying return on their investment.

41. Mitchell Reed, interviewed by Ryan A. Brasseaux and Erik Charpentier, January 17, 2004.

42. Ancelet, *Cajun Music*, 21.

43. Pierre V. Daigle, *Tears, Love and Laughter: The Story of the Cajuns and Their Music*, 4th ed. (Ville Platte, LA: Swallow Publications, 1987), 105.

44. Falcon interview.; for a more in-depth analysis of Leonard Garfield "Len" Spenser's career, see William Howland Kenney, *Recorded Music in American Life: The Phonograph and Popular Memory, 1890–1945* (New York: Oxford University Press, 1999), 34–35.

45. Cajuns were keenly aware of American popular trends, as evidenced by Soileau's reference to Bing Crosby. Soileau interview.

46. Gronow, "Ethnic Recordings," 8; Daigle, *Tears, Love and Laughter*, 105–106.

47. On November 13, 1928, socialites and public officials judged an accordion contest between Joe Falcon and five challengers in Port Barre, LA. St. Landry Parish Sherriff Chas Thibodeaux, W. B. Prescott, George Perrault, and T. H. Casanova presided as officiators. *Opelousas News* (November 8, 1928).

48. Released as Columbia 15301-D; Harry Oster, "Acculturation in Cajun Folk Music," *McNeese Review* 10 (Winter 1958):13; Lauren C. Post, *Cajun Sketches from the Prairies of Southwest Louisiana* (Baton Rouge: Louisiana State University Press, 1974), 161.

49. Oster, "Acculturation in Cajun Folk Music," 13.

50. Marais Bouleur was a notoriously violent rural oil patch near Mire, LA, where frontier values and morals persisted even with the introduction of the petroleum industry. Barry Jean Ancelet, "Rednecks, Roughnecks and the Bosco Stomp: The Arrival of the Oil Industry in the Marais Bouleur," *Attakapas Gazette* 22 (Spring 1987): 29–34.

51. Cleoma's four recording sessions took place on December 22, 1934, in New York City, March 12, 1936, and February 21, 1937, in New Orleans, and December 15, 1937, in Dallas, Texas. For a description of Cleoma's injury, see Savoy, *Cajun Music*, 90–91.

52. Randy Falcon interviewed by Pat Johnson, 2006. See also Kevin S. Fontenot and Ryan André Brasseaux, "Cleoma Breaux Falcon (1906–1941): The Commercialization of Cajun Music," in *Louisiana Women: Their History, Their Lives*, ed. Janet Allured and Judith F. Gentry (Athens: University of Georgia Press, forthcoming).

53. Only a handful of women became professional commercial recording artists before 1950, including pianist Johnny Manuel, who performed with Cajun swing musician Harry Choates, and Joe Falcon's second wife, drummer Theresa Falcon.

54. For more on performing gender, see Judith Butler, *Gender Trouble: Feminism and the Subversion of Identity* (New York: Routledge, 1990).

55. Loula Falcon Langlinais, interviewed by Ryan A. Brasseaux and Pat Johnson, June 20, 2006; see also Fontenot and Brasseaux, "Cleoma Breaux Falcon (1906–1941)."

56. Soileau interview; Humphry, "Fais Do-Do, a Cajun Romp," 7.

57. Loula Falcon Langlinais, interviewed by Ryan A. Brasseaux and Pat Johnson, June 20, 2006; see also Fontenot and Brasseaux, "Cleoma Breaux Falcon (1906–1941)."

58. Savoy, *Cajun Music*, 90–91.

59. For information regarding white women singing vernacular Southern music, see Kristine M. Mccusker, *Lonesome Cowgirls and Honky Tonk Angels: The Women of Barn Dance Radio* (Urbana: University of Illinois Press, 2008); Mary A. Bufwack and Robert K. Oermann, *Finding Her Voice: Women in Country Music, 1800–2000* (Nashville, TN: Vanderbilt University Press, 2003); Kristine M. Mccusker and Diane Pecknold, eds., *A Boy Named Sue: Gender and Country Music* (Jackson: University Press of Mississippi, 2004); Charles K. Wolfe and James E. Akenson, eds., *The Women of Country Music: A Reader* (Lexington: University Press of Kentucky, 2003).

60. Yolanda Broyles-Gonzáles, *Lydia Mendoza's Life in Music/La Historia De Lydia Mendoza* (New York: Oxford University Press, 2003), 54.

61. Randy Falcon, interviewed by Pat Johnson, 2006; see also Fontenot and Brasseaux, "Cleoma Breaux Falcon (1906–1941)."

62. Pamela Grundy, "'We Always Tried to Be Good People': Respectability, Crazy Water Crystals, and Hillbilly Music on the Air, 1933–1935," *Journal of American History* 81, No. 4 (March 1995): 1600–1603; John Atkins, "The Carter Family," in *Stars of Country Music: Uncle Dave Macon to Johnny Rodriguez*, ed. Bill C. Malone and Judith McCulloh (Urbana: University of Illinois Press, 1975), 101, 108.

63. Zwonitzer and Hirshberg, *Will You Miss Me When I'm Gone?*, 70–71. Cleoma recorded A. P. Carter's "Bonnie Blue Eyes" on February 21, 1937, for the Decca label (Decca 17034).

64. Sara Carter left professional music for the privacy of civilian life. Cleoma, of course, died tragically young. Zwonitzer and Hirshberg, *Will You Miss Me When I'm Gone?*, 180–181, 246–247, 250.

65. Malone, *Country Music U.S.A.*; Nolan Porterfield, *Jimmie Rodgers: The Life and Times of America's Blue Yodeler* (Urbana: University of Illinois Press, 1992), 98–101, 107–113; Charles Wolfe, "The Legend That Peer Built: Reappraising the Bristol Sessions," in *The Country Reader: Twenty-Five Years of the Journal of Country Music*, ed. Paul Kingsbury (Nashville, TN: Country Music Foundation Press and Vanderbilt University Press, 1996), 3–20; Atkins, "The Carter Family," 96–97.

66. Soileau interview.

67. Ibid.

68. Ibid.

69. Ibid.

70. Seemann, "Le Gran Mamou."

71. Some musicologists have incorrectly identified Frank Dietlein as "Frank Deadline." Members of the Dietlein family were prominent figures in Upelousas, LA. Frank peddled luxury items, including jewelry and phonograph technology, and served on the board of directors of the Opelousas Motion Picture Company. Opelousas *Clarion-News* (December 23, 1916).

72. While the name of the field agent remains a mystery, Seemann postulates that it could have been Victor's famous artist and repertory (talent scout) man Ralph Peer. Seemann, "Le Gran Mamou."

73. Ibid.; Donald Lee Nelson, "'Mama, Where You At?': The Chronicle of Maius LaFleur," *John Edwards Memorial Foundation Quarterly* 19, No. 70 (Summer 1983): 77.

74. Mary Alice Fontenot and Vincent Riehl, *The Cat and St. Landry* (Baton Rouge, LA: Claitor's, 1972), 18.

75. Ville Platte *Gazette*, "Leo Soileau, Old Ace, Remembers" (May 2, 1974).

76. Nelson, "'Mama, Where You At?,'" 77.

77. Ann Allen Savoy, liner notes, "Leo Soileau: From Cajun Classic to Innovator," *Early American Cajun Music: The Early Recordings of Leo Soileau*, [disk] 2041 (Newton, NJ: Yazoo, 1999), 4.

78. Soileau and LaFleur also recorded "La Valse Criminelle," the criminal's waltz, (Victor 21770) during their Atlanta session. Nelson, "'Mama, Where You At?,'" 77–78.

79. The details surrounding Mayeuse LaFleur's tragic life and recording career are sketched out in Nelson, "'Mama, Where You At?'".

80. Ibid., 78.

81. Ibid.

82. As quoted in Savoy, "Leo Soileau," 5.

83. Kennedy and McNutt, *Little Labels—Big Sound*, xiv, 2–3, 8.

84. Roy Gonzales recorded "Attendre Pour un Train" (Waiting for a Train—Paramount 12807), "Un Fussi Qui Brille" (Paramount 12807), "Anuiant et Bleue" (I'm Lonely and Blue—Paramount 12823), "Choctaw Beer Blues" (Paramount 12823), and rejects "Dor Mon Enfant Dor" (Sleep, Baby, Sleep) and "Ma Maison Aupres de Leau " ("My Home Near the Water").

85. Ray Brassieur, "Notes Concerning Moise Robin," typescript in author's possession (includes a log of an 1987 interview with Robin by Ron Brown and Faron Serrette); Kevin S. Fontenot, "Cajun Musicians, Cajun Mystic: The Improbable Legacy of Moise Robin," presented at the annual meeting of the Louisiana Historical Association March 27, 2006.

86. For a discussion of rural poverty in the American South, see C. Vann Woodward, *The Burden of Southern History* (Baton Rouge: Louisiana

State University Press, 1993); Lawrence Goodwyn, *The Populist Moment: A Short History of the Agrarian Revolt in America* (New York: Oxford University Press, 1978).

87. John H. Cowley, "Moonshine and Mosquitoes: The Story of Dewey Segura," in *Accordions, Fiddles, Two Step and Swing: A Cajun Music Reader*, ed. Ryan A. Brasseaux and Kevin S. Fontenot (Lafayette: Center for Louisiana Studies, University of Louisiana at Lafayette, 2006), 379–381.

88. Lucien "Dale" Breaux, interviewed by Patricia Johnson, May 30, 2006.

89. The releases included four songs: "The Waltz of Our Little Town," "The Acadian Waltz, "The Pretty Girls Don't Want Me," and "Do You Think Work Is Hard." Ron Brown, "Playing in the Shadows: Early Cajun Recording Artists," in *Accordions, Fiddles, Two Step and Swing: A Cajun Music Reader*, ed. Ryan A. Brasseaux and Kevin S. Fontenot (Lafayette: Center for Louisiana Studies, University of Louisiana at Lafayette, 2006), 349–350.

Chapter 3

1. Lafayette *Daily Advertiser* (March 23, 1929), p. 3.

2. There is some discrepancy about the spelling of the vocalist's name. The Lafayette newspaper printed the surname as Mufzar. Richard Spottswood lists the musicians as Muszar in his discography *Ethnic Music on Records*, vol. 1 (Urbana: University of Illinois Press, 1990). For aural examples of Pellerin's recordings, see Bob Pinson Recorded Sound Collection, Country Music Hall of Fame and Museum, Nashville, TN.

3. Tony Russell, (Nashville Tenn.), *Country Music Records: A Discography, 1921–1942* (Oxford: Oxford University Press, 2004), 684–685.

4. During the late nineteenth and early twentieth centuries, Longfellow's *Evangeline* was required reading for school children in curricula around the United States.

5. Judge Felix Voorhies's publication *Acadian Reminiscences* (1907)—marketed as the "true story of Evangeline"—stimulated a booming tourism industry in St. Martinville centered on Henry W. Longfellow's Acadian heroine. Felix Voorhies, *Acadian Reminiscences* (Boston: Palmer Company, 1907); Carl A. Brasseaux, *In Search of Evangeline: Birth and Evolution of the Evangeline Myth* (Thibodaux, LA: Blue Heron Press, 1988); Miriam Cooper and Bonnie Herndon, *Dark Lady of the Silents: My Life in Early Hollywood* (Indianapolis, IN: Bobbs-Merrill, 1973), 154–157; "The Screen," *New York Times* (August 20, 1919); Albert Proctor, "Andre A. Olivier Carefully Guards Tale of Evangeline," *The Progress* (October 7, 1938), 16, from the Louisiana and Lower Mississippi Valley Collection, Special Collections Dept., Louisiana State University at Baton Rouge; "Famous Poem Screened," *New York Times* (July 7, 1929); Crowley *Signal* (March 9, 1929; March 16, 1929; March 23, 1929); Napoleonville *Assumption Pioneer* (March 16, 1929).

6. Lauren C. Post, *Cajun Sketches from the Prairies of Southwestern Louisiana* (Baton Rouge: Louisiana State University Press, 1974); Harry Hansen, ed., *Louisiana: A Guide to the State* (New York: Hastings House, 1971), 60–79.

7. Recordings featuring the twin fiddling of the Soileau cousins (Alius and Leo Soileau), the robust harmonica playing of Leonville resident Artleus Mistric, and Syndey Landry's African-American–influenced solo guitar performance of "La Blouse Francaise" (French Blues) further reflect

the synthetic nature of Cajun culture and the heterogeneity of musical expression within the community.

8. Hansen, *Louisiana*, 179.

9. Michael Tisserand, *The Kingdom of Zydeco* (New York: Arcade, 1998), 4.

10. As quoted in Ann Allen Savoy, *Cajun Music: A Reflection of a People*, Vol. 1 (Eunice, LA: Bluebird Press, 1984), 96.

11. As quoted in Savoy, *Cajun Music*, 40.

12. Ann Allen Savoy, liner notes, "Leo Soileau: From Cajun Classic to Innovator," *Early American Cajun Music: The Early Recordings of Leo Soileau* [disk], 2041 (Yazoo, 1999), 2.

13. Leo Soileau, interviewed by Ralph Rinzler, October 20, 1965, RI1.024, Ralph Rinzler Collection, Archive of Cajun and Creole Folklore, University of Louisiana at Lafayette (hereafter cited as Soileau interview); Joe Darby, "Leo Soileau Remembers Little Boy Who Snuck His Papa's Fiddle," New Orleans *Times Picayune* (August 25, 1975).

14. Savoy, *Cajun Music*, 128.

15. Soileau interview; Savoy, "Leo Soileau," 3.

16. As quoted in Savoy, *Cajun Music*, 54.

17. Ibid.; Pierre V. Daigle, *Tears, Love, and Laughter: The Story of the Cajuns and Their Music*, 4th ed. (Ville Platte, LA: Swallow Publications, 1987), 115–117.

18. The musicians recorded six sides for Brunswick: "Bayou Pom Pom One Step," "La Valse de Church Point," "Petit Tes Canaigh," "Perrodin Two Step," "Valse de la Louisianne," and "Valse de Pointe Noire." Savoy, *Cajun Music*, 54; Daigle, *Tears, Love, and Laughter*, 116.

19. BeauSoleil bass player Mitchell Reed, a former understudy of McGee's, believes that the ornamentation employed by McGee is derived from old Irish compositions. Barry Jean Ancelet and Elmore Morgan, *The Makers of Cajun Music* (Austin: University of Texas Press, 1984), 35; Mitchell Reed, interviewed by Ryan A. Brasseaux and Erik Charpentier on January 17, 2004 (hereafter cited as Reed interview); Savoy, *Cajun Music*, 48, 52; Ann Allen Savoy, liner notes, *The Complete Early Recordings of Dennis Mcgee, with Ernest Fruge and Sady Courville, 1929–1930* [disk], 2012 (Newton, NJ: Yazoo, 1994), 3–4.

20. The back cover of the Yazoo release *The Complete Early Recordings of Dennis Mcgee, 1929–1930* features a quote from Marc Savoy, illustrating perfectly the prevailing attitude toward McGee by the end of the twentieth century: "Languages have dictionaries—Cajun music had Dennis McGee." André Gladu, *La Reel du Pendu* [film] (Montreal: Canada National Film Board, 1972); Les Blank and Chris Strachwitz, *Jai Été au Bal (I Went to the Dance Last Night): The Cajun and Zydeco Music of Louisiana* [film] (Fort Worth, TX: Brazos Films, 1989); *New York Times* (October 6, 1989); Michael Doucet, interviewed by Ryan A. Brasseaux and Erik Charpentier on September 7, 2004; *Cajun and Creole Masters* [disk], CDT-138 (New York: Music of the World, 1995); Ancelet and Morgan, *The Makers of Cajun Music*; Savoy, "The Complete Early Recordings of Dennis McGee," 3; Savoy, *Cajun Music*, 48.

21. Spires notes that the fingerboard of McGee's fiddle was worn from years of using his left index finger to produce an ornamental slide. Will Spires, liner notes, *The Complete Early Recordings of Dennis Mcgee, with Ernest Fruge and Sady Courville, 1929–1930* [disk], 2012 (Newton, NJ: Yazoo, 1994), 23–25.

22. The Tribute to Cajun Music festival simulated McGee's rise in popularity in south Louisiana during the 1970s and 1980s. Barry Jean Ancelet and Philip Gould, *One Generation at a Time: Biography of a Cajun and Creole Festival* (Lafayette: Center for Louisiana Studies, University of Louisiana at Lafayette, 2007).

23. Rocky L. Sexton and Harry Oster, "Une 'Tite Poule Grasse ou la Fille Aînée [A Little Fat Chicken or the Eldest Daughter]: A Comparative Analysis of Cajun and Creole Mardi Gras Songs," *Journal of American Folklore* 114, No. 452 (2001): 221–222.

24. The Louisiana territory refers to La Salle's original land claim defined by the Mississippi River and all the lands drained by the waterway—a mammoth slice of North America that stretched from Appalachia to the Rocky Mountains, and from the Gulf Coast to Canada.

25. Carl A. Brasseaux, trans. and ed., *A Comparative View of French Louisiana, 1699 and 1762: The Journals of Pierre Le Moyne D'Ibberville and Jean-Jacques-Blaise D'Abbadie* (Lafayette: Center for Louisiana Studies, University of Southwestern Louisiana, 1981), 100–101, 114, 122; field notes collected by John Laudun in 2004 describing fiddler Varise Connor's record collection in Lake Arthur Louisiana, digital copy of notes in author's possession.

26. See Ron Brown, liner notes, *Blind Uncle Gaspard, Delma Lachney, John Bertrand: Early American Cajun Music* [disk] (Newton, NJ: Yazoo, 1999) for the best documentation and biographical information for Blind Uncle Gaspard and Delmna Lachney.

27. Brown, *Blind Uncle Gaspard, Delma Lachney, John Bertrand*, 3.

28. Ron Brown notes that Delma Lachney's French Canadian great-grandfather migrated from Québec, Canada, during the early nineteenth century. Lachenaye was the original spelling of the surname. Brown, *Blind Uncle Gaspard, Delma Lachney, John Bertrand*, 3–4.

29. Ibid., 5.

30. Ibid.

31. Ibid., 3–6. Conflicting stories have created a debate about the author of "Baoille" (Vocalion 5280). Ron Brown maintains "it is likely that Delma Lachney composed it—he sings the song on the record and, according to several sources, reference in the lyrics is made to his mother and to his first wife, Estelle." However, another source argues that Gaspard penned the tune for the lover he could never have. The duo recorded eight other sides for Vocalion: "Marksville Blues," "Baltimore Waltz" (Vocalion 5320), "Je Me Trouve une Jolie Fille," (Vocalion 5347), "Riviere Rouge" (Red River) (Vocalion 5281), "La Louisiana," "Cher Ami Ma Vie Est Ruini" (Vocalion 5302), "La Danseuse," and "Bebe et la Gambleur" (Vocalion 5303).

32. Following Lachney and Gaspard's performances, the musicians encountered a situation similar to Joe Falcon's first recording experience, as the reluctant record executives eventually cut a check to Guy Goudeau for $300, perhaps because the unfamiliar French arrangements may have seemed alien and unmarketable. However, their records apparently sold well enough that the musicians made the trip to New Orleans two months later to record again for Vocalion. On March 5, 1929, Lachney and Gaspard reunited to wax four more sides: two duets—"Je M'En Vas dans le Chemin" (Vocalion 5314) and "Avoyelles" (Vocalion 5314)—and two solo performances featuring Gaspard on guitar and vocal—"Sur la Bord de l'Eau" (On the Riverside) (Vocalion 5333) and "Natchitoches" (Vocalion 5333). Ibid., 5.

33. Producer T-Bone Burnett revived the Gaspard arrangement of "Assi dans la Fenetre da Ma Chambre" in 2002 for the Warner Brother's film *Divine Secrets of the Ya-Ya Sisterhood*. Allison Krauss contributed an English translation of the song on the soundtrack. *Divine Secrets of the Ya-Ya Sisterhood* [CD], Columbia Records, 2002.

34. Ancelet, Barry Jean, "Cajun Music," *Journal of American Folklore* 107, No. 424 (Spring 1994): 285–303 at 296.

35. Savoy, *Cajun Music*, 24–25.

36. Harry Oster, *Folksongs of the Louisiana Acadians* [disk], 359 (El Cerrito, CA: Arhoolie, 1994).

37. Ralph Rinzler, *Louisiana Cajun French Music from the Southwest Prairies, 1964–1967* [CD], Vols. 1 and 2, 6001 and 6002 (Cambridge, MA: Rounder, 1989).

38. Brenda Daigle, "Acadian Fiddler Dennis McGee and Acadian Dances," *Attakapas Gazette* 7 (September 1972): 138.

39. Reed interview (Reed was an understudy of McGee's).

40. Sady Courville asked that his name not appear on the recordings, fearing his recordings might have a negative reception west of the Atchafalaya Basin. As a new and relatively untested Cajun musicial market opened, Courville's hesitancy stemmed from the stigma attached to all things Cajun. The Brunswick representatives complied, labeling the musician as 'Second Fiddle' on all but one of the records. Savoy, *Cajun Music*, 40–41.

41. Ibid., 54.

42. Tisserand, *The Kingdom of Zydeco*, 59–60.

43. Ibid., 36.

44. Amédé Ardoin and Dennis McGee recorded six sides during their first session: "Two Step de Mama" (Columbia 40514-F), "La Valse a Abe" (Columbia 40511-F), "Two Step de Eunice" (Columbia 40511-F), "Two Step de Prairie Soileau" (Columbia 40515-F), "Madam Atchen" (Columbia 40515-F), and "Taunt Aline" (Columbia 40514-F).

45. On November 19, 1930, Ardoin and McGee recorded "Amadie Two Step" (Brunswick 576), "Valse a Austin Ardoin" (Brunswick 576), "Blues de Basile" (Brunswick 531), "Valse À Thomas Ardoin" (Brunswick 531), "Two Step d'Elton" (Brunswick 513), and "Valse de Gueydan" (Brunswick 513) in New Orleans, LA. On November 20, 1930, the duo recorded "Valse a Alice Poulard" (Brunswick 495), "One Step d'Oberlin" (Brunswick 495), "Valse de Opelousas" (Brunswick 559), and "One Step des Chameaux" (Brunswick 559).

46. At the end of his musical career, Ardoin clearly crossed social boundaries that appropriated public displays of interracial sexual behavior when a group of Cajun dancegoers nearly beat the accordionist to death. Ardoin's assailants perceived an intimate encounter between the musician and a white woman as a violation of accepted sexual behavior in a white-only courtship space.

47. Tisserand, *The Kingdom of Zydeco*, 63; Garry Boulard, *Louis Prima* (Urbana: University of Illinois Press, 2002), 10–11, 18; Phil Pastras, *Dead Man Blues: Jelly Roll Morton Way Out West* (Berkeley: University of California Press, 2001), 10.

48. Mina Monroe and Kurt Schindler, *Bayou Ballads: Twelve Folk-Songs from Louisiana* (New York: G. Schirmer, 1921), vii; Shane Bernard and Julia Guirard, "'Colinda': Mysterious Origins of a Cajun Folksong," *Journal of Folklore Research* 29 (1992): 37–52.

49. Monroe, *Bayou Ballads*, vii; Savoy, *Cajun Music*, 15, 50; Daigle, "Acadian Fiddler Dennis McGee and Acadian Dances," 139.

50. Savoy, "The Complete Early Recordings of Dennis McGee," 18–20.

51. Baton Rouge *Morning Advocate* (June 7, 1959); Harry Oster, "Acculturation in Cajun Folk Music," *McNeese Review* 10 (Winter 1958): 19–23.

52. Amédé Ardoin presumably sat at the rear of the vehicle, in the bus's "colored" section. When the musicians reached the outer limits of the city, the bus boarded the Hoboken ferry. Icy water from the Hudson River leached into the bus as the damaged transport vessel began to sink. Water levels reached the passengers knees before another ferry rescued the travelers. Jared M. Snyder, liner notes, *Amédé's Recordings* (El Cerrito, CA: Arhoolie, 1995), 14.

53. Released as Decca 17004. For the Afro-Creole influence on Joe Falcon, see Lauren C. Post, "Joseph C. Falcon, Accordion Player and Singer: A Biographical Sketch," *Louisiana History* 11 (1970): 68–70.

54. Accordionist Lawrence Walker recorded the blues sides accompanied by fiddler Elton Walker and guitarists Junior Broussard and Aldus Broussard (or Norris Mire). Bluebird released the recording as Bluebird B-2199. Robert Sacré, *Musiques Cajun, Créole et Zydeco* (Paris: Presses Universitaires de France, 1995), 37–39.

55. Alan Lomax, *The Folk Songs of North America, in the English Language* (Garden City, NY: Doubleday, 1960), 577–578.

56. Nathan Abshire and the Rayne-Bo Ramblers (Norris Savoy, fiddle; LeRoy "Happy Fats" LeBlanc and Warnest Schexnyder, guitars) recorded six sides in New Orleans for Bluebird on August 10, 1935: "Valse de Riceville," "One Step de Morse" (Bluebird B-2174); "French Blues," "Gueydan Breakdown" (Bluebird B-2177); "One-Step de Lacassine," and "La Valse de Doutte Dachuninen" (Bluebird B-2178).

Chapter 4

1. The archive has since changed its name to the Archive of Folk Culture (http://www.loc.gov/folklife/archive.html, accessed June 27, 2007). Here I use the contemporary appellation in currency at the time the Lomaxes surveyed Louisiana. The father and son team collected most of their Cajun material between July and August of 1934.

2. Alan A. Lomax, John A. Lomax, *Our Singing Country: A Second Volume of American Ballads and Folk Songs* (New York: Macmillan, 1941), xv.

3. New Iberia was a bustling commercial center situated along the Bayou Têche near the eastern edge of Cajun Country. For more on New Iberia, see Glenn R. Conrad, ed., *New Iberia: Essays on the Town and Its People* (Lafayette: Center for Louisiana Studies: University of Louisiana at Lafayette, 1979).

4. Alan Lomax, liner notes, *Cajun and Creole Music: The Classic Louisiana Recordings, 1934/1937*, 11661-1843-2 (Cambridge, MA: Rounder Records, 1999), n.p.; John A. Lomax, *Adventures of a Ballad Hunter* (New York: Macmillan, 1947). For information on McIlhenny as ballad hunter, see Nolan Porterfield, *Last Cavalier: The Life and Times of John A. Lomax, 1867–1948* (Urbana: University of Illinois Press, 1996), 322–323; James Conaway, "On Avery Island, Tabasco Sauce Is the Spice of Life," *Smithsonian* (May 1984), 72–82, and "Salt and Pepper Flavor This Island," *Southern Living* (March 1989), 34–35.

5. Joseph C. Hickerson, "Early Field Recordings of Ethnic Music," in *Ethnic Recordings in America: A Neglected Heritage* (Washington, DC: American Folklife Center, Library of Congress, 1982), 70.

6. Some estimates "indicate upward of fifteen thousand American Indian" recordings existed throughout the United States by the early 1930s. Hickerson, "Early Field Recordings of Ethnic Music," 68. Lomax et al. (*Our Singing Country*, xiv) recognized the historic significance of their field recordings and its advantages for the methodology of musicological fieldwork:

> The collector with pen and notebook can capture only the outline of one song, while the recorder, having created an atmosphere of easy sociability, confines the living song, without distortion and in its fluid entirety, on a disc. Between songs, sometimes between stanzas, the singers annotate their own song. The whole process is brief and pleasurable. They are not confused by having to stop and wait for the pedestrian pen of the folklorist: they are able to forget themselves in their songs and to underline what they wish to underline. Singing in their homes, in their churches, at their dances, they leave on these records imperishable spirals of their personalities, their singing styles, and their cultural heritage. The field recording, as contrasted with the field notebook, shows the folksong in its three dimensional entirety, that its, with whatever rhythmic accompaniment there may be (hand-clapping, foot-patting, and so on), with its instrumental background, and with its folk harmonization.

7. Lomax, *Cajun and Creole Music*.

8. I have borrowed Richard White's notion of the "middle ground" as a process that operates on the premise of mutual and creative misunderstandings. Richard White, "Creative Misunderstandings and New Understandings," *William and Mary Quarterly* 63, No. 1 (January 2006): 10, and *The Middle Ground: Indians, Empires, and Republics in the Great Lakes Region, 1650–1815* (Cambridge: Cambridge University Press, 1991).

9. Robin D. G. Kelley, "Notes on Deconstructing 'The Folk,'" *American Historical Review* 97, No. 5 (December 1992): 1402.

10. Porterfield, *Last Cavalier*, 128.

11. American anthropology and folklore began to reconsider its attitude toward fieldwork in the United States under the influence of Franz Boas, Zora Neal Hurston, Hortense Powdermaker, and other researchers interested in vernacular American culture. John and Alan Lomax were important figures in the movement regarding folk music, particularly after John published *Cowboy Songs* in 1910. John A. Lomax, *Cowboy Songs* (New York: Sturgis and Walton, 1910); Lomax, *Adventures of a Ballad Hunter*; Porterfield, *Last Cavalier*; Bruce M. Knauft, *Genealogies for the Present in Cultural Anthropology* (New York: Routledge, 1996), 9–40; Regna Darnell, *Invisible Genealogies: A History of Americanist Anthropology* (Lincoln: University of Nebraska Press, 2001); Zora Neal Hurston, *Mules and Men* (New York: Harper Perennial, 1990); Hortense Powdermaker, *After Freedom: A Cultural Study in the Deep South* (Madison: University of Wisconsin Press, 1993).

12. Benjamin Filene, *Romancing the Folk: Public Memory and American Roots Music* (Chapel Hill, NC: UNC Press, 2000), 49.

13. Porterfield, *Last Cavalier*, 111.

14. As quoted in Porterfield, *Last Cavalier*, 323, 324.

15. New Iberia *Weekly Iberian* (April 28, 1938).

16. Marais Bouleur is a rural working-class Cajun neighborhood in Acadia Parish, near present-day Mire, LA. Donald J. Hebert, *L'Eglise du Marais Bouleur, 1872 to 1991: History of the Church at Marais Bouleur, Mire, Louisiana* (Rayne, LA: Hebert Publications, 1991); Barry Jean Ancelet, "Rednecks, Roughnecks and the Bosco Stomp: The Arrival of the Oil Industry in the Marais Bouleur," *Attakapas Gazette* 22 (Spring 1987): 29–34.

17. Irène Thérèse Whitfield, *Louisiana French Folk Songs* (Baton Rouge: Louisiana State University Press, 1939), 22.

18. Lomax Collection, Archive of Cajun and Creole Folklore: AAFS 11 B-side, AAFS 12 single-faced disk, AAFS 14 A-side, AAFS 14 B-side, LO1.001; AAFS 15 B-side, AAFS 16 A-side, AAFS 16 B-side, AAFS 17 single-faced disk, LO.002; AAFS 24 A-side, AAFS 26 A-side, AAFS 26 B-side, LO.003; AAFS 27 A-side, AAFS 27 B-side, AAFS 28 A-side, AAFS 28 B-side, AAFS 29 A-side, AAFS 29 B-side, LO1.004; AAFS 30 A-side, AAFS 30 B-side, AAFS 31 A-side, AAFS 32 A-side, AAFS 32 B-side, LO1.005; AAFS 33 A-side, AAFS 33 B-side, AAFS 34 A-side, AAFS 34 B-side, LO1.006; AAFS 35 A-side, AAFS 35 B-side, AAFS 36 single-faced disk, AAFS 37 A-side, AAFS 37 B-side, LO1.007; AAFS 39 B-side, LO1.008; AAFS 42 A-side, AAFS 42 B-side, LO1.009; AAFS 83b1, LO1.011.

19. Comeaux lived at Route 4, Box 117, New Iberia, LA, according to the field recording annotations. AAFS 33a1, AAFS 33a2, AAFS 33a3, AAFS 33b1, AAFS 33b2, AAFS 33b3, AAFS 34a1, AAFS 34a2, AAFS 34a3, AAFS 34a4, AAFS 34b1, AAFS 34b2, LO1.006, Lomax Collection, Archive of Cajun and Creole Folklore.

20. Lomax et al. cite Elita (Elida) Hoffpauir as one of the finest singers they encountered in the United States in *Our Singing Country*: "Elida Hofpauir, fifteen, who knew a bookful of French and Cajun ballads, who worked in a tomato canning factory and wanted a dollar 'store-bought' dress for a present" (xi). In a more contemporary newspaper interview published in the *Weekly Iberian* in April of 1938, Lomax explained that Hoffpauir worked in a fish-canning factory. I state that she worked in a fish (not tomato) canning factory based on the New Iberia *Weekly Iberian*, April 28, 1938.

21. New Iberia *Weekly Iberian* (April 28, 1938).

22. Ibid.

23. Lomax Collection, Archive of Cajun and Creole Folklore: AAFS 32 A-side, AAFS 32 B-side, LO1.005; AAFS 38A, LO1.008. Despite the French origin of Julien's repertoire, these ballads may reflect the Hoffpauir family's North American experience, not their European roots. The Hoffpauirs first immigrated to New Orleans in the 1770s from Alsace, then a German principality. By the 1780s, the family had relocated to the Opelousas district along Louisiana's western prairies. The Bayou Country's multiethnic Francophone community eventually absorbed the Alsatians. In light of the Acadian genealogical connection to western France and Poitou, and the incredible amount of cross-cultural borrowing taking place in south Louisiana during the nineteenth and twentieth centuries, the Hoffpauirs undoubtedly learned a portion of their repertoire from the surrounding wealth of folkloric material in south Louisiana. Furthermore, Elita engaged the region's industrial economy. Her employment in a local factory and her desire to participate in mass consumption, juxtaposed with her ballad repertoire, interjected serious complications in the Lomaxian isolation model.

Descendants of Thomas Hoffpauir, Family Treemaker Online, http://fami lytreemaker.genealogy.com/users/h/o/f/Charles-R-Hoffpauir/ODT2-0001. html?Welcome=1077029249, accessed on February 17, 2004.

24. Lomax, *Cajun and Creole Music*, n.p.; see also New Iberia *Weekly Iberian* (April 28, 1938).

25. Shane K. Bernard, *The Cajuns: Americanization of a People* (Jackson: University Press of Mississippi, 2003), xx–xxi; H. W. Gilmore, "Social Isolation of the French Speaking People of Rural Louisiana," *Social Forces* 12, No. 1 (1933): 78–84; Ancelet, "Rednecks, Roughnecks and the Bosco Stomp," 29–34; Barry Jean Ancelet, *Cajun Music: Its Origins and Development* (Lafayette: Center for Louisiana Studies, University of Southwestern Louisiana, 1989); Ann Allen Savoy, *Cajun Music: A Reflection of a People*, Vol. 1 (Eunice, LA: Bluebird Press, 1984); Vaughan B. Baker, "The Acadians in Antebellum Louisiana: A Study of Acculturation," in *The Cajuns: Essays on Their History and Culture*, ed. Glenn R. Conrad (Lafayette: Center for Louisiana Studies, University of Southwestern Louisiana, 1978), 115–128; New Iberia *Weekly Iberian* (April 6, 1939).

26. A local legend asserts that a child riding a tricycle accidentally bumped into Brasseaux, who proceeded to destroy the tricycle by jumping up and down on it in the streets of Erath. Ancelet, *Cajun and Creole Music*, n.p.

27. The only picture I have ever seen of Isaac Sonnier and Fénélon Brasseaux, both dressed in their Army uniforms, is published in Curney J. Dronet, *A Century of Acadian Culture: The Development of a Cajun Community: Erath (1899–1999)* (Erath, LA: Acadian Heritage and Culture Foundation, 2000), 52. Unfortunately, in 2005, Hurricane Rita (the storm that ravished Cajun Country two weeks after Katrina) washed away the image when Erath's Acadian Museum flooded.

28. Alan Lomax described "Je M'endors" as a "highly original Franco-American blues like song." The song's hybrid nature is a product of south Louisiana's cultural melting pot. AAFS 17a2, LO1.002, Lomax Collection, Archive of Cajun and Creole Folklore; Lomax, *Cajun and Creole Music*, n.p.; Ancelet, *Cajun and Creole Music*, n.p.

29. AAFS-11 B-side, LO1.001, Lomax Collection, Archive of Cajun and Creole Folklore.

30. Both the Lomaxes and Barry Ancelet transcribed and translated materials from the collection. I have included the Ancelet transcription, which may be closer to the original intentions of Mr. Bornu, because Ancelet has a better grasp of Cajun French and its cultural context. Ancelet, *Cajun and Creole Music*, n.p.

31. Illiteracy was widespread within the working-class Cajun population until mandatory schooling went into effect. Any schooling children did receive after 1921 was in English. Carl A. Brasseaux, "Acadian Education: From Cultural Isolation to Mainstream America," in *The Cajuns: Essays on Their History and Culture*, ed. Glenn R. Conrad (Lafayette: Center for Louisiana Studies, University of Southwestern Louisiana, 1978), 212–224; Bernard, *The Cajuns*, 19.

32. For nineteenth-century bilingualism among Cajuns, see W. W. Pugh, "Bayou Lafourche from 1820 to 1825—Its Inhabitants, Customs and Pursuits," *Louisiana Planter and Sugar Manufacturer* (September 29, 1888), 143; A. R. Waud, "Acadians of Louisiana," *Harper's Weekly* (October 20, 1866), 670; James H. Dormon, "A Late Nineteenth Century View of Acadiana: Charles Dudley Warner's 'The Acadian Land,'" *Attakapas Gazette* 7 (1972): 168; Frederick Law Olmsted, *A Journey through Texas: Saddle-Trip*

on the Southwestern Frontier: With a Statistical Appendix (New York: Dix, Edwards, and Co., 1857), 401–403.

33. English instructions designed for newly arrived immigrants from Southern and Eastern Europe applied equally to native-born "foreign" language groups such as American Indians, Latinos, and Cajuns. Bernard, *The Cajuns*, 33; Brasseaux, "Acadian Education"; for other the effects of Progressive Era English language education on ethnic and immigrant populations in America, see Michael McGerr, *A Fierce Discontent: The Rise and Fall of the Progressive Movement in America, 1870–1920* (New York: Oxford University Press, 2005), 77–117; Matt Garcia, *A World of Its Own: Race, Labor, and Citrus in the Making of Greater Los Angeles, 1900–1970* (Chapel Hill, NC: UNC Press, 2001), 87–120; George J. Sánchez, *Becoming Mexican American: Ethnicity, Culture, and Identity in Chicano Los Angeles, 1900–1945* (New York: Oxford University Press, 1995), 87–107; and K. Tsianina Lomawaima, *They Called It Prairie Light: The Story of Chilocco Indian School* (Lincoln: University of Nebraska Press, 1995). On immigration and Americanization, see Robert A. Carlson, *The Americanization Syndrome: A Quest for Conformity* (London: Croom Helm, 1987); Philip Gleason, "American Identity and Americanization," in *Concepts of Ethnicity*, ed. William Peterson, Philip Gleason, and Michael Novak (Cambridge, MA: Belknap/Harvard University Press, 1982), 57–143; Mel van Elteren, *Americanism and Americanization: A Critical History of Domestic and Global Influence* (Jefferson, NC: McFarland, 2006); and Matthew Frey Jacobson, *Barbarian Virtues: The United States Encounters Foreign Peoples at Home and Abroad, 1876–1917* (New York: Hill and Wang, 2000).

34. American Indians had a similar English-language educational experience. As Susan U. Philips illustrates, Native Americans students' use of English posed a variety of difficult situations for their instructors. Indeed, the students spoke "Indian English," not the Standard English of their teachers.

> Although many people on the reservations still speak an Indian language, today all of the Warm Springs children in school are monolingual speakers of English. The dialect of English they speak, however, is not the Standard English of their teachers but one that is distinctive to the local Indian community, and that in some aspects of grammar and phonology shows influence from the Indian languages spoken on the reservation.

By the end of the twentieth century, Cajun school children were overwhelmingly monolingual Anglophones, often translating French grammatical structures and vocabulary into English. For example, the south Louisiana phrase "come see" (come here) is a direct translation from the French *viens voir*. In some instances, monolingual Cajuns incorporate specific French terms, such as *envie* (to crave), pass (from the French *passer*), and *honte* (embarrassed) within English phrases. Susan U. Philips, "Participant Structures and Communicative Competence: Warm Springs Children in Community and Classroom," in *Linguistic Anthropology: A Reader*, ed. Alessandro Duranti (Malden, MA: Blackwell Publishers, 2001), 305. For a discussion of Cajun English, see Sylvie DuBois and Barbara Horvath, "Let's tink about dat: Interdental Fricatives in Cajun English," *Language Variation and Change* 10, No. 3 (1998): 245–261, "From Accent to Marker in Cajun English: A Study of Dialect Formation in Progress," *English World Wide* 19, No. 2 (1998): 161–188, and "When the Music Changes, You Change Too: Gender and Language Change in Cajun English," *Language Variation and Change* 11 (1999): 287–313; Sylvie Dubois, "Verbal Morphology in Cajun Vernacular English: A Comparison with Other Varieties of Southern English," *Journal of English Language and Linguistics* 31, No. 1 (2003): 1–26; Shana L. Walton, "Flat Speech and Cajun Ethnic Identity in Terrebonne Parish, Louisiana" (Ph.D. Dissertation, Tulane University, 1994).

35. AAFS 11b2, LO1.001, Lomax Collection, Archive of Cajun and Creole Folklore; Lomax, *Cajun and Creole Music*, n.p.; Alan Lomax, *The Folk Songs of North America in the English Language* (Garden City, NY: Doubleday, 1960), 355–356. Contemporary ethnographies conducted by the Works Progress Administration further illustrate the tremendous impact of Western movies on the Cajun community. Cajuns attending picture shows imbibed American popular culture through a one-way dialogue afforded by the mass medium.Lyle Saxon, et al., *Gumbo Ya-Ya: A Collection of Louisiana Folk Tales* (New York: Bonanza, 1954), 202; Lomax et al., *Our Singing Country*, 194.

36. AAFS 15b1, LO1.002, Lomax Collection, Archive of Cajun and Creole Folklore.

37. AAFS 12 single-faced disk, LO1.001, Lomax Collection, Archive of Cajun and Creole Folklore.

38. Perhaps the most remarkable instrumental performances in the Archive of American Folk Song's south Louisiana collection feature Cajuns demonstrating colonial-era instrumental conventions. On June 29, 1934, the Lomaxes recorded two compositions in New Iberia featuring clarinetist Henri Decuir and fiddler Delmar Hebert. According to the annotation following the performance, Decuir (born 1863) insisted that the septuagenarian duo specialized in "colonial music." They offered two distinctly Old World arrangements rendered on clarinet and fiddle—a sound that apparently persisted since the 1780s under the radar of the commercial Cajun market. The lingering memory of reed and string arrangements carried over through an unidentified waltz performed with the accompaniment of Hebert's children. The musicians claimed that the tune was the first waltz introduced to Louisiana during the French regime. Both instruments remained in the musical landscape, though in different capacities. The clarinet found a voice in local jazz ensembles, while fiddles resonated with the sounds of various dance music traditions. AAFS 24b2, LO1.003; AAFS 41 B-side, LO1.009; AAFS 41b2, Lomax Collection, Archive of Cajun and Creole Folklore. For a brief reference to clarinet and fiddle in Cajun music, see Ancelet, *Cajun Music*, 15; Margaret O'Brien-Molina to Ryan André Brasseaux, personal communication [e-mail], January 18, 2004. Southwest Louisiana was also a hotbed for jazz musicians. The Lomaxes recorded the Evangeline Band—a jazz ensemble that featured clarinet, cornet, and trombone—on June 13, 1934. AAFS 41a1, AAFS 41a2, LO1.008, Lomax Collection, Archive of Cajun and Creole Folklore.

39. Lomax Collection, Archive of Cajun and Creole Folklore: AAFS 20a1, AAFS 20a2, AAFS 20a3, AAFS 21a1, AAFS 21a2, AAFS 21a3, AAFS 21a4, LO1.002; AAFS 21b1, AAFS 21b2, AAFS 21b3, LO1.003.

40. "Sitting On Top of the World" was recorded in Shreveport, LA, by the black Mississippi string band the Mississippi Sheiks, popular among both African Americans and Southern whites. Stephen R. Tucker, "Louisiana Folk and Regional Popular Music Traditions on Records and the

Radio: An Historical Overview with Suggestions for Future Research," in *Accordions, Fiddles, Two Step and Swing: A Cajun Music Reader*, ed. Ryan A. Brasseaux and Kevin S. Fontenot (Lafayette: Center for Louisiana Studies, University of Louisiana at Lafayette, 2006), 233. A fiddler usually listed as Wayne Perry recorded 38 commercial sides for the Bluebird and Decca labels in 1937 and 1938 with three different incarnations of Joe Werner's Cajun Swing ensemble: Joe's Acadians, Joe Werner and the Ramblers, and the Louisiana Rounders. All three groups featured Perry on fiddle, Joe Werner on guitar, vocal, and on most sides harmonica, and Julius "Papa Cairo" Lamperez on either guitar or electric steel guitar. Perry's knowledge of both Blues and Anglo-American material featured in the Lomax recordings would have facilitated the transition to Cajun swing, if he is indeed the fiddler from the Joe Werner sessions.

41. Mitchell Reed, interviewed by Ryan A. Brasseaux and Erik Charpentier, January 17, 2004.

42. New Iberia *Weekly Iberian* (April 28, 1938).

43. Anne Bailey, *Invisible Southerners: Ethnicity in the Civil War* (Macon: University of Georgia Press, 2006), 7.

44. "State Plans for Louisiana for Developing Regional and Community Festivals," Lauren Chester Post Papers, Acc. No. 2854, 7:11–19, Box 2, Folder 58, Special Collections, Hill Memorial Library, Louisiana State University.

45. Cajun-born Dean of Administration James F. Broussard and noted sociologist T. Lynn Smith served as advisers. Post then selected Supervisor of Music for New Orleans Public Schools Mary Conway and George H. Gardiner of the Lafayette Chamber of Commerce as his assistants. "Report on Louisiana's Part in the National Folk Festival Held in Dallas, Texas As Part of the Texas Centennial." Lauren Chester Post Papers, Acc. No. 2854, 7:11–19, Box 2, Folder 58, Special Collections, Hill Memorial Library, Louisiana State University.

46. Lauren Chester Post grew up outside of Duson, LA, where the future cultural geographer learned to straddle his Anglo American ancestry and the Cajun cultural landscape around him. Post also knew the world beyond south Louisiana. After enlisting in the U.S. Navy during World War I, he accepted his first assignment at Newport, RI (one of the nation's folk music hubs during the second half of the twentieth century), before receiving technical training at Harvard University's Radio School. His radio skills paid off on board the U.S.S. *Whipple*, during his doctoral studies at the University of California at Berkeley, and later during his field expeditions into the Bayou Country. He returned to his childhood home every summer to photograph and interview Cajun bands and record songs after accepting an appointment in the geography department at Louisiana State University, which facilitated and funded the Cajun programming at the National Folk Festival. Irène Whitfield Holmes, "In Memoriam: Lauren Chester Post," *Louisiana Folklore Miscellany* 4 (1976–1980): 7.

47. "State Plans for Louisiana for Developing Regional and Community Festivals," Lauren Chester Post Papers, Acc. No. 2854, 7:11–19, Box 2, Folder 58, Special Collections, Hill Memorial Library, Louisiana State University.

48. The entourage included: Lauren C. Post, chairman; Irène Thérèse Whitfield, who served as interpreter for the weavers and as a critic for folk music formally; tenor vocalist Elmore Sonnier, who also acted as interpreter and general handyman; Madam Alphe and Adolphina Benoit

representing local weaving custom; nineteen members of the "Evangeline Band" and costumed dance troupe; and Southern University's African American Quartet. Their respective entourages, including substitutes, troupe directors, chaperones, vocal coaches, and assistants rounded out the delegation. Lauren Chester Post Papers, Acc. No. 2854, 7:11–19, Box 2, Folder 58, Special Collections, Hill Memorial Library, Louisiana State University. See also Michael Ann Williams, *Staging Tradition: John Lair and Sarah Gertrude Knott* (Urbana: University of Illinois Press, 2006).

49. Walker hailed from Duson; Norris Mire and Ardus Broussard from Rayne. Sidney Sr., Sidney Jr., and Evelyn Broussard all made the trip from Lake Arthur.

50. Lauren C. Post, "General Plan of the National Folk Festival," Lauren Chester Post Papers, Acc. No. 2854, 7:11–19, Box 2, Folder 58, Special Collections, Hill Memorial Library, Louisiana State University.

51. The Chicago School of sociology was a major force disseminating information about ethnic and immigrant groups living in Chicago through the voice of cultural authority. Ideas about poverty, crime, and other characteristics of ghetto life came to life under the direction of Robert E. Park. Robert E. Park, Ernest W. Burgess, and Roderick D. McKenzie, *The City: Suggestions for Investigation of Human Behavior in the Urban Environment* (Chicago: University of Chicago, 1925); Martin Blumer, *The Chicago School of Sociology: Institutionalization, Diversity, and the Rise of Sociological Research* (Chicago: University of Chicago, 1986); for more on ethnics and their connection to leftist circles in both the American North and South, see Paul Avrich, *The Haymarket Tragedy* (Princeton, NJ: Princeton University Press, 1984); David Montgomery, *The Fall of the House of Labor: The Workplace, the State, and American Labor Activism, 1865–1925* (Cambridge: Cambridge University Press, 1989); Zaragosa Vargas, *Labor Rights Are Civil Rights: Mexican American Workers in Twentieth-Century America* (Princeton, NJ: Princeton University Press, 2007); Robin D. G. Kelley, *Hammer and Hoe: Alabama Communists During the Great Depression* (Chapel Hill, NC: UNC Press, 1990); Lizabeth Cohen, *Making a New Deal: Industrial Workers in Chicago, 1919–1939* (Cambridge: Cambridge University Press, 1990); Glenda Elizabeth Gilmore, *Defying Dixie: The Radical Roots of Civil Rights, 1919–1950* (New York: W. W. Norton, 2008); Randi Storch, *Red Chicago: American Communism at Its Grassroots, 1928–35* (Urbana: University of Illinois Press, 2007); Michael Denning, *The Cultural Front: The Laboring of American Culture in the Twentieth Century* (London: Verso, 1997).

52. National Folk Festival Souvenir Program, Lauren Chester Post Papers, Acc. No. 2854, 7:11–19, Box 2, Folder 58, Special Collections, Hill Memorial Library, Louisiana State University.

53. According to Michael Ann Williams, some of the nation's top academics—e.g., Zora Neal Hurston and Benjamin Botkin—molded Sarah Gertrude Knott's conceptualization of folklore. Williams, *Staging Tradition*, 20–22. For other pertinent discussions, see also Jane S. Becker, *Selling Tradition: Appalachia and the Construction of an American Folk, 1930–1940* (Chapel Hill, NC: UNC Press, 1998); Richard A. Peterson, *Creating Country Music: Fabricating Authenticity* (Chicago: University of Chicago Press, 1997).

54. My thinking here represents the intersection of David Whisnant's provocative assertion that political motivations inspired individuals to attach the folk label to the so-called isolated population of Appalachia, and what historians Eric Hobsbawm and Terrence Ranger term the "invention of

tradition." The moniker "folk" whitewashed impoverished "crackers" and "hillbillies" living in the upland South. By inventing a tradition concerned with characterizing these "backward" peoples through the uplifting, but equally marginalizing term "folk," Americans came to image a people who still spoke Elizabethan English and preserved Old World ballads. This new tradition involved constructing a consumable facade around a marginalized population. I suggest that Whisnant's argument holds true for the Cajun experience albeit in a Francophone context. That is, ethnic groups also experienced a kind of cultural uplift through the political act of naming groups such as Cajuns as the "folk." David E. Whisnant, *All That Is Native and Fine: The Politics of Culture in an American Region* (Chapel Hill, NC: UNC Press, 1995); Eric Hobsbawm and Terence Ranger, eds., *The Invention of Tradition* (Cambridge: Cambridge University Press, 1992).

55. Radio transcription (text only) from Lauren Chester Post Papers, Acc. No. 2854, 7:11–19, Box 2, Folder 58, Special Collections, Hill Memorial Library, Louisiana State University.

56. Ibid.

57. Kevin S. Fontenot and Ryan A. Brasseaux, "King of the Dancehalls: Accordionist Lawrence Walker," in *Accordions, Fiddles, Two Step and Swing: A Cajun Music Reader*, ed. Ryan A. Brasseaux and Kevin S. Fontenot (Lafayette: Center for Louisiana Studies, University of Louisiana at Lafayette, 2006), 425–429.

58. "Acadian Band Makes Hit at National Folk Festival," Lauren Chester Post Papers, Acc. No. 2854, 7:11–19, Box 2, Folder 58, Special Collections, Hill Memorial Library, Louisiana State University. Meanwhile, Madam Alphe Benoit and her daughter Adolphina demonstrated traditional carding, spinning, and weaving techniques on a 500-pound loom for 14 hours a day. LSU alums Irène Thérèse Whitfield and Elemore Sonnier, and the chairman's wife, Valerie Post, took turns translating for the Francophone weavers. Although Post accurately represented Cajun dance music's folk qualities at the festival, he cast the monolingual working-class Benoit family as a romantic stereotype by dressing them in costumes modeled after outdated fashions.

59. Lauren C. Post, "Lake Arthur Musicians and Singers Win Praise at National Folk Festival," newspaper clipping, Lauren Chester Post Papers, Acc. No. 2854, 7:11–19, Box 2, Folder 58, Special Collections, Hill Memorial Library, Louisiana State University. See also "Acadian Band Makes Hit at National Folk Festival," Lauren Chester Post Papers. Lyle Saxon, co-author of the Louisiana Writers Project publication *Gumbo Ya-Ya*, proclaimed that the Cajun delegation offered one of the best performances at the festival. Lyle Saxon correspondence to Dean James Broussard, June 19, 1936, Lauren Chester Post Papers, Acc. No. 2854, 7:11–19, Box 2, Folder 58, Special Collections, Hill Memorial Library, Louisiana State University.

60. Ibid.

61. Lauren C. Post, *Cajun Sketches from the Prairies of Southwest Louisiana* (Baton Rouge: Louisiana State University Press, 1974), 159–160.

62. Sidney S. Broussard to Lauren C. Post, June 26, 1936, Lauren Chester Post Papers, Acc. No. 2854, 7:11–19, Box 2, Folder 58, Special Collections, Hill Memorial Library, Louisiana State University.

63. Sarah Gertrude Knott to Lauren C. Post, June 25, 1936, Lauren Chester Post Papers, Acc. No. 2854, 7:11–19, Box 2, Folder 58, Special Collections, Hill Memorial Library, Louisiana State University.

64. Sarah Gertrude Knott to Aldus Broussard, March 27, 1937; Sarah Gertrude Knott correspondence to Wade Bernard, March 27, 1937; Lauren Chester Post Papers, Acc. No. 2854, 7:11–19, Box 2, Folder 58, Special Collections, Hill Memorial Library, Louisiana State University.

65. William A. Owens, *Tell Me a Story, Sing Me a Song: A Texas Chronicle* (Austin: University of Texas Press, 1983), 119.

66. William A. Owens, *Texas Folk Songs* (Austin: Texas Folklore Society, 1950), 20.

67. Ibid., 20.

68. In south Louisiana, a potato kiln is a warehouse used to store harvested potatoes, especially sweet potatoes. Ibid., 20.

69. Ibid., 18.

70. Owens et al., *Tell Me a Story, Sing Me a Song*, 122.

71. Ibid., 121.

72. The song is commonly known as "J'ai Passé Devant ta Porte."

73. Ibid., 148.

74. Owens, *Texas Folk Songs*, 21.

75. Whitfield, *Louisiana French Folk Songs*.

76. Rachel Adams, *Sideshow U.S.A.: Freaks and the American Cultural Imagination* (Chicago: University of Chicago Press, 2001), 25–59.

77. Kathleen Hoover and John Cage, *Virgil Thomson: His Life and Music* (New York: Thomas Yoseloff, 1959), 208.

78. "Ania Dorfmann, Pianist, Heard with Orchestra," *Philadelphia Enquirer* (27 November 1948), MSS 29A, Box 146, Series No. VII.A, Folder 24, 1948, Virgil Thomson Papers, Irving S. Gilmore Music Library, Yale University.

79. MSS 29, Box 75, Series No. III, Folder 27, Pulitzer Prize, Virgil Thomson Papers, Irving S. Gilmore Music Library, Yale University.

Chapter 5

1. Luderin Darbone, interviewed by Ryan A. Brasseaux and Carl A. Brasseaux, July 12, 2003.

2. Ibid.

3. As quoted in Ben Sandmel, liner notes, *Luderin Darbone's Hackberry Ramblers, Early Recordings: 1935–1950* [disk], 7050 (El Cerrito, CA: Arhoolie, 2003), 6.

4. Luderin Darbone, interviewed by Ryan A. Brasseaux and Carl A. Brasseaux, July 12, 2003.

5. Ben Sandmel doubled as the Hackberry Ramblers drummer and manager. As quoted in Sandmel, *Luderin Darbone's Hackberry Ramblers*, 6.

6. Lizabeth Cohen, *Making a New Deal: Industrial Workers in Chicago* (Cambridge: Cambridge University Press, 1990), 145.

7. Bill C. Malone, *Country Music U.S.A.: A Fifty Year History* (Austin: University of Texas Press, 1968), 172; Michael Mendelson, "Benny Thomasson and the Texas Fiddling Tradition," *John Edwards Memorial Foundation Quarterly* 10, No. 35, Part 3 (Autumn 1974); Charles Wolfe, "Tracking the Lost String Bands," *Southern Exposure* 2–3 (1977): 11–20; W. K. McNeil, "Five Pre-World War II Arkansas String Bands: Some Thoughts on Their Recording Success," *John Edwards Memorial Foundation Quarterly* 20, No. 74 (Fall/Winter 1984): 68–75; Kevin Sanders, "Ragtime's Influence on Early Country Music," *Rag Times* 34, No. 3 (September 2000): 2–8; Patrick Henry Bogan, Jr., "East Texas Serenaders," in *The Handbook of Texas Music*,

ed. Roy R. Barkley (Austin: Texas State Historical Association for Studies in Texas History at the University of Texas at Austin, 2003), 89–90.

8. Varise Connor as quoted in Raymond François, *Yé Yaille, Chère: Traditional Cajun Dance Music* (Ville Platte, LA: Swallow Publications, 1990), 15. Country historian Bill Malone maintains that minstrelsy played an important role in the development of these small string combos by popularizing the fiddle and banjo, which became standard instrumentation for many Southern ensembles. The banjo, however, did not factor into Cajun music until the Cajun swing era, when musician relegated the instrument to the rhythm section as in the jazz tradition. Bill C. Malone, *Singing Cowboys and Musical Mountaineers: Southern Culture and the Roots of Country Music* (Athens: University of Georgia Press, 1993).

9. Ancelet, *Cajun Music*, 15.

10. Ron Yule, *When the Fiddle Was King: Early Country Music from the North and West Regions of Louisiana* (Natchitoches, LA: Northwestern State University Press, 2006), 58, 65–66. The Creole Ramblers—another Cameron Parish Creole ensemble, featuring tenor banjo player Dallas LeBeouf, fiddler Andrew LeBeouf, and guitarist Crawford Vincent—performed their interpretation of Jimmie Rodgers's repertoire until the late 1930s, when the group began to emulate Bob Wills and Cliff Bruner. Considering Cameron Parish's proximity to east Texas, the country undercurrents inherent in the Fawvors' and the Creole Ramblers' musical stylings diffused through cross-cultural pollination.

11. Pat Harrison, liner notes, *Cajun: Early Recordings* [CD], C JSP7726 (London: JSP Records, 2004); Sacré, *Musiques Cajun, Créole et Zydeco*, 37–39 ; Pierre V. Daigle, *Tears, Love and Laughter: The Story of the Cajuns and Their Music*, 4th ed. (Ville Platte, LA: Swallow Publications, 1987), 140; Savoy, *Cajun Music*, 206.

12. Luderin Darbone, "A Brief History of the Hackberry Ramblers," in *Accordions, Fiddles, Two Step and Swing: A Cajun Music Reader*, ed. Ryan A. Brasseaux and Kevin S. Fontenot (Lafayette: Center for Louisiana Studies, University of Louisiana at Lafayette, 2006), 399.

13. Cajun audiences flocked to hear both black and white entertainers. Afro-Creole orchestras such as the Yelping Jazz Hounds, Wicked Jazz 7, Black Eagles Jazz Band, the Banner Orchestra, and Black Diamond Band performed in and around their home communities, often catering to middle-class white audiences who provided the financial support that sustained these combos. White musicians such as Bill Landry, whose orchestra enjoyed widespread popular in the Bayou Country playing the latest standards in American jazz, also attracted large Cajun audiences. *Lafayette Daily Advertiser* (February 21, 1922); Thibodaux *Lafourche Comet* (June 1, 1922; January 21,1926; August 26, 1926); Ville Platte *Weekly Gazette* (October 10, 1925; September 19, 1925); Crowley *Signal* (August 6, 1927), 7; *Opelousas News*, February 9, 1928; Denis Hebert, "The Hebert Family and the Music of Acadiana," *Attakapas Gazette* 23, No. 3 (Fall 1988): 104; Austin Sonnier, Jr., *Second Linin': Jazzmen of Southwest Louisiana, 1900–1950* (Lafayette: Center for Louisiana Studies, University of Southwestern Louisiana, 1989), 10; Sara Le Menestrel, "The Color of Music: Social Boundaries and Stereotypes in Southwest Louisiana French Music," *Southern Cultures* 13 (Fall 2007): 87–105; Barbara Smith Corrales, "Prurience, Prostitution, and Progressive Improvements: The Crowley Connection, 1909–1918," *Louisiana History* 45, No. 10 (Winter 2004): 37–70; Alicia P. Long, *The Great Southern Babylon: Sex, Race, and*

Respectability in New Orleans, 1865–1920 (Baton Rouge: Louisiana State University Press, 2004); Al Rose, *Storyville, New Orleans, Being an Authentic, Illustrated Account of the Notorious Red-Light District* (Tuscaloosa: University of Alabama Press, 1974).

14. Gene Thibodeaux, *Rice, Railroads and Frogs: A History of Rayne, Louisiana* (Church Point, LA: Plaquemine Brûlée Press, 2001), 146.

15. *Lafayette Daily Advertiser* (October 3, 1929).

16. Accordionist Octa Clark had not been immune to the Jazz Age, either. His repertoire included "The Black Eagle Two-Step," a song the accordionist learned from legendary jazzman Bunk Johnson, who played for a stint with the African-American Crowley-based Black Eagle orchestra. Todd Mouton, "Love or Folly? Cajun Trailblazers BeauSoleil Celebrate 20 Years Together," *OffBeat* (January 1997), 45; Sonnier, *Second Linin,'* 10.

17. Luderin Darbone, interview by Ryan A. Brasseaux, Erik Charpentier, and Carl A. Brasseaux, January 3, 2004; Sandmel, *Luderin Darbone's Hackberry Ramblers*, 7.

18. Dave Oliphant, "Texas Jazz 1920–50," in *The Roots of Texas Music*, ed. Lawrence Clayton and Joe W. Specht (College Station: Texas A&M University Press, 2003), 37–65.

19. Darbone interview.

20. Cary Ginell, "The Development of Western Swing," *John Edwards Memorial Foundation Quarterly* 20, No. 74 (Fall/Winter 1984): 58–67, and Ginell and Roy Lee Brown, *Milton Brown and the Founding of Western Swing* (Urbana: University of Illinois, 1994), xxx–xxxi. For the most comprehensive work on Bob Wills, see Charles R. Townsend, *San Antonio Rose: The Life and Music of Bob Wills* (Urbana: University of Illinois Press, 1976).

21. Bill C. Malone, *Don't Get above Your Raisin': Country Music and the Southern Working Class* (Urbana: University of Illinois Press, 2002), 35; Bernard, *The Cajuns*, 38.

22. Bernard, *The Cajuns*, 37.

23. Dana Davids Olien and Roger M. Olien, *Oil in Texas: The Gusher Age, 1895–1945* (Austin: University of Texas Press, 2002), 29–30; John Edward Brantly, *History of Oil Well Drilling* (Houston: Gulf Publishing Company, 1971), 234; Kenny A. Franks and Paul F. Lambert, *Early Louisiana and Arkansas Oil: A Photographic History, 1901–1946* (College Station: Texas A&M University Press, 1982), 17–21.

24. Franks and Lambert, *Early Louisiana and Arkansas Oil*, 183–184.

25. Those predominately Cajun parishes affected include Acadia, Ascension, Assumption, Calcasieu, Cameron, Evangeline, Iberia, Iberville, Jefferson Davis, Lafayette, Lafourche, St. Charles, St. James, St. John the Baptist, St. Landry, St. Martin, St. Mary, Terrebonne, Vermilion, and West Baton Rouge. Franks and Lambert, *Early Louisiana and Arkansas Oil*, 183; Barry Jean Ancelet and Elmore Morgan, *The Makers of Cajun Music* (Austin: University of Texas Press, 1984), 32–33; Luderin Darbone, interviewed by Ryan A. Brasseaux and Carl A. Brasseaux, July 12, 2003 (hereafter cited as Darbone interview).

26. Barry Jean Ancelet, *Cajun Music: Its Origins and Development* (Lafayette: Center for Louisiana Studies, University of Southwestern Louisiana, 1989), 33; Charlie Seeman, *Le Gran Mamou: A Cajun Music Anthology, the Historic Victor/Bluebird Sessions 1928–1941* (Nashville, TN: Country Music Foundation, 1990), n.p.

27. Sandmel, *Luderin Darbone's Hackberry Ramblers*, 3.

28. Ibid.; Darbone interview.

29. Sandmel, *Luderin Darbone's Hackberry Ramblers*, 3.

30. Ibid., 4.

31. Darbone interview.

32. Edgar A. Schuler, *Survey of Radio Listeners in Louisiana* (Baton Rouge: Louisiana State University General Extension Division, 1943); Shane K. Bernard, *The Cajuns: Americanization of a People* (Jackson: University Press of Mississippi, 2003), 20.

33. Cajun fiddler/bandleader Hadley Castille, interviewed by Marce Lacouture, broadcast on KRVS 88.7 FM, Lafayette and Lake Charles, LA (NPR affiliate) on September 2, 2003, from 1–2 P.M.—on program *Lagniappe*, CD transcript of the broadcast in the author's possession.

34. *Lafayette Daily Advertiser* (September 4, 1924); Lafayette *Advertiser* (April 10, 1929). In 1929, the newspaper reported that clear stations from Tulsa, Oklahoma; Minneapolis, Minnesota; Cleveland, Ohio; and Ft. Wayne, Indiana, could be picked up on radios in Cajun Country.

35. Gene Fowler and Bill Crawford, *Border Radio: Quacks, Yodelers, Pitchmen, Psychics, and Other Amazing Broadcasters of the American Airwaves* (Austin: University of Texas Press, 2002).

36. Luderin Darbone, interviewed by Ryan A. Brasseaux and Carl A. Brasseaux, July 7, 2003. Shane K. Bernard argues in his book *The Cajuns* that "most Cajuns remained culturally isolated from the rest of America for nearly the entire first half of the twentieth century, even as radio made its way into south Louisiana during the 1920s and 1930s" (xxi). Clearly, as Luderin Darbone's statement acknowledges, Cajun swing was shaped in large part by the latest currents in American music. Radio was *the* conduit through which the Hackberry Ramblers discovered and absorbed the latest hillbilly and Western swing compositions—not only for their own amusement, but also to satisfy an audience that listened to the same emissions.

37. C. Joseph Pusateri, *Enterprise in Radio: WWL and the Business of Broadcasting in America* (Washington, DC: University Press of America, 1980), 126–127; Stephen R. Tucker, "Louisiana Folk and Regional Popular Music Traditions on Records and the Radio: An Historical Overview with Suggestions for Future Research," in *Louisiana Folklife: A Guide to the State*, ed. Nicholas R. Spitzer (Baton Rouge: Louisiana Folklife Program, 1985), 224–226.

38. *Shreveport Times* (March 8, 1925). Louisiana country music historian Stephen Tucker maintains that the first evidence of folk material broadcast by KWKH took place on March 8, 1925. Tucker, "Louisiana Folk," 224. See also Ann Allen Savoy, *Cajun Music: A Reflection of a People*, (Eunice, LA: Bluebird Press, 1984); Elizabeth Mae Roberts, "French Radio Broadcasting in Louisiana" (M.A. thesis, Louisiana State University, 1959), 36, 53; Luderin Darbone, "A Brief History of the Hackberry Ramblers," in *Accordions, Fiddles, Two Step and Swing: A Cajun Music Reader*, ed. Ryan A. Brasseaux and Kevin S. Fontenot (Lafayette: Center for Louisiana Studies, University of Louisiana at Lafayette, 2006), 400.

39. Darbone, "A Brief History of the Hackberry Ramblers," 399.

40. By the time Cajuns felt the full brunt of radio's impact, Cajun swing was standard programming on KVOL and KPLC. Diversity on the air waves continued to grow through the end of World War II, when Acadiana's radio stations featured a variety of live Louisiana music programming that included string band music, country and western, and accordion-based ensembles, on variety shows such as LeRoy LeBlanc and Oran Guidry's

Happy and Doc's Talent Show broadcast on Opelousas station KSLO. Shane Bernard and Julia Girourard, "'Colinda': Mysterious Origins of a Cajun Folksong," *Journal of Folklore Research* 29 (1992): 39; Roberts, "French Radio Broadcasting in Louisiana"; Beth Norwod, "French Broadcasting in Louisiana," *Southern Speech Journal* 30, No. 1 (1964): 46–54.

41. Leo Soileau, interviewed by Ralph Rinzler, October 10, 1965, RI1.024, Ralph Rinzler Collection, Archive of Cajun and Creole Folklore, University of Louisiana at Lafayette.

42. Crowley *Acadian-Signal* (October 6, 1938).

43. Contest winners included Contredanse Francaise from Mamou, First Prize—$35.00; Happy Fats and his Rayne-Bo Ramblers, Second Prize—$25.00; Doc and the Sons of the Acadians, Third Prize—$10.00; and Leo Soileau and his Rhythm Boys, Fourth Prize—$5.00. Plans for the Crowley Rice Festival, Louise V. Olivier Collection, No. 1880, Box 12, LA and Lower Mississippi Valley Collection, Hill Memorial Library, Louisiana State University, Baton Rouge.

44. Happy Fats and his Rayne-Bo Ramblers were based out of Rayne, LA. Personnel including Leroy "Happy Fats" Leblanc (singer, director, bass fiddle), Lewis Arceneaux (tamborine and washboard), Ray Clark (fiddle), Joseph Broussard (banjo), Sandy Norman (guitar), and Bobby Thibodaux (piano). Ibid.

45. Leo Soileau and His Rhythm Boys were based out of Basile, LA. Personnel included Leo Soileau (vocal, fiddle), Jessie Morhinveg (mandolin), Sammy Lusco (piano), Jerry Baker (guitar), and Sam Baker (drums) [scratched out: Ben Nicholson (banjo), Beethoven Miller (banjo)]. Ibid.

46. The Louisiana Hillbillies were based out of Crowley, LA. Personnel included Julius Lamperez (Hawaiian-style lap steel guitar), Andrus Thibodaux (fiddle, singer), Ray Guidry (banjo), Alphé Stutes (guitar), Hector Stutes (bass fiddle) [handwritten note—"In case of necessity"], and Warren Fo[r]eman (tenor guitar). Ibid.

47. The Merrymakers were based out of Eunice, LA. Personnel included J. B. Fuselier (singer, fiddle), Percy Oge (guitar), Elric Young (guitar), and Pete Duhon (bass fiddle). Ibid.

48. Joseph Falcon and His Silver Bells String Band were based out of Crowley, LA. Personnel included Joe Falcon (accordion and drums), Cleoma Falcon (guitar), Bob Mathews (banjo), Clifford Breaux (fiddle), and Allen Gilbert (guitar). Ibid.

49. Loula Falcon Langlanais, interviewed by Ryan A. Brasseaux and Pat Johnson, June 20, 2006.

50. According to musicologist Harry Oster, the jazz roots of "You Keep a Knockin'" are planted in the seedy New Orleans red light district Storyville, where several infamous jazz artists, including Jelly Roll Morton, enjoyed lucrative careers. Crowley *Daily Signal* (October 3, 1960; September 20, 1963); Harry Oster, *Folksongs of the Louisiana Acadians* [disk], 359 (El Cerrito, CA: Arhoolie, 1994); Charlie Redlich, interviewed by Ryan A. Brasseaux, May 5, 2005.

51. Shane K. Bernard, *Swamp Pop: Cajun and Creole Rhythm and Blues* (Jackson: University Press of Mississippi, 1996), 47.

52. As quoted in Barry Ancelet, "Dewey Balfa: Cajun Music Ambassador," *Louisiana Life* (September–October 1981): 78.

53. Mitchell Reed, personal communication, June 2004.

54. Barry Jean Ancelet, "Negotiating the Mainstream: The Creoles and Cajuns in Louisiana," *French Review* 80, No. 6 (May 2007): 1241.

Chapter 6

1. *Port Arthur News* (September 11, 1926). I thank Shane K. Bernard for calling my attention to the article.

2. The Great Depression further suffocated yeomen and sharecroppers following the agricultural depression of 1920.

3. See Anthony Harkins, *Hillbilly: A Cultural History of an American Icon* (New York: Oxford University Press, 2004).

4. R. L. Daniels, "The Acadians of Louisiana," *Scribner's Monthly* 19 (1879–1880): 383.

5. Thad St. Martin, "Letters and Comment—Cajuns," *Yale Review* 26 (June 1937): 859–862.

6. Cary Ginell, *Milton Brown and the Founding of Western Swing* (Urbana: University of Illinois Press, 1994), 178.

7. Leo Soileau, interviewed by Ralph Rinzler, October 20, 1965, RI1.024, Ralph Rinzler Collection, Archive of Cajun and Creole Folklore, University of Louisiana at Lafayette (hereafter cited as Soileau interview).

8. Ruth Sheldon, *Bob Wills: Hubbin' It* (Nashville, TN: Country Music Foundation Press, 1995), 47.

9. A. R. Waud, "Acadians of Louisiana," *Harper's Weekly* (October 20, 1866), 670.

10. George Washington Cable, "Notes on Acadians in Louisiana," 126, Cable Collection, Manuscripts Division, Tulane University Library, New Orleans, LA.

11. As quoted in William Ivy Hair, *Bourbonism and Agrarian Protest: Louisiana Politics, 1877–1900* (Baton Rouge: Louisiana State University Press, 1969), 135. To place Louisiana into a national context regarding immigration and economics, see Matthew Frey Jacobson, *Barbarian Virtues: The United States Encounters Foreign Peoples at Home and Abroad, 1876–1917* (New York: Hill and Wang, 2000).

12. Neil Foley, *The White Scourge: Mexicans, Blacks, and Poor Whites in Texas Cotton Culture* (Berkeley: University of California Press, 1997), 85, 64–65; see also Jack Temple Kirby, *Rural Worlds Lost: The American South, 1920–1960* (Baton Rouge: Louisiana State University Press, 1987).

13. Cajuns later appropriated the term "coonass" as a marker of working-class culture. See Dorice Tentchoff, "Ethnic Survival under Anglo-American Hegemony: The Louisiana Cajuns," *Anthropological Quarterly* 53, No. 4 (October 1980): 229–241; Carl A. Brasseaux, "Grand Texas: The Cajun Migration to Texas," in *The French in Texas*, ed. François Lagarde (Austin: University of Texas Press, 2003), 273–286; Shane K. Bernard, *The Cajuns: Americanization of a People* (Jackson: University Press of Mississippi, 2003), 96–97; Shana Walton, "Louisiana's Coonasses: Choosing Race and Class over Ethnicity," in *Signifying Serpents and Mardi Gras Runners: Representing Identity in Selected Souths*, ed. R. Celeste Ray and Luke E. Lassiter (Athens: University of Georgia Press, 2003), 38–50, http://www.cajunculture.com/Other/coonass.htm, accessed February 13, 2008.

14. David R. Roediger, *The Wages of Whiteness: Race and the Making of the American Working Class* (London: Verso, 1991), 13.

15. Barry Jean Ancelet and Elmore Morgan, *Cajun and Creole Music Makers* (Jackson: University Press of Mississippi, 1999), 40.

16. Ann Allen Savoy, *Cajun Music: A Reflection of a People* (Eunice, LA: Bluebird Press, 1984), 52.

17. Soileau interview.

18. David Goodhew, "Working-Class Respectability: The Example of Western Areas of Hohannesburg, 1930–55," *Journal of African History* 41 (2000): 266.

19. For a discussion of the economic ramifications associated with whiteness, see George Lipsitz, *The Possessive Investment in Whiteness: How White People Profit from Identity Politics* (Philadelphia: Temple University Press, 1998); Roediger, *The Wages of Whiteness.*

20. Gene Autry represented the ultimately white Southern working-class hero. His Hollywood image was one of the only respectable Southern archetypes portrayed to American audiences. The Texas native's films, and subsequent series such as those featuring Roy Rogers, left a favorable impression on both Cajun swing and Western swing musicians, as evidenced by the costume shift in both genres. See Douglas B. Green, *Singing in the Saddle: The History of the Singing Cowboy* (Nashville, TN: Vanderbilt University Press and Country Music Foundation Press, 2002); and Holly George-Warren, *Public Cowboy No. 1: The Life and Times of Gene Autry* (New York: Oxford University Press, 2007).

21. Norman Cohen, "The Skillet Lickers: A Study of a Hillbilly String Band and Its Repertoire," *Journal of American Folklore* 78, No. 309 (July-September 1965): 241.

22. Foley, *The White Scourge*, 63.

23. For a brief discussion of respectability among Cajun and Creole musicians, see Sara Le Menestrel, "The Color of Music: Social Boundaries and Stereotypes in Southwest Louisiana French Music," *Southern Cultures* 13 (Fall 2007), 100–104. For a theoretical discussion of respectability in analogous contexts in the Afro-Caribbean see, Peter J. Wilson, "Reputation and Respectability: A Suggestion for Caribbean Ethnology," *Man* 4, No. 1 (March 1969): 70–84, *Oscar: An Inquiry into the Nature of Sanity?* (Prospect Heights, IL: Waveland Press, 1992), 113–142, and *Crab Antics: A Caribbean Case Study of the Conflict between Reputation and Respectability* (Prospect Heights, IL: Waveland Press, 1995), 94–121. For the hierarchal relationships between Anglo, ethnic, and poor whites, see Foley, *The White Scourge*; David G. Gutiérrez, *Walls and Mirrors: Mexican Americans, Mexican Immigrants, and the Politics of Ethnicity* (Berkeley: University of California Press, 1995); Carl A. Brasseaux, *Acadian to Cajun: Transformation of a People, 1803–1877* (Jackson: University Press of Mississippi, 1992); and Bernard, *The Cajuns.*

24. David R. Roediger, *Working toward Whiteness: How America's Immigrants Became White. The Strange Journey from Ellis Island to the Suburbs* (New York: Perseus Books Group, 2006), 8.

25. Manuel H. Peña, *The Mexican American Orquesta: Music, Culture, and the Dialectic of Conflict* (Austin: University of Texas Press, 1999), 99.

26. Ibid., 100–101. Conjunto is an accordion-based dance music, generally performed in Spanish, that parallels accordion-based Cajun dance music. Manuel H. Peña, *The Texas-Mexican Conjunto: History of a Working-Class Music* (Austin: University of Texas Press, 1985).

27. Alain Larouche, "The Cajuns of Canal Yankee: Problems of Cultural Identity in Lafourche Parish," in *French America: Mobility, Identity, and Minority Experience across the Continent*, ed. Dean R. Louder and Eric Waddell (Baton Rouge: Louisiana State University Press, 1993), 276.

28. Lizabeth Cohen, *Making a New Deal: Industrial Workers in Chicago, 1919–1939* (Cambridge: Cambridge University Press, 1990), 158.

29. Ibid., 156.

30. Pamela Grundy, "'We Always Tried to Be Good People': Respectability, Crazy Water Crystals, and Hillbilly Music on the Air, 1933–1935," *The Journal of American History* 81, No. 4 (March 1995): 1603.

31. Luderin Darbone, "A Brief History of the Hackberry Ramblers," in *Accordions, Fiddles, Two Step and Swing: A Cajun Music Reader*, ed. Ryan A. Brasseaux and Kevin S. Fontenot (Lafayette: Center for Louisiana Studies, University of Louisiana at Lafayette, 2006), 402–403; Louis Michot, interviewed by Ryan A. Brasseaux and Erik Charpentier, June 26, 2006; Sandmel, Ben, *Luderin Darbone's Hackberry Ramblers, Early Recordings: 1935–1950* [disk] (El Cerrito, CA: Arhoolie, 2003), 11; Stephen R. Tucker, "Louisiana Folk and Regional Popular Music Tradition on Records and the Radio: An Historical Overview with Suggestions for Future Research," in *Accordions, Fiddles, Two Step and Swing: A Cajun Music Reader*, ed. Ryan A. Brasseaux and Kevin S. Fontenot (Lafayette: Center for Louisiana Studies, University of Louisiana at Lafayette, 2006), 237.

32. Soileau interview.

33. Joe Darby, "Leo Soileau Remembers Little Boy Who Snuck His Papa's Fiddle," New Orleans *Times Picayune* (August 25, 1975).

34. Tony Russell, "Leo Soileau," *Old Time Music* 27 (1977): 9; John Broven, *South to Louisiana: The Music of the Cajun Bayous* (Gretna, LA: Pelican Publishing, 1983), 20–21.

35. Soileau interview.

36. Ibid.

37. Russell, "Leo Soileau," 5.

38. I am deeply indebted to my colleague and music historian Kevin Fontenot for calling to my attention the frustration and tension inherent in the sides recorded by Leo Soileau and Moïse Robin.

39. As quoted in Raymond François, *Yé Yaille, Chère: Traditional Cajun Dance Music* (Ville Platte, LA: Swallow Publications, 1990), 75.

40. There is some discrepancy as to when Leo Soileau formed his first Cajun swing ensemble. Ann Savoy gives two different dates: 1932 in the Yazoo liner notes to the *Early Recordings of Leo Soileau*, and 1934 in her book *Cajun Music*. John Broven also cites the formation of the Three Aces in 1934. If 1932 is correct, the Three Aces would constitute the first Cajun swing outfit to organize. On the other hand, 1934 situates the group's emergence after the formation of the Hackberry Ramblers in 1933. Ann Allen Savoy, "Leo Soileau: From Cajun Classic to Innovator," *Early Recordings of Leo Soileau*, *Early American Cajun Music* (Yazoo, 1999 2041), 8; Broven, *South to Louisiana*, 20.

41. Bill C. Malone and David Stricklin, *Southern Music, American Music* (Lexington: University of Kentucky Press, 1979), 85.

42. Cajun Country artists such as fiddler Rufus Thibodeaux and Doug Kershaw were both featured artists on WSM's Grand Ole Opry radio program, the popular keepers of country music tradition. In 2006, Cajun guitarist and vocalist Jimmy C. Newman celebrated 50 years as an official member of the Opry. Moreover, the North American Country Music Association inducted Newman into their International Hall of Fame on March 12, 2000. Bob Pinson, "The Bob Wills Recordings: A Comprehensive Discography," in Charles R. Townsend, *San Antonio Rose: The Life and Music of Bob Wills* (Urbana: University of Illinois Press, 1976), 339; Sheldon, *Bob Wills*, 81; Opry Member Jimmy C. Newman, in Meet the Opry, http://www.opry.com/MeetTheOpry/Members.aspx?id=92, accessed

August 19, 2006. See also Bill C. Malone, *Country Music U.S.A.: A Fifty Year History* (Austin: University of Texas Press, 1968).

43. Decca session logs maintain that O. P. Shreve and Johnny Roberts were the new members of the Four Aces replacing Tony Gonzales. It is unclear what instruments these musicians played.

44. Russell, "Leo Soileau," 6–7.

45. Soileau interview.

46. Ibid.

47. Savoy, *Cajun Music*, 129; Johnnie Allan, *Memories: A Pictoral History of South Louisiana Music*, Vols. 1 and 2, *1920s–1990s* (Lafayette, LA: JADFEL Publishing, 1995), 140, 149; Charles Wolfe, *A Good-Natured Riot: The Birth of the Grand Ole Opry* (Nashville, TN: Vanderbilt University Press, 1999), 250–251; Carolyn F. Griffith, "Czech and Polish Music in Texas before World War II," in *The Roots of Texas Music*, ed. Lawrence Clayton and Joe W. Specht (College Station: Texas A&M University Press), 175–191; James P. Leary, *Polkabilly: How the Goose Island Ramblers Redefined American Folk Music* (New York: Oxford University Press, 2006), 3–38.

48. Kevin Fontenot, personal communication, June 9, 2005.

49. Luderin Darbone, interviewed by Ryan A. Brasseaux, Erik Charpentier, and Carl A. Brasseaux, January 31, 2004.

50. Russell, "Leo Soileau," 6.

51. As quoted in Sandmel, *Luderin Darbone's Hackberry Ramblers*, 3.

52. Darbone, "A Brief History of the Hackberry Ramblers," 399.

53. Luderin Darbone, interviewed by Ryan A. Brasseaux and Carl A. Brasseaux, July 12, 2003.

54. Between 1936 and 1938, the Hackberry Ramblers recorded at the Bluebird label's New Orleans studios on February 19, 1936; October 17, 1936; February 22, 1937; September 10, 1937; April 1, 1938; and October 22, 1938.

55. Luderin Darbone, interviewed by Ryan A. Brasseaux, Erik Charpentier, and Carl A. Brasseaux, January 31, 2004.

56. In 1951, "Wondering" resurfaced in the American musical landscape when Louisiana Hayride star Webb Pierce scored a national smash hit with the composition that he learned from the Werner recording. Malone, *Country Music U.S.A.*, 234.

57. Bill C. Malone, *Don't Get Above Your Raisin': Country Music and the Southern Working Class* (Urbana: University of Illinois Press 2002), 117–148.

58. John Broven, "The Bayou Buckaroo: LeRoy 'Happy Fats' LeBlanc," in *Accordions, Fiddles, Two Step and Swing: A Cajun Music Reader*, ed. Ryan A. Brasseaux and Kevin S. Fontenot (Lafayette: Center for Louisiana Studies, University of Louisiana at Lafayette, 2006), 409.

59. Ibid.

60. The sessions took place on the following dates: August 8, 1935; September 10, 1937; April 2, 1938; October 23, 1938; February 14, 1940; and October 8, 1941. All of the sessions took place in New Orleans except for the group's last two dates, which took place in Dallas, Texas.

61. The Rayne-Bo Ramblers include the Bessie Smith lyric "I got the world in a jug, the stopper's in my hand" from the song "Downhearted Blues," and the Jimmie Rodgers's lyric "You may see me talking walking down that railroad track" from "Anniversary Blue Yodel (Blue Yodel Number 7)."

62. Broven, *South to Louisiana*, 26.

63. Ibid.

64. Nicholas R. Spitzer, liner notes, *Octa Clark and Hector Duhon: The Dixie Ramblers, Ensemble Encore, the Men and Their Music* [disk], LP 6011 (Cambridge, MA: Rounder Records, 1983).

65. As quoted in Spitzer, *Octa Clark and Hector Duhon*.

66. Ancelet and Morgan, *The Makers of Cajun Music*, 113.

67. As quoted in Spitzer, *Octa Clark and Hector Duhon*.

68. Savoy, *Cajun Music*, 142–143. Charlie Seeman, liner notes, *Raise Your Window: A Cajun Music Anthology, the Historic Victor/Bluebird Session, 1928–1941* (Nashville, TN: Country Music Foundation, 1993), n.p.; Chris Strachwitz, liner notes, *Cajun Breakdown: Cajun String Bands of the 1930s*, 7014 (El Cerrito, CA: Arhoolie, 1997).

69. As quoted in Lawrence Cohn, liner notes, *Cajun*, Vol. 1. *Abbeville Breakdown 1929–1939*, CK 46220 (New York: Roots N' Blues, 1990), 9.

70. Simon Schexnider, son of Rayne-Bo Rambler drummer and Cajun country-and-western and swamp pop musician Warren Storm [born Warren Schexnider] hit the national charts with "Prisoner's Song" in 1958. Shane K. Bernard, *Swamp Pop: Cajun and Creole Rhythm and Blues* (Jackson: University Press of Mississippi, 1996), 140–141.

71. H. F. Mooney, "Popular Music since the 1920s: The Significance of Shifting Taste," *American Quarterly*, Vol. 20, No. 1 (Spring, 1968), pp. 67–85.

72. As quoted in Sandmel, *Luderin Darbone's Hackberry Ramblers*, 11.

Chapter 7

1. Hadley Castille was born into a musical French-speaking family. Castille's encounter with "Jole Blon" was so profound that he spent his professional musical career studying Cajun swing and Harry Choates' fiddle style. Interview with Cajun fiddler/bandleader Hadley Castille, conducted by Marce Lacouture, broadcast on KRVS 88.7 FM, Lafayette and Lake Charles, LA (NPR affiliate) on September 2, 2003, 1–2 P.M. on the emission *Lagniappe*.

2. "Jole Blon" is also sometimes rendered "Jolie Blond" and "Jolie Blonde." Norris Melancon, interviewed by Ryan A. Brasseaux on June 16, 2002, in Pointe Noire, Acadia Parish, LA. Before the tremendous success of "Jole Blon," Happy Fats and the Rayne-Bo Ramblers enjoyed a regional hit about a popular but notoriously violent Cajun dance hall, "Au Bal Chez 'Tit Maurice" (At the Dance at the Little Maurice Dance Hall). Local bands "covered" the Rayne-Bo Ramblers' tune until public demand for "Jole Blon," as Norris Melancon remembers, "knocked [Au Bal Chez 'Tit Maurice] out."

3. Burke begins the audio book version by stating: "This novel, *Jolie Blon's Bounce*, deals, in part, with the origin of a song that has been an obsession with me for many years. Some people say the song 'Jole Blon' is the 'Cajun national anthem.' But, it's a haunting story. It deals with an irrevocable sense of loss, a loss perhaps of the Cajun culture, but personal loss in the author of the song, a fellow named Harry Choates" James Lee Burke and Mark Hammer, *Jolie Blon's Bounce*, unabridged audio book (New York: Simon and Schuster Audio, 2002).

4. The first independent Louisiana record companies, such as Khoury, Goldband, Fais-Do-Do, and later Swallow, Jin, Lanor, and La Louisiane, were able to sustain their businesses because of the tremendous commercial success of other pioneering independent labels like Gold Star.

Choates' recording expanded the market for Louisiana music by engaging a new potential audience. Other regional forms—such as swamp pop, swamp blues, and Louisiana soul—flourished on these indy labels and achieved nationwide commercial success during the late 1950s and 1960s. See John Broven, *South to Louisiana: The Music of the Cajun Bayous* (Gretna, LA: Pelican Publishing, 1983); and Shane K. Bernard, "J. D. Miller and Floyd Soileau: A Comparison of Two Small Town Recordmen of Acadiana," *Louisiana Folklife Journal* 15 (December 1991); "Twisting at the Fais Do Do: Swamp Pop in South Louisiana," www.louisianavoices.org/creole_art_swamp_pop.html, accessed January 28, 2003 [the article first appeared in the Louisiana Folklife Festival booklet 1995], and *Swamp Pop: Cajun and Creole Rhythm and Blues* (Jackson: University Press of Mississippi, 1996).

5. Kevin Fontenot, interviewed by author, July 4, 2004.

6. By the late 1940s, a diverse class of future all-star musicians—including Dean Martin, B. B. King, and Lightnin' Hopkins—all embarked on their musical careers. Lewis M. Killian, "The Adjustment of Southern White Migrants to Northern Urban Norms," *Social Forces* 32, No. 1 (October 1953): 66–70; Bill C. Malone, *Country Music U.S.A.: A Fifty-Year History* (Austin: University of Texas Press, 1968), 184–208; James N. Gregory, *The Southern Diaspora: How the Great Migrations of Black and White Southerners Transformed America* (Chapel Hill, NC: UNC Press, 2005), and *American Exodus: The Dust Bowl Migration and Okie Culture in California* (New York: Oxford University Press, 1989); James R. Grossman, *Land of Hope: Chicago, Black Southerners, and the Great Migration* (Chicago: University Of Chicago Press, 1991).

7. For an excellent synopsis of the role independent record labels played in shaping American music, see the introduction to Rick Kennedy and Randy McNutt, *Little Labels—Big Sound: Small Record Companies and the Rise of American Music* (Bloomington: Indiana University Press, 1999). About Southern music's impact on the national music scene, see Bill C. Malone and David Stricklin, *Southern Music, American Music* (Lexington: University Press of Kentucky, 1979).

8. Wade Fruge, quoted in Ann Allen Savoy, *Cajun Music: A Reflection of a People*, Vol. 1 (Eunice, LA: Bluebird Press, 1984), 46.

9. According to Amédé Breaux's stepson Shine Mouton, CleomaCleoma composed the lyric and taught the words to Amédé. Savoy, *Cajun Music*, 80; Barry Jean Ancelet, *Cajun Music: Its Origins and Development* (Lafayette: Center for Louisiana Studies, University of Southwestern Louisiana, 1989), 25.

10. Irène Thérèse Whitfield, *Louisiana French Folk Songs* (New York: Dover Publications, 1969), 81.

11. New Iberia *Weekly Iberian* (April 13, 1939); Laurent Carrière, interviewed by Carl A. Brasseaux, Church Point, LA, July 3, 1978.

12. Broven, *South to Louisiana*, 29–30. Kevin Coffey, liner notes, *Jole Blon: 23 Artists One Theme* [disk], BCD 16618 AJ (Hambergen, Germany: Bear Family Records, 2003), 2–10; Ben Sandmel, liner notes, *Luderin Darbone's Hackberry Ramblers, Early Recordings: 1935–1950* (El Cerrito, CA: Arhoolie Records, 2003), 9–10; John Whitehead and Ben Sandmel producers *"Make 'Em Dance": The Hackberry Ramblers' Story* [VHS film] (St. Paul, MN: Fretless Pictures, 2003).

13. Edwin Duhon, interviewed by Ryan A. Brasseaux and Carl A. Brasseaux, May 16, 2003.

14. Napoleonville *Assumption Pioneer* (January 22, 1921). The first automobiles in Cajun Country shocked many of its residents. The Lafayette *Advertiser* reported on March 8, 1905, three years before the emergence of the Model T Ford:

> Something of a sensation was created Saturday by the appearance of an automobile on the streets. As it passed everybody stopped to look, and the question was asked everywhere, "Have you seen the automobile?" While in front of the Gordon Hotel it attracted quite a crowd who examined it with a great deal of interest. Contrary to expectation, while passing over the streets where numbers of horses were hitched, it caused very few to become frightened: but somebody's saddle horse in Buchanan street didn't like the "funny thing" a bit, and waved his tail vigorously as he took his sudden and emphatic farewell. The automobile belongs to Mr. Herbert Billeaud, of Broussard, and the trip from Broussard here was in the nature of a trial trip. He was accompanied by Messrs. Andre and Paul Billeaud and Palmer Abbott of New Orleans, who is agent for the company from whom the automobile was purchased. The automobile is called the Oldsmobile.

LafayetteBy the 1920s, couples frequently used automobiles for "petting parties," or sexual escapades in parked vehicles; Ville Platte *Weekly Gazette* (August 30, 1924).

15. As quoted in Andrew Brown, *Harry Choates: Devil in the Bayou, the Gold Star Recordings* [disk], BCD 16355 (Hambergen, Germany: Bear Family Records, 2002), 31. Choates began his recording career with LeRoy "Happy Fats" LeBlanc, who toyed with the idea of recording "Jole Blon" with his group the Rayne-Bo Ramblers during the 1940s. With the onset of World War II, however, Choates had taken flight and Steve Sholes of RCA records told a disappointed LeBlanc that the session had to be canceled because of wartime shellac rationing. In the meantime, Happy Fats told Louisiana music expert John Broven, Choates "went off to Houston, he left the band and got in with a fellow by the name of Bill Quinn. And he made 'Jole Blon' and it was a million seller." As quoted in Broven, *South to Louisiana*, 31.

16. Andrew Brown writes that the series was divided into several numerically catalogued categories. These matrix numbers determined the genre: 100 (gospel), 400 (Spanish), 500 (square dances), 600 (blues), 700 (vanity or custom releases), and 1,300 (hillbilly and Cajun). Brown, *Harry Choates*, 35.

17. Jimmie Foster's Swingsters included James "Jimmie" Foster (bass), Harry Choates (fiddle/guitar/vocal), Esmond A. "Eddie" Pursley (acoustic lead guitar), B. D. Williams (rhythm guitar), Charles "Charley" Slagle (tenor banjo), and William D. "Bill" Slay (piano). B. D. Williams also played with Leo Soileau. Andrew Brown and Kevin Coffey write that the session took place on or around March 31, 1946. In Brown's interview with Charley Slagle, the musician recalled that the recording took "an entire Sunday afternoon." As March 31, 1946 fell on a Sunday, I have used the specific date. Brown, *Harry Choates*, 36–37; Coffey, *Jole Blon*, 2–12.

18. Bill Quinn could not read or write the French language. He consistently misspelled French song titles on his Gold Star releases. "La Value Zulbaugh" is apparently "La Valse Zulbaugh," or the Zulbaugh waltz. Broven, *South to Louisiana*, 29–31.

19. Broven, *South to Louisiana*, 29–31.

20. Randy Whatley, "Cajun Fiddler Harry Choates," Baton Rouge *Sunday Advocate Magazine* (February 4, 1983), 32; Brown, *Harry Choates*, 13.

21. Ancelet, *Cajun Music*, 29; Carl A. Brasseaux, "Grand Texas: The Cajun Migration to Texas," in *The French in Texas*, ed. François Lagarde (Austin: University of Texas Press, 2003), 273–286.

22. Brown, *Harry Choates*. Brown maintains that legends circulating about Choates selling the rights of the song to Quinn for $50 (or $100) and a bottle of booze are unfounded. Quinn also claimed authorship of "Basile Waltz." The Melody Boys also featured from time to time steel guitarist Julius "Papa Cairo" Lamperez and pianist Johnnie Ruth Smyrl, Joe Manuel's wife.

23. Brown, *Harry Choates*, 35.

24. Ibid., 32–44. By 1942, *Billboard* magazine began to devote some attention to country and hillbilly music. After years of neglect, *Billboard* established a succession of columns for country records, beginning with "Western and Race" (January 1942), "American Folk Records" (February 1942), and "Most Played Juke Box Folk Records" (1944). Malone, *Country Music U.S.A.*, 191.

25. Brown, *Harry Choates*, 32–44; Coffey, *Jole Blon*, 2–12.

26. See Michael H. Hunt, *Ideology and U.S. Foreign Policy* (New Haven, CT: Yale University Press, 1987), 46–91; Matthew Frey Jacobson, *Whiteness of a Different Color: European Immigrants and the Alchemy of Race* (Cambridge, MA: Harvard University Press, 1998).

27. A. R. Waud, "Acadians of Louisiana," *Harper's Weekly* (October 20, 1866), 670. Some of the most common Anglo criticisms of the Cajun community focused on perceived breeches of Victorian culture, including lack of education, based on their inability to speak English, and lack of ambition or interest in the acquisition of material goods, the driving force behind capitalism and the Protestant work ethic. This cultural complex became increasing more complicated within the Southern context. As Reilly demonstrates, Cajun self-sufficient yeoman farmers posed a serious threat "to the order and tranquility of the slave regime" and sharecropping system—two odious economic systems that thrived on dependent labors. For other examples of negative descriptions of the Cajun community, see W. H. Sparks, *The Memories of Fifty Years: Containing Brief Biographical Notices of Distinguished Americans, and Anecdotes of Remarkable Men; Interspersed with Scenes and Incidents Occurring during a Long Life of Observation Chiefly spent in the Southwest* (Philadelphia: E. Claxton and Company, 1882); Timothy F. Reilly, "Early Acadiana through Anglo-American Eyes, Part I," *Attakapas Gazette* 7, No. 3 (Spring 1977): 3–20, and "Early Acadiana through Anglo-American Eyes, Part II," *Attakapas Gazette* 7, No. 3 (Fall 1977): 159–176.

28. A regular performer in south Louisiana and east Texas, Mullican recorded his first interpretation of the Cajun waltz before Modern transformed Choates' version into a hit. Coffey, *Jole Blon*.

29. Ibid., 9.

30. As quoted in Brown, *Harry Choates*, 42; Coffey, *Jole Blon*, 21.

31. See Brasseaux, "Grand Texas"; Shana Walton, "Louisiana's Coonasses: Choosing Race and Class over Ethnicity," in *Signifying Serpents and Mardi Gras Runners: Representing Identity in Selected Souths*, ed. R. Celeste Ray and Luke E. Lassiter (Athens: University of Georgia Press, 2003), 38–50. Louisiana Hayride expert Tracey E. W. Laird explains that

Mullican invented nonsensical lines in place of French lyrics because he could not speak French. Tracey E. W. Laird, "Country Chameleons: Cajuns on the Louisiana Hayride" in *Accordions, Fiddles, Two Step and Swing: A Cajun Music Reader*, ed. Ryan A. Brasseaux and Kevin S. Fontenot (Lafayette: Center for Louisiana Studies, University of Louisiana at Lafayette, 2006), 273–278.

32. Kevin Fontenot, personal communication [e-mail], June 4, 2004.

33. Coffey, *Jole Blon*.

34. King 761, recorded on December 30 or 31, 1947. The musicians from the session include Aubrey "Moon" Mullican (piano/vocal), "Mutt" Collins (electric guitar), James Dee "Deacon" Anderson (steel guitar), Ray "Shang" Kennedy (bass), Johnny Holland (drums), James Guy "Cotton" Thompson (fiddle), and Clyde Brewer (fiddle/French vocal). Coffey, *Jole Blon*, 68.

35. Ibid.

36. Mexican Joe is a character inspired by the Jim Reeves tune by the same name. Like Latinos, Irish, Italians, and Poles, Cajuns did not fully enjoy white privilege. See Jacobson, *Whiteness of a Different Color*.

37. Coffey, *Jole Blon*.

38. This English spoken-word dialogue comes at the end of the composition, following the tunes' French lyrics. J. D. Miller released "New Jolie Blond" as Fais-Do-Do 1005.

39. Brunswick Records released Waylon Jennings' debut solo effort as Brunswick 9-55130. The session featured Waylon Jennings (vocal), Buddy Holly (guitar), George Atwood (bass), Bo Clarke (drums), King Curtis (saxophone), and the Roses (vocal chorus). Holly and Jennings apparently learned the tune from a reissued version of "Jole Blon," because Buddy Dee, who reissued Choates' original Gold Star recording on his own D label, is given credit by Brunswick as the author of the tune. Holly intended to record "Jole Blon" himself, but offered it to Jennings as a way to jumpstart his friend's solo career. Ellis Amburn, *Buddy Holly: A Biography* (New York: St. Martin's Press, 1995), 185–186; Coffey, *Jole Blon*, 72.

40. Amburn, *Buddy Holly*, 186.

41. For a discussion of sex and the blues, see Carol Batker, "'Love Me Like I Like to Be': The Sexual Politics of Hurston's Their Eyes Were Watching God, the Classic Blues, and the Black Women's Club Movement," *African American Review* 32 (Summer 1998): 199–213; Angela Y. Davis, *Blues Legacies and Black Feminism: Gertrude "Ma" Rainey, Bessie Smith, and Billie Holiday* (New York: Vintage, 1999).

42. Hazel V. Carby, "Policing the Black Woman's Body in an Urban Context," *Critical Inquiry* 18 (Summer 1992): 745–746.

43. For a discussion of mass cultural texts as legitimating the status quo, see Frederic Jameson, "Reification and Utopia in Mass Culture," *Social Text* 1 (Winter 1979): 141; Margaret T. McFadden, "'America's Boy Friend Who Can't Get a Date': Gender, Race, and the Cultural Work of the Jack Benny Program, 1932–1946," *Journal of American History* 80 (June 1993): 113–134.

44. Peggy Pascoe, "Miscegenation Law, Court Cases, and Ideologies of 'Race' in Twentieth-Century America," *Journal of American History* 83 (June 1996): 44–69. Miscegenation in Louisiana has long been common practice. For discussions of miscegenation and the Bayou State, with an emphasis on the Creole of color community, see Alecia P. Long, *The Great Southern Babylon: Sex, Race, and Respectability in New Orleans, 1865–1920* (Baton Rouge: Louisiana State University Press, 2004). A Creole of color

from Louisiana became the focal point of the collapse of California's miscegenation law: Dara Orenstein, "Void for Vagueness: Mexicans and the Collapse of Miscegenation Law in California," *Pacific Historical Review* 74 (2005): 367–407.

45. As quoted in Gerda Lemer, ed., *Black Women in White America: A Documentary History* (New York: Random House, 1972), 170.

46. Joanne Meyerowitz, "Beyond the Feminine Mystique: A Reassessment of Postwar Mass Culture, 1946–1958," *Journal of American History* 79 (March 1993): 1457.

47. See Winthrop D. Jordan, *White over Black: American Attitudes toward the Negro, 1550–1812* (New York: Norton, 1977); Evelyn Brooks Higginbotham, "African-American Women's History and the Metalanguage of Race," *Signs* 17, No. 2 (Winter 1992): 251–274; Eric Lott, "Love and Theft: The Racial Unconscious of Blackface Minstrelsy," *Representations* No. 39 (Summer 1992): 25–27; William J. Mahar, *Behind the Burnt Cork Mask: Early Blackface Minstrelsy and Antebellum American Popular Culture* (Urbana: University of Illinois Press, 1999), 268–328. William J. Mahar writes that the American perception of ethnic sexuality persisted although white mores in the United States evolved, particularly in major urban centers where new sexual freedoms provided by the disintegration of traditional courtship rituals and the establishment of prostitution districts. The characterization of nonwhites as morally loose, however, was already prevalent in American popular culture before the Civil War. As the antebellum minstrel musical repertoire demonstrates, the Anglo-Protestant view of sexual exploits among the "colored" was perhaps less of a social commentary than an erotic fantasy for white men. Black-faced whites performed tunes with implicit references to sexual intimacy between African-American characters for young white male audiences. Compositions such as "The yellow rose of Texas beats the belles of Tennessee," "Black Eyed Susianna" (1846), "Belle of Baltimore" (1848), and "I'll Throw Myself Away" (1852) portray African Americans as lustful, sexually active beings who "dance by de light of de moon," a characterization that played to white fantasies about sexual freedom. Indeed, sexuality underscored even the most chaste minstrel extravaganzas during the nineteenth century. Some songs focused on exotic "yaller gals," a reference to unmarried working women of mixed race. Like the romantic image of Creole women living in the Crescent City, yaller gals—and later Jole Blon—became caricatures onto which white males attached their fantasies about women and sexuality.

48. Ignorant, violent, and sexually disturbed poor whites became an established stereotype expressed in American popular culture throughout the twentieth century. Rural working-class folks felt the brunt of these slanderous interpretations in American pop cultural manifestations such as *Ma and Pa Kettle*, the *Beverly Hillbillies*, *Petticoat Junction*, *Gilligan's Island*, *Dukes of Hazard*, and the motion picture *Deliverance*. Erskine Caldwell's 1932 novel *Tobacco Road* is one of the most famous examples of sexual deviance portrayed in American popular culture. The novel's characters engage in voyeurism, masturbation, underage sex, and infidelity. Caldwell ultimately underscores the lack of moral awareness among rural poor whites in America, particularly in the South. Americanized Cajun pop culture expression such as Walter Coquille's Mayor of Bayou Pom Pom, and later Justin Wilson's comedy routines were rooted in the promotion of stereotypical caricatures of working-class Cajuns. "Li'l Abner,"

http://www.lil-abner.com/, accessed June 11, 2004; Erskine Caldwell, *Tobacco Road* (New York: Grosset and Dunlap, 1932). For an extensive exploration of working-class white southern stereotypes, see Anthony Harkins, *Hillbilly: A Cultural History of an American Icon* (New York: Oxford University Press, 2004).

49. Coffey, *Jole Blon*.

50. Ibid.

51. Ibid.

52. Ibid.

53. William A. Owens, *Texas Folk Songs* (Austin: Texas Folklore Society, 1950), 21.

54. Del-Fi 4110, issued in 1958, featured "Donna"/"La Bamba."

55. Rod Bernard and Clifton Chenier, *Boogie in Black and White* [disk], LP 9014 (Ville Platte, LA: Jin Records, 1976).

56. Rounder Select reissued the Flatlander's debut album in 1990 as *More a Legend Than a Band*. Their Moon Mullican–inspired rendition of "Jole Blon" features Steve Wesson on musical saw. Colin Escott, *The Flatlanders: More a Legend Than a Band* [CD], CD SS 34 (Cambridge, MA: Rounder Records, 1990). Bruce Springsteen and the E Street Band can be heard rehearsing "Jole Blon" on the bootleg series Lost Masters Volume XIII: Restless Days (The Telegraph Hill Rehearsals Volume III) recorded on January 11, 1980, in Holmdel, New Jersey. In 1981 alone, the E Street Band performed the tune in concert 17 times in the United States and Great Britain. Springsteen and Gary U.S. Bonds collaborated on the Bonds's release "Jole Blon" in 1981. The song was released as the 7" single EMI 8089 "Jole Blon"/"Just Like a Child." http://home.theboots.net/the boots/newlook/lost masters/lmv13.html, http://www.xs4all.nl/~maroen/ engels/lyrics/joleblon.htm, and http://www.springsteenlyrics.com/lyrics/j/ joleblon.php, accessed November 7, 2008. http://nebraska_99.tripod.com/ guestappear.html, accessed on 6/30/04.

57. Brown, *Harry Choates*, 45–46.

Chapter 8

1. Ray Abshire, interviewed by Ryan A. Brasseaux and Erik Charpentier for the "Cajun and Creole Hour" radio program. The emission aired on October 9, 2003, on KRVS 88.7 FM, Lafayette, Lake Charles, LA, from Noon to 1:00 P.M. Ray Abshire, personal communication [e-mail], April 21, 2006, 7:12 P.M.

2. Ibid.

3. Susan J. Douglas, *Listening In: Radio and the American Imagination* (New York: Times Books, 1999), 355.

4. Hadley Cantril and Gordon Allport, *The Psychology of Radio* (New York: Harper and Brothers, 1935), 3.

5. For a discussion of *Amos 'n' Andy*'s popularity, see Melvin Patrick Ely, *The Adventures of Amos and Andy: A Social History of an American Phenomenon* (New York: Free Press, 1991). Jimmie Rodgers pretended to visit the Carter Family rural home in Virginia while actually recording in Louisville, Kentucky, and humorist Walter Coquille in character as the "Mayor" addressed his constituency on New Orleans radio station WWL from the fictitious "Bayou Pom Pom." See Nolan Porterfield, *Jimmie Rodgers: The Life and Times of America's Blue Yodeler* (Urbana: University of Illinois Press, 1992), 290–294.

6. My deployment of the term "imagined communities" is derived from Benedict Anderson, *Imagined Communities: Reflections on the Origin and Spread of Nationalism* (London: Verso, 1991).

7. Bill C. Malone, *Country Music U.S.A.* (Austin: University of Texas Press, 2002) 153–155; for a further discussion of the rise of honky-tonk, see Jeremy J. Lange, *Smile When You Call Me Hillbilly: Country Music's Struggle for Respectability, 1939–1954* (Athens: University of Georgia Press, 2004).

8. Cantril and Allport, *The Psychology of Radio*, 19.

9. Ibid., vii. Josh Kun describes an individual's ability to create a new mental world through a sonic stimulus as "audiotopia." See Kun, *Audiotopia: Music, Race, and America* (Berkeley: University of California Press, 2005).

10. Cantril and Allport, *The Psychology of Radio*, 7.

11. Ibid.

12. Ibid., 259.

13. I am grateful to Kevin S. Fontenot for generously sharing his materials and insights regarding musical traditions in Louisiana, Texas, and Oklahoma. Kevin S. Fontenot, *No Label on the Juke Box: Musical Interaction in the Honky Tonk Corridor 1900–1950* (Lafayette, LA: Louisiana Historical Association, 2004).

14. Ibid.

15. Gerald Lynch, *Roughnecks, Drillers, and Tool Pushers: Thirty-Three Years in the Oil Fields* (Austin: University of Texas Press, 1987), 46.

16. Dean R. Louder and Michael Leblanc, "The Cajuns of East Texas," in *French America: Mobility, Identity, and Minority Experience Across the Continent*, ed. Dean R. Louder and Eric Waddell (Baton Rouge: Louisiana State University Press, 1993), 311.

17. Andrew Brown, liner notes, *Harry Choates: Devil in the Bayou, the Gold Star Recordings* [CD], BCD 16355 (Hambergen, Germany: Bear Family Records, 2002), 7.

18. Carl A. Brasseaux, "Grand Texas: The Cajun Migration to Texas," in *The French in Texas*, ed. François Lagarde (Austin: University of Texas Press, 2003), 276.

19. Louder and Leblanc, "The Cajuns of East Texas," 311.

20. Brown, *Harry Choates*, 24.

21. Andrew Brown identified the nightclubs in East Orange. the Grove Dinner Club, the Night Owl Club, Buster's Night Club, Club Irving, Felix DeMary's Dinner Club, the Flamingo, Stompin' Henry's, and the Blue Lake Club. Brown, *Harry Choates*, 24.

22. As quoted in ibid., 27.

23. Ibid.

24. Ibid.

25. Ibid., 18.

26. Kevin Coffey, liner notes, *Cliff Bruner and His Texas Wanderers* [disk], Bear Family BCD 15932 EI (Hambergen, Germany: Bear Family Records, 1997) 29.

27. Ibid., 31.

28. Brown, *Harry Choates*, 62. For a discussion of folk justice, see Barry Jean Ancelet, Jay D. Edwards, and Glen Pitre, *Cajun Country* (Jackson: University Press of Mississippi, 1991), 101–114.

29. Brown, *Harry Choates*, 4; for more on Choates' life and career see Kevin Coffey, "Harry Choates," *The Journal of the American Academy for the Preservation of Old-Time Country Music* 31 (February 1996): 13–15.

30. For more on Cajuns and WWII, see Shane K. Bernard, *The Cajuns: Americanization of a People* (Jackson: University Press of Mississippi, 2003); and Jason P. Theriot, "Cajuns in World War II, 1940–1947," M.A. Thesis, University of Houston, 2006. See also Jason P. Theriot's important three-volume oral history series, *To Honor Our Veterans: An Oral History of World War II Veterans from the Bayou Country* (Lafayette, LA: Jason P. Theriot, 2002–2005), which he organized by the war's different theaters.

31. Elizabeth Mae Roberts, "French Radio Broadcasting in Louisiana," M.A. thesis, Louisiana State University, 1959, 89.

32. Mrs. Wildis Bertrand to Hackberry Ramblers, June 24, 1944, Goldband Records, #20245, Southern Folklife Collection, Manuscripts Department, Wilson Library, University of North Carolina at Chapel Hill. The Southern Folklife Collection at UNC-Chapel Hill houses a substantial collection of fan mail written to the Hackberry Ramblers.

33. Rena Belle Dyke to Hackberry Ramblers, June 26, 1944; Emile Broussard to Hackberry Ramblers, n.d., Goldband Records, #20245, Southern Folklife Collection, Manuscripts Department, Wilson Library, University of North Carolina at Chapel Hill.

34. Historian Mae Ngai maintains that ethnic groups in the United States experienced a momentary feeling of being fully American during armed military conflict, a scenario she dubs "wartime citizen." *Impossible Subjects: Illegal Aliens and the Making of Modern America* (Princeton, NJ: Princeton University Press, 2005), 175–201. For more on the ethnic experience during WWII and their cultural ramifications back home, see Bernard, *The Cajuns*; and George J. Sánchez, *Becoming Mexican American: Ethnicity, Culture, and Identity in Chicano Los Angeles, 1900–1945* (New York: Oxford University Press, 1995).

35. John Broven, "The Bayou Buckaroo: LeRoy 'Happy Fats' LeBlanc," in *Accordions, Fiddles, Two Step and Swing: A Cajun Music Reader*, ed. Ryan A. Brasseaux and Kevin S. Fontenot (Lafayette: Center for Louisiana Studies, University of Louisiana at Lafayette, 2006). See also Irène Whitfield Holmes, "Acadian Music and Dances," *Attakapas Gazette* 11 (Winter 1976): 181–185.

36. Cantril and Allport, *The Psychology of Radio*, 259.

37. Ibid., 14.

38. Roberts, "French Radio Broadcasting in Louisiana," 92, 132–134, 136, 139–140.

39. Ibid., 142–143.

40. Fontenot, "No Label on the Juke Box."

41. See Stephen R. Tucker, "Louisiana Folk and Regional Popular Music Traditions on Records and the Radio: An Historical Overview with Suggestions for Future Research," in *Louisiana Folklife: A Guide to the State*, ed. Nicholas R. Spitzer (Baton Rouge: Louisiana Folklife Program, 1985), 230.

42. Rick Kennedy and Randy McNutt, *Little Labels—Big Sound: Small Record Companies and the Rise of American Music* (Bloomington: Indiana University Press, 1999), xvi.

43. As quoted in John Broven, *South to Louisiana: The Music of the Cajun Bayous* (Gretna, LA: Pelican Publishing, 1983), 37.

44. Miller's impact on American music has not been fully realized. Kitty Wells's smash "It Wasn't God Who Made Honky Tonk Angels" highlighted Miller's songwriting abilities, while African-American blues artists such as Slim Harpo made the maverick's production skills famous, particularly when the Rolling Stones covered two Harpo selections on *England's*

Newest Hit Makers and *Exile on Main Street*, respectively. Several other local labels emerged as a direct result of his trailblazing efforts, including Swallow records in Ville Platte.

45. As quoted in Bruce Bastin, liner notes, *Fais Do Do Breakdown: Happy, Doc and The Boys and Lee Sonnier*, Vol. 1, SLY 609 (Bexhill-On-Sea, East Sussex, England: Flyright, 1986), n.p.

46. Shane Bernard and Julia Guirouard, "'Colinda': Mysterious Origins of a Cajun Folksong," *Journal of Folklore Research* 29 (1992): 37–52. The record's B-side, "Colinda," became a fixture in the corridor's repertoire, in large part through the efforts of country musician and politician Jimmie Davis. Both LeBlanc and Guidry campaigned with Davis during his gubernatorial rallies in south Louisiana. The relationship forged between the Anglo governor and his Cajun backup band extended beyond the campaign trail. In 1949, Doc Guidry provided the fiddle track and helped translate the French lyrics for the Louisiana governor's English country rendition of "Colinda." Davis's cross-pollinated country version was a clear manifestation of the pervasive interaction across ethnic boundaries that connected the musical cultures flourishing within the region. More such cultural experiments developed as other independent labels attempted to exploit the region's rich musical landscape.

47. Bastin, *Fais Do Do Breakdown*.

48. Lee Sonnier and the Acadian All-Stars continued to record for Miller before Iry LeJeune waxed his seminal "Love Bridge Waltz." Written in the same vein as Ernest Tubb's "Soldier's Last Letter," Sonnier's "War Widow Waltz" became Miller's first hit for the newly founded Feature label. The recording's female vocalist, Laura Broussard, a relative and bandmate of Aldus Broussard who performed with Lawrence Walker at the 1936 National Folk Festival, sang to Cajun widows who experienced the myriad of conflicting emotions wrought by the war: patriotism, love separation, longing, and despair. "My husband left/He left to fight for our country," Broussard sang in a melancholy tone, "It hurts me to hear my little children/always crying for their father." Miller recalled, "I've seen women crying listening to it on a jukebox." Translation of Broussard's vocal by author: "Mon marie il est parti/il est parti pour se battre pour notre pays"; "Ça ça m' fait du mal des attend mes tits enfants, tout le tempo après plurer demander pour leur papa." Bastin, *Fais Do Do Breakdown*.

49. "Evangeline Special" was the flipside to the record. The complete Oklahoma Tornado lineup included Ben Oldag (bass), Dudley Champagne (drums), Bennie Hess (guitar), Virgel Bozeman (guitar), and Floyd Leblanc (fiddle and guitar). Ron Yule, *Iry Lejeune: Wailin' the Blues Cajun Style* (Natchitoches, LA: Northwestern State University Press, 2007), 20–22.

50. Barry Jean Ancelet first proposed this idea in "Cajun Music: An Effective Barometer of Louisiana French Society" in *Louisiana Tapestry: The Ethnic Weave of St. Landry Parish*, ed. Vaughan B. Baker and Jean T. Kreamer (Lafayette: Center for Louisiana Studies, University of Southwestern Louisiana, 1982), 44; and then more explicitly in Ancelet and Elmore Morgan, *The Makers of Cajun Music* (Austin: University of Texas Press, 1984), 27.

51. Ann Allen Savoy, liner notes, *Iry LeJeune: The Definitive Collection* [CD], CDCHD 428 (London: Ace Records, 2004).

52. Iry LeJeune performed as a fiddler on only one side during his short recording career, an issue entitled "Duralde Waltz." The accordionist was

certainly accustomed to the prevalent fiddle sound featured at local *bals de maison* and dance halls. See Yule, *Iry Lejeune*, 14–15.

53. Ibid., 14.

54. According to Ron Yule,

Floyd Leblanc was an accomplished fiddle player when he met Iry Lejeune. He had begun playing the fiddle in his youth along with his two brothers on homemade fiddles and guitars. They played at country dances demonstrating their great musicianship from their hometown of Mermentau to Lake Charles, where they eventually moved. During World War II, while serving in the military, Floyd met Virgel Bozeman, in San Antonio, and soon they formed the Oklahoma Tornadoes, a country style group. They continued to play after the war traveling throughout the south to play at clubs. (Ibid., 20–22)

55. As quoted in ibid., 20. LeJeune toured with the Tornadoes in Houston around the time of the "Love Bridge Waltz" session. He later accompanied the group on an extended tour that took the group through Oklahoma, New Orleans, and eventually Nashville. LeJeune felt that his music was not appropriately showcased and returned to Cajun Country by bus.

56. Ron Brown, personal communication [e-mail], July 26, 2005.

57. O. T. stood for Oklahoma Tornado.

58. John Broven, liner notes, *Cajun Honky Tonk: The Khoury Recordings—the Early 1950s* [CD], CD 427 (El Cerrito, CA: Arhoolie, 1995), 3.

59. Cantril and Allport, *The Psychology of Radio*, 260.

60. As quoted in Michael Simmons, "Doug Kershaw: The Real Deal in Cajun Fiddle," *Fiddler Magazine* 10 (Spring 2003): 4.

61. As quoted in Tracey E. W. Laird, "Country Chameleons: Cajuns on the Louisiana Hayride," in *Accordions, Fiddles, Two Step and Swing: A Cajun Music Reader*, ed. Ryan A. Brasseaux and Kevin S. Fontenot (Lafayette: Center for Louisiana Studies, University of Louisiana at Lafayette, 2006), 276.

62. *Louisiana Hayride* announcer Horace Logan announced over the auditorium's public address system that "the old lonesome Drifting Cowboy is coming home again." As quoted in Tracey E. W. Laird, *Louisiana Hayride: Radio and Roots Music Along the Red River* (New York: Oxford University Press, 2005), 97.

63. Ibid., 99.

64. Brown, *Harry Choates*, 65.

65. Barry Jean Ancelet and Elmore Morgan, *Cajun and Creole Music Makers* (Jackson: University Press of Mississippi, 1999), 49–53; Elijah Wald, John Junkerman, and Theo Pelletier, *River of Song: A Musical Journey down the Mississippi* (New York: St. Martin's Press, 1999), 266–280; Ann Allen Savoy, *Cajun Music: A Reflection of a People* (Eunice, LA: Bluebird Press, 1984); Broven, *South to Louisiana*, 235–237.

66. Chris Strachwitz, liner notes, *Chuck Guillory and the Rhythm Boys* [disk], LP 5039 (El Cerrito, CA: Arhoolie, 1988), n.p.

67. In 1949, the steel guitarist waxed the English-language "Big Texas #2," followed by the French remake of his original composition "Kooche Kooche," after forming his own group, Papa Cairo and His Boys. The personnel included Lamperez on vocal and steel, Don Lane on xylophone, Murphy Smith on fiddle, Herman Durbin on piano, Albert Roy on guitar, possibly Pete Duhon on bass, and Curly Mertz on percussion. Kevin Coffey, liner notes, *Swingbillies: Hillbilly and Western Swing on*

Modern/Colonial/Flair 1947–52 [disk] (London: Ace Records, 2004), 9; Broven, *South to Louisiana*, 34–35.

68. See Laird, *Louisiana Hayride*; Horace Logan and Bill Sloan, *Elvis, Hank, and Me: Making Musical History on the Louisiana Hayride* (New York: St. Martin's Press, 1998); Stephen R. Tucker, "'Louisiana Saturday Night': A History of Louisiana Country Music," Ph.D. dissertation, Tulane University, 1995.

69. Laird, "Country Chameleons," 273–278.

70. LeRoy "Happy Fats" LeBlanc, *What Has Made South Louisiana God's Special Country: Stories and Pictures of Traditional Cajun Music and Musicians, Radio and Television Stations, Our Language, Our Leaders, Our Customs and Culture, Our Festivals, and the Places of Business Who Have Made This Land "God's Special Country"* (Lafayette, LA: Acadiana Printing). The Rayne Public Library has the only extant copy I have ever seen—a photocopy tucked away in a vertical file.

71. Ibid.

72. Irène Whitfield Holmes maintains that Happy Fats LeBlanc "was a member of the 'Louisiana Hayride' from 1946 to 1950 and made two personal appearances at the 'Grand Ole Opry.'" "Acadian Music and Dances," 185.

73. As quoted in Broven, "The Bayou Buckaroo," 412–413.

74. "I love my Mommy and my Poppy, I love them oh so well
But the one I love better is my little Lulu Bell.

> [Chorus] She's a sweet little cajinne [Cajun], with a winkle in
>   her eye
> And it almost breaks my heart, when I gotta say goodbye.
> I can still see her standing, with a crawfish in each hand
> We gonna have a gumbo, cause she's looking for the pan
> I'm gonna catch a lot of catfish, and in the month of June
> I'm gonna marry Lulu, and have a Cajun honeymoon.
> She's my Lulu, my pretty Little Lulu/When I holler You-hoo,
>   I'm callin you hoo
> Oh my Lulu, my pretty Little Cajinne/You are the girl of my
>   dreams.
> We'll raise some pennon rouge [hot peppers], and file
>   gumbo too
> And maybe in a year or so, a tax reduction or two
> You'll plow and sweep and the house you'll keep, I'll grant
>   you every wish
> I'll sit on the banks of the muddy Bayou, and catch a few
>   catfish.

LeBlanc, *What Has Made South Louisiana God's Special Country.*

75. Hadacol was based out of Lafayette, LA, on the southwestern corner of the Honky-Tonk Corridor.

76. Colin Escott, *Hank Williams: The Biography* (Boston: Little, Brown, 1995), 117. See also Colin Escott, liner notes, *The Health and Happiness Shows*, P2 17862 (Los Angeles: Poly Gram Records, 1993).

77. Floyd Martin Clay, *Coozan Dudley LeBlanc: From Huey Long to Hadacol* (Gretna, LA: Pelican Publishing, 1973), 172; George Berry, interviewed by Ryan A. Brasseaux and Erik Charpentier, September 5, 2001.

78. Laird, *Louisiana Hayride*, 96.

79. John Broven, *South to Louisiana*, 35.

80. Cantril and Allport, *The Psychology of Radio*, 3.

81. Ibid., 19.

82. Ibid., 21.

83. Leo Soileau, interviewed by Ralph Rinzler October 20, 1965, RI1.024, Ralph Rinzler Collection, Archive of Cajun and Creole Folklore, University of Louisiana at Lafayette.

84. All three musicians became well acquainted in 1945, when Martin "Bull" Leger opened the Cajun Kitchen café on Broad Street in Lake Charles, LA. The Honky-Tonk Corridor hotspot served as a musical magnet, hosting jam sessions frequented by the likes of Lawrence Walker, Nathan Abshire, Iry LeJeune, and steel guitarist Atlas Fruge. LeJeune often "warmed up" before his KPLC radio spots and performances at local dance clubs. Yule, *Iry Lejeune*, 27.

85. Jeff Hannusch, "Masters of Louisiana Music: Nathan Abshire," *Off-Beat* 16, No. 10 (October 2003): 25.

86. For Williams's influence on D. L. Menard, see Ancelet and Morgan, *Cajun and Creole Music Makers*, 49–53; Wald and Junkerman, *River of Song*, 266–280; http://www.acadianmuseum.com/legends.php?viewID=108, accessed July 23, 2008; http://www.lsue.edu/acadgate/music/menard.htm, accessed July 23, 2008.

Epilogue

1. Jan Risher, "How to Celebrate a Grammy Win?" *Times of Acadiana* (February 13, 2008).

2. Herman Fuselier, "Live from the Grammys: Musicians Poised to Make History," *Lafayette Daily Advertiser* (February 10, 2008).

3. Herman Fuselier, "Live from the Grammys: Musicians poised to make history," *Lafayette Daily Advertiser*, February 10, 2008.

4. In the zydeco camp, Queen Ida (1982), Clifton Chenier (1983), and Rockin Sidney (1985) all won Grammys. BeauSoleil, featuring Michael Doucet, won in 1997 for *L'Amour ou la Folie*, thus becoming the only Cajun band to ever win a Grammy award. Other Cajun bands, including the Hackberry Ramblers, the Basin Brothers, and Steve Riley and the Mamou Playboys, have also enjoyed Grammy nominations. Scott McLennan, "Let's Get Cajun; Basin Brothers Keeping Tradition Alive," *Telegram and Gazette* (March 3, 1994); Bill Syken, "Folklore, Living, Breathing and Singing," *New York Times* (February 28, 1999); Ben Ratliff, "With a Twang and a Teardrop," *New York Times* (26 February 1998); Barry Jean Ancelet, "Cajun Music," *Journal of American Folklore* 107 (Spring 1994): 285–303; Charles J. Stivale, *Disenchanting Les Bons Temps: Identity and Authenticity in Cajun Music and Dance* (Durham, NC: Duke University Press, 2003), 41, 59.

5. As quoted in Steve Hochman, "Rock the Vote," *Independent* (February 6, 2008). 5.

6. Shaun Hearen, "Q & A: Ann Savoy," *Acadian* [St. Landry edition] (April 2006), 29.

7. "Louisiana's French-Speaking Culture, Once Derided, Now Is the Spice of Life," *USA Today* (February 26, 1999).

8. Minnie Kelley, "Acadian South Louisiana," *Journal of Geography* 33, No. 3 (March 1934): 83; Walter M. Kollomorgen and Robert W. Harrison, "French-Speaking Farmers of Southern Louisiana," *Economic Geography* 22 (July 1946): 155; Barry Jean Ancelet, "Rednecks, Roughnecks and the

Bosco Stomp: The Arrival of the Oil Industry in the Marais Bouleur," *Attakapas Gazette* 22 (Spring 1987): 29–34, and *Cajun Music: Its Origins and Development* (Lafayette: Center for Louisiana Studies, University of Southwestern Louisiana, 1989), 16–17; Ann Allen Savoy, *Cajun Music: A Reflection of a People* (Eunice, LA: Bluebird Press, 1984), xi; James H. Dorman, *The People Called Cajuns: An Introduction to an Ethnohistory* (Lafayette: Center for Louisiana Studies, University of Southwestern Louisiana, 1983), 25; Pierce F. Lewis, *New Orleans: The Making of an Urban Landscape* (Santa Fe, NM: Center for American Places, 2003), 13.

9. Harry Oster, "Acculturation in Cajun Folk Music," *McNeese Review* 10 (Winter 1958): 12.

10. Ibid., 13; *LSU Daily Reveille* (May 14, 1959); Baton Rouge *Morning Advocate* (June 7, 1959).

11. Elizabeth Brandon, "The Socio-cultural Traits of the French Folksong in Louisiana," *Revue de Louisiane/Louisiana Review* 1 (1972): 21.

12. Shane K. Bernard, *The Cajuns: Americanization of a People* (Jackson: University Press of Mississippi, 2003), xxi.

13. Ibid., 20–21.

14. Ibid., 148.

15. Richard A. Peterson, *Creating Country Music: Fabricating Authenticity* (Chicago: University of Chicago Press, 1997); Jane S. Becker, *Selling Tradition: Appalachia and the Construction of an American Folk, 1930–1940* (Chapel Hill, NC: UNC Press, 1998); Michael Ann Williams, *Staging Tradition: John Lair and Sarah Gertrude Knott* (Urbana: University of Illinois Press, 2006); Regina Bendix, *In Search of Authenticity: The Formation of Folklore Studies* (Madison: University of Wisconsin Press, 1997).

16. Richard Handler and Jocelyn Linnekin, "Tradition, Genuine or Superfluous," *Journal of American Folklore* 97, No. 385 (1984): 273.

17. Ibid., 273–274.

18. W. T. Stead, *The Americanisation of the World; or, The Trend of the Twentieth Century* (London: H. Marckley, 1902); see also Carol Aronovici, "Americanization: Its Meaning and Function," *American Journal of Sociology* 25, No. 6 (1920): 702.

19. Cajuns recontextualizing American popular culture is not an isolated incident. American historian Rob Kroes has observed the same behavioral pattern among Europeans exposed to American popular culture. Rob Kroes, "American Empire and Cultural Imperialism: A View from the Receiving End," in *Rethinking American History in a Global Age*, ed. Thomas Bender (Berkeley: University of California Press, 2002), 300.

20. For more on the broad reach of American culture see Charles Bright and Michael Geyer, "Where in the World Is America? The History of the United States in the Global Age," in *Rethinking American History in a Global Age*, ed. Thomas Bender (Berkeley: University of California Press, 2002), 67–69; for more on Cajuns engaging American culture, see Barry Jean Ancelet and Elmore Morgan, *The Makers of Cajun Music* (Austin: University of Texas Press, 1984); Barry Jean Ancelet, "Cajun Music," in *American Musical Traditions*, Vol. 4, *European American Music*, ed. Jeff Todd Titon and Bob Carlin (New York: Schirmer Reference, 2002), 31–39; Kip Lornell, *Introducing American Folk Music: Ethnic and Grassroot Traditions in the United States*, 2nd ed. (Boston: McGraw-Hill, 2002), 193.

21. As quoted in Hochman, "Rock the Vote"; for the complicated relationship between Creoles (black) and Cajuns (white), see Mark Mattern, "Stirring Up the Roux: Negotiating Cajun Identity and Relations with Black

Creoles," in *Acting in Concert: Music, Community, and Political Action* (New Brunswick, NJ: Rutgers University Press, 1998), 101–118, and "Let the Good Times Unroll: Music and Race Relations in Southwest Louisiana," *Black Music Research Journal* 17, No. 2 (Autumn 1997), 159–168; Carl A. Brasseaux, "Creoles: A Family Portrait in Black and White," in *French, Cajun, Creole, Houma: A Primer on Francophone Louisiana* (Baton Rouge: Louisiana State University Press, 2005), 85–116.

22. Hochman, "Rock the Vote."

23. Louise Meintjes, "Paul Simon's Graceland, South Africa, and the Mediation of Musical Meaning," *Ethnomusicology* 34 (Winter 1990): 37–73.

24. Herman Fuselier, "Grammy Victory Means It's Time to Get in the Game," *Lafayette Daily Advertiser* (February 15, 2008).

25. Hochman, "Rock the Vote."

26. Ibid.

27. Becker, *Selling Tradition*, 5.

28. Barry Jean Ancelet, "The Theory and Practice of Activist Folklore: From Fieldwork to Programming," in *Working the Field: Accounts from French Louisiana*, ed. Jacques Henry and Sara LeMenestrel (Westport, CT: Praeger, 2003), 81–100, and "The Center for Acadian and Creole Folklore: An Experiment in Guerrilla Academics," in *Sounds of the South*, ed. Daniel W. Patterson (Durham, NC: Duke University Press, 1991), 148–154; Barry Jean Ancelet and Philip Gould, *One Generation at a Time: Biography of a Cajun and Creole Festival* (Lafayette: Center for Louisiana Studies, University of Louisiana at Lafayette, 2007); Mark Mattern, "Cajun Music, Cultural Revival: Theorizing Political Action in Popular Music," *Popular Music and Society* 22 (Summer 1998): 31–49, and Mattern, *Acting in Concert*.

29. Mattern, *Acting in Concert*, 79.

30. Ancelet, "The Center for Acadian and Creole Folklore," 148–154; Ancelet and Gould, *One Generation at a Time*; Ancelet, "The Theory and Practice of Activist Folklore," 81–100; Barry Jean Ancelet, "L'oeuvre et l'ouvrage de Jean Arceneaux, poète Louisianais," *Études de lingusitique appliquée* 70 (April-June 1988): 13–19; Mathé Allain and Barry Jean Ancelet, "Feu de Savane: A Literary Renaissance in French Louisiana," *Southern Exposure* 9 (Summer 1981): 4–10; Mathé Allain, "Écrasez l'infâme : l'école en question chez les jeunes activists cadiens," *Études de lingusitique appliquée* 70 (Avril-Juin 1988): 7–12, and "Twentieth-Century Acadians," in *The Cajuns: Essays on Their History and Culture*, ed. Glen R. Conrad (Lafayette: Center for Louisiana Studies, University of Southwestern Louisiana, 1978), 141; David Barry, "A French Literary Renaissance in Louisiana: Cultural Reflections," *Journal of Popular Culture* 23 (Summer 1989): 47–64; Olivier Marteau, "Entretien 'carnavalesque' avec Jean Arceneaux et Barry Jean Ancelet," *Etudies Francophone, Dossier Thematique: Louisiane numero double* 21, Nos. 1 and 2 (printempts-automne) (Lafayette: University of Louisiana at Lafayette, 2006), 196–204; Barry Jean Ancelet, "Cajun Music: An Effective Barometer of Louisiana French Society," in *Louisiana Tapestry: The Ethnic Weave of St. Landry Parish*, ed. Vaughan B. Baker and Jean T. Kreamer (Lafayette: Center for Louisiana Studies, University of Southwestern Louisiana, 1982), 41–48.

31. W. Fitzhugh Brundage, "Le Reveil de la Louisiane: Memory and Acadian Identity, 1920–1960," in *Where These Memories Grow: History, Memory and Southern Identity*, ed. W. Fitzhugh Brundage (Chapel Hill, NC: UNC Press, 2000), 272.

32. At the Festivals Acadiens, the largest Cajun music festival in Cajun Country, *only* bands that sing primarily in French are invited to perform on the "main" stage. If a band emphasizes English during a performance, an unwritten rule demands that they are not welcome back until they make amends. Those popular bilingual Cajun bands that emphasize English lyrics, especially the Bluerunners, Horace Trahan and the New Osson Express, and Jamie Bergeron and the Kicking Cajuns, are conspicuously absent from festival schedules. The widely popular accordionist Wayne Toups, who began his career singing French songs, did not appear at the festival when he began to emphasize English-language compositions. Furthermore, regular performers that issue hit songs with English lyrics—such as the Richard LeBeufs' regional hit "Who Stole My Monkey" and selections from the Mamou Playboys' *Bayou Ruler* album—were not invited back the year after their records stimulated much local acclaim. To consult the year-by-year lineups of festival performers on the main stage of the Festivals Acadiens, bands scheduled by the activist collective "Rubber Boots Incorporated," see Ancelet and Gould, *One Generation at a Time*.

33. Dorman, *The People Called Cajuns*, 76.

34. See Ryan A. Brasseaux and Erik Charpentier, "Fabricating Authenticity: The Cajun Renaissance and Steve Riley and the Mamou Playboys," in *Accordions, Fiddles, Two Step and Swing: A Cajun Music Reader*, ed. Ryan A. Brasseaux and Kevin S. Fontenot (Lafayette: Center for Louisiana Studies, University of Louisiana at Lafayette, 2006), 487–495. Authenticity debates in Cajun music circles parallel those discussions that play out in country music. These issues, however, are complicated by the ethnic group's particular deployment of historical memory. Like authenticity, memory is a socially and culturally constructed phenomenon that interprets the past for contemporary concerns. See Peterson, *Creating Country Music*; Jolie Jensen, *Nashville Sound: Authenticity, Commercialization, and Country Music* (Nashville, TN: Country Music Foundation and Vanderbilt University Press, 1998); Richard M. Dorson, *Folklore and Fakelore: Essays toward a Discipline of Folk Studies* (Cambridge, MA: Harvard University Press, 1976); Bendix, *In Search of Authenticity*; W. Fitzhugh Brundage, "Introduction: No Deed But Memory" and "Le Reveil Acadien: Memory and Acadian Identity, 1920–1960," in *Where These Memories Grow: History, Memory and Southern Identity*, ed. W. Fitzhugh Brundage (Chapel Hill, NC: UNC Press, 2000), 1–28, 271–298.

35. Barry Ancelet, Jay D. Edwards, and Glen Pitre, *Cajun Country* (Jackson: University Press of Mississippi, 1991), 158 (emphasis original).

36. The linguistic and cultural activists affiliated with the preservationist group Action Cadienne maintain the notion that "it is impossible to conceive of a culture without being able to speak its language." Bernard, *The Cajuns*, 148. For discussions of Cajun ethnicity in the late twentieth century, see Jacques M. Henry and Carl L. Bankston, III, "Louisiana Cajun Ethnicity: Symbolic or Structural?" *Sociological Spectrum* 19 (1999): 223–248, *Blue Collar Bayou: Louisiana Cajuns in the New Economy of Ethnicity* (Westport, CT: Praeger, 2002), and "The Silence of the Gators: Cajun Ethnicity and Intergenerational Transmission of Louisiana French," *Journal of Multilingual and Multicultural Development* 19, No. 1 (1998): 1–23.

37. Mark Mattern, "Cajun Music, Cultural Revival," 43.

38. The oversimplification presented in previous musical studies stemmed, in part, from limited availability of resources before the music

industry initiated a campaign to reintroduce on compact disk the scattered remains of south Louisiana's Cajun musical past buried deep in the grooves of 78 rpm recordings. During the 1990s and the first years of the twenty-first century, important new resources, in the form of expansive discographies and scores of vintage Cajun material reissued on compact disk by domestic and European labels, suddenly brought into focus the full breadth of commercial Cajun music between 1928 and 1941. These materials radically affected and profoundly informed the vantage point from which this study materialized. The perspective offered in this volume presents an alternative view of the Cajuns and their music, a view that hopes to broaden the horizons and possibilities of future research by considering the development and evolution of the genre through a lens that simultaneously acknowledges its meaning within a local context and the music's connection to regional and national trends.

39. Steve Knopper, "2007: From Bad to Worse," *Rolling Stone* (February 7, 2008), 17.

40. Fuselier, "Local Fans Anticipate Grammy Winner."

41. The projected median household incomes for 2003 in these three parishes were as follows: Evangeline, $23,576; St. Landry, $25,520; Avoyelles, $25,402—compared with the U.S. average, $43,318. U.S. Census Bureau, http://quickfacts.census.gov/qfd/states/22/22039.html, accessed March 12, 2007; http://quickfacts.census.gov/qfd/states/22/22097.html, accessed November 6, 2008; http://quickfacts.census.gov/qfd/states/22/22009.html, accessed November 6, 2008.

42. Bankston and Henry, "The Silence of the Gators," 1–23.

43. Hochman, "Rock the Vote."

44. As quoted in Hochman, "Rock the Vote."

Bibliography

Oral History, Photographic, and Archival Collections

Archive of Cajun and Creole Folklore, Center for Cultural and Eco-Tourism, Edith Garland Dupré Library, University of Louisiana at Lafayette, Lafayette, LA: Barry Jean Ancelet Collection, Alan Lomax Collection, Ralph Rinzler Collection, Senior Service America Collection.

Archivo General de Indias, Papeles Procedentes de Cuba, Edith Garland Dupré Library, University of Louisiana at Lafayette, Lafayette, LA.

Cajun and Creole Music Collection, Edith Garland Dupré Library, University of Louisiana at Lafayette, Lafayette, LA.

Farm Security Administration, Office of War Information Photograph Collection, Prints and Photographs Division, Library of Congress, Washington, DC.

Federal Writers' Collection, Cammie G. Henry Research Center, Watson Memorial Library, Northwestern State University, Natchitoches, LA.

Freeland Archive, Acadia Parish Library, Crowley, LA.

George Washington Cable Collection, Manuscripts Division, Tulane University Library, New Orleans, LA.

Goldband Collection, Southern Folklife Collection, Wilson Library, University of North Carolina at Chapel Hill, Chapel Hill, NC.

Lauren Chester Post Papers, Special Collections, Hill Memorial Library, Louisiana State University, Baton Rouge, LA.

Louise V. Olivier Collection, Louisiana and Lower Mississippi Valley Collection, Hill Memorial Library, Louisiana State University, Baton Rouge, LA.

Sam Tarleton Papers, Archives and Special Collections, Frazar Memorial Library, McNeese State University, Lake Charles, LA.

Sarah Gertrude Knott Papers, Manuscripts and Archives, Kentucky Library and Museum, Western Kentucky Library, Bowling Green, KY.

Virgil Thomson Papers, Irving S. Gilmore Music Library, Yale University, New Haven, CT.

Newspapers

Abbeville (LA) *Meridional*, 1879–1922.
Abbeville (LA) *Progress*, 1923.

Baton Rouge *Morning Advocate*, 1959.
Baton Rouge *Sunday Advocate Magazine*, 1983.
Crowley (LA) *Acadian-Signal*, 1938.
Crowley (LA) *Daily Signal*, 1955–1963.
Crowley (LA) *Signal*, 1896–1927.
Every Saturday, 1871.
Frank Leslie's Illustrated Newspaper 1877.
Frank Leslie's Popular Monthly, Vol. 12, 1876.
Jennings (LA) *Daily Times-Record*, 1910.
Lafayette (LA) *Advertiser*, 1896–1931.
Lafayette (LA) *Daily Advertiser*, 2008.
Lafayette (LA) *Gazette*, 1894.
LSU Daily Reveille, 1959.
Morgan City (LA) *Attakapas Register*, 1877.
Napoleonville (LA) *Assumption Pioneer*, 1930.
New Iberia (LA) *Enterprise*, 1904–1924.
New Iberia (LA) *Weekly Iberian*, 1938–1939.
New Orleans *Bee*, 1862.
New Orleans *Times Picayune*, 1975.
New York Times, 1989, 1998–1999
Opelousas (LA) *Clarion*, 1900–1905.
Opelousas (LA) *Clarion-News*, 1916–1932.
Opelousas (LA) *Clarion-Progress*, 1924–1925.
Opelousas (LA) *Courier*, 1856–1906.
Opelousas (LA) *News*, 1928.
Opelousas (LA) *St. Landry Clarion*, 1911–1913.
Port Arthur (LA) *News*, 1926.
Rayne (LA) *Signal*, 1886.
Shreveport Times, 1925.
St. Martinville (LA) *Weekly Messenger*, 1912.
Worcester (LA) *Telegram and Gazette*, 1994.
Times of Acadiana, 2008.
Thibodaux (LA) *Lafourche Comet*, 1919–1939.
Thibodaux (LA) *Sentinel*, 1869–1875.
USA Today, 1999.
Ville Platte (LA) *Gazette*, 1974.
Ville Platte (LA) *Weekly Gazette*, 1921–1925.
West Baton Rouge *Sugar Planter*, 1860.

Secondary Sources

Abshire, Ray. *Cajun and Creole Hour* [audio recording in author's possession]. Lafayette, LA: KRVS 88.7 FM, 2003.
Adams, David Wallace. *Education for Extinction: American Indians and the Boarding School Experience 1875–1928*. Lawrence: University of Kansas Press, 1995.
Adams, Rachel. *Sideshow U.S.A.: Freaks and the American Cultural Imagination*. Chicago: University of Chicago Press, 2001.
Allain, Mathé. "Écrasez l'infâme: l'école en question chez les jeunes activists cadiens." *Études de lingusitique appliquée* 70 (April–June 1988): 7–12.
———. "Twentieth-Century Acadians." *The Cajuns: Essays on Their History and Culture*. ed. Glen R. Conrad. Lafayette: Center for Louisiana Studies, University of Southwestern Louisiana, 1978.

Allain, Mathé, and Barry Jean Ancelet. "Feu de Savane: A Literary Renaissance in French Louisiana." *Southern Exposure* 9 (Summer 1981): 4–10.

Allan, Johnnie. *Memories: A Pictoral History of South Louisiana Music*, Vols. 1 and 2, *1920s–1990s*. Lafayette, LA: JADFEL Publishing, 1995.

Amburn, Ellis. *Buddy Holly: A Biography*. New York: St. Martin's Press, 1995.

American Folklife Center. *Ethnic Recordings in America: A Neglected Heritage*. Studies in American Folklife No. 1. Washington, DC: American Folklife Center, Library of Congress, 1982.

"The American Folklife Center." Library of Congress, http://www.loc.gov/folklife/, accessed 2007.

Ancelet, Barry Jean. *Cajun and Creole Folktales: The French Oral Tradition of South Louisiana*. Jackson: University Press of Mississippi, 1994.

———. *Cajun and Creole Music: The Classic Louisiana Recordings, 1934/1937* [disk]. Cambridge, MA: Rounder Records, 1999.

———. "Cajun Music." *American Musical Traditions*. Vol. 4. *European American Music*, ed. Jeff Todd Titon and Bob Carlin. New York: Schirmer Reference, 2002, 31–39.

———. "Cajun Music." *Journal of American Folklore* 107, No. 424 (Spring 1994): 285–303.

———. "Cajun Music: An Effective Barometer of Louisiana French Society," in *Louisiana Tapestry: The Ethnic Weave of St. Landry Parish*, ed. Vaughan B. Baker and Jean T. Kreamer. Lafayette: Center for Louisiana Studies, University of Southwestern Louisiana, 1982, 41–48.

———. *Cajun Music: Its Origins and Development*. Lafayette. Center for Louisiana Studies, University of Southwestern Louisiana, 1989.

———. "The Center for Acadian and Creole Folklore: An Experiment in Guerrilla Academics" *Sounds of the South*, ed. Daniel W. Patterson. Durham, NC: Duke University Press, 1991, 148–154.

———. "Dewey Balfa: Cajun Music Ambassador." *Louisiana Life* (September–October 1981), 78–85.

———. "L'oeuvre et l'ouvrage de Jean Arceneaux, poète Louisianais." *Études de lingusitique appliquée* 70 (April-June 1988): 13–19.

———. "*Ote Voir Ta Sacrée Soutane*: Anti-clerical Humor in Louisiana French Oral Tradition." *Louisiana Folklore Miscellany* 7 (1985): 26–33.

———. "Negotiating the Mainstream: The Creoles and Cajuns in Louisiana." *French Review* 80, No. 6 (May 2007): 1235–1255.

———. "Rednecks, Roughnecks and the Bosco Stomp: The Arrival of the Oil Industry in the Marais Bouleur." *Attakapas Gazette* 22 (Spring 1987): 29–34.

———. "The Theory and Practice of Activist Folklore: From Fieldwork to Programming." *Working the Field: Accounts from French Louisiana*, ed. Jacques Henry and Sara LeMenestrel. Westport, CT: Praeger, 2003, 81–100.

———. "Zydeco/Zarico: Beans, Blues and Beyond." *Black Music Research Journal* 8 (1988): 33–49.

Ancelet, Barry Jean, Jay Dearborn Edwards, and Glen Pitre. *Cajun Country*. Folklife in the South Series. Jackson: University Press of Mississippi, 1991.

Ancelet, Barry Jean, and Philip Gould. *One Generation at a Time: Biography of a Cajun and Creole Festival*. Lafayette: Center for Louisiana Studies, University of Louisiana at Lafayette, 2007.

Ancelet, Barry Jean, and Elmore Morgan. *Cajun and Creole Music Makers*. Jackson: University Press of Mississippi, 1999.

———. *The Makers of Cajun Music*. Austin: University of Texas Press, 1984.

Anderson, Benedict. *Imagined Communities: Reflections on the Origin and Spread of Nationalism*. London: Verso, 1991.

Aronovici, Carol. "Americanization: Its Meaning and Function." *American Journal of Sociology* 25, No. 6 (1920): 695–730.

Atkins, John. "The Carter Family," in *Stars of Country Music: Uncle Dave Macon to Johnny Rodriguez*. ed. Bill C. Malone and Judith McCulloh. Urbana: University of Illinois Press, 1975.

Avrich, Paul. *The Haymarket Tragedy*. Princeton, NJ: Princeton University Press, 1984.

Ayer, Edward L. *The Promise of the New South: Life after Reconstruction*. New York: Oxford University Press, 2007.

Bailey, Anne J. "Invisible Southerners: Ethnicity in the Civil War." Macon: University of Georgia Press, 2006.

Baker, Vaughan B. "The Acadians in Antebellum Louisiana: A Study of Acculturation." *The Cajuns: Essays on Their History and Culture*, ed. Glenn R. Conrad. Lafayette: Center for Louisiana Studies, University of Southwestern Louisiana, 1978, 115–128.

Ballard, Cordelle Kemper. "Steamboats on the Bayou." *Attakapas Gazette* 19 (1984): 8–10.

Bankston, Carl L., III, and Jacques M. Henry. "The Silence of the Gators: Cajun Ethnicity and Intergenerational Transmission of Louisiana French." *Journal of Multilingual and Multicultural Development* 19, No. 1 (1998): 1–23.

Barde, Alexandre. *The Vigilante Committees of the Attakapas*, ed. David Edmonds and Dennis Gibson, trans. Henrietta Guilbeau Rogers. Lafayette, LA: Acadiana Press, 1981.

Barkley, Roy R. *The Handbook of Texas Music*. Austin: Texas State Historical Association and Center for Studies in Texas History at the University of Texas at Austin, 2003.

Barry, David. "A French Literary Renaissance in Louisiana: Cultural Reflections." *Journal of Popular Culture* 23 (Summer 1989): 47–64.

Bastin, Bruce. *Fais Do Do Breakdown: Happy, Doc and The Boys and Lee Sonnier*. Vol. 1, SLY 609 [liner notes] (Flyright, 1986), n.p.

———. *Red River Blues: Blues Tradition in the Southeast*. Urbana: University of Illinois Press, 1986.

Batker, Carol. "'Love Me Like I Like to Be': The Sexual Politics of Hurston's Their Eyes Were Watching God, the Classic Blues, and the Black Women's Club Movement." *African American Review* 32 (Summer 1998): 199–213.

Baudier, Roger. *The Catholic Church in Louisiana*. New Orleans: A. W. Hyatt Stationery Mfg. Co., 1939.

Becker, Jane S. *Selling Tradition: Appalachia and the Construction of an American Folk, 1930–1940*. Chapel Hill, NC: UNC Press, 1998.

Bender, Thomas, ed. *Rethinking American History in a Global Age*. Berkeley: University of California Press, 2002.

Bendix, Regina, *In Search of Authenticity: The Formation of Folklore Studies*. Madison: University of Wisconsin Press, 1997.

Bernard, Rod, and Clifton Chenier. *Boogie in Black and White*. Ville Platte, LA: Jin Records, 1976.

Bernard, Shane K. *The Cajuns: Americanization of a People*. Jackson: University Press of Mississippi, 2003.

———. "J. D. Miller and Floyd Soileau: A Comparison of Two Small Town Recordmen of Acadiana." *Louisiana Folklife* 15 (December 1991): 12–20.

———. *Swamp Pop: Cajun and Creole Rhythm and Blues*. American Made Music Series. Jackson: University Press of Mississippi, 1996.

Bernard, Shane K., and Julia Girouard. "'Colinda': Mysterious Origins of a Cajun Folksong." *Journal of Folklore Research* 29 (1992): 37–52.

Berry, George. Interview with the author. September 5, 2001.

Bienvenu, Marcelle, Carl A. Brasseaux, and Ryan A. Brasseaux. *Stir the Pot: The History of Cajun Cuisine*. New York: Hippocrene Books, 2005.

Blanchet, Catherine. "Acadian Instrumental Music." *Louisiana Folklore Miscellany* 3, No. 1 (April 1970): 70–75.

Blank, Les, and Chris Strachwitz. *J'ai Été au Bal (I Went to the Dance Last Night): The Cajun and Zydeco Music of Louisiana* [film]. Fort Worth, TX: Brazos Films, 1989.

Blumer, Martin. *The Chicago School of Sociology: Institutionalization, Diversity, and the Rise of Sociological Research*. Chicago: University of Chicago, 1986.

Bogan, Jr., Patrick Henry. "East Texas Serenaders," in *The Handbook of Texas Music*, ed. Roy R. Barkley. Austin: Texas State Historical Association for Studies in Texas History at the University of Texas at Austin, 2003, 89–90.

Bond, Bradley G., ed. *French Colonial Louisiana and the Atlantic World*. Baton Rouge: Louisiana State University Press, 2005.

Boulard, Garry. *Louis Prima*. Urbana: University of Illinois Press, 2002.

Brandon, Elizabeth. "The Socio-cultural Traits of the French Folksong in Louisiana." *Revue de Louisiana/Louisiana Review* 1 (1972): 19–52.

Brantly, John Edward. *History of Oil Well Drilling*. Houston, TX: Gulf Publishing Company, 1971.

Brasseaux, Carl A. *Acadian to Cajun: Transformation of a People, 1803–1877*. Jackson: University Press of Mississippi, 1992.

———. "Acadian Education: From Cultural Isolation to Mainstream America." *The Cajuns: Essays on Their History and Culture*, ed. Glenn R. Conrad. Lafayette: Center for Louisiana Studies, University of Southwestern Louisiana, 1978, 212–224.

———, trans and ed. *A Comparative View of French Louisiana, 1699 and 1762: The Journals of Pierre Le Moyne D'iberville and Jean-Jacques-Blaise D'abbadie*. Lafayette: Center for Louisiana Studies, University of Southwestern Louisiana, 1979.

———"Creoles: A Family Portrait in Black and White," in *French, Cajun, Creole, Houma: A Primer on Francophone Louisiana*. Baton Rouge: Louisiana State University Press, 2005, 85–116.

———. *The Founding of New Acadia: The Beginnings of Acadian Life in Louisiana, 1765–1803*. Baton Rouge: Louisiana State University Press, 1987.

———. *French, Cajun, Creole, Houma: A Primer on Francophone Louisiana*. Baton Rouge: Louisiana State University, 2005.

———. "Grand Texas: The Cajun Migration to Texas." *The French in Texas*, ed. François Lagarde. Austin: University of Texas Press, 2003: 273–286.

———. *Scattered to the Wind: Dispersal and Wanderings of the Acadians, 1755–1809*. Lafayette: Center for Louisiana Studies, University of Southwestern Louisiana, 1991.

————. *In Search of Evangeline: Birth and Evolution of the Evangeline Myth*. Thibodaux, LA: Blue Heron Press, 1988.

Brasseaux, Carl A., and Keith P. Fontenot. *Steamboats on Louisiana's Bayous: A History and Directory*. Baton Rouge: Louisiana State University Press, 2004.

Brasseaux, Carl A., Claude F. Oubre, and Keith P. Fontenot. *Creoles of Color in the Bayou Country*. Jackson: University Press of Mississippi, 1996.

Brasseaux, Ryan A. "Early Twentieth-Century Reminiscences of Eve Lavergne Castille." *Louisiana History* 66, No. 1 (Winter 2005): 65–88.

Brasseaux, Ryan A., and Kevin S. Fontenot, eds. *Accordions, Fiddles, Two Step and Swing: A Cajun Music Reader*. Lafayette: Center for Louisiana Studies, University of Louisiana at Lafayette, 2006.

Bright, Charles and Michael Geyer. "Where in the World Is America? The History of the United States in the Global Age," in *Rethinking American History in a Global Age*. ed. Thomas Bender. Berkeley: University of California Press, 2002.

Broven, John. "The Bayou Buckaroo: LeRoy 'Happy Fats' LeBlanc," in *Accordions, Fiddles, Two Step and Swing: A Cajun Music Reader*. ed. Ryan A. Brasseaux and Kevin S. Fontenot. Lafayette: Center for Louisiana Studies, University of Louisiana at Lafayette, 2006.

————. *Cajun Honky Tonk: The Khoury Recordings—the Early 1950s* [disk]. El Cerrito, CA: Arhoolie, 1995.

————. *South to Louisiana: The Music of the Cajun Bayous*. Gretna, LA: Pelican Publishing, 1983.

Brown, Andrew. *Harry Choates: Devil in the Bayou, the Gold Star Recordings* [disk]. Hambergen, Germany: Bear Family Records, 2002.

Brown, Ron. *Blind Uncle Gaspard, Delma Lachney, John Bertrand: Early American Cajun Music* [liner notes, disk]. Newton, NJ: Yazoo, 1999.

————. "Playing in the Shadows: Early Cajun Recording Artists," in *Accordions, Fiddles, Two Step and Swing: A Cajun Music Reader*. ed. Ryan A. Brasseaux and Kevin S. Fontenot. Lafayette: Center for Louisiana Studies, University of Louisiana at Lafayette, 2006.

Broyles-Gonzales, Yolanda. *Lydia Mendoza's Life in Music/La Historia de Lydia Mendoza: Norteno Tejano Legacies*. New York: Oxford University Press, 2003.

Brundage, W. Fitzhugh, ed., "Introduction: No Deed but Memory," in *Where These Memories Grow: History, Memory and Southern Identity*. ed. W. Fitzhugh Brundage. Chapel Hill, NC: UNC Press, 2000, 1–28.

————. "Le Reveil Acadien: Memory and Acadian Identity, 1920–1960," in *Where These Memories Grow: History, Memory and Southern Identity*. ed. W. Fitzhugh Brundage. Chapel Hill, NC: UNC Press, 2000, 271–298.

————. *Where These Memories Grow: History, Memory and Southern Identity*. Chapel Hill, NC: UNC Press, 2000.

Bufwack, Mary A., and Robert K. Oermann, *Finding Her Voice: Women in Country Music, 1800–2000*. Nashville, TN: Vanderbilt University Press, 2003.

Butler, Judith, *Gender Trouble: Feminism and the Subversion of Identity*. New York: Routledge, 1990.

Cable, George Washington. "Creole Slave Dances: The Dance in Place Congo." *Century Magazine* 31 (November 1885–April 1886): 519–522.

Cajun and Creole Masters [disk]. New York: Music of the World, 1995.

Caldwell, Erskine. *Tobacco Road*. New York: Grosset and Dunlap, 1932.

Cantril, Hadley, and Gordon Allport. *The Psychology of Radio*. New York: Harper and Brothers, 1935.

Carby, Hazel V. "Policing the Black Woman's Body in an Urban Context." *Critical Inquiry* 18 (Summer 1992): 738–755.

Carlson, Robert A. *The Americanization Syndrome: A Quest for Conformity*. London: Croom Helm, 1987.*Catalog of the Southwestern Louisiana Industrial Institute, Lafayette, LA., Containing List of Officers, Teachers, and Students, 1902–1903*. New Orleans: L. Grahm Co., 1902.

Castille, Hadley. *Lagniappe*. Audio recording. Lafayette, LA: KRVS 88.7 FM, 2003.

Chiasson, Anselme et al. "Le Folklore Acadien," in *L'Acadie des Maritimes*. ed. Jean Daigle. Moncton, New Brunswick: Chaire d'études acadiennes, Université de Moncton, 1993.

Clay, Floyd Martin. *Coozan Dudley Leblanc: From Huey Long to Hadacol*. Gretna, LA: Pelican Publishing, 1973.

Clayton, Lawrence, and Joe W. Specht, eds. *The Roots of Texas Music*. College Station, TX: Texas A&M University Press, 2003.

Coffey, Kevin. *Cliff Bruner and His Texas Wanderers* [disk]. Hambergen, Germany: Bear Family Records, 1997.

———. "Harry Choates." *The Journal of the American Academy for the Preservation of Old-Time Country Music* 31 (February 1996): 13–15.

———. *Jole Blon: 23 Artists One Theme* [disk]. Hambergen, Germany: Bear Family Records, 2003.

———. *Swingbillies: Hillbilly and Western Swing on Modern/Colonial/Flair 1947–52* [disk]. London: Ace Records, 2004.

Cohen, Lizabeth, *A Consumers' Republic: The Politics of Mass Consumption in Postwar America*. New York: Alfred A. Knopf, 2003.

———. *Making a New Deal: Industrial Workers in Chicago, 1919–1939*. Cambridge: Cambridge University Press, 1990.

Cohen, Norman. "Early Pioneers," in *Stars of Country Music: Uncle Dave Macon to Johnny Rodriguez*, ed. Bill C. Malone and Judith McCulloh. Urbana: University of Illinois Press, 1975.

———. "The Skillet Lickers: A Study of a Hillbilly String Band and Its Repertoire." *Journal of American Folklore* 78, No. 309 (July-September 1965): 229–244.

Cohen, Norm and Paul F. Wells. "Recorded Ethic Music: A Guide to Resources," in *Ethnic Recordings in America: A Neglected Heritage*. Washington, DC: American Folklife Center, Library of Congress, 1982.

Cohn, Lawrence. *Cajun*. Vol. 1. *Abbeville Breakdown 1929–1939* [disk]. New York: Roots N' Blues, 1990.

Comeaux, Malcolm L. "The Cajun Accordion." *Revue de Louisiane/Louisiana Review* 7, No. 2 (Winter 1978): 117–128.

———. "The Cajun Dance Hall." *Material Culture* 20 (2000): 37–56.

———. "Introduction and Use of Accordions in Cajun Music." *Louisiana Folklore Miscellany* 7 (1999): 27–41.

Conrad, Glenn R., ed. *The Cajuns: Essays on Their History and Culture*. Lafayette: Center for Louisiana Studies, University of Southwestern Louisiana, 1978.

———. *New Iberia: Essays on the Town and Its People*. Lafayette: Center for Louisiana Studies, University of Southwestern Louisiana, 1979.

"D. L. Menard." Contemporary Cajun, Creole, and Zydeco Musicians, http://www.lsue.edu/Acadgate/Music/Menard.Htm. 2008.

Conaway, James. "On Avery Island, Tabasco Sauce Is the Spice of Life." *Smithsonian* (May 1984), 72–82.

———. "Salt and Pepper Flavor This Island." *Southern Living* (March 1989), 34–35.

Cooper, Miriam, and Bonnie Herndon. *Dark Lady of the Silents: My Life in Early Hollywood*. Indianapolis, IN: Bobbs-Merrill, 1973.

Corrales, Barbara Smith. "Prurience, Prostitution, and Progressive Improvements: The Crowley Connection, 1909–1918." *Louisiana History* 45, No. 10 (Winter 2004): 37–70.

Cowley, John H. "Moonshine and Mosquitoes: The Story of Dewey Segura," in *Accordions, Fiddles, Two Step and Swing: A Cajun Music Reader*. ed. Ryan A. Brasseaux and Kevin S. Fontenot. Lafayette: Center for Louisiana Studies, University of Louisiana at Lafayette, 2006, 379–382.

Daigle, Brenda. "Acadian Fiddler Dennis McGee and Acadian Dances." *Attakapas Gazette* 7, No. 3 (1972): 124–143.

Daigle, Jean, ed. *L'acadie Des Maritimes*. Moncton, New Brunswick: Chaire d'études acadiennes, Université de Moncton, 1993.

Daigle, Pierre V. *Tears, Love, and Laughter: The Story of the Cajuns and Their Music*. 4th ed. Ville Platte, LA: Swallow Publications, 1987.

Daniels, R. L. "The Acadians of Louisiana." *Scribner's Monthly* 19 (1879–1880), 383–392.

Darbone, Luderin. "A Brief History of the Hackberry Ramblers," in *Accordions, Fiddles, Two Step and Swing: A Cajun Music Reader*. ed. Ryan A. Brasseaux and Kevin S. Fontenot. Lafayette: Center for Louisiana Studies, University of Louisiana at Lafayette, 2006.

Darby, William. *A Geographical Description of the State of Louisiana Presenting a View of the Soil, Climate, Animal, Vegetable and Mineral Productions: Illustrative of Its Natural Physiognomy, Its Geographical Configuration, and Relative Situation: With an Account of the Character and Manners of the Inhabitants: Being an Accompaniment to the Map of Louisiana*. Philadelphia: John Melish, 1816.

Darnell, Regna. *Invisible Genealogies: A History of Americanist Anthropology*. Lincoln: University of Nebraska Press, 2001.

Davis, Angela Y. *Blues Legacies and Black Feminism: Gertrude "Ma" Rainey, Bessie Smith, and Billie Holiday*. New York: Vintage, 1999.

de la Houssaye, Sidonie. *Pouponne and Balthazar*, trans. J. John Perret. Lafayette: Center for Louisiana Studies, University of Southwestern Louisiana, 1983.

de Laussat, Pierre Clément. *Memoirs of My Life to My Son during the Years 1803 and after, Which I Spent in Public Service in Louisiana as Commissioner of the French Government for the Retrocession to France of That Colony and for Its Transfer to the United States*. Baton Rouge: Louisiana State University Press, 1978.

Debien, Gabrielle. "The Acadians in St. Domingue," in *The Cajuns: Essays on Their History and Culture*. ed. Glen R. Conrad. Lafayette: Center for Louisiana Studies, 1979.

Del Sesto, Steven L. "Cajun Music and Zydeco: Notes on the Music of Southern Louisiana." *Louisiana Folklore Miscelany* 4 (1976–1980): 88–101.

Denning, Michael. *The Cultural Front: The Laboring of American Culture in the Twentieth Century*. London: Verso, 1997.

Divine Secrets of the Ya-Ya Sisterhood [CD], Columbia Records, 2002.

DeWitt, Mark F. "In the Cajun Idiom: Mutual Influences of Dance Music Style and Diatonic Accordion Technique." *Musical Performance* 3, Parts 2–4 (2001): 185–214.

————. "The Diatonic Button Accordion in Ethnic Context: Idiom and Style in Cajun Dance Music." *Popular Music and Society* 26, No. 3 (2003): 305–330.

Ditch, Jay K., ed., and George F. Reinecke, trans. "Early Louisiana French Life and Folklore from the Anonymous Breaux Manuscript." *Louisiana Folklore Miscellany* 2, No. 3 (May 1966): 1–58.

Dole, Gérard. *Louisiana Creole Music* [disk]. Washington, DC: Folkways Records, 1978.

Dorman, James H. "A Late Nineteenth Century View of Acadiana: Charles Dudley Warner's 'The Acadian Land.'" *Attakapas Gazette* 7 (1972): 157–169.

————. *The People Called Cajuns: An Introduction to an Ethnohistory*. Lafayette: Center for Louisiana Studies, University of Southwestern Louisiana, 1983.

Dorson, Richard M. *Folklore and Fakelore: Essays toward a Discipline of Folk Studies*. Cambridge, MA: Harvard University Press, 1976.

Douglas, Susan J. *Listening In: Radio and the American Imagination*. New York: Times Books, 1999.

Dronet, Curney J. *A Century of Acadian Culture: The Development of a Cajun Community: Erath (1899–1999)*. Erath, LA: Acadian Heritage and Culture Foundation, 2000.

DuBois, Sylvie. "Verbal Morphology in Cajun Vernacular English: A Comparison with Other Varieties of Southern English." *Journal of English Language and Linguistics* 31, No. 1 (2003): 1–26.

DuBois, Sylvie, and Barbara Horvath. "From Accent to Marker in Cajun English: A Study of Dialect Formation in Progress." *English World Wide* 19, No. 2 (1998): 161–88.

————. "Let's Tink about Dat: Interdental Fricatives in Cajun English." *Language Variation and Change* 10, No. 3 (1998): 245–261.

————. "When the Music Changes, You Change Too: Gender and Language Change in Cajun English." *Language Variation and Change* 11 (1999): 287–313.

Duranti, Alessandro, ed. *Linguistic Anthropology: A Reader*. Blackwell Anthologies in Social and Cultural Anthropology. Malden, MA: Blackwell, 2001.

Eccles, W. J. *The Canadian Frontier 1534–1760*. Albuquerque: University of New Mexico Press, 1983.

Ely, Melvin Patrick. *The Adventures of Amos and Andy: A Social History of an American Phenomenon*. New York: Free Press, 1991.

Epstein, Dena J. Polacheck. *Sinful Tunes and Spirituals: Black Folk Music to the Civil War*. Urbana: University of Illinois Press, 1977.

Escott, Colin. *The Flatlanders: More a Legend Than a Band* [disk]. Cambridge, MA: Rounder Records, 1990.

————. *Hank Williams: The Biography*. Boston: Little, Brown, 1994.

————. *The Health and Happiness Shows* [disk]. Los Angeles: PolyGram Records, 1993.

Faragher, John Mack. *A Great and Noble Scheme: The Tragic Story of the Expulsion of the French Acadians from Their American Homeland*. New York: W. W. Norton, 2005.

Filene, Benjamin. *Romancing the Folk: Public Memory and American Roots Music*. Cultural Studies of the United States. Chapel Hill, NC: UNC Press, 2000.

Foley, Neil. *The White Scourge: Mexicans, Blacks, and Poor Whites in Texas Cotton Culture*. Berkeley: University of California Press, 1997.

Foner, Eric. *Reconstruction: America's Unfinished Revolution, 1863–1877*. New York: Harper Collins, 2002.

Fontenot, Kevin, S. and Ryan A. Brasseaux. "Cleoma Breaux Falcon (1906–1941): The Commercialization of Cajun Music," in *Louisiana Women: Their History, Their Lives*, ed. Janet Allured and Judith F. Gentry. Athens: University of Georgia Press, forthcoming.

Fontenot, Kevin S. "Country Music's Confederate Grandfather: Henry C. Gilliland," in *Country Music Annual 2001*. ed. Charles K. Wolfe and James E. Akenson, Lexington: University Press of Kentucky, 2001, 190–206.

———. *No Label on the Juke Box: Musical Interaction in the Honky Tonk Corridor 1900–1950*. Unpublished paper in the author's possession, 2004.

Fontenot, Kevin S. and Ryan A. Brasseaux. "King of the Dancehalls: Accordionist Lawrence Walker," in *Accordions, Fiddles, Two Step and Swing: A Cajun Music Reader*. ed. Ryan A. Brasseaux and Kevin S. Fontenot. Lafayette: Center for Louisiana Studies, University of Louisiana at Lafayette, 2006, 425–429.

Fontenot, Mary Alice, and Vincent Riehl. *The Cat and St. Landry*. Baton Rouge, LA: Claitor's, 1972.

Fortier, Alcée. *Louisiana Studies*. New Orleans, LA: F. F. Hansell and Bros., 1894.

Fowler, Gene and Bill Crawford. *Border Radio: Quacks, Yodelers, Pitchmen, Psychics, and Other Amazing Broadcasters of the American Airwaves*. Austin: University of Texas Press, 2002.

François, Raymond E. *Yé Yaille, Chère: Traditional Cajun Dance Music*. Lafayette, LA: Swallow Publications, 1990.

Franklin, Benjamin. *The Autobiography and Other Writings by Benjamin Franklin*. New York: Bantam, 1982.

Franks, Kenny Arthur, and Paul F. Lambert. *Early Louisiana and Arkansas Oil: A Photographic History, 1901–1946*. College Station: Texas A&M University Press, 1982.

Garcia, Matt. *A World of Its Own: Race, Labor, and Citrus in the Making of Greater Los Angeles, 1900–1970*. Chapel Hill, NC: UNC Press, 2001.

Gastoué, Amédée. *Le Cantique Populaire en France*. Lyon, France: Editions Musicales Janin, 1924.

Gaudet, Marcia G. *Tales from the Levee: The Folklore of St. John the Baptist Parish*. Louisiana Folklife Series. Lafayette: Center for Louisiana Studies, University of Southwestern Louisiana, 1984.

Gaudet, Marcia, and James C. McDonald, eds. *Mardi Gras, Gumbo and Zydeco: Readings in Louisiana Culture*. Jackson: University Press of Mississippi, 2003.

George-Warren, Holly. *Public Cowboy No. 1: The Life and Times of Gene Autry*. New York: Oxford University Press, 2007.

Gilmore, Glenda Elizabeth. *Defying Dixie: The Radical Roots of Civil Rights, 1919–1950*. New York: W. W. Norton, 2008.

Gilmore, H. W. "Social Isolation of the French Speaking People of Rural Louisiana." *Social Forces* 12, No. 1 (1933): 78–84.

Ginell, Cary. "The Development of Western Swing." *John Edwards Memorial Foundation Quarterly* 20, No. 74 (Fall/Winter 1984): 58–67.

Ginell, Cary, and Roy Lee Brown. *Milton Brown and the Founding of Western Swing*. Music in American Life. Urbana: University of Illinois Press, 1994.

Gladu, André. *La Reel Du Pendu* [film]. Montreal, Canada: National Film Board, 1972.

Glassie, Henry. *All Silver and No Brass: An Irish Christmas Mumming*. Philadephia: University of Pennsylvania Press, 1983.

Gleason, Philip. "American Identity and Americanization," in *Concepts of Ethnicity*,. Cambridge, MA: Belknap/Harvard University Press, 1982, 57–143.

Goodhew, David. "Working-Class Respectability: The Example of Western Areas of Hohannesburg, 1930–55." *Journal of African History* 41 (2000): 241–266.

Goodwyn, Lawrence. *The Populist Moment: A Short History of the Agrarian Revolt in America*. New York: Oxford University Press, 1978.

Graham, Philip. *Showboats: The History of an American Institution*. Austin: University of Texas Press, 1951.

Grand Ole Opry. Members, http://www.opry.com/MeetTheOpry/Members. Aspx?Id=92. Accessed 2007.

Green, Archie. "Hillbilly Music: Source and Symbol." *Journal of American Folklore* 78, No. 309 (July–September, 1965): 204–228.

Green, Douglas B. *Singing in the Saddle: The History of the Singing Cowboy*. Nashville, TN: Vanderbilt University Press and Country Music Foundation Press, 2002.

Greenberg, Kenneth. *Honor and Slavery: Lies, Duels, Noses, Masks, Dressing as a Woman, Gifts, Strangers, Humanitarianism, Death, Slave Rebellions, the Proslavery Argument, Baseball, Hunting, and Gambling in the Old South*. Princeton, NJ: Princeton University Press, 1997.

Gregory, James N. *American Exodus: The Dust Bowl Migration and Okie Culture in California*. New York: Oxford University Press, 1989.

———. *The Southern Diaspora: How the Great Migrations of Black and White Southerners Transformed America*. Chapel Hill, NC: UNC Press, 2005.

Griffith, Carolyn F. "Czech and Polish Music in Texas before World War II," in *The Roots of Texas Music*, ed. Lawrence Clayton and Joe W. Specht. College Station: Texas A&M University Press, 175–191.

Gronow, Pekka. "Ethnic Recordings: An Introduction," in *Ethnic Recordings in America: A Neglected Heritage*. Washington, DC: American Folklife Center, Library of Congress, 1982.

Grossman, James R. *Land of Hope: Chicago, Black Southerners, and the Great Migration*. Chicago: University Of Chicago Press, 1991.

Grundy, Pamela. "'We Always Tried to Be Good People': Respectability, Crazy Water Crystals, and Hillbilly Music on the Air, 1933–1935." *Journal of American History* 81, No. 4 (March 1995): 1591–1620.

Gushee, Lawrence. *Pioneers of Jazz: The Story of the Creole Band*. New York: Oxford University Press, 2005.

Gutiérrez, David G. *Walls and Mirrors: Mexican Americans, Mexican Immigrants, and the Politics of Ethnicity*. Berkeley: University of California Press, 1995.

Hair, William Ivy. *Bourbonism and Agrarian Protest: Louisiana Politics, 1877–1900*. Baton Rouge: Louisiana State University Press, 1969.

Hall, Gwendolyn Midlo. *Africans in Colonial Louisiana: The Development of Afro-Creole Culture in the Eighteenth Century*. Baton Rouge: Louisiana State University Press, 2005.

Handler, Richard, and Jocelyn Linnekin. "Tradition, Genuine or Superfluous." *Journal of American Folklore* 97, No. 385 (1984): 273–291.

Hannusch, Jeff. "Masters of Louisiana Music: Nathan Abshire." *OffBeat* 16, No. 10 (October 2003): 24–26.

Hansen, Harry, ed. *Louisiana: A Guide to the State*. New York: Hastings House, 1971.

Harkins, Anthony. *Hillbilly: A Cultural History of an American Icon*. New York: Oxford University Press, 2004.

Harrison, Pat. *Cajun: Early Recordings* [disk]. London: JSP Records, 2004.

Hearen, Shaun. "Q & A: Ann Savoy." *Acadian* [St. Landry edition] (April 2006): 28–29.

Hebert, Denis. "The Hebert Family and the Music of Acadiana." *Attakapas Gazette* 23, No. 3 (Fall 1988): 99–110.

Hebert, Donald J. *L'eglise Du Marais Bouleur, 1872 to 1991: History of the Church at Marais Bouleur, Mire, Louisiana*. Rayne, LA: Hebert Publications, 1991.

Henry, Jacques M., and Carl L. Bankston, III. *Blue Collar Bayou: Louisiana Cajuns in the New Economy of Ethnicity*. Westport, CT: Praeger, 2002.

———. "Louisiana Cajun Ethnicity: Symbolic or Structural?" *Sociological Spectrum* 19, No. 1 (1999): 223–248.

Higginbotham, Evelyn Brooks. "African-American Women's History and the Metalanguage of Race." *Signs* 17, No. 2 (Winter 1992): 251–274.

Hobsbawm, Eric, and Terrance Ranger, eds. *The Invention of Tradition*. Cambridge: Cambridge University Press, 1992.

Hochman, Steve. "Rock the Vote." *Independent* (February 6, 2008).

Holmes, Irène Whitfield. "Acadian Music and Dances." *Attakapas Gazette* 11 (Winter 1976): 181–185.

———. "In Memoriam: Lauren Chester Post." *Louisiana Folklore Miscellany* 4 (1976–1980): 7–8.

Hoover, Kathleen, and John Cage. *Virgil Thomson: His Life and Music*. New York: Thomas Yoseloff, 1959.

Huber, Leonard Victor. *Creole Collage: Reflections on the Colorful Customs of Latter-Day New Orleans Creoles*. Lafayette: Center for Louisiana Studies, University of Southwestern Louisiana, 1980.

Huber, Patrick J., and Kevin S. Fontenot. "A 'Cajan' Music Mystery: Dr. James F. Roach and the Commercial Recording of 'Guée Gué Solingaie.'" Unpublished paper in author's possession, n.d.

Humphrey, Mark. *Cajun Dance Party: Fais Do-Do* [disk]. New York: Columbia Legacy, 1994.

Hunt, Michael H. *Ideology and U.S. Foreign Policy*. New Haven, CT: Yale University Press, 1987.

Hurston, Zora Neal. *Mules and Men*. New York: Harper Perennial, 1990.

Hyde, Samuel C. *Pistols and Politics: The Dilemma of Democracy in Louisiana's Florida Parishes, 1810–1899*. Baton Rouge: Louisiana State University Press, 1996.

Israel, Fred L. ed. *1897 Sears Roebuck Catalogue*. New York: Chelsea House Publishers, 1968.

Jacobson, Matthew Frey. *Barbarian Virtues: The United States Encounters Foreign Peoples at Home and Abroad, 1876–1917*. New York: Hill and Wang, 2000.

———. *Whiteness of a Different Color: European Immigrants and the Alchemy of Race*. Cambridge, MA: Harvard University Press, 1998.

Jameson, Frederic. "Reification and Utopia in Mass Culture." *Social Text* 1 (Winter 1979): 130–148.

Jensen, Jolie. *Nashville Sound: Authenticity, Commercialization, and Country Music*. Nashville, TN: Country Music Foundation and Vanderbilt University Press, 1998.

Jordan, Winthrop D. *White over Black: American Attitudes toward the Negro, 1550–1812*. New York: Norton, 1977.

Keeler, Ralph, and A. R. Waud. "On the Mississippi." *Every Saturday* 2, No. 75 (June 3, 1871): 524–526.

Kelley, Minnie. "Acadian South Louisiana." *The Journal of Geography* 33, No. 3 (March 1934): 81–90.

Kelley, Robin D. G. "Notes on Deconstructing 'The Folk.'" *American Historical Review* 97, No. 5 (December 1992): 1400–1408.

———. *Hammer and Hoe: Alabama Communists during the Great Depression*. Chapel Hill, NC: UNC Press, 1990.

Kennedy, Rick, and Randy McNutt. *Little Labels—Big Sound: Small Record Companies and the Rise of American Music*. Bloomington: Indiana University Press, 1999.

Kenney, William Howland. *Recorded Music in American Life: The Phonograph and Popular Memory, 1890–1945*. New York: Oxford University Press, 1999.

Killian, Lewis M. "The Adjustment of Southern White Migrants to Northern Urban Norms." *Social Forces* 32, No. 1 (October 1953): 66–70.

Kingsbury, Paul, ed. *The Country Reader: Twenty-Five Years of the Journal of Country Music*. Nashville, TN: Country Music Foundation Press and Vanderbilt University Press, 1996.

Kirby, Jack Temple. *Rural Worlds Lost: The American South, 1920–1960*. Baton Rouge: Louisiana State University Press, 1987.

Knauft, Bruce M. *Genealogies for the Present in Cultural Anthropology*. New York: Routledge, 1996.

Knopper, Steve. "2007: From Bad to Worse." *Rolling Stone* (February 7, 2008): 15–18.

Kollomorgen, Walter M., and Robert W. Harrison. "French-Speaking Farmers of Southern Louisiana." *Economic Geography* 22, No. 3 (July 1946): 153–160.

Kroes, Rob. "American Empire and Cultural Imperialism: A View from the Receiving End," in *Rethinking American History in a Global Age*, ed. Thomas Bender. Berkeley: University of California Press, 2002.

Kun, Josh. *Audiotopia: Music, Race, and America*. Berkeley: University of California Press, 2005.

Laird, Tracey E. W. "Country Chameleons: Cajuns on the Louisiana Hayride" in *Accordions, Fiddles, Two Step and Swing: A Cajun Music Reader*. ed. Ryan A. Brasseaux and Kevin S. Fontenot. Lafayette: Center for Louisiana Studies, University of Louisiana at Lafayette, 2006, 273–278.

———. *Louisiana Hayride: Radio and Roots Music along the Red River*. New York: Oxford University Press, 2005.

Lange, Jeremy J. *Smile When You Call Me Hillbilly: Country Music's Struggle for Respectability, 1939–1954*. Athens: University of Georgia Press, 2004.

Larouche, Alain. "The Cajuns of Canal Yankee: Problems of Cultural Identity in Lafourche Parish," in *French America: Mobility, Identity, and Minority Experience across the Continent*. ed. Dean R. Louder and Eric Waddell. Baton Rouge: Louisiana State University Press, 1993.

Leary, James P. *Polkabilly: How the Goose Island Ramblers Redefined American Folk Music*. New York: Oxford University Press, 2006.

"Lebanese Tribute to Bruce Springsteen," http://www.Springsteenlyrics. com/Lyrics/J/Joleblon.php," accessed. 2008.

LeBlanc, LeRoy "Happy Fats." *What Has Made South Louisiana God's Special Country: Stories and Pictures of Traditional Cajun Music and Musicians, Radio and Television Stations, Our Language, Our Leaders, Our Customs and Culture, Our Festivals, and the Places of Business Who Have Made This Land 'God's Special Country.'* Lafayette, LA: Acadiana Printing.

Le Menestrel, Sara. "The Color of Music: Social Boundaries and Stereotypes in Southwest Louisiana French Music." *Southern Cultures* 13 (Fall 2007): 87–105.

Lemer, Gerda, ed. *Black Women in White America: A Documentary History*. New York: Random House, 1972.

Lewis, Pierce F. *New Orleans: The Making of an Urban Landscape*. Sante Fe, NM: Center for American Places, 2003.

"Li'l Abner." http://www.lil-abner.com, accessed 2004.

Lipsitz, George. *The Possessive Investment in Whiteness: How White People Profit from Identity Politics*. Philadelphia: Temple University Press, 1998.

"Living Legends." Acadian Museum, http://www.acadianmuseum.com/ legends.php. Accessed 2008.

Logan, Horace, and Bill Sloan. *Elvis, Hank, and Me: Making Musical History on the Louisiana Hayride*. New York: St. Martin's Press, 1998.

Lomawaima, K. Tsianina. *They Called It Prairie Light: The Story of Chilocco Indian School*. Lincoln: University of Nebraska Press, 1995.

Lomax, Alan. *Cajun and Creole Music: The Classic Louisiana Recordings, 1934/1937* [liner notes]. Cambridge, MA: Rounder Records, 1999.

Lomax, Alan. *The Folk Songs of North America, in the English Language*. Garden City, NY: Doubleday, 1960.

Lomax, John A. *Adventures of a Ballad Hunter*. New York: Macmillan, 1947.

———. *Cowboy Songs*. New York: Sturgis and Walton, 1910.

Lomax, John A., Alan A. Lomax. *Our Singing Country: A Second Volume of American Ballads and Folk Songs*. New York: Macmillan, 1941.

Long, Alecia P. *The Great Southern Babylon: Sex, Race, and Respectability in New Orleans, 1865–1920*. Baton Rouge: Louisiana State University Press, 2004.

Long, Richard A. "Creole." *Harvard Encyclopedia of American Ethnic Groups*. Cambridge. MA: Belknap Press, Harvard University Press, 1980.

Lornell, Kip. *Introducing American Folk Music: Ethnic and Grassroot Traditions in the United States*. 2nd ed. Boston: McGraw-Hill, 2002.

———. *Virginia Traditions: Non-Blues Secular Black Music* [disk]. Ferrum, VA: Blue Ridge Institute Records, 1976.

Lornell, Kip, and J. Roderick Moore. "Clarence Tross: Hardy Country Banjoist." *Goldenseal* 2, No. 3 (1976): 7–13.

Lott, Eric. "Love and Theft: The Racial Unconscious of Blackface Minstrelsy." *Representations* No. 39 (Summer 1992): 25–27.

Louder, Dean R. and Michael Leblanc. "The Cajuns of East Texas," in *French America: Mobility, Identity, and Minority Experience Across the Continent*. ed. Dean R. Louder and Eric Waddell. Baton Rouge: Louisiana State University Press, 1993.

Louder, Dean R., and Eric Waddell, eds. *French America: Mobility, Identity, and Minority Experience across the Continent*. Baton Rouge: Louisiana State University Press, 1993.

Lyle Saxon, Edward Dreyer, and Robert Tallant. *Gumbo Ya-Ya: A Collection of Louisiana Folk Tales*. New York: Bonanza, 1954.

Lynch, Gerald. *Roughnecks, Drillers, and Tool Pushers: Thirty-Three Years in the Oil Fields*. Personal Narratives of the West Series. Austin: University of Texas Press, 1987.

Mahar, William J. *Behind the Burnt Cork Mask: Early Blackface Minstrelsy and Antebellum American Popular Culture*. Music in American Life. Urbana: University of Illinois Press, 1999.

Malone, Bill C. *Country Music U.S.A.* Austin: University of Texas Press, 2002.

———. *Country Music U.S.A.: A Fifty-Year History*. Austin: University of Texas Press, 1968.

———. *Don't Get above Your Raisin': Country Music and the Southern Working Class*. Music in American Life. Urbana: University of Illinois Press, 2002.

———. *Singing Cowboys and Musical Mountaineers: Southern Culture and the Roots of Country Music*. Mercer University Lamar Memorial Lectures Vol. 34. Athens: University of Georgia Press, 1993.

Malone, Bill C., and Judith McCulloh, eds. *Stars of Country Music: Uncle Dave Macon to Johnny Rodriguez*. Music in American Life. Urbana: University of Illinois Press, 1975.

Malone, Bill C., and David Stricklin. *Southern Music/American Music*. Lexington: University Press of Kentucky, 2003.

Marteau, Olivier. "Entretien 'carnavalesque' avec Jean Arceneaux et Barry Jean Ancelet." *Etudies Francophone, Dossier Thematique: Louisiane numero double* 21 Nos. 1 and 2 (printemps-automne). Lafayette, LA: Université de Louisiane a Lafayette, 2006, 196–204

Mattern, Mark. *Acting in Concert: Music, Community, and Political Action*. New Brunswick, NJ: Rutgers University Press, 1998.

———. "Cajun Music, Cultural Revival: Theorizing Political Action in Popular Music." *Popular Music and Society* 22 (Summer 1998): 31–48.

———. "Let the Good Times Unroll: Music and Race Relations in Southwest Louisiana." *Black Music Research Journal* 17, No. 2 (Autumn 1997): 159–168.

Mccusker, Kristine M. *Lonesome Cowgirls and Honky Tonk Angels: The Women of Barn Dance Radio*. Urbana: University of Illinois Press, 2008.

Mccusker Kristine M., and Diane Pecknold eds. *A Boy Named Sue: Gender and Country Music*. Jackson: University Press of Mississippi, 2004.

McFadden, Margaret T. "'America's Boy Friend Who Can't Get a Date': Gender, Race, and the Cultural Work of the Jack Benny Program, 1932–1946." *Journal of American History* 80 (June 1993): 113–134.

McGerr, Michael. *A Fierce Discontent: The Rise and Fall of the Progressive Movement in America, 1870–1920*. New York: Oxford University Press, 2005.

McNeil, W. K. "Five Pre-World War II Arkansas String Bands: Some Thoughts on Their Recording Success." *John Edwards Memorial Foundation Quarterly* 20, No. 74 (Fall/Winter 1984): 68–75.

Meintjes, Louise. "Paul Simon's Graceland, South Africa, and the Mediation of Musical Meaning." *Ethnomusicology* 34 (Winter 1990): 37–73.

Melancon, Norris. Interview with the author. July 30, 2005.

Mendelson, Michael. "Benny Thomasson and the Texas Fiddling Tradition." *John Edwards Memorial Foundation Quarterly* 10, No. 35, Part 3 (Autumn 1974).

Meyerowitz, Joanne. "Beyond the Feminine Mystique: A Reassessment of Postwar Mass Culture, 1946–1958." *Journal of American History* 79 (March 1993): 1455–1482.

Mitchell, Pablo. *Coyote Nation: Sexuality, Race, and Conquest in Modernizing New Mexico, 1880–1920.* Chicago: University of Chicago Press, 2005.

Monroe, Mina, and Kurt Schindler. *Bayou Ballads: Twelve Folk-Songs from Louisiana.* New York: G. Schirmer, 1921.

Montgomery, David. *The Fall of the House of Labor: The Workplace, the State, and American Labor Activism, 1865–1925.* Cambridge: Cambridge University Press, 1989.

Mouton, Todd. "Love or Folly? Cajun Trailblazers BeauSoleil Celebrate 20 Years Together." *OffBeat* (January 1997), 45.

Nelson, Donald Lee. "'Mama, Where You At?': The Chronicle of Maius Lafleur." *John Edwards Memorial Foundation Quarterly* 19, No. 70 (Summer 1983): 76–79.

Ngai, Mae. *Impossible Subjects: Illegal Aliens and the Making of Modern America.* Princeton, NJ: Princeton University Press, 2005.

Norwod, Beth. "French Broadcasting in Louisiana." *Southern Speech Journal* 30, No. 1 (1964): 46–54.

Olien, Diana Davids, and Roger M. Olien. *Oil in Texas: The Gusher Age, 1895–1945.* Clifton and Shirley Caldwell Texas Heritage Series No. 3. Austin: University of Texas Press, 2002.

Oliphant, Dave. "Texas Jazz 1920–50," in *The Roots of Texas Music.* ed. Lawrence Clayton and Joe W. Specht. College Station: Texas A&M University Press, 2003, 37–65.

Olmsted, Frederick Law. *A Journey in the Seaboard Slave States in the Years 1853–1854, with Remarks on Their Economy.* Vol 2. New York: G. P. Putnam's Sons, 1904.

———. *A Journey through Texas: Saddle-Trip on the Southwestern Frontier: With a Statistical Appendix.* New York: Dix, Edwards, and Co., 1857.

Orenstein, Dara. "Void for Vagueness: Mexicans and the Collapse of Miscegenation Law in California." *Pacific Historical Review* 74 (2005): 367–407.

Oster, Harry. *Folksongs of the Louisiana Acadians* [disk]. El Cerrito, CA: Arhoolie, 1994.

———. "Acculturation in Cajun Folk Music." *McNeese Review* 10 (Winter 1958): 19–23.

Oster, Harry, and Revon Reed. "Cajun Mardi Gras in Louisiana." *Louisiana Folklore Miscellany* 1, No. 4 (1960): 1–17.

Owens, William A. *Texas Folk Songs.* Publications of the Texas Folklore Society No. 23. Austin: Texas Folklore Society, 1950.

Owens, William A. *Tell Me a Story, Sing Me a Song: A Texas Chronicle.* Austin: University of Texas Press, 1983.

Ownby, Ted. *Subduing Satan: Religion, Recreation, and Manhood in the Rural South, 1865–1920.* Fred W. Morrison Series in Southern Studies. Chapel Hill, NC: UNC Press, 1990.

Park, Robert E., Ernest W. Burgess, and Roderick D. McKenzie. *The City: Suggestions for Investigation of Human Behavior in the Urban Environment.* Chicago: University of Chicago, 1925.

Pascoe, Peggy. "Miscegenation Law, Court Cases, and Ideologies of 'Race' in Twentieth-Century America." *Journal of American History* 83 (June 1996): 44–69.

Pastras, Phil. *Dead Man Blues: Jelly Roll Morton Way Out West.* Berkeley: University of California Press, 2001.

Patterson, Daniel W. ed., *Sounds of the South*. Durham, NC: Duke University Press, 1991.

Peña, Manuel H. *The Mexican American Orquesta: Music, Culture, and the Dialectic of Conflict*. Austin: University of Texas Press, 1999.

———. *The Texas-Mexican Conjunto: History of a Working-Class Music*. Austin: University of Texas Press, 1985.

Peterson, Richard A. *Creating Country Music: Fabricating Authenticity*. Chicago: University of Chicago Press, 1997.

Petitjean, Irene M. "'Cajun' Folk Songs of Southwestern Louisiana." Master's Thesis, Columbia University, 1930.

Philips, Susan U. "Participant Structures and Communicative Competence: Warm Springs Children in Community and Classroom," in *Linguistic Anthropology: A Reader*, ed. Alessandro Duranti. Malden, MA: Blackwell Publishers, 2001.

Pinson, Bob. "The Bob Wills Recordings: A Comprehensive Discography," in *San Antonio Rose: The Life and Music of Bob Wills*. Charles R. Townsend. Urbana: University of Illinois Press, 1976.

Porterfield, Nolan. *Jimmie Rodgers: The Life and Times of America's Blue Yodeler*. Urbana: University of Illinois Press, 1992.

———. *Last Cavalier: The Life and Times of John A. Lomax, 1867–1948*. Folklore and Society. Urbana: University of Illinois Press, 1996.

Post, Lauren C."Acadian Folkways." *Louisiana State University Alumni News* 12, No. 4 (April 1936): 7–9, 26–27.

———. *Cajun Sketches from the Prairies of Southwest Louisiana*. Baton Rouge: Louisiana State University Press, 1974.

——— "Joseph C. Falcon, Accordion Player and Singer: A Biographical Sketch." *Louisiana History* 11 (1970): 63–88.

Powdermaker, Hortense. *After Freedom: A Cultural Study in the Deep South*. Madison: University of Wisconsin Press, 1993.

Pratt, Mary Louise. *Imperial Eyes: Travel Writing and Transculturation*. London: Routledge, 1992.

Prentiss, George Lewis. *A Memoir of S. S. Prentiss*. Vol. 1. New York: Scribner, 1899.

Prévos, André. "Afro-French Spirituals about Mary Magdalene." *Louisiana Folklore Miscellany* 4 (1976–1980): 41–53.

Prichard, Walter, Fred B. Kniffen, and Clair A. Brown, eds. "Southern Louisiana and Southern Alabama in 1819: The Journal of James Leander Cathcart." *Louisiana Historical Quarterly* 28 (July 1945): 735–921.

Pugh, W. W. "Lafourche from 1820 to 1825—Its Inhabitants, Customs and Pursuits." *Louisiana Planter and Sugar Manufacturer* (September 29, 1888): 143.

Pusateri, C. Joseph. *Enterprise in Radio: WWL and the Business of Broadcasting in America*. Washington, DC: University Press of America, 1980.

Ray, R. Celeste, and Luke E. Lassiter. *Signifying Serpents and Mardi Gras Runners: Representing Identity in Selected Souths*. Southern Anthropological Society Proceedings No. 36. Athens: University of Georgia Press, 2003.

Reilly, Timothy F. "Early Acadiana through Anglo-American Eyes, Part I." *Attakapas Gazette* 7, No. 3 (Spring 1977): 3–20.

———. "Early Acadiana through Anglo-American Eyes, Part II." *Attakapas Gazette* 7, No. 3 (Fall 1977): 159–176.

Richardson, Lisa E. "The Public and Private Domains of Cajun Women Musicians in Southwest Louisiana," in *Accordions, Fiddles, Two Step and Swing: A Cajun Music Reader*. ed. Ryan A. Brasseaux and Kevin S. Fontenot. Lafayette: Center for Louisiana Studies, University of Louisiana at Lafayette, 2006.

Rinzler, Ralph. *Louisiana Cajun French Music from the Southwest Prairies, 1964–1967*, Vols. 1 and 2 [disk]. Cambridge, MA: Rounder Records, 1989.

——. *Louisiana Cajun French Music from the Southwest Prairies, 1964–1967*, Vol. 2 [disk]. Cambridge, MA: Rounder Records, 1989.

Roberts, Elizabeth Mae. "French Radio Broadcasting in Louisiana." M.S. thesis, Louisiana State University, 1959

Robin, C. C. *Voyage to Louisiana, 1803–1805*, trans. Stuart O. Landry, Jr. New Orleans, LA: Pelican Publishing, 1966.

Roediger, David R. *Working toward Whiteness: How America's Immigrants Became White. The Strange Journey from Ellis Island to the Suburbs*. New York: Perseus Books, 2006.

——. *The Wages of Whiteness: Race and the Making of the American Working Class*. London: Verso, 1991.

Roman, Marguerite. "Les Acadiens Au XXe Siècle." *Comptes Rendus de l'Athénée Louisianais* (March 1924) : 12–23.

Rose, Al. *Storyville, New Orleans, Being an Authentic, Illustrated Account of the Notorious Red-Light District*.Tuscaloosa: University of Alabama Press, 1974.

Roseberry, William. *Anthropologies and Histories: Essays in Culture, History, and Political Economy*. New Brunswick, NJ: Rutgers University Press, 1989.

Ross, Sally, and J. Alphonse Deveau. *The Acadians of Nova Scotia Past and Present*. Halifax, NS: Nimbus, 1992.

Russell, Tony. "Leo Soileau." *Old Time Music* 27 (1977): 5–9.

Russell, Tony.*Country Music Records: A Discography, 1921–1942*. New York: Oxford University Press, 2004.

Sacré, Robert. *Musiques Cajun, Créole et Zydeco*. Paris: Presses Universitaires de France, 1995.

Saldívar, Ramón. *The Borderlands of Culture: Américo Paredes and the Transnational Imaginary*. Durham, NC: Duke University Press, 2006.

Sánchez, George J. *Becoming Mexican American: Ethnicity, Culture, and Identity in Chicano Los Angeles, 1900–1945*. New York: Oxford University Press, 1995.

Sanders, Kevin. "Ragtime's Influence on Early Country Music." *Rag Times* 34, No. 3 (September 2000): 2–8.

Sandmel, Ben., *Luderin Darbone's Hackberry Ramblers, Early Recordings: 1935–1950* [liner notes, disk]. El Cerrito, CA: Arhoolie, 2003.

Savoy, Ann Allen. *Cajun Music: Alive and Well in Louisiana* [Louisiana Folklife Festival Booklet]. Baton Rouge: Louisiana Division of the Arts, Department of Culture, Recreation and Tourism 1990.

——. *Cajun Music: A Reflection of a People*. Eunice, LA: Bluebird Press, 1984.

——.*The Complete Early Recordings of Dennis McGee, with Ernest Fruge and Sady Courville, 1929–1930* [liner notes, disk]. Newton, NJ: Yazoo, 1994.

——. *Edius Naquin: Ballad Master* [audio cassette]. New Orleans: New Orleans Jazz and Heritage Foundation, Inc., n.d.

——. *Iry Lejeune: The Definitive Collection* [disk]. London: Ace Records, 2004.

———. "Leo Soileau: From Cajun Classic to Innovator," *Early American Cajun Music: The Early Recordings of Leo Soileau* [liner notes, disk]: Newton, NJ: Yazoo, 1999.

Schuler, Edgar A. *Survey of Radio Listeners in Louisiana*. Baton Rouge: Louisiana State University General Extension Division, 1943.

Seeman, Charlie. *Le Gran Mamou: A Cajun Music Anthology, the Historic Victor/Bluebird Sessions 1928–1941*. Nashville, TN: Country Music Foundation, 1990.

———. *Raise Your Window: A Cajun Music Anthology, the Historic Victor/Bluebird Session, 1928–1941*. Nashville, TN: Country Music Foundation, 1993.

Sexton, Rocky L. "Cajuns, Germans, and Les Americans: A Historical Anthropology of Cultural Demographic Transformations." Ph.D. dissertation, University of Iowa, 1996.

———. "Ritualized Inebriation, Violence, and Social Control in Cajun Mardi Gras." *Anthropological Quarterly* 74, No. 1 (January 2001): 28–38.

Sexton, Rocky, and Harry Oster. "Une 'Tite Poule Grasse ou la Fille Aînée [a Little Fat Chicken or the Eldest Daughter]: A Comparative Analysis of Cajun and Creole Mardi Gras Songs." *Journal of American Folklore* 114, No. 452 (2001): 204–224.

Sheldon, Ruth. *Bob Wills: Hubbin' It*. Nashville, TN: Country Music Foundation Press, 1995.

Simmons, Michael. "Doug Kershaw: The Real Deal in Cajun Fiddle." *Fiddler Magazine* 10 (Spring 2003).

Shugg, Roger Wallace. *Origins of Class Struggle in Louisiana: A Social History of White Farmers and Laborers during Slavery and After, 1840–1875*. Baton Rouge: Louisiana State University Press, 1966.

Smalley, Eugene V. "Sugar-Making in Louisiana." *Century Illustrated Monthly Magazine* 35 (November 1887-April 1888): 100–120.

Snyder, Jared M. "Squeezebox: The Legacy of the Afro-Mississippi Accordionists." *Black Music Research Journal* 17, No. 1 (Spring 1997): 37–57.

———. *Amédé's Recordings* [disk]. El Cerrito, CA: Arhoolie, 1995.

Sonnier, Austin M. *Second Linin': Jazzmen of Southwest Louisiana, 1900–1950*. Louisiana Life Series No. 3. Lafayette: Center for Louisiana Studies, University of Southwestern Louisiana, 1989.

Sparks, W. H. *The Memories of Fifty Years: Containing Brief Biographical Notices of Distinguished Americans, and Anecdotes of Remarkable Men; Interspersed with Scenes and Incidents Occurring during a Long Life of Observation Chiefly Spent in the Southwest*. Philadelphia: E. Claxton and Co., 1882.

Spires, Will. *The Complete Early Recordings of Dennis Mcgee, with Ernest Fruge and Sady Courville, 1929–1930* [liner notes, disk].: Newton, NJ: Yazoo, 1994.

Spitzer, Nicholas R., ed. "Documenting Tradition: Louisiana Folklife and Media," in *Louisiana Folklife: A Guide to the State*. ed. Spitzer. Baton Rouge: Louisiana Folklife Program, 1985.

———. *Louisiana Folklife: A Guide to the State*. Baton Rouge: Louisiana Folklife Program, 1985.

———.*Octa Clark and Hector Duhon: The Dixie Ramblers, Ensemble Encore, the Men and Their Music* [liner notes, disk], LP 6011. Cambridge, MA: Rounder Records, 1983.

Spottswood, Richard K. *Ethnic Music on Records: A Discography of Ethnic Recordings Produced in the United States, 1893 to 1942.* 7 vols. Music in American Life. Urbana: University of Illinois Press, 1990.

"State and Country QuickFacts." U.S. Census Bureau, http://quickfacts.census.gov/qfd/states/22000.html. Accessed 2008.

Stead, W. T. *The Americanization of the World; or, The Trend of the Twentieth Century.* New York: H. Marckley, 1902.

Stivale, Charles J. *Disenchanting Les Bons Temps: Identity and Authenticity in Cajun Music and Dance.* Durham, NC: Duke University Press, 2003.

St. Martin, Thad. "Letters and Comment—Cajuns." *Yale Review* 26 (June 1937): 859–862.

Storch, Randi. *Red Chicago: American Communism at its Grassroots, 1928–35.* Urbana: University of Illinois Press, 2007.

Strachwitz, Chris. *Cajun Breakdown: Cajun String Bands of the 1930s* [disk]. El Cerrito, CA: Folklyric, 1997.

———— "Cajun Country," in *The American Folk Music Occasional,* ed. Strachwitz and Pete Welding. Vol. 1. New York: Oak Publishers, 1970.

————. *Chuck Guillory and the Rhythm Boys* [disk]. El Cerrito, CA: Arhoolie, 1988.

Stromquist, Shelton. *Re-inventing "The People": The Progressive Movement, the Class Problem, and the Origins of Modern Liberalism.* Urbana: University of Illinois Press, 2006.

Suarez, Raleigh Anthony. "Rural Life in Louisiana, 1850–1860." Ph.D. dissertation, Louisiana State University, 1954.

Tallant, Robert. *Voodoo in New Orleans.* London: Collier-Macmillan, 1969.

Tentchoff, Dorice. "Ethnic Survival under Anglo-American Hegemony: The Louisiana Cajuns." *Anthropological Quarterly* 53, No. 4 (October 1980): 229–241.

Theriot, Jason P. "Cajuns in World War II, 1940–1947." M.A. Thesis, University of Houston, 2006.

————. *To Honor Our Veterans: An Oral History of World War II Veterans from the Bayou Country,* Vol. 1, *The Pacific War.* Lafayette, LA: Jason P. Theriot, 2002.

————. *To Honor Our Veterans: An Oral History of World War II Veterans from the Bayou Country,* Vol. 2, *The Mediterranean Campaign.* Lafayette, LA: Jason P. Theriot, 2003.

————. *To Honor Our Veterans: An Oral History of World War II Veterans from the Bayou Country,* Vol. 3, *The European Theater.* Lafayette, LA: Jason P. Theriot, 2005.

Thériot, Marie del Norte, and Catherine Brookshire Blanchet. *Les Danse Rondes: Louisiana French Folk Dances.* Lafayette, LA: Tribune Printing Plant, 1955.

Thibodeaux, Gene. *Rice, Railroads and Frogs: A History of Rayne, Louisiana.* Church Point, LA: Plaquemine Brûlée Press, 2001.

Tisserand, Michael. *The Kingdom of Zydeco.* New York: Arcade, 1998.

Titon, Jeff Todd, and Bob Carlin, eds. *American Musical Traditions.* 5 vols. New York: Schirmer Reference, 2002.

Townsend, Charles R., *San Antonio Rose: The Life and Music of Bob Wills.* Urbana: University of Illinois Press, 1976.

Tucker, Stephen R. "Louisiana Folk and Regional Popular Music Tradition on Records and the Radio: An Historical Overview with Suggestions for Future Research," in *Accordions, Fiddles, Two Step and Swing: A Cajun Music Reader.* ed. Ryan A. Brasseaux and Kevin S. Fontenot.

Lafayette: Center for Louisiana Studies, University of Louisiana at Lafayette, 2006.

———. "Louisiana Folk and Regional Popular Music Traditions on Records and the Radio," in *Louisiana Folklife: A Guide to the State*. ed. Nicholas R. Spitzer. Baton Rouge: Louisiana Folklife Program, 1985, 223–40.

———. "'Louisiana Saturday Night': A History of Louisiana Country Music." Ph.D. dissertation, Tulane University, 1995.

Ulmer, Grace. "Economic and Social Development of Calcasieu Parish, Louisiana, 1840–1912." *Louisiana Historical Quarterly* 32 (July 1949): 596–599.

Usner Daniel H., Jr. *American Indians in the Lower Mississippi Valley: Social and Economic Histories*. Lincoln: University of Nebraska Press, 2003.

———. *Indians, Settlers, and Slaves in a Frontier Exchange Economy: The Lower Mississippi Valley before 1783*. Chapel Hill, NC: UNC Press, 1992.

Vandal, Gilles. *Rethinking Southern Violence: Homicides in Post-Civil War Louisiana, 1866–1884*. The History of Crime and Criminal Justice Series. Columbus: Ohio State University Press, 2000.

van Elteren, Mel. *Americanism and Americanization: A Critical History of Domestic and Global Influence*. Jefferson, NC: McFarland, 2006.

Vargas, Zaragosa. *Labor Rights Are Civil Rights: Mexican American Workers in Twentieth-Century America*. Princeton, NJ: Princeton University Press, 2007.

Voorhies, Felix, *Acadian Reminiscences*. Boston: Palmer Company, 1907.

Wald, Elijah, John Junkerman, and Theo Pelletier. *River of Song: A Musical Journey down the Mississippi*. New York: St. Martin's Press, 1999.

Waller, Altina L. *Feud: Hatfields, Mccoys, and Social Change in Appalachia, 1860–1900*. Chapel Hill, NC: UNC Press, 1988.

Walton, Shana. "Louisiana's Coonasses: Choosing Race and Class over Ethnicity," in *Signifying Serpents and Mardi Gras Runners: Representing Identity in Selected Souths*. ed. R. Celeste Ray and Luke E. Lassiter. Athens: University of Georgia Press, 2003, 38–50.

———. "Flat Speech and Cajun Ethnic Identity in Terrebonne Parish, Louisiana." Ph.D. Dissertation, Tulane University, 1994.

Ware, Carolyn E. *Cajun Women and Mardi Gras: Reading the Rules Backwards*. Urbana: University of Illinois Press, 2006.

Watts, Edward. *In This Remote Country: French Colonial Culture in the Anglo-American Imagination, 1780–1860*. Chapel Hill: University of North Carolina, 2006.

Waud, A. R. "Acadians of Louisiana." *Harper's Weekly* (October 20, 1866): 670.

Weiland, Ione. "Typical Household: Lafayette Parish, 1825–1835." *Attakapas Gazette* 9 (March 1974).

Whisnant, David E. *All That Is Native and Fine: The Politics of Culture in an American Region*. Chapel Hill, NC: UNC Press, 1995.

White, Doris. "Jouré My Lord." *Louisiana Folklore Miscellany* 4 (1976–1980): 143–145.

White, Richard. "Creative Misunderstandings and New Understandings." *William and Mary Quarterly* 63, No. 1 (January 2006): 9–14.

———. *The Middle Ground: Indians, Empires, and Republics in the Great Lakes Region, 1650–1815*. Cambridge: Cambridge University Press, 1991.

Whitehead, John. *"Make 'Em Dance": The Hackberry Ramblers' Story* [film]. St. Paul, MN: Fretless Pictures, 2003.

Whitfield, Irène Thérèse. *Louisiana French Folk Songs*. 3rd ed. New York: Dover Publications, 1969.

———. *Louisiana French Folk Songs*., Baton Rouge, LA: Louisiana State University Press, 1939.

Williams, Michael Ann. *Staging Tradition: John Lair and Sarah Gertrude Knott*. Urbana: University of Illinois Press, 2006.

Wilson, Peter J. *Crab Antics: A Caribbean Case Study of the Conflict between Reputation and Respectability*. Prospect Heights, IL: Waveland Press, 1995.

———. *Oscar: An Inquiry into the Nature of Sanity?* Prospect Heights, IL: Waveland Press, 1992.

———. "Reputation and Respectability: A Suggestion for Caribbean Ethnology." *Man* 4, No. 1 (March 1969): 70–84.

Wolfe, Charles. *A Good-Natured Riot: The Birth of the Grand Ole Opry*. Nashville, TN: Vanderbilt University Press, 1999.

Wolfe, Charles. "The Legend That Peer Built: Reappraising the Bristol Sessions," in *The Country Reader: Twenty-Five Years of the Journal of Country Music*, ed. Paul Kingsbury. Nashville, TN: Country Music Foundation Press and Vanderbilt University Press, 1996, 3–20.

———. "Tracking the Lost String Bands." *Southern Exposure* 2–3 (1977): 11–20.

Wolfe, Charles K., and James E. Akenson, eds., *Country Music Annual 2001*. Lexington: University of Kentucky Press, 2001.

———. *The Women of Country Music: A Reader*. Lexington: University Press of Kentucky, 2003.

Wolfe, Charles K., and Kip Lornell. *The Life and Legend of Leadbelly*. New York: HarperCollins, 1992.

Wolfe, Charles, and Ted Olson, eds. *The Bristol Sessions: Writings about the Big Bang of Country Music*. Jefferson, NC: McFarland, 2005.

Woodward, C. Vann. *The Burden of Southern History*. Baton Rouge: Louisiana State University, 1993.

Wyatt-Brown, Bertram. *Southern Honor: Ethics and Behavior in the Old South*. New York: Oxford University Press, 1983.

Yule, Ron. *Iry Lejeune: Wailin' the Blues Cajun Style*. Natchitoches, LA: Northwestern State University Press, 2007.

———. *When the Fiddle Was King: Early Country Music from the North and West Regions of Louisiana*. Natchitoches, LA: Northwestern State University Press, 2006.

Zwonitzer, Mark, and Charles Hirshberg. *Will You Miss Me When I'm Gone?: The Carter Family and Their Legacy in American Music*. New York: Simon and Schuster, 2002.

Index

Abbeville, 35, 54, 133, 144, 147, 154, 184, 189
Abshire, Nathan, 76, 85–89, 150, 156, 179, 180, 192, 193, 197–199, 204, 206, 221, 226
Acadian, 5–12, 15, 27, 28, 30–32, 34, 40, 58, 60, 70, 73–76, 79, 82, 85, 97, 104, 106–108, 123, 125, 127, 128, 131, 135, 139, 140–144, 147, 150, 169, 170, 172, 183, 187, 193–194, 197, 210, 211, 216, 223, 224, 227
Acadian exiles, 6–9, 15, 17, 27–30, 32
Acadia Parish, 3, 34, 46, 49, 59, 92, 95, 100, 103, 120, 126–128, 133, 148, 157, 192
Acadie (Acadia), 8, 9, 32
a cappella, 9, 30, 33–35, 47, 48, 81, 98, 97, 109, 110, 147, 212
accordion, 4, 10, 16, 18–23, 38, 42, 44, 49, 50, 56, 57, 60–70, 73, 75–88, 95, 97, 103, 104, 107, 109, 113, 115, 117, 119, 120, 128, 129, 134, 136, 138, 141, 144–146, 152, 156, 159, 163, 170, 171, 178–182, 191, 192–198, 206, 207, 209, 214, 218, 220, 222, 226
  Afro-Creoles use of, 20, 21, 136
  brands of, 22
  chromatic piano accordion, 114, 115
  importation of, 19, 21, 22
accordion contest, 60, 78, 119
Acuff, Roy, 6, 165, 169, 177, 178, 204
African American, 11, 13, 16–17, 20, 21, 33, 38, 54, 55, 65, 67, 69, 73, 74,

75, 79, 84–86, 95, 111, 116, 119, 120, 136, 155, 165, 172, 181–183
Afro-Creole, 11, 16–18, 20, 21, 33, 50, 56–58, 66, 67, 76–79, 83–86, 119, 135, 136, 143, 183, 195, 197, 215, 220–224, 227, 228
agriculture, 5, 6, 9, 10, 11, 14, 29, 30, 37, 38, 39, 41, 48, 51, 55, 60, 65, 69, 70, 75–77, 80, 81, 116, 109, 122, 123, 132–136, 140, 152, 154, 156, 157, 168, 182, 195
alcohol, 19, 28, 34, 35, 37, 40, 46, 47, 51, 61, 62, 71, 91, 95, 163, 172–174, 187, 223
  moonshine, 65, 67, 69, 184
Allan, Johnnie, 129
Alleman, Tony, 109, 118
Alley Boys of Abbeville, 24, 134, 144, 153, 154, 191, 221
Allport, Gordon, 25, 180, 182, 183, 190, 198, 204, 205
Americanization, 4, 7, 9, 24, 46, 61, 84, 88, 97, 98, 162, 163, 166, 176, 213
Amos'n' Andy, 140, 149, 180
amplification, 46, 113–115, 154, 180
Ancelet, Barry Jean, 25, 46, 97, 110, 130, 216, 219, 220, 227
Anglophone, 6, 10, 11, 15, 100, 117, 122, 160, 170, 218
Ardoin, Amédé, 50, 56–58, 76–78, 83–86, 136, 143, 195, 197, 220–223, 228
Armstrong, Louis, 67, 73, 84
assimilation, 6, 7, 94, 195, 215, 216

Atlanta, GA, 12, 51, 55, 65, 73–75, 161
authenticity, 94, 105, 107, 212–216
automobiles, 80, 97, 98, 115, 162
Autry, Gene, 137
Avalon Club, 179, 180, 190
Avoyelles Parish, 78–82, 218

"The Back Door," 200, 207
bal de noce, 42, 61
Balfa, Dewey, 102, 130
ballads, 9, 30, 31, 32, 45, 48, 58, 64,
    75, 81, 82, 91, 95–99, 103,
    104, 109, 110, 162
bals de maison, 9, 10, 30, 31, 35–38, 40,
    42–48, 69, 80, 161
banjo, 12, 13, 16–17, 21, 23, 73, 75,
    115, 141, 150, 153, 156, 163, 212
Barde, Alexander, 16, 45
Barnum, P. T., 111
Basile, LA, 65–67, 146, 163, 164,
    179, 190
bass (upright), 23, 80, 115, 129, 141, 144,
    148–150, 156, 170, 185, 194, 226
Baton Rouge, LA, 12, 15, 97, 103, 127,
    135, 140, 196
Bayou Blue, LA, 109
Bayou Lafourche, LA, 9, 14, 36, 37,
    39, 54
Bayou Têche, LA, 14, 16, 53, 74, 109
Beaumont, TX, 60, 122, 123, 146, 184,
    186, 187
BeauSoleil, 210, 220
Bellard, Douglas, 56, 228
Bernard, Rod, 129, 177, 207
Bernard, Shane K., 122, 129, 177
"Big Texas," 160, 179, 180, 200, 201,
    204, 224
Billboard, 6, 164, 169
Blanchet, Catherine, 16, 36
Bluebird (record label), 56, 58, 60, 78,
    86–88, 118, 143, 144, 147, 148,
    150–153, 156, 197, 221
blues, 6, 23, 54, 56, 61, 68, 75, 83–88, 97,
    98, 101, 110, 117, 118, 121, 129, 130,
    143, 149, 150–153, 163, 170, 172,
    176, 179, 186, 187, 191, 197, 198,
    200, 204, 206, 207, 211, 221–226
Bond, Johnny, 175
boogie, 144, 169, 177
Brandon, Elizabeth, 33, 211, 227
Brasseaux, Carl A., 9, 10
Brasseaux, Fenelon, 97
Breaux, Amédé, 19, 71, 88, 149, 161,
    169, 170, 195

Breaux, Cleoma, 16, 23, 49, 50, 52, 55,
    58–64, 69, 70, 76, 86, 109, 112,
    128, 129, 143, 158, 161, 217, 219,
    221, 223, 228
Breaux Brothers, 58, 70, 71, 81, 85,
    219, 221
Bristol Sessions, 55, 64, 68
Broussard, Ardus, 104, 106, 107
Broussard, Evelyn, 104
Broussard, Sidney Jr., 104, 107
Broussard, Sidney Sr., 104
Brown, Milton, and the Musical
    Brownies, 121, 141, 186, 189, 191,
    193, 200
Brown, Ron, 71, 80, 197, 222
Bruner, Cliff, and his Texas Wanderers,
    134, 144, 162, 185, 186, 192,
    201, 225
Burrow, George, 49, 51, 59, 69
Burrus Flour Mill, 116, 139

Cable, George Washington, 17–18,
    43, 135
cage aux chiens, 46, 47
Cain's Ballroom, 190
Cajun honky tonk, 25, 159, 181, 182,
    189, 191–194, 197, 198, 206, 207,
    219, 223, 225, 226
Cajun swing, 159–163, 166, 169, 170,
    176–177, 182, 185, 189, 191,
    193–197, 198, 200, 201, 205–206,
    212, 214, 216, 219, 220–226
calliope, 14, 15
Cameron Parish, 117, 118
cantiques, 30, 32, 33, 36, 48, 110
Cantril, Hadley, 180, 182, 183, 190, 198,
    204, 205
Carson, Fiddlin' John, 55, 64, 69
Carter Family, 55, 63, 64, 139, 193, 210
Castille, Hadley, 125, 157
Catholicism, 6, 11, 13, 29, 32–36, 63,
    131, 137, 138, 167, 168, 173, 183,
    211, 218
Chicago, IL, 51, 70, 80, 81, 107, 116,
    125, 143, 148, 149
Choates, Harry, 3, 24, 129, 130, 141,
    144, 151, 152, 157–171, 176–178,
    182, 185–187, 193–195, 199–201,
    205, 216, 220, 224–226
Church. *See* Catholicism; Protestantism
Civil War, 6, 9, 10, 11, 16–19, 29, 30, 34,
    36, 42, 43, 80, 217
clarinet, 9, 15–16, 120, 121, 212
Coffey, Kevin, 159, 166, 169, 225

Cohen, Lizabeth, 52, 116, 139
Columbia (record label), 49, 50, 53, 54, 56, 59, 60, 64, 69, 71, 78, 83, 102, 106, 109, 117, 161, 180, 182, 209, 221, 222
Comeaux, Malcolm, 20, 22, 25, 32
complaintes, 30, 31, 42, 48
conjunto, 138, 145
consumerism, 16, 19, 21–23, 52, 55, 59, 60, 62, 66, 68, 96, 113, 122, 145, 193, 197, 205
contests, band, 60, 78, 119, 127, 128, 130, 139, 152, 162
    dance, 38, 39, 119
Cooley, Spade, 145, 155
coonass, 111, 136, 168, 186, 187
"Corinne, Corinna," 86, 109, 146, 153
cotton, 6, 14, 39, 55, 65, 70, 75–77, 132, 134–136, 140, 152, 154, 156, 157, 168, 195
country-and-western music, 23, 24, 61, 122, 125, 137, 139, 142–144, 149, 166, 168–174, 178–181, 185, 192, 194, 196, 202, 210, 211, 219, 220, 221, 224, 226. *See also* hillbilly
courtship, 10, 23, 28–30, 40–42, 44, 46, 48, 63, 161, 162, 176
Courville, Sady, 77, 78, 82–84, 117, 125, 161, 222
cowboy songs, 61, 75, 94, 95, 97, 100, 104, 109, 110, 111, 144
cracker, 111, 136, 173. *See also* coonass
Credeur, Joe, 56
Creole Hour, 127, 128
Crowley, LA, 38, 47, 62, 96, 97, 100, 107, 119, 120, 126–128, 130, 141–143, 147, 148, 170, 185, 190, 193, 201, 226
cultural authority, 102, 209, 214, 215, 216

Dacus, William "Smokey," 142
Daigle, Pierre Varmin, 59
Dallas, TX, 57, 70, 92, 103, 104, 106, 107, 109, 117, 121, 129, 142, 151, 170, 181, 183, 184, 189, 200
dance hall, 3, 5, 6, 10, 16–18, 21, 23, 29, 30, 35, 36, 37, 41, 45–50, 52, 60, 62, 65, 66, 69, 70, 71, 76, 77, 80, 85, 86, 88, 91, 113, 114, 117, 119, 130, 136, 139, 143, 144, 146, 147, 149, 153–155, 161, 168, 176–179, 180, 183–186, 192, 194, 201, 202, 205, 207, 217, 226

dance hall sound. *See* Cajun honky tonk
Daniel, R. L., 40, 47, 131
danse ronde, 32, 36
Davis, Governor Jimmie, 61, 84, 140, 144, 145, 149, 192, 202
Davis, Quincy, 179
"Dear Old Sunny South by the Sea," 115, 154
Decca (record label), 56, 58, 60, 61, 76, 85, 86, 128, 129, 143, 144, 148, 169, 201, 224, 228
deportation. *See Grand Derangement*
Dietlein, Frank, 65, 67
Disk Jockey, 164, 177, 190, 191
Dixie Ramblers, 44, 134, 144, 149, 152, 153
Doucet, Michael, 210, 220
Doucet, Oscar, 56, 74
drums, 115, 128, 129, 130, 142, 143, 148, 154, 197
Duhon, Buddy, 186, 187, 225
Duhon, Edwin, 114, 146, 148, 162
Duhon, Hector, 45, 120, 129, 152
Dunn, Bob, 186, 187, 200

early commercial era, 23, 49, 52, 55, 56, 58, 65, 73, 75, 76, 79, 82, 85–87, 88, 117, 143, 152, 154, 162, 194, 205, 219, 220–224
education, 7, 12, 13, 63, 74, 82, 94, 97–99, 115, 127, 128, 134, 137, 145–147, 154, 165, 196, 218
electricity, 37, 85, 108, 115
ethnography. *See* fieldwork
Eunice, LA, 77, 81, 119, 227
Evangeline, 67, 74, 91, 104, 106, 107, 172
    film, 7, 75
    Henry Wadsworth Longfellow's poem, 74
    parish, 77, 79, 81, 82, 218
    rural community and oil field, 44, 113, 122, 133, 196, 197
Evangeline troupe, 104, 106, 107

factories, 75, 96, 104, 116, 121, 132, 133, 139, 196
Fais Do Do, 48, 221
    label, 6, 178, 193, 198, 205
    orchestra contest, 127
Falcon, Joe, 23, 49, 50, 51, 52, 55, 58, 59, 60–63, 65, 66, 69, 70, 76, 77, 81, 86, 106, 109, 126, 143, 158, 217, 219, 221, 223
    and Silver String Band, 128, 227

fan mail, 188, 189
Fawvor, Dudley, 117–119, 152, 223
Fawvor, James, 83, 117–119, 152, 223
fiddle, 4, 38, 45, 102, 106, 120, 152,
    156, 158, 162, 185, 220, 222, 225
  as lead instrument, 16, 21, 117
  seconder style, 66, 83
folklore, 3, 9, 16–17, 20, 21, 24, 33, 36,
    45, 50, 57, 59, 60, 61, 65, 68, 70, 78,
    81, 82, 91–112, 127, 130, 134, 152,
    153, 161, 164, 165, 173, 175, 176,
    182, 187, 192, 197, 198, 209–216,
    219–224, 227
  ethnography, 33, 76, 81, 91, 92–95,
    108, 109, 215, 222, 227
  field recordings, 91, 92, 95–98,
    100–102, 108–110, 227
  gatekeepers, 95, 109, 186
Fontenot, Canray, 86, 130
Fontenot, Kevin S., 183, 191
Fontenot, Mary Alice, 65
foodways, 27, 28, 34–37, 39, 110, 132,
    166, 169, 173, 174, 193
Francophone, 5, 6, 9, 10, 15–16, 25, 29,
    34, 59, 79, 97, 99, 107, 115, 116,
    118, 123, 131, 145, 160, 167, 207,
    212, 217, 224, 227
French colonialism, 7, 8, 9, 10, 27, 28,
    29, 30, 33, 76, 79, 81, 82, 84, 101
Fruge, Columbus, 68, 219
Fruge, Ernest, 77, 78, 83, 85, 222
Fruge, Wade, 161, 222
Fuselier, J. B., 128, 153, 221, 224

Gaspard, Alcide "Blind Uncle," 75, 76,
    78–82, 219, 222
gender and Cajun culture, 7, 31, 40, 41,
    62–64, 93, 96, 149, 172, 173
Gennett (record label), 54, 67, 142, 223
Gilliland, Henry, 55
Ginell, Cary, 134
glissando, 78, 155
Gold Star (record label), 163–166, 178,
    194, 201, 225
Golden Triangle (Texas), 60, 69, 108,
    118, 122, 123, 131, 146, 163, 166,
    178, 184, 185, 186, 187
Gonzales, Roy, 67, 68, 223
Gonzales, Tony, 24, 120, 142, 143, 212
Graceland, 214
Grammy Awards, 209, 210, 214, 218
Grand Derangement, 6, 8, 9, 15, 17, 27,
    28, 30, 79

Grand Ole Opry, 125, 142, 144, 149,
    165, 169, 191, 199, 202, 203, 227
Great Depression, 16, 23, 36, 52, 56,
    57, 70, 75, 83, 84, 85, 91, 101, 105,
    110, 113, 116, 122, 133, 136, 137,
    155, 161, 180, 215
Great Migration, 105, 116, 172
"Gué Gué Solingaie," 58, 59
Guidry, Bixy, 56, 66
Guidry, Oran "Doc," 120, 128, 151, 169,
    189, 193, 202, 203
Guillory, Chuck, 200, 201, 224
guitar, 16, 21–23, 38, 49, 50, 56, 61–64,
    67, 68, 73, 75, 76, 80–82, 84, 87, 88,
    95, 104, 109, 113–120, 128, 129,
    134, 148, 149, 150–156, 181, 193,
    196, 197, 200, 201, 205, 207, 225
  twin guitars, 141, 143, 144, 146, 147,
    150, 152, 163, 170, 175, 193, 195
gumbo, 34, 35, 37, 39, 110, 166, 169
guns, 43–45

habitants, 9, 10, 29
Hackberry Ramblers, 24, 114, 119–122,
    125–127, 134, 137, 139, 140, 146,
    147–149, 150, 152, 153, 155, 156,
    158, 162, 169, 188–191, 212, 219,
    221–224
Hadacol, 149, 188, 203, 204, 228
Haiti. *See* Saint-Domingue
Happy Fats. See LeRoy "Happy Fats"
    LeBlanc
Harlem, 54–55, 61
harmonica, 13, 19–21, 56, 75, 109, 147,
    169, 221, 224
Hawaiian music (influence of), 23, 154,
    156. *See also* steel guitar
"Health and Happiness Show," 204
"High Society," 115, 120, 152, 153
hillbilly, 5, 6, 23, 45, 52, 55, 57, 64, 65,
    81, 84, 86, 101, 107, 115, 117, 118,
    121, 125–130, 139, 141, 143–148,
    150, 153, 154, 160, 167, 185, 194,
    224, 226
  as slur, 11, 131, 135, 168 (*see also*
    coonass; cracker)
"Hip et Tyho," 106
hobo, 69, 147, 149, 150
Hoffpauir, Elita, 96, 99
Holly, Buddy, 170, 177
Hollywood, 62, 75, 137, 189, 215
home music. *See* ballads, *cantiques*,
    complaintes

honky tonk, 5, 6, 24, 47, 61, 114, 144, 147, 156, 168, 172, 173, 177, 179, 183–185, 187, 188, 194, 196, 199, 201, 204, 206
    musical style, 25, 159, 181, 182, 189, 191–198, 200, 202, 206, 207, 219, 223, 225, 226
honky tonk corridor, 6, 24, 183, 184, 187–189, 191, 192, 194, 196, 197, 200–202, 204
honor culture, 30, 40, 43, 44, 187
horse and buggy, 83, 152
Houston, TX, 85, 121, 141, 144, 161, 163, 164, 178, 183, 193, 194, 196, 205, 226
Hutto, Bill, 202, 203, 226
hybridity, 100, 102, 212

improvisation, 87, 115, 119, 120, 154, 187, 194
"I'm Walking the Floor Over You," 188, 189
industrialization, 5, 84, 116, 130, 132, 134, 162, 183, 184, 189
interracial bands, 18, 57, 83, 84, 120, 136, 172
Irish culture (influence of), 11, 34, 78, 79, 82, 96, 143, 211
isolation, 47, 75, 89, 93, 95–97, 101, 102, 105, 175, 182, 209–212, 214, 215–217
"It's a Sin to Tell a Lie," 61, 223

jail, 143, 153, 154, 187
"Jambalaya (On the Bayou)," 199, 200, 203, 204, 227
jazz, 4, 5, 13, 20, 23, 24, 38, 61, 67, 73, 75, 84, 86, 87, 95, 98, 101, 107, 115–117, 119–122, 126, 129, 130, 137, 142–144, 150, 151, 155, 156, 167, 187, 191, 193, 199
Jenkins, Ike, 120
Jennings, Waylon, 6, 165, 170, 171
Jim Crow, 83, 84, 119, 136
    dance style, 38
jitterbug, 38, 121
"Jole Blon," 6, 24, 157–161, 163–178, 182, 187, 189, 192, 194, 195, 199, 200–203, 205, 212, 220, 225
Jolly Boys of Lafayette, 120, 223
Jolson, Al, 67, 144. See also minstrelsy
jukebox, 110, 157, 161, 164, 176, 186, 197–201

Kegely, Will, 197
Kershaw, Doug and Rusty, 3, 159, 170, 199, 202, 226
KFDM (Beaumont, TX), 123, 146
Khoury, George, 178, 182, 192, 197, 198, 205, 226
King, Peewee, 144
knives, 30, 43, 44
Knott, Sarah Gertrude, 92, 93, 103, 104–108, 110, 111, 210, 215
KPLC (Lake Charles, LA), 126, 140, 189, 197
KRLD (Dallas, TX), 106, 189
Kroeber, Alfred, 111
KVOL (Lafayette, LA), 126, 139, 140, 154, 190, 201
KVOO (Tulsa, OK), 189
KWKH, 6, 125, 126, 140, 189, 202, 227

"La Bamba," 177
labor, 5, 27, 28, 40, 41, 51, 60, 62, 76, 77, 82, 93, 96, 105, 109, 121, 122, 132–137, 144, 145, 149, 179, 183, 205
Lachney, Delma, 79, 80, 81, 219, 222
Lafayette, LA, 12, 15, 17, 20, 23, 47–50, 52, 54, 59–60, 64, 66, 70–74, 87, 103, 106, 108, 109, 119, 120, 123–126, 128, 139, 140, 144, 151, 156, 158, 164, 167, 178, 183, 185, 189, 190, 201, 203, 204, 212, 221, 223, 225, 227
"Lafayette (Allon a Luafette)," 49, 50, 52, 71, 106, 109, 158, 178, 212, 221, 223
LaFleur, Mayeuse, 64–67, 197, 221, 222
Lake Charles, LA, 13, 53, 77, 119, 123, 126, 127, 140, 141, 145, 146, 149, 170, 188–189, 192, 197, 200, 226
"La Marseillaise," 109, 110, 127
Lamperez, Julius "Papa Cairo," 128, 156, 185, 200, 201, 204, 224
language, 3, 5, 6, 7, 9, 10, 15, 24, 43, 54, 55, 58, 59, 61, 69, 70, 82, 108, 123, 125, 145, 160, 166–168, 174, 180, 188, 205, 211, 212, 216, 219
    bilingualism, 68, 99, 100, 101, 145, 153, 158, 187, 190, 207, 212, 213, 216, 218, 228
    See also French
"La Valse de Gueydan," 143, 162, 220
Leadbelly. See Huddie "Leadbelly" Ledbetter
LeBlanc, Dudley J., 149, 188, 203, 204

LeBlanc, Floyd, 195, 196, 226
LeBlanc, LeRoy "Happy Fats," 87, 129,
    149, 150–152, 156, 169, 189, 193,
    195, 198, 201–203, 206, 212, 225
Ledbetter, Huddie "Leadbelly," 21
Lee, Russell, 29, 37, 41, 47, 119,
    133, 201
LeJeune, Angelas, 50, 66, 77, 83,
    195, 228
LeJeune, Iry, 3, 84, 159, 182, 192, 195,
    196, 205, 206, 225
"Les Veuve de al Coulee," 151, 152, 228
Library of Congress, 91
Light Crust Doughboys, 121, 139,
    150, 189
Li'l Abner, 173
Lomax, Alan, 70, 91–103, 106–111,
    210, 215, 220, 227
Lomax, John, 70, 91–103, 106,
    108–111, 210, 215, 220, 227
Long, Huey, 97, 132, 182
Louisiana French Folk Songs, 95,
    110, 111
Louisiana Hayride, 6, 149, 159, 174,
    179, 189, 198–200, 202, 203,
    226, 227
Louisiana Hillbillies, 128
Louisiana Purchase, 9, 10, 39, 211
Louisiana School for the Blind, 196
Louisiana State University, 95, 103,
    104, 106, 109, 110, 123, 127, 228
Louisiana Story, 7, 111, 112
"Love Bridge Waltz," 195, 197, 198,
    205, 206
"Lulu's Back in Town," 61, 128,
    129, 223
Lydia Mendoza, 63

"Ma Blonde est Parti," 86, 88, 161,
    169, 171
Malone, Bill C., 122, 142, 149, 181
Mamou, LA, 45, 81, 82, 143, 147, 185,
    220, 227
mandolin, 16, 115, 144, 148, 156
Manuel, Joe, 163
Marais Bouleur, 61, 96
Mardi Gras, 31–36, 38
Marksville, LA, 80, 191
Matassa, Cosmo, 193
mazurka, 18, 38, 56, 78, 82, 85, 106
McGee, Dennis, 38, 42, 46, 50, 52, 56,
    57, 70, 75–77, 82, 89, 117, 125,
    136, 149, 197, 221–223

Meche, Leon, 49, 59
Memphis, TN, 51, 55, 68, 149,
    154, 214
Menard, D. L., 200, 207
"Mercredi Soir Passé," 81, 82
Merrymakers, 128, 134, 144, 153, 221
Mexican Americans, 7, 63, 75, 125, 138,
    140, 169, 176, 177
    orquestas, 137, 138
microphone, 8, 49, 50, 51, 66–68, 109,
    120, 147, 153, 184
migration, 48, 105, 116, 135, 172, 184
Miller, Beethoven, 153
Miller, J. D., 149, 192–194, 197, 199,
    202, 204, 205
minstrelsy, 67, 144
Mississippi River, 14, 17–19, 32, 33,
    79, 81
Monroe, Mina, 58
Montgomery Ward, 59, 80, 139, 155
moonshine, 65, 67, 69, 184. See also
    alcohol
Morton, Ferdinand "Jelly Roll,"
    84, 121
Mufzar, Christine, 73, 74, 75
Mullican, "Moon" Aubrey, 144, 145,
    162, 165–169, 173, 185, 204

Naquin, Edius, 82
Nashville, TN, 125, 144, 203, 220, 227
Natchitoches, 81
National Folk Festival, 92, 93, 103–105,
    107, 108, 111
National Rice Festival, 38, 107,
    126–128, 130, 201
Native American, 7, 91, 104,
    111, 165
New Iberia, LA, 44, 91, 96, 108, 119,
    124, 181, 200
New Orleans, LA, 5, 14, 17, 19–24,
    34, 49, 50–53, 55, 58, 59, 68–70,
    78, 83–87, 103, 115, 117, 119,
    120–122, 125, 126, 140, 141, 143,
    147, 148, 151, 153, 155, 174, 183,
    184, 193, 196, 200
New York, NY, 49, 51, 55, 59, 60, 62,
    70, 71, 74, 76, 77, 86, 109, 116,
    119, 125, 145, 149, 181
Newman, Jimmy C., 159, 170, 199, 201,
    202, 207, 224, 226

Oberstien, Eli, 153
oil. See petroleum

Okeh (record label), 54, 56, 58, 64, 69, 73–75
Oklahoma Tornadoes, 194, 195, 196, 206
Oliver, Joseph "King," 67, 121
Olivier, Louise V., 107
one-step, 56, 85, 86, 88, 97, 198, 228
Opelousas, LA, 12, 16, 21, 22, 53, 65, 78, 119, 189, 226
Opera (record label), 6, 178, 182, 194–197, 206, 226
orality, 9, 31, 34, 35, 59, 96, 123, 180
Orange, TX, 118, 184, 185
Oster, Harry, 25, 33, 34, 61, 81, 82, 110, 211, 227
O.T. Records, 197
Our Singing Country, 95, 96
Owens, William, 92–94, 107–110, 176, 227

"Papa Cairo." *See* Julius Lamperez
Paramount (record label), 56, 67, 142, 162, 223
parc aux petits, 37, 41, 46, 48
Peer, Ralph, 54, 55, 64
Pellerin, Patrick, 73, 74, 75, 212
Perry, Wayne, 101, 102
petroleum, 5–7, 12, 24, 75, 85, 96, 98, 103, 111, 114, 115, 121–123, 127, 131–134, 136, 144–146, 149, 168, 172, 173, 183–185, 197
phonograph, 50, 52, 54–60, 67, 79, 80, 116, 195, 209
  cylinders, 53
  Thomas Edison, 53, 54
piano, 54, 58, 66, 73, 129, 144, 145, 149–151, 156, 158, 205
Picou, Alphonse, 120
"Pine Grove Blues," 88, 179, 198, 226
Place Congo, 17, 84
Pointe Noire, 77, 206
politics, 10, 15, 49, 84, 97, 132, 140, 145, 149, 182, 188, 203, 205, 210
polka, 18, 35, 38, 56, 75, 106, 144
Port Arthur, TX, 60, 69, 108, 131, 163, 178, 184, 188
Post, Lauren C., 16, 77, 92, 93, 103, 104, 106–108, 110, 215, 227
poverty, 11, 63, 69, 105, 132, 136, 160, 165, 173, 217, 218
Progressive Era, 7, 93, 99, 172, 182, 213
prohibition, 47, 183
prostitution, 21, 119, 175

Protestantism, 6, 7, 11, 20, 29, 32, 33, 64, 122, 131, 137, 160, 167, 173, 176, 183, 215, 218
Psychology of Radio, 182, 204
Pugh, W. W., 39, 40

Quinn, Bill, 163–166, 178, 192, 194, 201

race records, 54, 55, 57
radio, 3, 5–8, 24, 25, 50, 52, 58, 95, 100, 106, 116, 121–126, 129, 139, 140, 146, 147, 149, 152, 153, 155–159, 161, 166, 174, 179, 180–184, 188–190, 193, 197–207, 211, 212, 227
railroad, 5, 12, 22, 75, 126, 132, 172
Rainwater, Floyd, 146, 147, 156
Rayne, LA, 22, 49, 107, 114, 119, 127, 147, 150
Rayne-bo Ramblers, 87, 88, 119, 127, 128, 130, 134, 144, 149–152, 156, 189, 193, 197, 206, 221, 225
RCA, 143, 147, 148, 155
recording studio, 5, 8, 21, 49, 50, 51, 56, 58, 59, 63, 65–71, 75, 76, 78, 82, 83, 87, 106, 109, 117, 120, 123, 125, 128, 141–143, 146–148, 150, 151, 153, 157, 163, 170, 183, 184, 192–195, 197, 198, 205, 207, 226
record retailers (dime store), 52–54, 71, 80, 109, 156, 221, 226
respectability, 64, 134, 135, 137, 141, 142, 149, 154, 155, 218
Riley, Kirby, 56, 228
Rinzler, Ralph, 20, 60, 65, 81, 82, 110, 135, 227
Riverside Ramblers, 139, 140, 147, 148, 155
Roach, Dr. James F., 58, 59
Robertson, Eck, 55, 116
Robin, C. C., 9, 39
Robin, Moïse, 67, 68, 141, 223
rockabilly, 171, 207, 226, 227
Rodgers, Jimmie, 5, 55, 63–68, 84, 86, 115, 125, 142, 143, 150–152, 186, 210, 212, 223
roughneck, 96, 122, 132, 145, 155
royalties, 51, 165
Russell, Tony, 141, 143, 219

Saint-Domingue, 27–28
San Antonio, TX, 51, 55, 58, 63, 85, 109, 121, 149

Sandmel, Ben, 115, 122, 123, 224
Savoy, Ann, 22, 25, 83, 161, 195, 210, 222
Savoy, Marc, 84
saxophone, 121, 144, 170
Scott, LA, 109
Segura, Dewey, 20, 69, 70, 102, 221
sexuality, 25, 39, 40, 42, 46, 47, 160–162, 171–176
sharecropping, 10, 11, 55, 70, 133, 134, 136, 157, 218
Shiner, TX, 77, 145
showboats, 13, 14, 15, 185
Shreve, Floyd, 141, 143, 147
Shreveport, LA, 6, 21, 125, 126, 140, 159, 181, 183, 189, 199, 202, 203, 215, 227
Shuler, Eddie, 148, 166, 169, 170, 192, 197, 205, 223
Simon, Paul, 214, 215
slavery, 8–11, 17, 27–29, 84, 103, 136
Snow, Hank, 165, 169
Soileau, Leo, 50, 52, 60, 64–70, 76, 77, 112, 117, 119, 120, 127–130, 134–136, 139, 140, 141, 145, 147, 150–155, 163, 185, 187, 189, 191, 195, 220–223, 228
    Four Aces, 126, 137, 140, 143, 156, 197, 201, 205, 206, 212, 224
    and His Rhythm Boys, 140, 144, 185
    Three Aces, 126, 141, 142, 143, 147, 162
Sonnier, Elemore, 107, 109
Sonnier, Lennis, 113–115, 146, 147
Sons of the Acadians, 128, 144
Sparks, W. H., 43
Spindletop, TX, 85, 122, 185
Spitzer, Nicholas, ix, 45, 57, 152
Springsteen, Bruce, 6, 177
steel guitar, 23, 115, 128, 129, 144, 147, 148, 150, 151, 154, 156, 169, 170, 185–187, 194, 200, 201, 224
stereotypes, 7, 12, 74, 93, 95, 111, 137, 165, 171, 172, 173, 175, 176, 177
St. Landry Parish, 65, 78, 82, 209, 210, 218
St. Martinville, 18, 46, 74, 108, 119
Storm, Warren, 129, 130
string bands, 16–17, 38, 113, 115–118, 121, 125, 128, 129, 139, 153, 162, 182, 184, 206, 224. *See also* Cajun swing
Swallow (record label), 178, 220

"T'es Petite et T'es Mignonne," 117, 152
Texas, 5–7, 21, 23–25, 51, 57, 58, 60, 69, 75–77, 84–86, 92, 94, 97, 98, 100, 103, 108, 109, 115–126, 129–139, 142–146, 148, 149–155, 159–164, 166–170, 172, 174, 176–189, 192, 193, 196, 197, 200–202, 204, 206, 216, 224–226
Texas Centennial, 103, 108
Thomson, Virgil, 111, 112
"Tiger Rag," 115, 146
Tin Pan Alley, 54, 125
Tobacco Road, 173, 175
Trahan, Adam, 56, 71
transculturation, 4
triangle, 17, 18, 22, 63, 102, 104, 119
Tubb, Ernest, 149, 181, 188, 189, 199, 227
two-step, 38, 56, 161, 214, 221

Valens, Ritchie, 177
Victor (record label), 54–56, 64–68, 141, 147, 155, 174, 221
Ville Platte, 67, 126, 143, 147, 220
violence, 10, 16, 30, 43–46, 48, 131, 132
virtuosity, 83, 194
Vocalion (record label), 54, 56, 58, 67, 78, 81, 83, 85, 142, 144, 154

Walker, Lawrence, 3, 76, 83, 85, 86, 88, 89, 104, 106, 107, 118, 192, 206, 223, 226
Waller, Fats, 61, 73, 129, 212
waltz, 24, 35, 38, 40, 41, 50, 56, 66, 75, 81, 82, 85, 88, 117, 143, 146, 147, 152, 157–166, 169–172, 174–178, 195–198, 205, 206, 214, 225, 226
"Valse à Deux Temps," 38, 61, 106
washboard, 17, 150, 151
Waud, A. R., 18–19, 165
wedding dance. *See* bal de noce
Werner, Joe, 127, 147, 148, 151, 155, 201, 224
Western swing, 5, 6, 23, 24, 86–88, 109, 115–117, 119, 121–123, 125, 126, 129, 130, 134, 137, 139, 142–145, 151, 154–156, 160, 167, 169, 177–179, 185, 191–193, 206, 212, 216, 224, 225
whiteness, 6, 136, 137, 138, 142
Whitfield, Irène Thérèse, 25, 42, 92, 93, 95, 96, 103, 108–111, 161, 215

Williams, Hank, 149, 159, 179–181, 189, 192, 198–204, 206, 207, 212, 227

Wills, Bob, 5, 86, 109, 116, 121, 125, 130, 135, 142, 150, 152, 154, 165, 169, 178, 181, 186, 189, 190, 192, 193

WNOE (New Orleans, LA), 140

women, 21, 25, 28, 31, 37, 38, 40, 41, 62–64, 97, 149, 161, 162, 172, 176, 188, 223, 227

"Wondering," 147, 148, 152, 158

World War II, 6, 22–25, 38, 40, 42, 57, 84, 86–88, 101, 127, 129, 130, 148, 151, 154, 155, 157, 158, 160, 173, 176, 177, 179, 180, 182, 185, 187, 188, 190–194, 197, 200, 206, 207, 209, 216, 219, 222

WSM (Nashville, TN), 125, 144, 200, 203

WWL (New Orleans, LA), 125

yodel, 65, 68, 115, 146, 150, 154, 176, 199, 223

zydeco, 17, 177, 209, 210, 214, 215, 217, 220, 221, 228